THE HORSEMEN COMETH

Third Edition
Racing Towards the Midnight Cry
From Christ's parable of the Ten Maidens *Matthew 25:1-13*

Charles Pretlow

THE HORSEMEN COMETH
Gloom, Doom, or Glory
Third Edition *Racing Towards the Midnight Cry*
December 2015
Copyright © Charles Pretlow
First Edition December 2004 titled **Revelation Six Get Ready**
Second Edition June 2008,
    Retitled **The Horsemen Cometh** *Gloom, Doom, or Glory* with no alterations other than the preface.

All rights reserved. Printed in the United States of America. No part of this publication may be reproduced, stored in a retrieval system, or transmitted, in any form or by any means electronic, mechanical, photocopying, recording, or otherwise, without the prior written permission of the author.

All scripture references and quotes are from the Revised Standard Version of the Holy Bible unless otherwise noted.
Old Testament Section Copyright © 1952
New Testament Section Copyright © 1946, 1971
by Thomas Nelson Inc.

Cover art: The Four Horsemen, by Dr. Marilyn Todd-Daniels
Copyright © Woodsong Institute of Art. www.woodsonginstitute.com

ISBN 978-1-943412-04-4

Published by -
Wilderness Voice Publishing, LLC
Canon City, Colorado USA
www.wvpbooks.com

"A voice crying in the wilderness —
proclaiming the good news of the coming Kingdom!"

CONTENTS

About cover art and artist 5
3rd Edition *Racing Towards the Midnight Cry* 7
2nd Edition *When You See These Things Look Up* 11
Introduction 23

PART ONE: ABANDONED BY GOD ATTACKED BY SATAN

Prelude 27
Chapter 1: Crossing the Threshold of Abandonment 29
Chapter 2: Beware: Satan Demands to Sift Christians 59
Chapter 3: Doctrines of Men and Demons 79
Chapter 4: Tossed About and Carried Away 145
Chapter 5: The Self-Righteous: Fighting A Losing Battle 215

PART TWO: HOW TO STAND AND ENDURE TO THE END

Prelude 253
Chapter 6: Refiner's Fire and Fuller's Soap 255
Chapter 7: Purity That Shines In The Darkness 275
Chapter 8: Spiritual Warfare That Is Effective 289
Chapter 9: Standing in the Gap 205
Chapter 10: Winning The War 319

Answering The Question, "What should I do?" 343

Appendix A: Judgment, Premature Death, Wrath of God ... 345
Appendix B: The Human Psychic and Spirit Power 355

About The Author 367
Ministry Information 369
More Resources 371

THE FOUR HORSEMEN
By Dr. Marilyn Todd-Daniels

DR. MARILYN TODD-DANIELS, artist, writer and educator, has created thousands of works of fine art primarily in oil and watercolor, over a 40-year career.

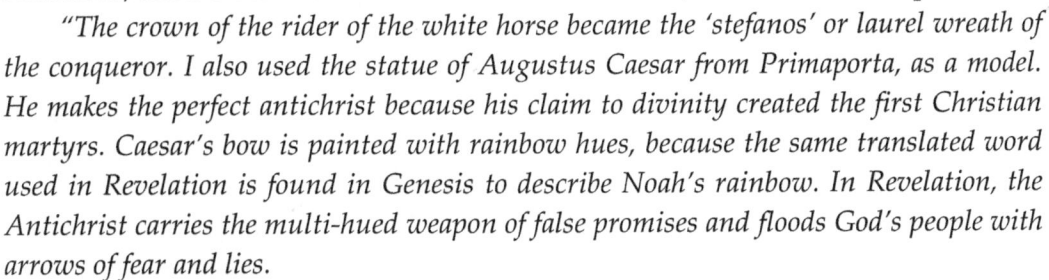

Her book *Thirty Nine Stripes*, is a work forged jointly in the fires of her personal victories and our public sorrows as a nation. Written and compiled over approximately one year following the events of September 11, 2001, Todd-Daniels tells a compelling story of her years of personal trials transformed into gracious victory through her paintings.

Of her painting, *The Four Horsemen*, used on the cover of *The Horsemen Cometh*, Todd-Daniels explains:

"The crown of the rider of the white horse became the 'stefanos' or laurel wreath of the conqueror. I also used the statue of Augustus Caesar from Primaporta, as a model. He makes the perfect antichrist because his claim to divinity created the first Christian martyrs. Caesar's bow is painted with rainbow hues, because the same translated word used in Revelation is found in Genesis to describe Noah's rainbow. In Revelation, the Antichrist carries the multi-hued weapon of false promises and floods God's people with arrows of fear and lies.

If these promises, illusions and lies are believed and followed, eventually our true dreams... originally gifts of God... will shrivel and die. Therefore Death's hand points to and implicates the counterfeit bow. Death rides a pale Arabian horse, alluding to 'bring death to all infidels.' Already its sting has begun to torment America and the final outcome is far from reconciled...

The red horse's rider is given the power to take peace from the earth. The horse, a German Hanovarian, was originally bred as a heavy-bodied warhorse. The dragon on the shield depicts wrath and anger. The bloody sword indicates the wars and devastation that follow when peace cannot be found. When Jesus Christ is not uppermost, there cannot be any lasting peace.

The black horse, a Scandinavian Friesian, is ridden by famine who carries a set of scales. 'As ye measure out, so shall ye be measured.' If one has been niggardly in regard to sharing God's gifts, a person's spirit will surely starve in the midst of plenty. The flood threatening to engulf the people is opposed by the image of the cross, which sheds the light, and Shekinah glory of Christ. Famine's dark reign is overcome.

As the painting neared completion, I began to be overcome with sorrow—the sense of impending judgment over America. As I fasted and painted, by Divine revelation, I sensed the Lord speaking. 'If you will judge yourself in the light of the cross, and repent, you will be spared the judgment of the four horsemen.' Thus, if the pale figures huddled in the foreground will turn and face the cross, crying out to the Lord in true repentance, rending their hearts rather than their garments, they can become whole."

Dr. Todd-Daniels web site: www.woodsonginstitute.com

Third Edition

Racing Towards the Midnight Cry

December 2015 update

THE APOSTLE JOHN'S REVELATION SPEAKS OUT TODAY
Come Out of Her My People—Revelation 18:4

The wicked and evil at heart in America now wallow in the rising tide of filth, like a dog rolling in carrion (rotting meat). This is exactly the condition Christ spoke of as being a major indication of his imminent return. (See Luke 17:22-31.)

And all the while God's people continue to play church, love prosperity, as they continue to be charmed asleep by false prophets and false teachers embracing this world's lies. Far too many only honor God with their lips allowing their heart of hearts to stay enthralled by the good life on earth.

Thus, God's people accommodate their beliefs and twist the Gospel to appease a culture that runs on sensuality and lust for pleasure.

Most Charismatic movements that many considered to be revivals and spiritual awakenings are nothing more than a display of human spiritualism produced by carnal activity. These false spiritual manifestations do have spiritual power driving these false awakenings—but it is not the power of God. The discerning saint must distinguish between a true move of God and false awakenings driven by the carnal spiritualism of men boosted by the power of the demonic.

REALIZATION OF THE TRUTH
When will God's People Wakeup, Raise their Heads and Straighten Up?

God's people, the Church of Jesus Christ are asleep to the hour because Christ's return has been delayed—in spite of Christ's consistent warnings in Scripture. Our Lord encouraged us to be aware of all the indicators that point to his return.

He said, *"And there will be signs in sun and moon and stars, and on the earth distress of nations in perplexity because of the roaring of the sea and the waves, people fainting with fear and with foreboding of what is coming on the world. For the powers of the heavens will be shaken. And then they will see the Son of Man coming in a cloud with power and great glory. <u>Now when these things begin to take place, straighten up and raise your heads, because your redemption is drawing near</u>"* (Luke 21:25-28).

Few realize the world and America is running head first into the brick wall of judgment. And a multitude of lost sinners and carnal-wayward Christians will be plunged into eternal darkness if God does not somehow wake his people up.

America and the world is in the process of being abandoned by God to gates of hell and the devil's fury. However, in these last days God will not abandon his people and the good-hearted lost sinner to darkness and hopelessness—leaving them asleep in their deceived and ignorant stupor.

How will the Lord awaken his sleeping church in time and bring a multitude of lost sinner and the backslidden to salvation and eternal security?

BREAKING THE REALIZATION THRESHOLD
The Midnight Cry Awakening with the 'Come Away' Message

Do not lose hope; for true servants of Christ are about to boldly pronounce in great power (in the true power of God) a final awakening of God's people. It will be the midnight cry Christ spoke of in the parable of the ten maidens (Mathew 25:1-13). *"But at midnight there was a cry, 'Here is the bridegroom! Come out to meet him"* (Matthew 25:6).

Hebrew tradition holds that the close servants of the bridegroom are those he entrusts to go forth and announce the bridegroom's coming. It is these very close servants who attend to the bridegroom and who intimately know his movements and plans.

Not all who serve Christ today have bowed down to the false. Soon the true servants of Christ will appear and cry out the good news of the coming kingdom, *"And this gospel of the kingdom will be proclaimed throughout the whole world as a testimony to all nations, and then the end will come"* (Matthew 24:14).

However, before this midnight cry takes place, it is required that more pressure come upon the world and a sleeping church. The signs, perplexities, and troubles must increase to break the sleepwalking stupor holding God's people spell bound.

Foreboding fear is building rapidly and will soon break the *realization threshold* where an uncountable multitude of sleeping spellbound Christians and lost sheep will be startled awake.

The end of the age pressures must continue to mount in order to cross the threshold that beaks total denial. Otherwise, many lost sinners and the lukewarm and deceived Christian will remain asleep. The coming midnight cry will come at a time when everything is falling apart, and this final cry will be blasted by the Holy Spirit and delivered forcefully through Christ's true servants.

Millions will be startled awake and called to come away from the lies of the false church, spiritual lethargy, and the love of this world (including America).

This gloomy forecast is accurate and is meant to pry the hearts of God's people from the love of this world and to come away from its hypnotic spell and look up, and not look back (in the heart) but forward to the glory of our coming King.

"And there will be signs in sun and moon and stars, and on the earth distress of nations in perplexity because of the roaring of the sea and the waves, people fainting with fear and

with foreboding of what is coming on the world. For the powers of the heavens will be shaken. And then they will see the Son of Man coming in a cloud with power and great glory. Now when these things begin to take place, straighten up and raise your heads, because your redemption is drawing near" (Luke 21:25-28).

THE FINAL MOVE OF GOD
Sustained by True Disciples, Persecution and Tribulation

In this darkening hour Christians are led astray by false hope perpetuated by weak and cowardly leadership. Few pastors warn according to what Christ taught of this hour, as most leaders pander to the Christian masses who want to hear only good things. Gross denial and passivity hold captive the people of God, reinforced by three major false doctrines:

1) Espousing that Christ's return is a long way off. 2) The lie that Christianity will usher in worldwide peace and prosperity so Christ can return. 3) And the most spellbinding myth portrays Jesus rescuing Christians before any serious trouble befalls the world (also known as the pre-tribulation rapture).

Thus most Christians are sound asleep because the relevant teachings of Christ concerning the end-of-this-age are ignored. Few are prepared, alert, strengthened, and abiding in Christ, giving them the ability to endure to the end.

"But watch yourselves lest your hearts be weighed down with dissipation and drunkenness and cares of this life, and that day come upon you suddenly like a trap. For it will come upon all who dwell on the face of the whole earth. But stay awake at all times, praying that you may have strength to escape all these things that are going to take place, and to stand before the Son of Man" (Luke 21:34-36).

The final awakening is coming soon, and our challenge is not to be deceived by spin-off counterfeit movements.

First, before the final awakening takes place, a key sign Christ spoke of must occur—unbridled persecution towards Christians, which will cause many *so-called* Christians to fall away. The message that the true body of Christ is about to embrace will be part of the reason for the coming great falling away. However, false leaders will try to subvert that message—the message of the good news of the coming kingdom and to come out from the false and away from the love of this world—the message of the midnight cry, *"Behold the bridegroom! Come out to meet him."*

These false servants mesmerizing God's people today are about to be exposed! Christ exposed the false leaders during his earthly ministry, so too, Christ will do the same during the last moments of this age. Malachi's prophesy was fulfilled by Christ and the first apostles, and a second fulfillment is about to occur: *"And now we call the arrogant blessed. Evildoers not only prosper but they put God to the test and they escape.' Then those who feared the LORD spoke with one another. The LORD paid attention and heard them, and a book of remembrance was written before him of those who feared the LORD and esteemed his name. 'They shall be mine, says the LORD of hosts, in the day when I make up my treasured possession, and I will spare them as a man spares his son who serves him. Then once more you shall see the distinction between the righteous and the wicked, between one who serves God and one who does not serve him'"* (Malachi 3:15-18).

True servants of Christ have been hidden in the wilderness, enduring the discipline of the Lord, learning to walk in fear of the Lord. Soon they will become recognized by the masses of Christianity and the world.

Then once again God's people and the world will be able to know the difference, *"between the righteous and the wicked, between one who serves God and one who does not serve him."*

But how will the Lord accomplish this separation between the true and the false?

There is coming a day when God acts, but first comes a cleansing to the body of Christ—the bride of Christ. Importantly, the spell of the false gospel and counterfeiting spiritualism must be broken and seen for what it is—magic thinking full of myths and heresies.

A PERSECUTION MADNESS HAS ALREADY BEGUN
Outspoken Christians are being Bashed and Driven into the Closet

Read on in this volume and get a clear picture of what we saw back in 2004. You will discover what God requires of you that he may guide, empower, and protect in the coming dark times.

Second Edition

When You See These Things, Look Up!

June 2008 update

How the second coming of Jesus Christ will unfold is a hot debate between many contemporary Christian authors and theologians. Unfortunately, most Christians have believed in a consensus of flawed theology concerning the rapture, the Great Tribulation, and the future of America.

There is a spell over the majority of sincere Christians, keeping their understanding darkened to the truth of Christ's return. Human nature wants to believe in the most favorable scenario concerning the end of this age and the coming of the Kingdom of God to earth.

The Apostle Paul warned, *"For the time is coming when people will not endure sound teaching, but having itching ears they will accumulate for themselves teachers to suit their own likings, and will turn away from listening to the truth and wander into myths"* (2 Timothy 4:3,4). Indeed, a great number of teachers preach myths and teach *magic thinking* doctrines concerning the things of God, especially how the end of this age will end. Few want to receive the truth laid out in Scripture, so false teachers pervert what Christ said concerning His coming. Most people like to hear soothing myths and conjecture of the most important event by God that is about to take place.

Of course, God knew this would be the case, so the end of this age will not come with a sudden bang! Christ said, *"And when you hear of wars and tumults, do not be terrified; for this must first take place, but the end will not be at once"* (Luke 21:9). What we are experiencing now, with all the earthquakes, wicked weather, wars, distress, and perplexity among the nations are what Christ called birth pangs. These are merciful warnings allowed by God to break the spell over a multitude of deceived Christians and non-believers alike.

Many will not take these warnings to heart, rather pretend all the trouble will eventually die down and the nations will resolve their differences. Then there will be many Christians who awake to these signs but choose to believe the myth that Christ will rapture (remove the true Christian from the earth) before the coming trouble brings any real discomfort to them.

Jesus called these Christians foolish as described in this passage, *"Then the kingdom of heaven shall be compared to ten maidens who took their lamps and went to meet the bridegroom. Five of them were foolish, and five were wise. For when the foolish took their lamps, they took no oil with them; but the wise took flasks of oil with their lamps. As the bridegroom was delayed, they all slumbered and slept. But at midnight* there was a cry, 'Behold, the bridegroom! Come out to meet him.' Then all those maidens rose and trimmed their lamps. And the foolish said to the wise, 'Give us some of your oil, for our lamps are going out.' But the wise replied, 'Perhaps there will not be enough for us and for you; go rather to the dealers and buy for yourselves.' And while they went to buy, the bridegroom came, and those who were ready went in with him to the marriage feast; and the door was shut. Afterward the other maidens came also, saying, 'Lord, lord, open to us.' But he replied, 'Truly, I say to you, I do not know you.' Watch therefore, for you know neither the day nor the hour" (Matthew 25:1-13).

It is time to look for the coming Kingdom of Heaven and His very soon coming. Christ warned, "So also, when you see these things taking place, you know that the kingdom of God is near" (Luke 21:31).

ABOUT THE TITLE CHANGE.
THE HORSEMEN COMETH – GLOOM, DOOM, OR GLORY!

The second revision of this book was published in December of 2004 and then titled *Revelation Six Get Ready – for the great and terrible day of the Lord is drawing near!*

The new titled reflects the urgency of the hour and the resistance that so many have in receiving the truth about the coming of Christ. The only addition to the book is this preface. As you read the main text you will see what was written is still timely, as much of the prophetic written has come to pass with still more unfolding daily.

The most disturbing is the predicted wickedness in society and the weak and sin-ridden condition of Christians, including the exposé of so many hypocritical and charlatan national Christian leaders.

One most prominent fallen leader was Ted Haggard. In several sections, we exposed the fruit of Haggard's leadership when we witnessed the heretical teachings and maddening activities within New Life Church in Colorado Springs in 2003, (see pages 94, 150, and 361). Then to our astonishment, we see confirmation in 2006 with Haggard's national disgrace. Haggard was president of the National Evangelical Association and worked with Focus on the Family in campaigning against homosexuality and other national immorality.

Haggard's hypocrisy and disgrace along with so many other heretical, greedy, and corrupt national ministries has helped create distain and distrust of Evangelical and Charismatic Christians. Haggard's secret sin became known just before the 2006 elections and undoubtedly affected the outcome.

Indeed, Haggard with so many other false teachers have fulfilled Peter's prophesy, *"But false prophets also arose among the people, just as there will be false teachers among you, who will secretly bring in destructive heresies, even denying the Master who bought them, bringing upon themselves swift destruction. And many will follow their licentiousness, and because of them the way of truth will be reviled. And in their greed they will exploit you with false words; from of old their condemnation has not been idle, and their destruction has not been asleep"* (2 Peter 2:1-3). The Gospel of Christ has now become reviled, maligned, ridiculed, and rejected because of greed and carnal hyper-faith driven, licentious national leaders and mega-church pastors.

Now the tide has turned with the Evangelical right loosing national credibility and influence. The floodgates of hell have opened wide spewing filth, perversion, and wickedness. The salt of the earth has lost is preserving influence, as Christ pronounced, *"You are the salt of the earth; but if salt has lost its taste, how shall its saltness be restored? It is no longer good for anything except to be thrown out and trodden under foot by men"* (Matthew 5:13).

Revulsion and persecution is coming to Evangelical Christians and the Conservative Right. The populace of America sees no difference between the wicked and the so-called on-fire Christian.

DIABOLICAL DARKNESS OVER THE LAND
The Preaching of Another Jesus

God is warning, but so few are taking heed. God's people are blind and walking in a satanic darkness that will destroy the faith of millions of so-called born-again, Spirit-filled, baptized Christians.

Few know the truth about the coming trouble. They have told lies and half-truths concerning the true Christ, sanctification, the works of the flesh, love of this world and the terrible trouble that must be endured leading to Christ's return.

Millions of deceived Christians believe they can spout Christ's name in prayer and spiritual warfare and get instant answers and victory. Several years ago, after reading the first release of this book, a Christian woman gave us an account of a terrifying dream she had. This woman is a sister to a staff member of our ministry. She discounted the truth and did not receive the message or the book. God in his faithfulness even warned her.

In her dream, she was walking around in a strange house with some other people she did not know, then suddenly all the doors and windows became locked. She tried getting out and the others turned demonic in appearance, which terrified her. Then she started commanding her freedom in the name of Jesus. Several times, she repeated – *"Open in the name of Jesus"*, and then the other people, now demonic in nature said to her, *"Your Jesus can't help you here."*

When she told the dream to her sister (our staff member), she thought the dream was a warning for one of her grandchildren. Our staff member set her straight, letting her know it was a warning for her, that she is following the wrong Jesus. She was horrified, but listened and agreed. However, she not take it to heart as she continues to embrace Joyce Meyers and Joel Osteen's teachings, a perverted Gospel that teaches many to enter by the wide gate and follow the easy path that leads to destruction with the myth that Christians will be raptured out of any trouble. (See Matthew 7:13,14 and Mark 13:24-27).

We have listened to many tell us of warning dreams that terrify but so few take heed, as they continue to believe the false teachers they enjoy listening to.

Does God warn in dreams? Yes, *"For God speaks in one way, and in two, though man does not perceive it. In a dream, in a vision of the night, when deep sleep falls upon men, while they slumber on their beds, then he opens the ears of men, and terrifies them with warnings, that he may turn man aside from his deed, and cut off pride from man; he keeps back his soul from the Pit, his life from perishing by the sword"* (Job 33:14-18).

Preaching a different Jesus is not new. The Apostle Paul warned the charismatic Christians in Corinth that they had readily submitted to a group of false apostles who came to them preaching another Jesus. Paul called them superlative apostles in that they elevated themselves above the original apostles, getting believers to accept a different Gospel and receive a different spirit—other than the true Gospel and the genuine Holy Spirit (see 2 Corinthians 11:3-15).

This same work of Satan has emerged in these last days again, just as Christ warned when he said, *"Take heed that no one leads you astray. For many will come in my name, saying, 'I am the Christ,' and they will lead many astray"* (Matthew 24:4,5).

In their spiritual hunger, multitudes in America have embraced a false gospel and received a false spirit by way of—as Paul called them, deceitful workmen, disguising themselves as apostles of Christ.

Mega-church and false charismatic movements have deceived many through a gospel that bids all to come and have life made easy, with the promise of riches, worldly success and emotional bliss that covers up depression and any other ill feeling.

Charlatan leaders sell what they call the power of God for tithes and offering. The Apostle Peter stopped this type of marketing and commercialization of the Gospel of Christ when he confronted Simon the Magician as recorded in the book of Acts.

You see, Simon had practiced magic in Samaria before the Apostles came to this land with the good news of Christ. In fact, Simon had a large following, but a multitude in Samaria believed on the Lord Jesus Christ, including Simon.

Simon was baptized and continued with Philip in ministry and was amazed by the signs and great miracles performed. Peter came down to Samaria after hearing that the Samaritans had received the Gospel and laid hands on the new believers that they might receive the Holy Spirit.

Here is what Simon does as recorded in the book of Acts, *"Now when Simon saw that the Spirit was given through the laying on of the apostles' hands, he offered* them money, saying, 'Give me also this power, that any one on whom I lay my hands may receive the Holy Spirit.' But Peter said to him, 'Your silver perish with you, because you thought you could obtain the gift of God with money! You have neither part nor lot in this matter, for your heart is not right before God. Repent therefore of this wickedness of yours, and pray to the Lord that, if possible, the intent of your heart may be forgiven you. For I see that you are in the gall of bitterness and in the bond of iniquity.' And Simon answered, 'Pray for me to the Lord, that nothing of what you have said may come upon me.'" (Acts. 8:18-24).

Peter stopped Simon from entering into buying and trading in the power of the Holy Spirit.

Today, thousands of Simon the Magician characters have stepped into pulpits and TV ministries all across America, selling and trading the power of God and commercializing the Gospel of Christ.

What they trade in is not the true Gospel or the true Holy Spirit, but rather a counterfeit work by Satan who has appeared to the masses as an angel of light to deceive a multitude of gullible, naïve and greedy Christians.

Satan, through these deceitful workmen, has cast a terrible darkness over the land. Another Jesus is being preached, creating a false gospel that has produced a gospel-hardened people who reject the true Gospel of Christ.

The Apostle Paul confronted the perverting of the true Gospel when he wrote to the Christians at Galatia. He wrote, *"I am astonished that you are so quickly deserting him who called you in the grace of Christ and turning to a different gospel—not that there is another gospel, but there are some who trouble you and want to pervert the gospel of Christ. But even if we, or an angel from heaven, should preach to you a gospel contrary to that which we preached to you, let him be accursed. As we have said before, so now I say again, If any one is preaching to you a gospel contrary to that which you received, let him be accursed. Am I now seeking the favor of men, or of God? Or am I trying to please men? If I were still pleasing men, I should not be a servant of Christ."* (Galatians 1:6-10).

He wrote, *let him be accursed*, concerning the person preaching a perverted Gospel.

Because of the depth of arrogance and rebellion of the so many deceived, the only way to restore the light of the true Gospel is through extreme trouble and persecution. And that is exactly what Christ predicted would come at the end of this age for the Christian, *"Then they will deliver you up to tribulation, and put you to death; and you will be hated by all nations for my name's sake. And then many will fall away, and betray one another, and hate one another. And many false prophets will arise and lead many astray. And because wickedness is multiplied, most men's love will grow cold. But he who endures to the end will be saved. And this gospel of the kingdom will be preached throughout the whole world, as a testimony to all nations; and then the end will come."* (Matthew 24:9-14).

The gross darkness that currently covers the land is from the false gospel and the preaching of another Jesus and it will only give way by the preaching of the coming Kingdom of God by true servants of the Lord Jesus Christ as persecution and trouble increases.

A Time When Men Faint in Fear

The nations of the world are perplexed with the extreme weather, earthquakes, ravaging floods, and hurricanes blamed by junk science as global warming. In truth, Jesus speaks of these events as birth pangs of the coming Kingdom of God. *"And there will be signs in sun and moon and stars, and upon the earth distress of nations in perplexity at the roaring of the sea and the waves, men fainting with fear and with foreboding of what is coming on the world; for the powers of the heavens will be shaken. And then they will see the Son of man coming in a cloud with power and great glory"* (Luke 21:25-27).

With years of wars and rumors of wars, the increase of perplexing issues in the Middle East, the renewal of the Cold War with Russia and China (few see this) and US economy on the brink of collapse, Christians should be awake and ready for the coming trouble leading to Christ's coming. Yet a false peace and security keeps most Americans and Christians in a stupor. The gradual escalation of all these troubles has desensitized millions to the fact that the world is now on the brink of the Great Tribulation that leads to Armageddon. The Apostle Paul wrote, *"But as to the times and the seasons, brethren, you have no need to have anything written to you. For you yourselves know well that the day of the Lord will come like a thief in the night. When people say, 'There is peace and security,' then sudden destruction will come upon them as travail comes upon a woman with child, and there will be no escape. But you are not in darkness, brethren, for that day to surprise you like a thief. For you are all sons of light and sons of the day; we are not of the night or of darkness. So then let us not sleep, as others do, but let us keep awake and be sober"* (1 Thessalonians 5:1-6).

Like lemmings headed for the cliff, masses of Christians have bought into the false peace and security, and shudder with fear at God's warnings; the roaring of the seas, wars and rumors of wars, false teachers and false prophets, with the increase of gross wickedness matching that of Sodom and Gomorrah.

God's people fear the truth, because they are not ready to give up the love of this world and submit to the Lordship of Christ. Many will be taken away in the coming sudden destruction. The delay in Christ's return and increased trouble is God trying to awaken His people from the spell of the false teachings, before it is too late.

The birth pangs of the coming Kingdom are about to become terrifying. Even now, there is little that any nation can do at stopping the mounting worldwide political chaos and economic woes that are ever growing with intensity and frequency from wars, food shortages, earthquakes, floods, and killer storms.

All the nations are powerless in stopping the slide towards a worldwide economic collapse and global political chaos.

We are in the final days leading up to the Great Tribulation and most Christians are unprepared for what is about to take place.

LIKE THE DAYS OF NOAH AND LOT

Even though the birth pangs are increasing, bringing on fear and discomfort, most ignore these signs and carry on with life, with business as usual. These unprecedented days of prosperity have given the masses and most Christians license to live like there is no life after death, no judgment to come; *"Let us eat and drink, for tomorrow we die."*

America has become a godless society as it was in the days of Noah and Lot. To the lukewarm and unbelieving Christian this should be the biggest sign of all. Filth and immorality has become blatant, legal, and acceptable throughout America. Indecency is everywhere eroding every institution, leaving nothing sacred and pure, and it only grows worse.

"As it was in the days of Noah, so will it be in the days of the Son of man. They ate, they drank, they married, they were given in marriage, until the day when Noah entered the ark, and the flood came and destroyed them all. Likewise as it was in the days of Lot -- they ate, they drank, they bought, they sold, they planted, they built, but on the day when Lot went out from Sodom fire and sulphur rained from heaven and destroyed them all— so will it be on the day when the Son of man is revealed. On that day, let him who is on the housetop, with his goods in the house, not come down to take them away; and likewise let him who is in the field not turn back. Remember Lot's wife." (Luke 17:26-32).

Now we live in a world of extreme contrasts, as in the Apostle John's revelation, *"'Come!' And I saw, and behold, a black horse, and its rider had a balance in his hand; and I heard what seemed to be a voice in the midst of the four living creatures saying, 'A quart of wheat for a denarius, and three quarts of barley for a denarius; but do not harm oil and wine!'"* (Revelation 6:5,6).

There is no sensing of the coming destruction, even as fuel and food prices skyrocket, the demand for entertainment, celebrations, luxury items, fine dining and personal mobility ever increases. Like drunken sailors on liberty staggering from bar to bar oblivious of the repercussions of the next day.

Society's mad craving for more of everything with the prosperity gospel's intoxicating effects keeps millions of lost sinners and Christians numb to the

Holy Spirit's convictions. For He warns in every generation as Jesus taught, *"And when he comes, he will convince the world concerning sin and righteousness and judgment: concerning sin, because they do not believe in me; concerning righteousness, because I go to the Father, and you will see me no more; concerning judgment, because the ruler of this world is judged"* (John 16:8-11).

Yes, Satan has been judged and thrown out of heaven and he has come down to earth with great wrath determined to deceive the world and as many believers in Christ as possible. He wants God's people to stay blinded to the coming judgment and Great Tribulation, keeping as many as possible unprepared and weak.

The devil wants to throw a multitude into the valley of decision without understanding, hoping for many to choose and align with the coming Anti-Christ rule.

Therefore, life will be *troubling* and *as usual*, right up to the start of the Great Tribulation.

COME OUT FROM AMONGST THEM

The Apostle Paul's admonition is for us now, *"You are not restricted by us, but you are restricted in your own affections. In return—I speak as to children—widen your hearts also. Do not be mismated with unbelievers. For what partnership have righteousness and iniquity? Or what fellowship has light with darkness? What accord has Christ with Belial? Or what has a believer in common with an unbeliever? What agreement has the temple of God with idols? For we are the temple of the living God; as God said, 'I will live in them and move among them, and I will be their God, and they shall be my people. Therefore come out from them, and be separate from them, says the Lord, and touch nothing unclean; then I will welcome you, and I will be a father to you, and you shall be my sons and daughters, says the Lord Almighty.' Since we have these promises, beloved, let us cleanse ourselves from every defilement of body and spirit, and make holiness perfect in the fear of God"* (2 Corinthians 6:- 7:1).

Many of God's people are restricted from the fullness of Christ and His abundant life because of carnal and worldly affections. Many try to serve God and money together trying to maintain a romantic worldly life style. Christians suffer from defilements from their former life in the world and continue to be emotionally involved and spiritually enthralled with idolatrous living, even living in sin and perverted lifestyles. Gazing at the world's perverted lifestyle for titillation and fantasy, falling into secret sin and searching for Christian fellowship that accommodates the worlds ways. Many have lost their faith, since they reject their conscience repeatedly.

Now is the time to leave idolatry and sensuous living behind. Run to the true Christ, giving him permission to expose and cleanse all defilements and leave the lukewarm and apostate churches. Seek out fellowship with likeminded people and take no part in the unfruitful works of darkness.

"But you are a chosen race, a royal priesthood, a holy nation, God's own people, that you may declare the wonderful deeds of him who called you out of darkness into his marvelous light. Once you were no people but now you are God's people; once you had not received mercy but now you have received mercy. Beloved, I beseech you as aliens and exiles to abstain from the passions of the flesh that wage war against your soul. Maintain good conduct among the Gentiles, so that in case they speak against you as wrongdoers, they may see your good deeds and glorify God on the day of visitation" (1 Peter 2:9-12).

THEN THEY WILL DELIVER YOU UP

As the birth pangs of the coming Kingdom become more intense, there will come a worldwide persecution madness towards the true Christian and the religious-conservative movement.

Due to the exposed hypocrisy and corruption of so many Christian national leaders, already a deep disregard and even hatred has become prevalent with liberal and independent voters across America.

Furthermore, with the Bush administration's push to bring an Evangelical form of Democratic-Capitalism to Iraq and Afghanistan by way of war, much of the world has the perception that American Christianity is trying to convert the world politically. With America's continued appropriate support of Israel and the escalating war on terrorism, the world is moving closer to the end of the age battle of Armageddon. (Fighting evil while living wickedly before the Lord is an open invitation for judgment.) The world wants peace and perceives that America and Israel stand in opposition to world peace.

In reality, the world is in the grip of a heavenly war between the forces of hell and God's angelic hosts that will soon result in the final religious war enlisting the world to turn against Christianity.

Soon, in America, Christians will need to guard against random acts of hatred, the burning and desecration of churches and murder. In the near future, it will no longer be fashionable to wear Christian slogans on clothing, or to display Christian bumper stickers; a fear of verbal and even physical attacks will become an everyday threat.

All the growth in Christianity experienced in America and other places around the world over the last 40 years will be reduced in great numbers. The body of Christ, through the coming persecution will become comprised of the sincere and truly called-of-God sold-out disciple. The false Christian and the counterfeit leaders will fall away from Christ and be used of Satan to persecute the true Christian through betrayal.

"Then they will deliver you up to tribulation, and put you to death; and you will be hated by all nations for my name's sake. And then many will fall away, and betray one another, and hate one another And many false prophets will arise and lead many astray. And because wickedness is multiplied, most men's love will grow cold. But he who endures to the end will be saved." (Matthew 24:9,13).

Are you prepared to endure to the end of this coming onslaught of persecution?

THE FINAL TRUE MOVE OF GOD

The coming persecution will be used of God as a means of house cleaning and purification for the body of Christ. During the height of the birth pangs and persecution, a sovereign true move of God will begin and be facilitated through a holy and distinct group of Christian workers and leaders who serve God alone and fear no man. Armed with sound doctrine while preaching all that Christ taught and proclaiming the truth of the coming Kingdom of God in the true power of God, this will mark the beginning of the final harvest of souls, which will gain incredible voice throughout the world.

The message that Christians must endure the Great Tribulation and be used in the final great harvest of souls will finally begin to make sense to the sincere Christian. Millions of Christians who formerly were deceived by the pre-tribulation rapture false doctrine will wake up and spread the good news of the coming Kingdom of God.

The final true move of God will be another by-product of the coming persecution and not be hijacked by false leaders, as in the past.

"And this gospel of the kingdom will be preached throughout the whole world, as a testimony to all nations; and then the end will come" (Matthew 24:14).

JUDGMENT OF THE UNITED STATES OF AMERICA

The end will come with the commencement of the Great Tribulation period. This final travail of trouble will be a major evangelistic tool in God's hands to gather in a multitude before the rapture at the end of the Great Tribulation, just before the wrath of God falls upon the world. (See Revelation 7:9-14).

What will be the catalyst that ignites the end and mark the beginning of the Great Tribulation? —Judgment of the USA.

Few see judgment coming to America and those who have warned are maligned and ridiculed, even accused of being unpatriotic and divisive.

False peace and security, false doctrines, as well as extreme idolatry of the American dream have blinded most Christians to the reality that America has crossed the line of Biblical immorality and wickedness.

Russia and China are building their military prowess to attack America and control the world. The cold war is back and is hotter than ever. These two enemies of freedom and democracy believe that Communism will succeed only if they control the world and its resources. America is standing in the way of world dominance.

Once America is attacked and defeated, the end will begin. Few see this coming – few will be ready in time to endure such destruction and calamity.

Yes, when people will say, *"There is peace and security"* then sudden destruction will come!

YOUR REDEMPTION IS VERY NEAR!

Jesus said, *"Now when these things begin to take place, look up and raise your heads, because your redemption is drawing near. ... So also, when you see these things taking place, you know that the kingdom of God is near. ... But take heed to yourselves lest your hearts be weighed down with dissipation and drunkenness and cares of this life, and that day come upon you suddenly like a snare; for it will come upon all who dwell upon the face of the whole earth. But watch at all times, praying that you may have strength to escape all these things that will take place, and to stand before the Son of man"* (Luke 21:28-36).

We must take heed, become ready for the coming trouble, and pray to have strength to escape these things. Please note, [*May have strength*] is properly translated as [may have exceeding godliness to be deemed entitled or qualified] to escape the coming trouble.

It is time to look up and set our minds on the things of God and the coming Kingdom and pray for more time to get ready. Many believers will be martyred for their faith in Christ in the coming days, especially during the Great Tribulation period. If this is the case for you or I, we will have done our work and be received into the Kingdom of our God, before the rest. If we are called to endure to the end and be raptured, we will have ministered the Gospel according to God's will.

It is the wrath of God that is coming in which we will be spared. The Great Tribulation is Satan's last gasp at opposing God and Christ in this age. Christ said, *"And do not fear those who kill the body but cannot kill the soul; rather fear him who can destroy both soul and body in hell"* (Matthew 10:28).

The message of *The Horsemen Cometh – Gloom, Doom, or Glory!* is to help prepare the sincere Christian for the coming of Christ; that you and I may stand at His appearance without shame, thus at that moment, having done all to stand—let us stand therefore and glorify Christ our Lord!

INTRODUCTION

ABOUT THIS PROPHETIC MESSAGE

PLEASE read this with an attitude of testing, for we are admonished, *"Beloved, do not believe every spirit, but test the spirits to see whether they are of God; for many false prophets have gone out into the world"* (1 John 4:1).

As a minister of the Gospel, a shepherd responsible to feed God's sheep, I am compelled to warn. To warn about what the Lord has shown concerning the condition of His people and the things to come. To warn and encourage, not frighten, push or manipulate. To warn in such a manner as to drive Christians closer to the Lord and search the Scriptures for themselves; to encourage and help prepare the bride of Christ for the coming of the Lord and to help equip the saints to be true witnesses to a lost and dying world.

Jesus said, *"Blessed are you when men revile you and persecute you and utter all kinds of evil against you falsely on my account. Rejoice and be glad, for your reward is great in heaven, for so men persecuted the prophets who were before you. You are the salt of the earth; but if salt has lost its taste, how shall its saltness be restored? It is no longer good for anything except to be thrown out and trodden under foot by men. You are the light of the world. A city set on a hill cannot be hid. Nor do men light a lamp and put it under a bushel, but on a stand, and it gives light to all in the house. Let your light so shine before men, that they may see your good works and give glory to your Father who is in heaven"* (Matthew 5:11-16).

God's people are responsible for the condition of this nation. The indicators of judgment are all around us. We have had a sample of what is to come with all our troubles and the attack of 9/11.

When judgment looms over a nation, it begins with prosperity and lack of trouble. Through the last part of the eighties and through the nineties, prosperity grew and grew. Yet, we as a people, including far too many believers, took these prosperous times as a license to grow indulgent and wicked. A simple study of biblical accounts indicates increased prosperity as immorality grows unchecked is a strong indication that judgment follows very closely. Indeed, prosperity mixed with gross wickedness is a terrible sign that God has abandoned a nation to trouble, and this is true for individuals as well, including Christians.

The two decades preceding the Great Depression were full of prosperity, yet immorality, crime and wickedness grew very rapidly. The last two generations have forgotten what judgment is like for a nation headed towards a Sodomite society, as this nation was during the Roaring Twenties.

A nation that gives heed to the Lord and depends on God will have the Lord's hand of discipline guiding them. A humble nation will have problems that will bring out godly men and women who lead the people to the high ground. The people will want to hear the hard things and do what is right, even at the expense of profit, popularity and economic success.

However, when a nation crosses the line and rejects God altogether, that is when God no longer disciplines; there is no longer Divine providential blessing and reproof.

When the controlling majority and populace call "good evil and evil good" while casting off restraint, discipline and warning, that nation can expect to be a nation abandoned by God. Indeed, God abandoned America to the forces of hell as we witnessed the towers fall, great fires, numerous national crises and disasters. Unfortunately, even after these warnings the revelry is about to blast off into the final party, with society drinking up the last bottles of prosperity that God allows just before judgment.

"Or do you presume upon the riches of his kindness and forbearance and patience? Do you not know that God's kindness is meant to lead you to repentance? But by your hard and impenitent heart you are storing up wrath for yourself on the day of wrath when God's righteous judgment will be revealed" (Romans 2:4,5).

As you read this message, be mindful of the Scripture references that corroborate these insights, warnings and instructions. Treat this book as a sound guide or road map to help you prepare to endure the coming trouble. The serious Christian must be ready to endure to the end and do warfare for the Lord in these coming days as this age ends.

Indeed, the majority of Christians in the body of Christ are not ready to endure the coming trouble. Legitimate issues that have become cares of this world spellbind most Christians.

They have become overly involved in work, church and family, blinded to the handwriting on the wall. The result is that sincerest Christians in America are ill-prepared for what is about to take place.

In all the church growth and so-called revival movements across this great nation, a predominant lukewarm relationship with God persists. Except for a remnant, the church of America honors God with their lips, but their hearts are far from Him. The church of America has abandoned God for a watered-down gospel of prosperity and idolatry—love for the American dream is much stronger than love for God. Therefore, God has abandoned the church and turned this nation over to the god of prosperity and lust for success.

For years, warnings have rung out to the church—repent, repent, and repent—only to have a token response. A few have cried out, but that is not nearly enough!

Now God is warning! In review, we see extreme catastrophes, natural disasters and economic scares leading up to the 9/11 tragedy and terrorist attacks. The pattern over the last ten years is increased frequency and intensity in these warnings from God.

I believe we are teetering on the brink, and if not for a handful of intercessors and sold-out ministries and congregations, judgment would have already begun.

This nation is about to plunge into extreme trouble and it will affect every person in America. The church of America will stand before God with blood on their hands for lack of warning and not living as a true example of Christ's nature, as the body of Christ should.

The end-of-the-age prophecies are unfolding right before our eyes. The Mideast crisis will be the catalyst for great trouble, greater than the world has ever seen. Jesus said the end would be this way, and it would be a sign signifying His very soon return.

I am not an alarmist trying to scare people and thus promote some kind of tabloid ministry, preying on Christian ignorance concerning the last days. On the other hand, many are truly ignorant of what Christ taught concerning the end times, the condition of the church, the great tribulation and the fact that God will use the bride of Christ as a witness to the world during the Great Tribulation. How much of this troubled time we must endure, I am not sure? I do believe the rapture will not occur until a multitude of unsaved, backslidden and lukewarm Christians respond wholeheartedly to salvation and sanctification during this time. We must be ready to respond to Christ's coming—regardless of when—for He will come as a thief and catch many off guard.

That means we must be ready to endure tribulation and abide in Christ, standing confident and doing the perfect Will of the Lord.

Again, perhaps if enough of God's people respond in time with true repentance, a clean heart, prayer, and true intercession, we might have a heritage from the Lord to give to our children and grandchildren; if not, well, I can't imagine the terror and pain we, as God's people, will go through. What will be worse is that these things could have been minimized or even prevented, had enough of God's people taken heed to the warnings.

The Horsemen Cometh, for the great and terrible day of the Lord is drawing near! sounds out a warning with solid teachings and instruction on what the everyday sincere believer must do to walk through the coming times, victoriously!

To that end, I pray each reader be truly blessed, being made vessels of honor to glorify our Lord and King—that none of us be ashamed on the day of His appearance.

Amen and Amen.

PART ONE

ABANDONED BY GOD ATTACKED BY SATAN

PRELUDE

"REJOICE THEN, O heaven and you that dwell therein! But woe to you, O earth and sea, for the devil has come down to you in great wrath, because he knows that his time is short!" (Revelation 12:12).

"Now I saw when the Lamb opened one of the seven seals, and I heard one of the four living creatures say, as with a voice of thunder, 'Come!' And I saw, and behold, a white horse, and its rider had a bow; and a crown was given to him, and he went out conquering and to conquer. When he opened the second seal, I heard the second living creature say, 'Come!' And out came another horse, bright red; its rider was permitted to take peace from the earth, so that men should slay one another; and he was given a great sword. When he opened the third seal, I heard the third living creature say, 'Come!' And I saw, and behold, a black horse, and its rider had a balance in his hand; and I heard what seemed to be a voice in the midst of the four living creatures saying, 'A quart of wheat for a denarius, and three quarts of barley for a denarius; but do not harm oil and wine!' When he opened the fourth seal, I heard the voice of the fourth living creature say, 'Come!' And I saw, and behold, a pale horse, and its rider's name was Death, and Hades followed him; and they were given power over a fourth of the earth, to kill with sword and with famine and with pestilence and by wild beasts of the earth. When he opened the fifth seal, I saw under the altar the souls of those who had been slain for the word of God and for the witness they had borne; they cried out with a loud voice, 'O Sovereign Lord, holy and true, how long before thou wilt judge and avenge our blood on those who dwell upon the earth?' Then they were each given a white robe and told to rest a little longer, until the number of their fellow servants and their brethren should be complete, who were to be killed as they themselves had been. When he opened the sixth seal, I looked, and behold, there was a great earthquake; and the sun became black as sackcloth, the full moon became like blood, and the stars of the sky fell to the earth as the fig tree sheds its winter fruit when shaken by a gale; the sky vanished like a scroll that is rolled up, and every mountain and island was removed from its place. Then the kings of the earth and the great men and the generals and the rich and the strong, and every one, slave and free, hid in the caves and among the rocks of the mountains, calling to the mountains and rocks, 'Fall on us and hide us from the face of him who is seated on the throne, and from the wrath of the Lamb; for the great day of their wrath has come, and who can stand before it?'" (Revelation Six).

The Horsemen Cometh
Gloom, Doom, or Glory?

September 11th is a forewarning of what is to come. The NASA shuttle disaster was one more blow to America's national pride. Forest fires, destructive hurricanes, earthquakes, the roaring of the seas and the waves (tsunamis), terrorism, wars and rumors of war are perplexing our nation and the world. We have built our towers of Babel, reaped prosperity, and declared God irrelevant kicking His name out of almost every institution. Then we in turn sing *God Bless America*!

Most Christians in America have their hearts loaded down with the cares of this world, filled with the pride of life, lust of the eyes and lust of the flesh.

Today, Christ stands at the door of our Christian hearts and knocks, bidding us to open and allow Him to cleanse and sanctify. Most have rejected His pleadings and warnings. Few Christians are ready to endure the coming trouble prophesied in Revelation Six.

Jesus warned, *"But take heed to yourselves lest your hearts be weighed down with dissipation and drunkenness and cares of this life, and that day come upon you suddenly like a snare; for it will come upon all who dwell upon the face of the whole earth. But watch at all times, praying that you [may have strength] to escape all these things that will take place, and to stand before the Son of man"* (Luke 21:34-36).

CHAPTER 1

Crossing the Threshold of Abandonment

A STRONG DELUSION SENT FROM GOD

"The coming of the lawless one by the activity of Satan will be with all power and with pretended signs and wonders, and with all wicked deception for those who are to perish, because they refused to love the truth and so be saved. Therefore God sends upon them a strong delusion, to make them believe what is false, so that all may be condemned who did not believe the truth but had pleasure in unrighteousness" (2 Thessalonians 2:9-12).

In the Gospel of Matthew, Christ warned of a powerful but false spiritual awakening as the end of the age unfolds. Along with a false spiritual awakening, all governments of the world would become ensnared in an evil deceitful political system. This deception by false leaders, both Christian and political, would lead astray millions. Jesus underscored the coming deception to be so powerful, it would almost sway the elect of God—*Christians who have a true relationship with God*. (See Matthew 24:21-31).

The Holy Spirit of God and the Lord's angelic host have restrained the lawlessness and the Antichrist until the appointed time. To the discerning saint, that restraint is lifting, and millions of Christians are in grave risk of being caught up in a delusion sent by God to condemn the wicked.

Over these last 30 years the morality of America and the church of America has slid toward crossing the point of no return. There is a threshold that a nation and the people of God can cross, which incites judgment. A judgment where God abandons a people to the powers of hell, a people abandon to the deceptive rule of the wicked.

Even though Christian leaders and some political leaders decry this drowning flood of Sodom-like immorality—God is ignoring the cries, prayers and protests, allowing the power of the wicked to gain more and more ground. Why?

GOD WILL NO LONGER HOLD BACK THE TIDE

"Therefore God gave them up to the lusts of their hearts to impurity, to the dishonoring of their bodies among themselves, because they exchanged the truth about God for a lie and worshiped and served the creature rather than the Creator, who is blessed forever! ... And since they did not see fit to acknowledge God, God gave them up to a base mind and to improper conduct. They were filled with all manner of wickedness,

evil, covetousness, and malice. Full of envy, murder, strife, deceit, malignity, they are gossips, slanderers, haters of God, insolent, haughty, boastful, inventors of evil, disobedient to parents, foolish, faithless, heartless, ruthless. Though they know God's decree that those who do such things deserve to die, they not only do them but approve of those who practice them" (Romans 1:24,25 and 28-32).

The population of the United States is currently estimated at 292,609,500; with 53% Protestant, 26% Roman Catholic, 8% other Christian affiliation, 2% Jewish and 2% Muslim. Eighty-seven percent of the populace of this nation call themselves "Christian."

Jesus declared that Christians are the moral fiber of any nation. *"You are the salt of the earth... "You are the light of the world"* (Matthew 5:13,14).

"When I shut up the heavens so that there is no rain, or command the locust to devour the land, or send pestilence among my people, if my people who are called by my name humble themselves, and pray and seek my face, and turn from their wicked ways, then I will hear from heaven, and will forgive their sin and heal their land" (2 Chronicles 7:13,14).

I am addressing the 254,570,260 people who acknowledge God through Jesus Christ, His Son. You and I, as Christians in this great nation, are responsible for the moral condition of this nation; and that condition directly relates to God's favor or disfavor toward our land.

Indeed, during the last 30 years the morality of this country has slid toward a degenerate condition on a par with biblical accounts in which God judged nations and cities such as Israel, Babylon and Sodom and Gomorrah. Recent tragedies and disasters have tested this nation, and few equate these troubles as precursors to more severe judgments at the hand of God.

God is challenging America and God's people concerning their moral character. Throughout President Bill Clinton's years, this deception and moral decline accelerated. The outcome of the 2000 election was another failed test. The choice was leaner times with a moral president, or prosperity with a perverse president. The popular vote went to Al Gore; fortunately, this nation is a republic and the Electoral College system temporarily stopped political evil from taking this nation to sudden judgment, which would have led to a total abandonment by God.

President George W. Bush had difficult challenges with 9/11, the shuttle disaster, natural disasters, the war on terror and the Afghan-Iraq war. The perplexities' and crises' frequencies and intensities are ever-growing. There have been lulls between each cycle, but those lulls are less frequent and shorter.

The beginning of this millennium brought in more wickedness, lawlessness, homosexual marriage, removal of the Ten Commandments from public areas, national flash nudity and fouler talk on TV and radio.

The scandals in business, government and Christianity became frequent headlines in the news. Mayors, city administrators and judges took it upon themselves to sanction homosexual marriages. A mainline Christian denomination elected a homosexual bishop. Other liberal denominations are pressing for the same. The last four years have been truly incredible.

Voices of dissent grew louder in protest of this immoral decline. Battle lines were beginning to form.

Then the election campaigns began. The far-left element of the liberal Democrats drew upon every imaginable difficulty and issue to attack the Bush administration, conservative talk show hosts and Christian moral crusaders. Lies, innuendos, slander and over-the-top expressions of rage became campaign messages; an obvious media bias manufactured headlines, concocted stories, false documents and half-truths to influence the election. Movies were produced and shown to sway the masses. These were planned attacks to discredit the President.

During a campaign rally, a Senator John Kerry supporter interviewed by a TV reporter said, *"We have to get Bush out, the narrowed-minded Christians have no idea of the world picture."*

How Senator Kerry conducted his 2004 Presidential campaign is a snapshot into the future.

Indeed, the Antichrist world leader will use deception, lies, political power and signs and wonders to sway the masses.

The poll analysts indicate that the church vote kept Bush in office, a rare victory in the fight against America's declining morals. This is giving God's people more time to get ready but is also the catalyst for a coming persecution and trouble that Christ warned would come at the end of the age.

The Moral Majority is being resurrected, renamed *Faith and Values Coalition*. The lines have been drawn and these moral battles will break out into a full-fledged war. Already the far-left is gearing up.

You can count on a backlash against Christians, moral crusaders and the conservative right. This political victory will inspire enraged hate. Be prepared for an onslaught of evil, immorality and over-the-top and in-your-face hatred and protests.

This rage against Christians will start slowly but soon it will gain momentum. Churches will be vandalized, some burned to the ground by arsonists. Christians touting Christ with public display of jewelry, bumper stickers and Christian slogans will be attacked. Persecution madness has ignited, as the whole world decries America politically driven by the right-wing Christian evangelicals who are resisting the New World Order and peace.

The forces of hell are mounting a full assault on the righteous and God is allowing the restraint to lift. Why is God giving this nation over to the wicked and ignoring the prayers and efforts of God's people?

"Cry aloud, spare not, lift up your voice like a trumpet; declare to my people their transgression, to the house of Jacob their sins. Yet they seek me daily, and delight to know my ways, as if they were a nation that did righteousness and did not forsake the ordinance of their God; they ask of me righteous judgments, they delight to draw near to God. 'Why have we fasted, and thou seest it not? Why have we humbled ourselves, and thou takest no knowledge of it?' Behold, in the day of your fast you seek your own pleasure, and oppress all your workers. Behold, you fast only to quarrel and to fight and to hit with wicked fist. Fasting like yours this day will not make your voice to be heard on high" (Isaiah 58:1-4).

Satan has offered Americans and the church in America prosperity and peace. The cost has been morality, integrity, and character. Many in this nation, and far too many of God's people, one way or another, have sold themselves to the Evil One in order to maintain the *good times* and the American dream. Remember, Jesus said, *"For what does it profit a man, to gain the whole world and forfeit his life?"* (Mark 8:36).

If the economy were not in recovery, the Bush administration would probably not have been reelected, regardless of the moral issues.

The church is worried about the good life and prosperity rather than doing all of God's Will. Leadership in the church has laid heavy burdens on the people, raising money for extravagant building programs, greedy for members to pay the bills, while pointing the finger at sinners and speaking wickedly against the true servants of the Lord. Far too many Christian leaders are quick to declare the sins of the outsiders while preaching a shallow gospel. They give few answers that can truly restore the lost sinner. Wounds are glossed over, and the preaching and teaching of the cross and sanctification is avoided. Sermons avoid the harder teachings of Christ to increase the minister's popularity, tickle the ear, encourage church attendance and raise money. Very little is taught or preached concerning the deep roots of bitter jealousy and selfish ambition that is running rampant within the body of Christ.

God's people are to influence the nations in which they live, and we see this truth historically.

The root cause of the Great Depression and World War II can be traced to God's people. In America, God's people pushed to legislate morality through the Temperance Movement. The Constitution was amended; prohibition of liquor became law, which led to one of the most corrupt periods in this nation's history. Prosperity, technological breakthroughs and decadence were unprecedented.

Swift judgment fell upon this country as Wall Street crashed and the Great Depression swallowed up prosperity overnight.

During the same period after World War I, the nation of Germany suffered great humility from the war's defeat. God's people and church leadership gave no moral beacon to light the way through this darkness. Hitler mesmerized the German people, while most Protestant leaders said nothing in order to keep the state payroll coming to the pastors. Even today, taxes are collected from the populace to help fund the churches in Germany. The Catholic Church went so far as to actually sign a treaty with Hitler, in essence stating, *you leave us alone, we'll leave you alone*. The few Christians who withstood Hitler were driven out of the country, imprisoned or executed.

Again, God's people in this nation are deceived and distracted from the divine commission given by Christ, *as being salt of the earth.*

THIS NATION IS BEING BLESSED MORE THAN EVER

With all the prosperity, this nation has become more selfish and greedier than ever in its history. Large and small companies alike devise wicked plans to get more productivity and pay their workers less. Corporate executives have been exposed one after another, caught in illegal schemes motivated by greed and increases in stock market results; their ruthlessness has rocked this nation's financial stability.

Lying, cheating and adultery have become fashionable. Murder, rape, violence in our schools, along with witchcraft and all kind of wickedness fill our movie and TV screens. Now these evils have become almost everyday headlines on our nightly news. Criminals prey upon the weak and helpless, while more and more swindlers make their mark as the naïve and the gullible are taken in with get-rich gimmicks. Famous actors who once portrayed biblical characters now act in lewd and perverse films, yet the church still embraces them as special envoys that speak for Christ. Some are now reaping the consequences of their hypocrisy as they suffer various health problems and often, untimely deaths. All this is mocking God, and these people reap what they have sown.

Idolatry of work, money, sports, leisure, homes, cars, vacations, gambling, alcohol, drugs, sex, pornography and parties surpasses the previous level of indulgence. There is no fear of retribution from God whatsoever. Our national mockery of God has even shown up in a popular line of clothing with the slogan, "No Fear." Indeed, there is very little fear of God in society, or even in Christianity.

In one local emergency room recently, a lifeless four-month-old baby appeared with its mother. The mother said the baby had been asleep for 16 hours. She further said the child's breathing was funny when she put him down. The next day the hospital discovered that the child died from abuse and neglect, leading to a criminal investigation.

Serial murders, rapists and parents murdering their children are common news. Our minds are filled with horror upon horror. Remember Susan Smith who drowned her two children, Michael, and Alexander? I could list this kind of horror, one upon another on a national level, not to mention the state-by-state accounts that miss national media coverage. Yet we celebrate our victories, prosperity and technology while self-righteously imposing our brand of democracy and debauchery throughout the world. Christians in this country are deceived, unwilling to recognize that America is falling headlong toward catastrophic judgment.

WE HAVE CROSSED THE LINE

"No prosperity and no glory can save a nation that is rotten at heart."
President Theodore Roosevelt

This nation has come to the point of considering filth, perversion, and adultery as acceptable forms of lifestyle. What was once unacceptable and shocking when brought to public light has now become common. Flash nudity during primetime, perverted shows depicting extreme contests and lesbian and homosexual relationships as well as witchcraft on daytime soap operas are now popular. This is just the tip of the iceberg. In our 1996 presidential elections, Senator Robert Dole noted that there would be an outrage expressed by this nation concerning the immoral character of President Clinton. The following week he lamented, saying, *"There was no outrage!"*

The 2000 election should have been about restoring truth and justice to the White House, instead the popular vote went to the candidate who still has a shadow of lies over him.

In the 2004 campaign, lies, character attacks, hatred, and partisan finger-pointing went over the top. The battle line was the morality of this nation.

Again, Christians are pushing to legislate morality, while living as hypocrites before the world and unwilling to clean up their own house.

The flash point to which Israel (God's people) succumbed when Jesus walked the earth was hypocrisy. Again, it is hypocrisy driving the church in America toward harsh ejection by the Lord. The church is condemning the immorality without first cleansing herself. Instead, the scoffer and godless have exposed church and ministerial corruption and immorality repeatedly.

There is a remnant that is righteous, but for the most part the church of America seeks the Lord only to maintain a fleshly, self-indulgent lifestyle. There is an unwillingness to let go of the pleasures and material blessings. Most disregard Christ's admonition to *"store your treasures in heaven!"* The blessings given to the church of America have become idols! The *gospel* message presented by most churches is watered-down religious hype that calls believers to "give to get" and keep up the appearance of righteousness.

National ministries have pushed these heretical teachings to such an extreme that many bewildered Christians are turned-off and tuned-out. These struggling believers are tired of sorting through a maze of gimmicks and silly antics. Millions of wandering Christians and curious lost sinners are desensitized to the true Gospel of Christ by these charismatic sideshows and neurotic tabloid ministries.

Many teach shortcuts on how to obtain the abundant life, rather than the discipline of the Lord that brings true holiness. Too many pulpits are silent concerning sanctification of the believer and how to crucify the works of the flesh and the prevalent narcissistic self-life. Few live a life that glorifies God. The discipline that creates a holy life is sidestepped, while many put on the appearance of holiness. False and carnal teachings hinder the Holy Spirit from having full reign in the life of the individual Christian or the body-life in local churches.

Millions of Christians are lost, wandering in a wasteland. *"And Jesus went about all the cities and villages, teaching in their synagogues and preaching the gospel of the kingdom, and healing every disease and every infirmity. When he saw the crowds, he had compassion for them, because they were harassed and helpless, like sheep without a shepherd"* (Matthew 9:35,36).

These are Christ's warnings to every generation that goes astray. Many have written similar warnings. A popular Christian author, W. Phillip Keller, has written many books; one most read by many Christians worldwide is, *A Shepherd Looks at Psalm 23*. Written in the seventies, this book is still well-read and considered a Christian classic. It's still in print and is available on audiotape as well. The author, a shepherd by occupation, eloquently expounded Psalm 23, uplifting the reader to a deeper understanding of Christ's care and comfort as the Good Shepherd.

Yet in 1988 Brother Keller wrote *Predators in our Pulpits*, a powerful warning and exposé covering many of these same abuses in the church and society that have now become all the more pervasive and insidious. *Predators in our Pulpits* is out of print and rarely available as a used book. This work is just as important, if not more so, than *A Shepherd Looks at Psalm 23*. As prophesied, the last-day Christian desires only soothing messages and stops up their ears to the hard message, which can snatch their soul from the snares of hell. Yes, over these many years God's people were warned, but the warnings have been ignored.

GOD CONTINUES TO EXPOSE HIDDEN CORRUPTION AND EVIL

Christians are in love with America more than they love God. As the end of the age unfolds, the United States of America will be pulled into the coming New World Order that will soon accept the antichrist's rule. Yes, all nations will embrace Satan's lie, including Israel. The promise of peace and restoration of prosperity will draw America and millions of Christians in the final dark hours leading up to Christ's return. We see Europe taken in by a new union of nations soaked in socialistic ideology and filled with immorality. Canada succumbed to this political ideology many years ago and now, through a gradual seeping into our own culture and politics, the United States is on the brink of a social revolution, racing toward Satan's short-lived deception of the whole world – including the United States!

My father is a World War II veteran who put his life on the line many times as a survivor of Navy battles in the Pacific. He shot down a Japanese torpedo plane single-handed, put Marines on the beach at Peleliu, endured a terrible island battle and survived shipwrecking typhoons. He is a survivor of the Great Depression, a warrior for this country who lived on the edge, surviving only to lead a life of hardship. I grew up in an abusive and dysfunctional, but very patriotic, home. Part of the reason for my father's alcohol abuse and violence stemmed from the horrors of war. What he witnessed and partook of in his late teens caused nightmares throughout his life.

When I graduated from high school, I went to college and lasted through the football season, got behind in studies and ended up joining the Marine Corps in November of '69. I expected to go to Viet Nam and most likely die for my country. My family's patriotic values instilled a mindset of "the United States, right or wrong, do or die!"

I rejected the anti-war movement and the cynicism towards our country that many in my generation embraced. The Marine Corps became my passion. The discipline, training and advancement opportunities straightened me out, at least on a social level, but as a career Marine my morals were not at all exemplary. God spared me Viet Nam, though I made my life available to go. The Marines assigned me to be trained in electronic repair, where as an honor graduate, I became a telecommunication equipment repair instructor.

Miraculously, I came to know Christ while in the service of my country and was honorably discharged five years early from my first six-year reenlistment. I was called into full-time ministry in 1974 where the Lord prompted me to request an early release. God graciously moved upon the Marine Corps to accommodate my request and gave me an honorable discharge.

My oldest son spent seven years in the Coast Guard, a very demanding life and strenuous duty. My family has always been proud of America, but what he experienced under the Clinton years in the military is part of the decline of America's greatness and its continued plunge toward wickedness. My son witnessed cutbacks, cover-up of deadly mishaps and decline in leadership character within the new officer corps entering the Coast Guard.

Part of the judgment of God upon a wayward nation is the exposé of corruption and hidden wickedness. As mentioned earlier, the downfall of many of our past political heroes along with Watergate, Whitewater, and the impeachment of President Clinton, coupled with Enron and the prison scandal in Iraq, all point to an increased *judgment of exposure*. God is lifting up the skirts of America and showing the world and God's people its vile hidden wickedness.

The cynicism of the sixties and seventies is now directed at Christian institutions and ministries as well as most esteemed national institutions. From wayward Supreme Court justices to corrupt police, not one foundational pillar of our society is clean.

In the coming days you will see more exposure of corruption and wickedness in high places. Our military will not be exempt. During former President Ronald Reagan's years, the military had men and women of solid vision leading the way in restoring esteem for our government and the military branches. Now we learn of sex scandals in our military academies along with other covered up corruption.

This is just the beginning. You can expect God to show the world the wickedness concealed by corrupt generals and commanders within the military. America will be seen as being no different from the much-maligned third world countries where governments and their military govern and protect the elite and are rife with bribes, payoffs and abuse.

As the end of the age approaches many Christians will be caught napping and whimsically living in a fantasy world of nostalgia, wishing for the days when life was comfortable, peaceful and filled with wholesome values. Christians are spellbound with the lost American dream, hoping that the dream will turn America back to family values and clean living.

God is talking through all these exposures and national troubles saying, *Wake up Christians of America! The days are evil and America will follow the rest of the world's rebellion. Get ready to receive the coming Christ and his judgment upon the whole world–including America.*

Yes, we are to pray for godly leaders, our government and peace. We are to stand up for what is right. We are to vote for the most godly-principled people to be in office. But we must also lead godly lives, unencumbered, as exiles in a foreign country ready to leave in a twinkle of an eye! (See Hebrews 11:13-16).

To the contrary, much of church growth and evangelism is motivated by restoring America to its former glory so Christians can still have fun living in the world. Millions of dollars are poured into ministries and churches which promote an Americanized gospel that promises prosperity and restoration of America and the good life.

GOD'S PEOPLE ARE OVERBURDENED WITH EXORBITANT PROJECTS

The megachurch syndrome that affects thousands of ministers, church elders and board members has taken a toll on the sheep. God's people go along with the bigger-is-better mentality, counting people like cattle—the more people, the more success. The larger the building, the more people will come. This reasoning has consumed church after church. We read about one financial abuse after another as the sheep give and give to feed leadership's ego and monument-building lust. Denominations and local churches compete with each other in the appearance of success as they attempt to build the biggest congregation. It seems that a building project is the main goal for church growth.

The truth is, these ego monuments are built at the expense of the spiritual welfare of the congregation. When the *cross* is preached from the pulpit, the phonies leave, along with their checkbooks; and there goes the building expansion program! *"Let's preach the easy road gospel so no feelings are hurt. Let's not expose hidden sin and selfishness in the church; let's be careful not to ruffle the flesh,"* seems to be the pastors' constant refrain.

If you want to be a well-liked minister, work for the congregation and not for the Lord. Tell them what they want to hear. The numbers will increase, and you can get them to build the best church facility in your community. This is a temptation of Satan, and he continues to find plenty of takers.

God's people are in competition with each other over souls for church growth. God's people elect and appoint the best-looking, best-dressed, smoothest orator that money can buy so new converts will come in as Israel did when choosing Saul over the leadership of the prophet Samuel. They wanted a king to rule over them so they could buy him off. The king would tell them what they wanted to hear, as in the surrounding pagan nations. They chose the best looking and most athletic people. To the contrary, king Saul was a phony coward. King Saul ignored what God commanded and preferred to do what the people wanted him to. On the first mission for the Lord, Saul was to destroy all of the Amalekites. Instead, he disobeyed God, giving in to the will of the people of Israel. (See 1 Samuel 15).

A prophet of the Lord confronted this insecure coward. Even as the evidence of his disobedience trailed behind him, Saul still insisted that he had done God's

Will. Saul says that the people took the best of the Amalekites' sheep and cattle to *"sacrifice to the Lord your God."* You see, Saul was loyal and obedient to another god than the God of Israel, and that god was Saul, himself. Because of his insecurities (see 1 Samuel 10:22 and 15:17), Saul would not stand up to the people, even though he knew God would back him up. Saul did what the people wanted, not what God wanted, in order to maintain his popularity. On the way back from this failed mission, king Saul built a monument of himself.

Thus, today, as did king Saul, many pastors and leaders are making themselves kings over God's people, tickling their ears, placating, and pandering to their fleshly desires and ignoring the word of God. They are avoiding confrontations with sinful and selfish congregations. They are building ego monuments out of stone and mortar and not building disciples of Christ. They want their names to live on as the great pastor who built the greatest congregation and greatest church facility in the city!

Some of these pastors have led their congregations into debt with credit cards and second mortgages to get these building programs completed. God's people pray and weep over building programs while the severely wounded in their own families and in their communities go without help. Thousands of congregations play the game of Christian hypocrisy, looking good for God on the outside, but refusing to do the hard things that set the captives free. They avoid soiling their lives by touching the poor, the lost and the hurting neighborhood children for God. They look the other way as their neighbor flounders in a living hell.

Christ warned that many Christians will be rejected at the great judgment seat of Christ because they refused to help the truly downtrodden, those in prison and those considered lesser in society. (See Matthew 25:41-46).

GOD'S WOUNDED ARE STUCK IN THE MENTAL HEALTH SYSTEM

Through the years, church growth idolatry has grown and grown. Very few ministries attempt to build Christ-like character into the congregation. Rather, they seek out converts that will go along with their building and expansion programs. They skew their sermons and give special treatment to the rich. Preferential ministry is directed at the functional in society, while the hurting, the divorced, the crushed in spirit, the dysfunctional and the severely wounded are forced to get help from government programs, secular counseling and the world's mental health systems and asylums. Only a few true and faithful ministries stay the course and help the truly wounded and needy.

Most mental health patients across this nation suffer misdiagnoses of forgotten, hidden abuse inflicted during childhood. They are convinced that their problems cannot be cured, but with the right medication, their problem will be controlled. They struggle through life like zombies, overmedicated on prescribed antipsychotic drugs, believing that this sedated condition is the best they can ever achieve.

Many in the mental health profession are sincere and do help many, but when God is left out of the recovery process and demonic infestations are ignored, it's no wonder most mental health patients reach basic functionality through chemistry to survive only moment by moment.

The wounded inner spirit and the divided spirit of the mind sends distorted signals from forgotten or hidden trauma from childhood. Some of the hatred and rejection came upon them just after conception, as they sensed rejection from one or both parents in their spirit while still in the womb.

One Christian woman with whom our ministry helped told of a childhood spiritual wound she received from her father. As a young child, she witnessed her father beat to death their family pet dog with a baseball bat. He flew into a rage because the dog supposedly got too rough with her.

That and other vague memories came out in counseling. When we met her, she had been under the care of a local psychiatrist for over ten years. Her doctor had her on high doses of Lithium. She had been in abusive relationships and had been dependent on alcohol and drugs from the time she was in college.

In the book of James, there are scriptural guidelines for recovering from such wounds to the spirit. We worked with her but could only get so far. The painful truth about past bitterness and unresolved trauma was too hard for her to take in her drugged condition. After ten years of prescribed chemicals, she had become so passive and spiritually dead that she chose to stay medicated and leave her inner bitterness, jealousy, rage, fear and hatred alone. In her divided and drugged condition, she was content to stumble through life, pleading for prayer from others to help her succeed in just holding down a job.

The body of Christ has very little discernment or answers for the people who are carrying past abuse and trauma. Pastors are shocked that the youth of their congregation have severe problems created by dysfunctional Christian parents. For most Christian leaders, as long as the parents in their congregation look good on the outside, attend church and talk the talk, they never think to look deeper. They refuse to see the covered-up abuse, neglect, and hypocrisy in the home. From generation to generation, these adult children have staggered into church throughout the last century, perpetuating hypocrisy, hidden abuse, and selfishness. When they come to church, they learn to mimic Christ. If a new convert looks good enough on the outside, then often they acquire responsibilities they cannot bear and far too many become burnt-out. All this has piled up on this last day generation of Christians. No wonder Jesus said that many would fall away and spoke of a faithless last day church, *"Nevertheless, when the Son of man comes, will he find faith on earth?"* (Luke 18:8).

Yes, new converts burnout and crash constantly. They struggle from one false doctrine to another, trying to be set free from their past forgotten wounds still lodged in their spirits. God's wounded get more help from the world than from the church in general.

Most Christians who did not have these grievous wounds or who have their lives in order do not have a clue of how to minister to these people. It is no surprise that most churches across America have very little help to offer wounded Christians. These wounded Christians suffer from being double-minded or having a crushed spirit. The Bible has answers, but the church is often not equipped to help Christians with these spiritual problems. Instead, the wounded Christian goes outside the church for help.

There are ministries that have learned to help those wounded in spirit, but most congregations and pastors reject these ministries. On the other hand, many ministries that do attempt to learn how to help the wounded in spirit become caretakers and babysitters that pity these wounded into staying sick for years. They often use New Age methods or a 12-step knock-off program from Alcoholics Anonymous in an attempt to support and facilitate recovery. These programs are either spiritualistic in nature, opening doors to worse spiritual problems or, as in the case of the 12-step programs, leave out vital scriptures that the Holy Spirit can use to reach to the roots of bitterness and heal hidden wounds, most of which occurred during childhood.

AMERICAS' HIDDEN HOLOCAUST

This nation refuses to address a hidden epidemic and confront the hidden sin and wickedness directed at children. Child abuse and neglect are embedded in the subcultures of our society. Society and the church play a pretend game concerning the causes of dysfunctional families and abusive adults. We will raise millions of dollars for foreign missions to feed starving children overseas while over 12 million American children go hungry on a daily basis. We let the welfare system take care of our hurting children while we spend millions on elaborate sanctuaries and church parking lots.

New Christian couples with their families get very little guidance on Holy Spirit-led cleansing and inner transformation. Instead, these new Christians learn how to be religious abusers as spouses and parents. They learn how to fake it religiously, to play the "submit game" and never die to self in order to become equal joint heirs in the grace of life. They become hypocrites, raising rebellious children who learn to conceal bitterness, live in secret sin and suppress inner rage directed at their phony Christian parents.

The church does not have time to get involved with exposing and ministering to some of this nation's biggest sins: child abuse and neglect in the home.

Instead, God is depicted as a Santa Claus who will bring material blessings. Successful programs and youth ministries can never take the place of responsible loving parents who nurture their children in the things of God — at home during the week.

It is easier to give out *"turn or burn tracts"* than minister to crying children, hurting neighbors and the lost sinner. Many Christians do not know how to witness by example, far too many live selfish and jealous lives. These talk the talk but refuse to walk it out as Jesus prescribed. Vacation Bible school and Christian daycare workers often talk about Jesus rather than show how to live exemplary Christ-like lives. These programs replace the hard work of truly helping the children of this nation to know Jesus by reaching their parents. Very few intercessors are raised up to do battle with the Prince of Darkness in order to bring to light the hidden darkness that is in millions of families, including church families of this nation. True revival is the job of the body of Christ and it starts in the sanctuary.

This nation and the church are apathetic towards the holocaust of millions of unborn babies being aborted. And this nation continues to rack up the body count. Now we have developed an abortion pill, and experiments in cloning human embryos for medical research have started.

Our society has little regard for human life. The righteous have cried out and protested. They have prayed, fasted and wept. We have attempted to legally change the abortion laws and there have been very few victories.

Corrie Ten Boom, in 1975, at our college chapel in Seattle, recounted some of the Nazi horrors and said that it can happen again, right here in America. She was referring to government sanctioned abortions and loss of freedom in America. In Nazi Germany, the *death camps* were secret, yet we have our *death clinics* open to the public.

This is a horror that is an abomination unto the Lord. However, there is something worse than abortions that we, as the church, have either ignored or tolerated.

Abortion on demand is a symptom of a deeper root problem. I am afraid that we, as the salt of the earth, missed the mark. We are powerless in stopping the abortions for several reasons: the zealot approach, finger pointing, self-righteous hypocrisy and murderous tactics, to name a few. The worst reason is our own Christian hypocrisy and avoidance of our national hidden holocaust. A 1999 study showed there is a growing sexual abuse epidemic in America the public seldom hears about. The statistics cited in this 1999 study are frightening. Since this study, the exposure of the pedophilia in the Catholic Church and other denominations, and throughout society is epidemic in proportion. Millions are sexually victimized, causing emotional and spiritual damage beyond comprehension. Our national holocaust—our national tragedy—is child abuse, including neglect, hatred, and unspoken rejection of our children. Abortions are a symptom of this deeper root problem.

Jesus said, *"Suffer the children to come unto me."* What did He mean by this statement? Did Christ mean that we should tell them about Christ, salvation, do's and the don'ts so they will grow up faster than normal, so as not to be a problem? Or did Jesus expect Christian parents to live as an example that would impart faith to children, nurturing them and training them in the admonition of the Lord?

As with the disciples, when Christ admonished their callous attitude toward the little ones who wanted to be near Christ, most churches are also pushing aside children and teens. Most consider children a burden, rather than a blessing. Church and church families are entertaining them, buying them off and telling them to live a moral life so they will not be any more trouble than what they are already. It has backfired and we have more trouble than ever in the home because of Christian parental hypocrisy. Love-starved Christian children are growing up and becoming narcissistic adults with mental and emotional disorders. The megachurch answer is to cater to the narcissism. The church is often guilty of offering an easy road gospel that leads to destruction.

Thousands of Christians flood to evangelical, charismatic and Pentecostal churches looking for fire insurance and inner peace, with the emphasis on *"what can God do for me"* so they can become an overnight success. They look for a church that will entertain and babysit their children. The preaching of the Gospel has become mere *infomercials* bragging about how God (through their ministry) can miraculously make everything wonderful—*instantly*. If this does not happen, then that Christian has not exercised and/or developed enough faith, and they are not good enough to become one of the successful survival-of-the-fittest Christians.

Underneath all this hype and appearance of Christian character, the truth this generation is saying inwardly is, *"If we didn't have these kids, look how much further along we would be financially with far fewer hassles."* Churches separate the family with specialized programs that offer a smorgasbord of worldly family entertainment in order to keep the youth's attention. Too many churches have become baby-sitters, while tickling the ears of the parents.

Our fellowship provides nursery and care for small children, but as for the older teens, they attend service with their family. Parents should train their young children and teenagers in godly living in the home, by example. Far too often, the Sunday school teacher has this all-important task. An occasional youth group outing is good, but for the most part, church programs attack Christian family togetherness.

Child abuse, molestation, domestic violence, and youth crime are subjects often avoided in the pulpit. Christian parents find little practical help from the church in dealing with America's hidden holocaust or their own hidden tendencies toward spiritual rejection that sends out the destructive message, *"I wish I didn't have these kids!"* Instead, the church offers youth programs as a place to get rid of them, at least for a while, and for free!

Society has produced thousands of dysfunctional parents, including far too many Christian parents who subdue their spiritually rejected children through prescription medications. Millions of children suffer from Attention Deficit Disorder as well as other psychotic maladies, with little research done to pinpoint the true causes. One can speculate with a high degree of confidence that most causes stem from resentful, dysfunctional parents. A recent study suggests that younger children, when exposed to long periods of watching TV suffer from ADD. In October of 2004, the FDA ordered child alerts for antidepressants. Recent research concluded that there is an increased risk of suicidal thoughts leading to self-harm when children take prescribed antidepressants.

THE W.C. FIELDS SYNDROME

W.C. Fields, a comedian of our father's generation, had an infamous line, *"Anybody that hates kids and dogs can't be all bad."* Some progress has been made, but as a nation, we still struggle with inner hidden hatred and resentment toward children.

It has surfaced in abortions, children abandoned in daycares, undisciplined children or the extreme of abusive discipline. Children are often victims of sexual assault, mental and emotional torture, as well as bargaining chips in divorce.

Even in our public schools a pervasive abuse exists as illiteracy is often promoted along with immoral and narcissistic values. Thousands of children are made suspect by teachers looking for any symptom of ADD. These modern socialistic teachers are encouraged to get the parent's consent for testing, and if tested positive the child is put on medication and the school gets more federal funding.

Christian private schools are no exception, as they often foster hypocrisy and send high school graduates to Christian liberal colleges that are weak on the true Gospel and heavy on the social sciences and worldly teaching to keep federal grants in place. Children are pressured to perform in scholastics and sports to promote the schools' standings.

The major issue with this nation, as far as God's distaste goes, is our abandonment and hatred of our own children. Although child abuse, neglect and over-indulgences have been with us for years, now the results are culminating in the horrible destruction of the family.

Many ministries are calling America and the church to return to our ancestor's family values, but the previous generation's family lifestyle only looked good on the outside. They had an appearance of righteousness while hiding wickedness and all manner of evil. Many family ministries see the symptoms, but unfortunately do not deal with the root problem. The recent exposure of hidden sin at the highest levels in many of the prominent national ministries makes this point clear!

Our ministry has assisted many marriages; some experienced recovery, but some ended in divorce. Some spouses were evil, and divorce was the only solution. We assisted one young woman who was seeking legal help. She was seeking custody and protection from her husband, whom she discovered was molesting their children. This husband grew up in a Christian home where his parents were active in a major international youth ministry. We went with her to interview an attorney. He was in his late sixties and seemed objective. He listened to her difficult situation and her emotional challenges. He did not know that we, being there for her support, were ministers of the Gospel. He downplayed the molestations by injecting, *"You know, years ago, back in the Midwest, it was no big deal when the farmer was messing around with his daughters!"* We were appalled and I interjected, *"It was just as evil then as it is now!"* This man's moral views are not an exception, but rather the common hidden attitude, and this sickness permeates our society. Child abuse and molestation are not new to this generation but have been continually handed down from previous generations. National studies and the exposé within the Roman Catholic Church, with its widespread pedophilia and homosexuality, add credibility to the assertions in this book.

That is our heritage from our forefathers: cover up evil. God is lifting the veil that covers evil in the church and America. The secret sins of these last generations are being exposed.

Jesus warned, *"Beware of the leaven of the Pharisees, which is hypocrisy. Nothing is covered up that will not be revealed, or hidden that will not be known. Therefore whatever you have said in the dark shall be heard in the light, and what you have whispered in private rooms shall be proclaimed upon the housetops"* (Luke 12:1-3).

Hypocrisy has been our heritage. Yes, there were many godly homes, but too few in the previous generations. Church and godly families wanted the good life—the American Dream—while evil flourished and stayed hidden. The pursuit of money and success at the expense of our children is our heritage. Exposing and confronting evil was too difficult.

Each generation reaps in a greater way the previous generation's wickedness. Now, we as a nation and as a church are reaping terror from a truly lost generation.

Our own children have become terrorists. Driven by rage, children bring carnage to our schools in epidemic proportion. Since 1996 there have been some 28 school massacres by 30 different children who killed 6 educators, 43 fellow students and wounded 109.

A case to examine is the story of Kip Kinkel, a teenager who went on a shooting and killing spree at Thurston High School in Springfield, Oregon on May 21, 1998. He started out by killing his parents at home, and then went to school where he killed two more people and wounded 22 others.

Many studies tried to answer why Kip did this. Most concluded that there was perhaps no reason. The following were Kip's issues that, in his eyes left him few alternatives.

- He was an accidental conception in which his mother considered abortion. When the police arrested Kip, he kept crying out, *"I should have been aborted."*
- His older sister was a role model that was impossible to follow. Favoritism was very apparent, as his father constantly compared his daughter's achievements to Kip's failures, producing a powerful shame.
- His high school literature class wrote an essay on the modern movie rendition of *Romeo and Juliet,* filled with teen violence and murder.
- He was insecure and failed at being a "man." His father talked him into trying out for football, in which Kip failed.
- Girls he tried to date rejected him.
- Violence became a way of releasing stress.
- He became interested in guns.
- His psychiatrist discussed handgun ownership and bragged about his favorite semi-automatic handgun. Kip wanted one like it, and his father got him one to appease him.
- Finally, he got in trouble with the law over a handgun in school.
- Unable to face his dad, he killed to be free of a loveless, performance-orientated relationship with his parents, ending up at his school, killing and wounding many of his peers.

When the police entered the Kinkel home, a CD soundtrack of the above-mentioned movie, *Romeo and Juliet*, was playing loudly and continuously—an old Shakespeare tragedy played out in reality by Kip Kinkel.

This was not an abusive family; it was a perform-to-be loved family. It seemed that Kip never was successful in anything. He could never win his parents' (especially his father's) unconditional love and acceptance. These families, like millions of seemingly normal families, live with hidden desperation, struggling for unconditional acceptance.

When Kip fell short of perfection or failed, his parents emanated vibes, *"We should have never had him!"*

Millions of children are receiving surface love, but in their spirit they sense parental rejection. These rejected children feel they are burdens who should have never been born.

Today, most suffer quietly while they attend school and church, while thousands are stuck in asylums, mental health programs, all turning their pain, hate, and revenge inward to keep themselves from doing what Kip Kinkel did.

You will continue to see more and more teens and adults snap, as the rejected in society can no longer contain their stress. Snipers, serial killers, factory, government and church workers going *postal;* all point to society unraveling and going mad. The violence that permeates society brings out what is already deep within. These loveless "lost generation" children are everywhere, like time bombs ready to explode onto society. As they become older teens and adults, terrorism becomes the avenue of choice in expressing their rage.

Kip is accountable, as is anyone committing crime and murder. Nevertheless, this tragedy should have been prevented if his parents and community adults cared enough and learned how to show even a vestige of godly unconditional love and respect toward Kip.

God was gracious to me in my childhood, in spite of frequent molestation by babysitters, battered and emotionally abused, and attended over 18 schools before graduating from high school. I struggled to overcome sin, destructive relationships, and a failed marriage. There was so much negative influence in my life, to the point that many who knew me concluded and even said they thought, *"He will never make it."*

When I say that God was gracious to me, I mean this: there were three people in my life God used to intercede for me. When I was seven, a truly caring Christian family in my neighborhood invited me to dinner. The children were able to speak at the table and a sense of protection and love permeated the home. I never forgot that influence. I know they prayed for me. When I was 12, another neighbor also prayed for me and took my brother, my sister and me to church a few times. Her ministry had a great influence on me. She was a Baptist. Finally, when I was 15, an older widowed lady, Mrs. Jones, had a ministry of walking up and down our neighborhood. She talked with the kids about the Gospel. I could tell there was something special about her. She prayed and interceded for the children in our small town. She attended a local Pentecostal church and was simply a servant of the Lord Jesus. There was no fanfare or special recognition for these people.

Years later I returned to my hometown, where I graduated from high school. I was the counseling pastor of a local church. One day, from my office window, I saw Mrs. Jones walking by. By then she was elderly, but still walked the streets of my hometown, praying. I went out and greeted her and invited her in to visit. I briefly explained to her my life story, with all the trouble I went through on my way to know Jesus after my life had hit rock bottom. Then I explained to her how God had used her mightily through her prayers. This humble saint broke down and wept, and just kept praising Jesus. A few months later, Mrs. Jones died. There was no special funeral; no honor given that was due her—not that she wanted any of that, for she considered herself just a Christian worker who was true to the Lord.

These three people loved children; I am not talking about using children religiously, but sincerely standing in the gap for a lost generation. There are many still doing this kind of work, but not enough. The church refuses to do the hard, ugly, unpleasant work. If ministry does not get glory and applause from the pews, then seldom will you see hard work done.

If the churches these people attended had supported their work and made disciples for Jesus instead of converts to their denominations, I believe that many others just as I would not have suffered as hard a road in life before being awakened to the salvation of Christ.

This is the condition most churches are in today. Cover up and pretend, as they keep busy playing church. The truth is, too many Christian parents and churches treat children like *millstones around the neck*. Church daycares and Sunday schools have become mere depositories. Many daycare workers and Sunday school teachers try to teach them about God, only to have parents unravel Christ's teachings by hypocritical living.

The hidden holocaust of child abuse, neglect and rejection is not a secret any longer. God is lifting our skirts, as a nation and as Christians, exposing our secret wickedness.

A Sodomite Abduction Of Our Children

Jesus prophesied that a Sodom-like immorality would mark His soon return. America is racing toward this condition. The level of filth and perversion has become unimaginable from the standard set just a few years prior. Each year public and educational morals recede toward a demonic decadency, pressing our children into sexual bondage.

Grade school children often receive sex education without parental consent. The "sex-ed" directly opposes and nullifies parental input. Parents must make themselves aware of any program and fill out a form excusing their child's attendance. The curriculum is explicit and perverse, all under the guise of sexual diversity. Most public-school systems and the majority of secular child psychologists promote this early education to nullify sexual hang-ups and prejudice.

In reality, this creates a Sodomite society that grooms children to embrace sexual immorality without having to suppress a painful conscience.

Children are not safe on most streets in America without adult escorts. Children rape children, as the case in high school initiations. Prospective college athletes are enticed to attend schools through sexual favors and escort services. College spring breaks often degenerate into orgies.

The Internet is not safe. Pedophiles now hide in churches, befriending families, neighbors, and friends, searching for opportunities. Sexual predators, child abductors, molesters, rapists and other violent sexual criminals are increasing in number and in boldness. Judges are reluctant to incarcerate because of over-filled prison systems. Many liberal courts and perverse judicial rulings allow criminals to roam free. Young Carlie Brucia in Sarasota, Florida was a recent victim of a society racing toward sodomy. What is more terrifying—it will get worse.

AN IMMORAL NATION, A PHONY AND IDOLATROUS CHURCH THAT DESPISES LITTLE ONES

God abandoned Israel when the nation reached a point in idol worship that was unstoppable. At times, Baal, Asherah and Moloch worship permeated Israel's culture and worship. They honored God with their lips, but their hearts were far from really loving and obeying God. They took their idols into their hearts and their everyday living revolved around these false gods and household idols. When God sent prophets to warn and correct, Israel rejected, hated, stoned and even killed them. When the idol worship expanded to the sacrifice of children, God abandoned Israel to the forces of evil.

America's morals have sunk to this level of decay—even in the church. This nation and a great portion of the church embrace defiling passions, and live godless lives that sacrifice children and despise any authority that says stop or slow down.

What are some of our modern-day idols? We often idolize prosperity, money, convenience, success, pleasure, passion, work, leisure, entertainment, fun, excitement, sports, relationships and romance. Narcissistic spousal idolatry runs rampant in society and within the body of Christ, all in the name of marriage. Couples are obsessed with how to make sure their mates bring passion and happiness, demanding perfection, and if not, then divorce. All this adds up to avoiding the everyday, sometimes boring job of raising children properly and trusting God for basic needs, as well as the extras. These pursuits have caused divorce and the abandonment of our children.

Jesus said, *"Whoever humbles himself like this child, he is the greatest in the kingdom of heaven. Whoever receives one such child in my name receives me; but whoever causes one of these little ones who believe in me to sin, it would be better for him to have a great millstone fastened round his neck and to be drowned in the depth of the sea. Woe to the world for temptations to sin! For it is necessary that temptations come, but woe to the man by whom the temptation comes! And if your hand or your foot causes you to sin, cut it off and throw it away; it is better for you to enter life maimed or lame than with two hands or two feet to be thrown into the eternal fire. And if your eye causes you to sin, pluck it out and throw it away; it is better for you to enter life with one eye than with two eyes to be thrown into the hell of fire. See that you do not despise one of these little ones; for I tell you that in heaven their angels always behold the face of my Father who is in heaven"* (Matthew 18:5-10).

Recently, there was a so-called baptism of the Holy Spirit falling upon many youth groups in charismatic and Pentecostal fellowships. Parents felt secure as their teens became involved in teen groups where they experienced this supposed move of the Spirit of God.

Here is the most deceitful idol of all—the idol of power that most Christians are lusting after. They are looking for a special dose of *"Holy Spirit experience"* for themselves and their children, an experience that will produce lasting inner peace and pain-numbing euphoric feelings that will magically protect and change their inner life. In reality, these are false spirit experiences coming from a cross less gospel. This faddish movement makes life seem easier and creates magic thinking—a thinking that believes *"My children know God now and they are protected from all the world's vices,"* which frees parental consciences from guilt as they run after the things of this world.

In the many years of counseling families and teens, this is one of the biggest and subtlest sacrifices of children in the church.

It was brought to my attention that many of teens attending a Pentecostal church in our community were involved in activities similar to the Toronto Blessing. These teens were all excited and experienced spiritual touches. Word got out and the meetings began to swell in size. The local newspapers reported on this youth group and its activities and referred to it as a teen revival. This group even got some recognition on a national basis.

The claims were that these teens were coming to Jesus, staying out of trouble and getting off drugs.

The truth was that far too many of these teens were falling right back into their old lifestyles and habits. I became burdened for one young man and the Lord led me to stand in the gap for him. I knew that these false experiences were not helping him deal with his problems or bringing him closer to the true Christ.

About a year later, word got back to us that this young man was no longer involved with this group and was back into drugs. He made a connection with some teen gang members to supply them with some marijuana. He met with them late at night and went with them to a less frequented area just outside of town. Somehow, the deal fell through and these teens decided to kill him. They stabbed him several times and left him on the side of the road bleeding to death with a collapsed lung. By the grace of God, someone stopped and took him to the emergency room. It took him months to recover.

The point here is this: these so-called works and manifestations of the Lord just harden the heart of most teens caught up in these empty manifestations. These experiences are like drugs; the effects wear off and the old lifestyle switches back on. These teachings offer a false freedom and are really an alternative "feel good" that, like most feel-good experiences, leave nothing when they wear off; like a drug wearing off, it never changes or heals the inner person. This is not an isolated case.

THE CHURCH OF AMERICA IS SAYING TO GOD "DON'T BOTHER US, WE'RE HAVING FUN!"

In short, the church of America is saying: *Don't rock the boat; we're having fun playing church and being entertained.*

Truman and Jan Dillingham, a dear brother and sister in the Lord, have a traveling ministry and occasionally come to the Puget Sound area of the Northwest.

They deliver hard-hitting messages, dealing with true issues most ministries seldom address. Their ministry operates in the true gifts, building up those in their meetings. In 1991, Truman told of a prophetic dream he received from the Lord. In this dream he was preaching a *death-to-self* message, and those listening got up and walked away. In the dream, these Christians went behind a curtain. He walked over, drew open the curtain and saw a multitude of Christians sitting in front of a giant stage full of entertainers. That dream from the Lord was a prophetic warning that pointed to what has truly engulfed the body of Christ today.

Millions of Christians go to church looking for blessings, entertainment, and secure feelings. Millions of believers have come seeking and expecting a Hollywood effect, where praise and worship become self-absorbed spirit touches that supposedly set the personal spirit free. Concerts of prayer have sprung up nationwide only to end up in neurotic dance and chant meetings where outsiders would think they have entered a lunatic asylum. Hollywood-like plays and musicals (using secular music or erotic beat) have come to be expected in far too many church worship services.

Fellowships are informally controlled and manipulated by member cliques and carnal board members who push self-serving agendas. Gossip and busybodies undermine leadership, causing dissention and ruin true revival. These wolves in sheep's clothing love playing church, love controlling others and set themselves up as spiritual leaders walking in self-appointed authority.

Most pastors put up with these charlatans and wolves for fear of their salary and reputation. To survive, leadership must devise new and exciting entertainment, to bring in new converts for fast church growth and tirelessly wear themselves out catering to the Christian elitists who overtake and control thousands of congregations throughout America.

These controlling Christian members refuse to listen to the hard teachings of Christ, embrace the cross and die to their carnal-narcissistic agendas. As Paul wrote, *"For many, of whom I have often told you and now tell you even with tears, live as enemies of the cross of Christ. Their end is destruction, their god is the belly, and they glory in their shame, with minds set on earthly things"* (Philippians 3:18,19).

ABANDONED TO PROSPERITY

God has given over this nation and the church of America to prosperity. Most believe that material blessings, wealth, and health are signs of God's approval and protection. Millions of Christians embrace this lie. Leadership in the body of Christ has daubed with whitewash the true condition of God's people, and this false wall of protection is crumbling. Disaster looms for millions of Christians who are not prepared to navigate in the coming dark days.

The true wall of protection is a proper relationship with God. Christians really believe they are in a safety zone and are prepared to receive the coming Christ. False teachers and money-grabbing ministries teach Christians to live "high on the hog" and "go for all the gusto," not knowing that they have neglected their relationship with God. Multitudes of Christians have greedily consumed God's blessings, going after treasures on earth. *"Therefore we must pay the closer attention to what we have heard, lest we drift away from it. For if the message declared by angels was valid and every transgression or disobedience received a just retribution, how shall we escape if we neglect such a great salvation?"* (Hebrews 2:1-3).

Two centuries leading up to the Great Depression had the Industrial Revolution, World War I, and growth in technology, unprecedented prosperity and an extreme decline in morality. This period culminated into the decade called the Roaring Twenties. In 1919 the Temperance League, backed by Christian churches, succeeded in getting an amendment to the Constitution prohibiting the consumption and possession of alcohol or liquor. This self-righteous approach to combating the nation's sliding immorality led to the worst increase in organized crime and corruption ever.

The Roaring Twenties, depicted as the greatest decade of social change ever known in American history, is also known as the Jazz Age and the age that saw extreme mass consumption, liberal ideas, attacks on religious values and extreme rebellion against Victorian and moral ideals. There were few major catastrophes, but society experienced technological advances with mass production of the automobile, the telephone, and the airplane. Movies became a rage, with private ownership and capitalism driving the idea that anybody with a little "smarts" and luck could become a millionaire.

Sound familiar? Of course, we should see that the judgment of God was the Great Depression, starting with the stock market crash in 1929. Just before the Depression there was little visible trouble—just prosperity and wickedness. God gave no warning as to what was to come. America celebrated, embraced Darwinism (e.g., the Scopes trial), and became self-indulgent as American society transformed its morals.

The 1990s and the 1920s have an uncanny parallel. The discipline of God was mostly missing in these two decades—a time God abandoned this nation to the god of prosperity. This spiritually choked to death true faith, as false leadership opposed the true Gospel of Christ. The eighties and nineties saw the true Holy Spirit pushed out of many sanctuaries, and the idol of prosperity took God's place.

God has turned away, and the name *Ichabod* (the glory has departed) is on the doors of many congregations and fellowships across this nation.

Judgment is looming over this nation, and the majority of Christians are headed into trouble that will come without warning and with severe destruction! September 11 was a sample of things to come. There may be hope if true repentance comes to America and the church of America. This trouble has been staved off because some of God's people have awakened, become repentant and have truly sought the Lord for mercy and more time.

A Polluted Church Handed Down

We tend to blame the current generation for most of our woes. To the contrary, the open rebelliousness of the late sixties progressing to the current generation was handed down from the hypocrisy and the secret sins of our ancestors. The Great Depression dampened immorality and forced much of it underground. The Great Depression and the war brought America and Christians to a humbler and disciplined life. However, as God's blessings returned, the church—along with America—allowed hypocrisy and greed to creep back in. There has been warning after warning, but for the most part this nation and most Christian churches have refused to repent.

Leadership refuses to chase out the wicked from her midst and has left the church polluted and spiritually dead. Most of our church ancestry left a heritage of lies, legalism, licentious teachings and money-grabbing formulas that manipulate God's people for greedy church growth. Many who see this wickedness within the church are like Jonah, hiding in the ship, running from God, and asleep at their watch. They avoid criticism for speaking out against these deceitful things. Leadership looks the other way to preserve the tithe.

Paul wrote to the Christians at Corinth, trying to correct this same problem.

"I wrote to you in my letter not to associate with immoral men; not at all meaning the immoral of this world, or the greedy and robbers, or idolaters, since then you would need to go out of the world. But rather I wrote to you not to associate with anyone who bears the name of brother if he is guilty of immorality or greed, or is an idolater, reviler, drunkard, or robber—not even to eat with such a one. For what have I to do with judging outsiders? Is it not those inside the church whom you are to judge? God judges those outside. 'Drive out the wicked person from among you'" (1 Corinthians 5: 9-13).

Warning after warning has been given and rejected concerning a needful housecleaning in the church, across all denominations.

The Welsh revival 100 years ago was the beginning of a true revival that should have advanced to America. Instead, Satan squelched it with counterfeit gifts and extremism that portrayed participants as "mad" to the non-believers at large. Evan Roberts, a key leader in the beginning of this move of God, retreated to prayer as he saw this wicked scheme of Satan take over a true move of the Holy Spirit. I recommend *War on the Saints*, unabridged edition, written by Jessie Penn-Lewis, with Evan Roberts. Make sure you get the unabridged edition. Yes, the gifts are real, but they should not distract from the work of salvation, the cross, and sanctification. This false movement keeps plaguing the church, creating idolatry of "spiritual power" that short-circuits the work of the cross and true revival. This false work covers up sin in the camp and shuts down the true gift of prophecy that exposes evil and hidden issues of the heart within the church.

"The LORD passed before him, and proclaimed, 'The LORD, the LORD, a God merciful and gracious, slow to anger, and abounding in steadfast love and faithfulness, keeping steadfast love for thousands, forgiving iniquity and transgression and sin, but who will by no means clear the guilty, visiting the iniquity of the fathers upon the children and the children's children, to the third and the fourth generation'" (Exodus 34:6,7).

THE CHURCH IS NO LONGER SALT AND LIGHT

Jesus warned the church with these words found in Matthew 5:13-16, *"You are the salt of the earth; but if salt has lost its taste, how shall its saltiness be restored? It is no longer good for anything except to be thrown out and trodden under foot by men. 'You are the light of the world. A city set on a hill cannot be hid. Nor do men light a lamp and put it under a bushel, but on a stand, and it gives light to all in the house. Let your light so shine before men, that they may see your good works and give glory to your Father who is in heaven.'"* And in, Luke 14:34,35 Jesus said; *'Salt is good; but if salt has lost its taste, how shall its saltiness be restored? It is fit neither for the land nor for the dunghill; men throw it away. He who has ears to hear, let him hear.'"*

This generation of Christians has lost its flavor and light before men. Because of this, America is no longer influenced by God through the church to stay a moral course, and moreover, this nation and the church are blind to the evil that is about to come in increasing measure.

ON THE VERGE OF THE GREAT TRIBULATION

Jesus predicted that wars, rumors of wars, earthquakes and famines, were the beginning signs leading up to the Great Tribulation. One major indicator was intense persecution directed at Christians.

Through the centuries, Christians have suffered persecution, especially in the Eastern civilizations. Today we see the world enmeshed in turmoil driven by religious prejudice with intense hatred now directed at Christians. The Islamic and Jewish religions have fought each other for years. That hatred is currently spreading to include Western civilizations, especially in America and throughout Christianity.

During the last 20 years in America battle lines have formed defining evangelical Christianity and conservative politics as the same, which has the liberals in an uproar. The liberal left now attacks the conservative right as Christianity attempts to influence morality in government. This ideological difference is inciting ever-increasing bitter resentment, and evangelical Christians are about to become targets of hate and persecution.

Homosexual and lesbian politics, as well as the ACLU and other political organizations, have succeeded in evicting religion and God from American politics, government-funded institutions, and public schools. With the conservative agenda in the White House, the election of 2004 brought great heat in this battle.

The many moral battles in politics will soon be an all-out war. Persecution is coming to the Christians of America from other Americans. The polarizing between the forces of darkness and the forces of righteousness and morality is causing all Americans to take sides.

This is a major sign that Christ spoke of as a prelude to the Great Tribulation. Few American Christians see this sign as a warning of a collision with end-time prophecies such as immorality, widespread hatred and persecutions, which are now forefront in politics and everyday life.

Liberals, atheists, and false Christians want a One World Order where, in their minds, achievement of peace and prosperity come by following a socialistic political ideology. This is the work of Satan coming into power with all wicked deception. That which has restrained him is being removed and he will be allowed to make war on the saints. You can count on the coming trouble to throw the unprepared Christian into terrible turmoil. God is about to let the world see what kind of character is in the last-day Christian.

NUCLEAR WEAPONS OF MASS DESTRUCTION RESURRECTED

"But as to the times and the seasons, brethren, you have no need to have anything written to you. For you yourselves know well that the day of the Lord will come like a thief in the night. When people say, 'There is peace and security,' then sudden destruction will come upon them as travail comes upon a woman with child, and there will be no escape" (1 Thessalonians 5:1-3).

The tension and fear of global nuclear destruction finally ended when the Berlin wall fell. The whole world thought the Cold War was over. God abandoned America and most of the world to a false peace and security. Our wickedness grew with our prosperity, peace and security. America and Christians are still riding on a bubble of lies. The coming sudden destruction and terror will engulf the whole world. Just look what looms over our heads now!

Pakistan and India are in their own nuclear cold war. Pakistan is testing a missile capable of delivering a nuclear warhead. Iran is seeking nuclear weapons of mass destruction. North Korea has the bomb. China now has missiles that will reach the continental United States.

Perestroika (restructuring) is not working and *glasnost* (openness) is dying! President Vladimir Putin is resurrecting the old Marxist-Leninist-Stalinist totalitarian state. Old saber rattling between America and Russia is coming back with an escalating war of words. These are words that have weight, as Russia threatens peace and security with new missile technology that can purportedly out-maneuver Bush's new anti-missile defense system.

I was twelve when the world froze in terror during the Cuban missile crisis. As a sixth grader, we went through emergency drill after drill, hiding under our tables and standing against the walls of our school buildings. Neighbors were building bomb shelters underneath their homes. Unless you lived through this, it's hard to explain the feelings of terror and constant anxiety. All that fear and insecurity from such potential destruction seemed to just vanish when the Reagan-Bush administrations helped pressure Mikhail Gorbachev to accept free enterprise, tear down the iron curtain and create an open society.

Few see that the world is more dangerous than ever, with individual terrorists, rogue nations, and now China and Russia, concentrating their nuclear threat toward the United States. China's economy is growing and they are bidding for the world's limited resources. Russia's run at democracy was a miserable failure, and now Putin is exercising his authority to restore the iron grip of a centralized communist government. New alliances are forming, as America and the European Union must now compete more than ever with these godless socialistic societies. The prophecies of Daniel and the apostle John in Revelation, with their political alliance metaphors and symbols, begin to make sense.

With a constant terrorist threat, tracking aliens, terrorists, and drug traffic bank account activity demands innovative technology. The mark of the beast does not seem as distant as national identification systems are moving quickly to a biometric-based personal identification/verification technology. Next will be implanted identification technology ensuring that "you are who you say you are."

A Great Tribulation showdown will come out of seemingly nowhere and the United States will not have the protection of two great oceans as these resurrected superpowers aim for economic and political control of the world. What is worse, God's long-standing protection over America will be gone—since America has seen fit to remove all semblance of God from every government and public institution. Even America's Christians are filled with arrogance, pride, and self-righteousness while justifying the love of this world—honoring God with their lips but having hearts far from the true love of God.

Christian, will you continue to listen to lies from the pulpit and follow the false teachers? God has abandoned this nation and the lukewarm church to the god of this world. Will God abandon you or will you take heed and get ready?

"And he told them a parable: 'Look at the fig tree, and all the trees; as soon as they come out in leaf, you see for yourselves and know that the summer is already near. So also, when you see these things taking place, you know that the kingdom of God is near'" (Luke 21:29-31).

"But take heed to yourselves lest your hearts be weighed down with dissipation and drunkenness and cares of this life, and that day come upon you suddenly like a snare; for it will come upon all who dwell upon the face of the whole earth. But watch at all times, praying that you [may have strength] to escape all these things that will take place, and to stand before the Son of man" (Luke 21:34-36).

CHAPTER 2

Beware—Satan Demands to Sift the Last-Day Christian

BAPTISM OF FIRE OR SIFTED BY SATAN? IT'S YOUR CHOICE

MOST Christians avoid the discipline of Christ. It is religiously popular to work for God, appear righteous and look down on the lost and hurting. *"He also told this parable to some who trusted in themselves that they were righteous and despised others: 'Two men went up into the temple to pray, one a Pharisee and the other a tax collector. The Pharisee stood and prayed thus with himself, 'God, I thank thee that I am not like other men, extortioners, unjust, adulterers, or even like this tax collector. I fast twice a week, I give tithes of all that I get.' But the tax collector, standing far off, would not even lift up his eyes to heaven, but beat his breast, saying, 'God, be merciful to me a sinner!' I tell you, this man went down to his house justified rather than the other; for everyone who exalts himself will be humbled, but he who humbles himself will be exalted'"* (Luke 18:9-14).

Like the self-righteous Pharisee in Christ's comparison to the humble sinner, so it is with most Christians today, few of whom are truly humble.

The belief that Christ has instantly changed the nature of the born-again person has made many think in magic terms. Most deny they have any self-righteousness or reliance on self. If you have been looking down at those struggling in sin and overwhelmed in life, you have two choices to make: either buy from Christ gold refined in fire or expect Satan to sift you until you are thoroughly humbled.

"Therefore I counsel you to buy from me gold refined by fire, that you may be rich, and white garments to clothe you and to keep the shame of your nakedness from being seen, and salve to anoint your eyes, that you may see. Those whom I love, I reprove and chasten; so be zealous and repent" (Revelation 3:18,19).

If you think you can stand in the coming days without the true discipline of Christ, you can expect to experience trouble.

GOD'S RESTRAINT OF THE DEMONIC IS LIFTING

God is no longer restraining the demonic sources of filth and immorality that have seeped into our nation and its churches. Like a dam on the verge of bursting, the trickle has grown to an unstoppable rush, with the last restraint ready to break. Expect the floodgates of hell to open all the way very soon. We have all witnessed the obscene become the accepted norm. Through a slow process, this nation's inner character has been transformed to accept horror, evil and perverseness as legitimate lifestyles and appropriate entertainment.

Pressure for lifting same-sex marriage sanctions by church, state and at national levels is gaining momentum for acceptance. A major liberal Protestant denomination in 2003 elected an openly gay Bishop. We are seeing increasingly, a repulsive Sodom-like behavior spewed out everywhere. A recent radio news brief revealed the student government at the University of California, Berkley is attempting to pass an ordinance that allows public nudity on campus. Certain universities teach more on homosexuality than on economics. Some states have already passed same-sex marriage laws. Other liberal church denominations have also embraced this immorality and even some conservative churches are moving towards its acceptance. This increase in open immorality has been oozing into society drip by drip. Expect some major milestones in liberal interpretations of the Constitution that will cause a landslide of filth to come upon this nation very soon. Some liberal Democrats are making this a campaign issue.

THE JUDGMENT OF ABANDONMENT

The church has rejected the Lordship of Christ and His discipline, so the only thing left is the *judgment of abandonment*. God is giving the church and this nation what it wants. We have disregarded correction and reproof. Because we have rejected His Word, He now has given us over to the powers of darkness. God is about to turn this generation of Christians over to Satan for severe sifting. God will allow Satan to dump filth, violence, lust, prosperity and perversion on America and the church with no restraint.

JUDGMENT BEGINS WITH THE HOUSEHOLD OF GOD

"For the time has come for judgment to begin with the household of God; and if it begins with us, what will be the end of those who do not obey the gospel of God? And if the righteous man is scarcely saved, where will the impious and sinner appear?" (1 Peter 4:17, 18).

Millions of Christians have embraced the false gospel of cheap grace. Their lust and greed have made a shipwreck of their faith. Secret sin and hardened hearts permeate the body of Christ. God has warned, coaxed, wooed, and pleaded for repentance to the last three generations of Christians. Now judgment must come to purify the body of Christ.

Read the following passage from the book of Hebrews to get more insight concerning Christ, the Judge of God's people.

"For if we sin deliberately after receiving the knowledge of the truth, there no longer remains a sacrifice for sins, but a fearful prospect of judgment, and a fury of fire which will

consume the adversaries. A man who has violated the law of Moses dies without mercy at the testimony of two or three witnesses. How much worse punishment do you think will be deserved by the man who has spurned the Son of God, and profaned the blood of the covenant by which he was sanctified, and outraged the Spirit of grace? For we know him who said, 'Vengeance is mine, I will repay.' And again, 'The Lord will judge his people.' It is a fearful thing to fall into the hands of the living God" (Hebrews 10:26-31).

Yes, the majority of God's people in this nation have grieved, outraged, and chased the Holy Spirit out of God's sanctuaries. The church is about to reap what it has sown!

GIVEN OVER TO THE LUST OF KNOWLEDGE, POWER, PROSPERITY AND FREEDOM

The church in America has rejected the word of the cross and refused to die to self. Carnality and soulish religious experiences have taken the place of the cross. Instead of picking up our cross daily, suffering the work of inner sanctification, and growing up in the discipline of the Lord, we have sought after quick-fix shortcuts that help maintain the carnal self-life. We can still look religious and faithful on the outside and avoid the pain and suffering associated with the death of our old sin and carnal nature.

Christian literature, videos, and television shows have flooded the body of Christ with one teaching after another—one fad program after another. God's people are ever learning, but never obtaining the true grace of God. There are teachings on: How to pray, how to battle the enemy, how to win back this nation, how to save your marriage, how to get instant inner peace, how to work with angels, how-to-live-in-harmony with your family and neighbors, how to have great church growth—the list goes on and on. Some of this is of God, but most have fallen far short in discerning which teachings are the sound doctrines of Christ. False teachings prosper because the body of Christ wants the false teachings! We want to hear about the easy way, not about the narrow gate and the hard path that leads to life.

Hunger for spiritual power—not righteousness—has swept over many Christians. Millions of Christians are unsatisfied with their walk and think spiritual power will bring contentment and peace. Instead of hungering and thirsting after righteousness and embracing the cross, multitudes of Christians are taking shortcuts and entering the wide gate! Like Simon the Magician, many in the body of Christ seek after power for the wrong motives, embracing false doctrines until finally they get what they lusted after—spiritual power—but that power is not the Holy Spirit. (See 2 Corinthians 11:4.)

Lust for the good life that our affluent society offers has consumed most Christians. False prosperity teachings abound, and they seem to work. That is because God has abandoned millions of Christians to this idol of the heart, which is the love of money.

Jesus said: "Come unto me," "Take my yoke," and "Learn of me," but the church has said, *"Jesus, we believe, so come to us and entertain us, prosper us, bless us, and set us free! Set us free to do what we always wanted to do, to go where we want to go when we want!"*

We love Jesus for what we thought He promised to do for us concerning the so-called abundant life. Our love for Jesus is deep, as long as the material blessings hold out. When trouble and discipline come, when God applies the cross to our lives, our true lack of commitment of heart becomes obvious. Jesus allowed Peter to see the truth to break denial about his self-reliance, self-deception and pride. Christ did this by allowing Satan to sift Peter for a season; even then, Peter still struggled with insecurity and jealousy.

Remember the words that Jesus spoke to Peter. *"'Truly, truly, I say to you, when you were young, you girded yourself and walked where you would; but when you are old, you will stretch out your hands, and another will gird you and carry you where you do not wish to go.' (This he said to show by what death he was to glorify God). And after this he said to him, 'Follow me.' Peter turned and saw following them the disciple whom Jesus loved, who had lain close to his breast at the supper and had said, 'Lord, who is it that is going to betray you?' When Peter saw him, he said to Jesus, 'Lord, what about this man?' Jesus said to him, 'If it is my will that he remain until I come, what is that to you? Follow me!'"* (John 21:18-22).

The church wants knowledge, power, prosperity and freedom, without paying the price of total service and obedience to Christ. Christians want power and prestige to do what they want to do when they want, with no suffering or persecution. Jesus is saying to this generation of Christians: *"Do you love me more than these?"*

EXPECT MORE LAWFUL NUDITY

The next level of judgment will not be the economic crash (although that will come soon enough), but an avalanche of immoral acts backed by law. God is going to allow the filth of hell to vomit forth onto the lives of God's people. Only the pure at heart and the true lover of Christ will be protected. The lukewarm Christian and hypocrite will be overwhelmed.

We, as a nation and as a church, have come to the state arrived by at Nineveh—that immoral condition which forced God to judge that nation. Like that corrupt and wicked society, God is also against America. *"Behold, I am against you, says the LORD of hosts, and will lift up your skirts over your face; and I will let* nations look on your nakedness and kingdoms on your shame. I will throw filth at you and treat you with contempt, and make you a gazing stock"* (Nahum 3:5-6).

This flood of filth has begun, and we are already shocked, but we have not seen the worst of it. The avalanche of filth and perversion that is going to come will shock even the ungodly and wicked at first, but soon the majority will embrace it whole-heartedly.

Nudity will become legal in certain public venues protected by law. There is a new spiritual dimension Satan is inspiring in the land—the spirituality of nudity, a return to the Garden of Eden in the flesh, a spiritual awakening to public nakedness.

This is not a streaking or a fad of exhibitionism, but an added dimension of the satanic spirituality that is coming with this avalanche of filth. There will be no blushing, guilt or sense of wrongness. Satan is numbing the conscience of this nation and then searing it.

VEXATION OF THE SOUL
A SODOM AND GOMORRAH LUST-FEST IS COMING

Here is where the Christian must be prepared to persevere. The body of Christ is not prepared for what is about to be unleashed upon this nation. *The main reason for this warning is to hopefully awaken some, but time is running short; we must get ready now!* (See Ephesians 5:1-20).

Every true Christian must seek cleansing and separation. Even though this immorality will be flaunted in our face, if we are cleansed it will not affect us. *"To the pure all things are pure, but to the corrupt and unbelieving nothing is pure; their very minds and consciences are corrupted. They profess to know God, but they deny him by their deeds; they are detestable, disobedient, unfit for any good deed"* (Titus 1:15-16).

There is coming a new round of filth vomited from hell, directed at the lukewarm Christian and the doubled-minded saint. There will be Christian leaders exposed for sexual sins. The Jim and Tammy Bakker downfall, coupled with the Jimmy Swaggart exposé seemed unbelievable, but the coming backlash attack on Christians and many of the saints will be almost overwhelming. *Jim Bakker came out of his trouble apparently humbled, giving insight to others on how these false teachings set him up to fall and I hope and trust that Brother Swaggart is healed and restored.*

The coming flood of demonic sexual temptations will finally wake up many Christians to the fact that this society has become as Sodom. The world will finally begin to cross the line of judgment, completely. America's sexual preoccupations will become sexual obsessions. Pastors, church leaders, Christian men and women will have sexual temptations thrown at them when they least expect it. Many will fall into gross sin and sexual misconduct. A Sodom-like deluge of sexual predators will be knocking at the door of the Christian heart. Many Christians will open the door wide!

The event at the 2004 Super Bowl is a hint of the sexual nudity coming. Like Janet Jackson, other artists will continue to push the envelope of nudity and public graphic sexual lewdness. Millions of people, including children, instantly saw Jackson's breast. Even with this outrage, inch-by-inch, standards will continue to be lowered, allowing Sodom-like behavior.

No saint will be exempt. Those who refuse to embrace the truth about their own hidden impurities will not stand; any indulgent, fleshly sexual latent desires will overtake them! Only the cleansed will stand during this tidal wave of filth.

Why is this coming? Millions of Christians believe the blood of Jesus will protect them, no matter what comes at them, however they never allowed God to apply the work of the cross that brings death to their sin nature and carnal self-life. They played church instead, covering up the truth about their inner hidden desires.

"There are those who are pure in their own eyes but are not cleansed of their filth" (Proverbs 30:12). And, *"'Therefore come out from them, and be separate from them, says the Lord, and touch nothing unclean; then I will welcome you, and I will be a father to you, and you shall be my sons and daughters,' says the Lord Almighty. Since we have these promises, beloved, let us cleanse ourselves from every defilement of body and spirit, and make holiness perfect in the fear of God"* (2 Corinthians 6:17,18—7:1).

Now a flood of sexual filth is about to overwhelm millions of Christians. Like Lot, who was spellbound by Sodom's wickedness, so too the last-day Christian will have sexual predators knocking at the door of their hearts.

Dr. James Dobson, founder of Focus on the Family, interviewed a radio guest, Jim Taylor, who described what took place in an art class held on the campus of the University of Southern California. A prostitute who was attending the art class brought two lesbians to the class. They performed sex acts in front of the class, which was the prostitute's art project. Some of the students protested, but no appropriate action came against the department dean or the professor who sanctioned the immoral conduct.

With each wave of increased immorality and societal acceptance, unclean Christians will be forced to become purified or be driven into a lifestyle that is damning. The "wannabe" Christian will fall away from Christ or run with denominations that suit their particular sinful lifestyle.

In 2 Peter 2:4-11 it reads, *"For if God did not spare the angels when they sinned, but cast them into hell and committed them to pits of nether gloom to be kept until the judgment; if he did not spare the ancient world, but preserved Noah, a herald of righteousness, with seven other persons, when he brought a flood upon the world of the ungodly; if by turning the cities of Sodom and Gomorrah to ashes he condemned them to extinction and made them an example to those who were to be ungodly; and if he rescued righteous Lot, greatly distressed by the licentiousness of the wicked (for by what that righteous man saw and heard as he lived among them, he was vexed in his righteous soul day after day with their lawless deeds), then the Lord knows how to rescue the godly from trial, and to keep the unrighteous under punishment until the day of judgment, and especially those who indulge in the lust of defiling passion and despise authority. Bold and willful, they are not afraid to revile the glorious ones, whereas angels, though greater in might and power, do not pronounce a reviling judgment upon them before the Lord."*

The lewdness will be so powerful that many Christians will find themselves defenseless. The full armor of God that most Christians were led to believe they had put on (I must say, they attempt to magically put-on God's armor) will not stop this vexing evil that is about to be unleashed. The "quick-fix" doctrines that avoid inner sanctification and cleansing will be no match for this flood of filth. The perverse filth that Christians will be exposed to will penetrate the spirit and soul of those who avoided the fire of sanctification.

During September 2000, a prominent Christian leader who was a reformed homosexual was tempted to enter a homosexual bar while he visited Washington, DC on business. He tried to cover this up, and later admitted he went there on purpose. Why does this happen to so many Christians, even to those who try so hard to follow Christ and live-in righteousness?

This is due to the lack of instruction and sound doctrine that deals with hidden defilements and wounds to their spirit. There are defilements still lodged deep within. Many gloss over or ignore these hidden issues. Many avoid the painful work of the cross, which, if embraced, will allow the whole armor of God to become their own. The armor of God becomes inner Christ-like character, not some magic thinking put on by chanting false Christian incantations. No, instead, wounded Christians learn how to take the wide gate and the easy path. They are pure in their own eyes and believe they can stand. Again, as in Proverbs 30:12, they are pure in their own eyes.

"'Therefore come out from them, and be separate from them,' says the Lord, and touch nothing unclean; then I will welcome you, and I will be a father to you, and you shall be my sons and daughters,' says the Lord Almighty. Since we have these promises, beloved, let us cleanse ourselves from every defilement of body and spirit, and make holiness perfect in the fear of God" (2 Corinthians 6:17–7:1).

THE FINAL PARTY IS IN FULL SWING

A party spirit has swept this nation and has even crept into most churches. Mardi Gras-like festivals are springing up in increasing numbers. Many college spring breaks have become orgies. The annual Burning Man Festival in Nevada is an example of the growth of immorality and lewdness. The Louisiana Mardi Gras has become a spectacle of sordid public sexual acts. Gay Pride Mardi Gras are growing and receiving more and more media coverage—indeed America is becoming a Sodom-like society.

This same party spirit has pulled millions of Christians into a life that craves entertaining events, empty spiritual manifestations, fellowship socials, retreats and vacations. College and teen youth groups produce entertaining events and outings to keep the wavering Christian in the fold. Pastors pander to these latent desires, serving up entertaining praise, worship, group meetings and mission outings.

Christians bored with life become busybodies and gossips meddling in the affairs of others. Swayed by various impulses and carnal desires, these Christians run from meeting to meeting. They listen to anybody but never arrive at the knowledge of the truth. They never obtain the grace of God. They are malcontents who demand attention and entertainment from the pulpit. *"These are grumblers, malcontents, following their own passions, loud-mouthed boasters, flattering people to gain advantage. But you must remember, beloved, the predictions of the apostles of our Lord Jesus Christ; they said to you, "In the last time there will be scoffers, following their own ungodly passions It is these who set up divisions, worldly people, devoid of the Spirit"* (Jude 16-19).

SPELLBOUND CHRISTIANS WITH LINGERING CURIOSITY AND VOYEURISM

The vexing power of Sodom held Lot spellbound. That is where many Christians are now, held spellbound by their own uncleanness. Many Christians are outwardly appalled but inwardly interested in and gazing at the perverse activity with no expression of outrage. On the other hand, there is an outrage that is condemning, finger-pointing and hypocritical from the self-righteous, religious right. This outrage, like the Pharisees' self-righteous condemnation, is often a counter-balance suppression of hidden inner perverseness and lustful desires.

Two angels urged Lot to arise, take his family, and flee for their lives. However, Scripture states he lingered. *"So the men (angels) had to seize him and his wife and his two daughters by the hand, the Lord being merciful to him, and they brought him forth and set him outside the city... They said, 'Flee for your life; do not look back or stop any where in the valley; flee to the hills, lest you be consumed'"* (Genesis 19:15-17).

Lot's family carried the defilements of Sodom with them, for we see later how Lot's wife looked back, causing her death. (See Luke 17:26-37). Lot's own daughters got him drunk two nights in a row, slept with him, and each conceived a child. One child was Ben-ammi, the father of the Ammonites who made war against Israel. The other child, Moab, became the father of the Moabites; these people also were enemies of God's people. Even though Lot and his daughters were spared, the defilements of Sodom clung to them having far-reaching consequences.

This very issue is what overcame in the preceding example—the formerly gay Christian lingered over his former Sodom-like perverse lifestyle. He was looking back because the perverse issues and defilements that led him into this lifestyle in the first place were still within his spirit. The church and the ministries with which he was involved did not teach inner sanctification or getting down to the root of these latent perverse passions and allowing the Holy Spirit to thoroughly weed out and heal.

To emphasize, when we are born again we must become separate from old sinful life patterns, dig deep into our thoughts and attitudes concerning all of life in fear and trembling, cleansing ourselves of all past defilements. We must be renewed in the spirit of our minds and put off our old nature, which is like our former manner of life. (See 2 Corinthians 7:1 and Ephesians 4:22-32).

The eye is the lamp of the body, and as we expose ourselves to perversion and wickedness, our spirit and soul become desensitized and defiled. Many Christians walk in a light that is really darkness. Millions of believers expose themselves to the defiling light of the TV screen that penetrates to the core of their being. Deceived by a spiritual and religious pride, they gaze upon the wicked, thinking that they are immune to sin and its powers of destruction and defilement. They watch and become spellbound as demons re-flash defiling scenes across the minds, attacking to push these unprepared Christians into secret sin and foul inner fantasies to shipwreck their faith. Many will succumb and fall into sin and perversion as hell torments their souls, day and night. The result for many Christians will be a complete falling away. Remember what Jesus taught.

"Do not lay up for yourselves treasures on earth, where moth and rust consume and where thieves break in and steal, but lay up for yourselves treasures in heaven, where neither moth nor rust consumes and where thieves do not break in and steal. For where your treasure is, there will your heart be also. The eye is the lamp of the body. So, if your eye is sound, your whole body will be full of light; but if your eye is not sound, your whole body will be full of darkness. If then the light in you is darkness, how great is the darkness! No one can serve two masters; for either he will hate the one and love the other, or he will be devoted to the one and despise the other. You cannot serve God and mammon" (Matthew 6:19-24).

MAGIC FORMULAS WON'T WORK ANY MORE

Is there a vexation from what you are witnessing? Then there are defilements from your past still lodged within your soul and spirit. If you play church and practice a mental pretend game with yourself concerning the full armor of God, or plead the blood of Christ, or any other superstitious quick-fix gimmick, you are in for the shock of your life. If you believe you can just "praise" this attack off, you are mistaken. Merely because you tithe faithfully, attend church regularly, or are in the ministry, these activities will not exempt you from the oncoming satanic onslaught.

No, you must go through the discipline of the Lord. You must experience firsthand God's penetrating work in your heart and spirit where He tests, and sometimes sends fiery trials that purge, cleanse and heal the deep wounds and defilements in which many Christians still walk. You must allow Christ to expose defilements hidden within. Do not condemn yourself when the Lord exposes the hidden; do not be shocked but take ownership and confess to yourself the ugliness. Partner with likeminded Christians and hold each other accountable to press in, confess issues, pray with one another and trust in God's faithfulness.

This is humbling, but God will grant cleansing, healing and restoration. Humble yourself before God and He will exalt you. I will discuss in more detail how to cooperate with God in these tests and trials, and how to allow the Holy Spirit to cleanse carnal passions hidden deep within so many dear saints.

SATAN HAS BEEN PLAYING POSSUM

One of Satan's favorite tricks is to deceive. Like the Trojan horse, the enemy of our soul has come into our camp as an angel of light and a worker of righteousness. (See 2 Corinthians 11:12-15). Satan sends in false apostles, ministers and teachers who are deceitful and disguised as believers of Christ. The apostle Paul referred to these as superlative apostles who boast as though they worked as a true apostle. These same types of imposters are everywhere in the body of Christ today, and they amaze millions of Christians. Miracles abound, tricking many to believe false teachers and their false teachings. Signs and wonders follow these so-called great men and women of God, but in reality, the spiritual power brought forth is straight from hell. In many cases, Satan gladly exchanges an outer physical ailment for a hell-inspired doctrine. The physical ailments and problems seem healed, at least temporarily, but the soul and spirit are now in grave danger of severe deception empowered by a supernatural religious demon and/or demonic principality.

Leaders of these *angel of light* ministries that have invaded the body of Christ have a counterfeit faith about which the apostle Paul warned Timothy. (See 2 Timothy 3:1-9). Satan plays dead, like a possum, so that later he can really destroy the deceived. He will soon come calling on all those who have embraced the false doctrines and entertained demonic powers as the work of the Holy Spirit. Those who went along with these *angel of light* ministries will fall into trouble and temptation that will either destroy what faith is left or awaken the deceived believer to the truth. They will encounter trouble, as Satan will attempt to drag them down, but God is faithful and will save those who repent in time.

As for the *angel of light* ministries, payday is coming because God is not mocked! When trouble comes, these false teachers will not have a following any longer. When the sifting comes, God will raise up true servants and ministries. These will have the answers and the true power of God resting upon them. They will glorify Jesus, not themselves, and be used mightily to help the formerly deceived and lukewarm Christian receive repentance, as they put their hope in the living true Christ.

MILLIONS OF CHRISTIANS ARE DOUBLE-MINDED AND PASSIVE

Our wounds are grievous and in need of deep healing. However, as in the days of Jeremiah, so it is today. Far too many Christian leaders and Christian higher education institutions have turned God's wounded people over to secular healers who probe into their wounds scientifically, leaving God out of the therapy. Most of these hurting people receive help in the form of a pill and are told they will never be healthy, that they have an incurable mental disease.

Most ministries do not dare touch these hurting Christians. It is hard work and we are told that only the professionals can help. Pastors are not equipped to deal with the double-minded child of God, yet the Bible has the answers. The price to pay in ministering to the truly hurting is great, and few ministries choose to pay that price.

Instead, most churches cater to the so-called "good" and "normal" people. Church growth focuses on bringing in the already-have-it-together people. Preferential ministry is given and the hurting and dysfunctional are avoided and pushed aside. (See James 2:1-13). We have fallen to the state to which Israel had succumbed when judgment came to that nation.

"For from the least to the greatest of them, everyone is greedy for unjust gain; and from prophet to priest, every one deals falsely. They have healed the wound of my people lightly, saying, 'Peace, peace,' when there is no peace. Were they ashamed when they committed abomination? No, they were not at all ashamed; they did not know how to blush. 'Therefore they shall fall among those who fall; at the time that I punish them, they shall be overthrown,' says the LORD. Thus says the LORD: 'Stand by the roads, and look, and ask for the ancient paths, where the good way is; and walk in it, and find rest for your souls. But they said, 'We will not walk in it.' I set watchmen over you, saying, 'Give heed to the sound of the trumpet!' But they said, 'We will not give heed.' Therefore hear, O nations, and know, O congregation, what will happen to them. Hear, O earth; behold, I am bringing evil upon this people, the fruit of their devices, because they have not given heed to my words; and as for my law, they have rejected it" (Jeremiah 6:13-19).

The double-minded Christian is passive and disassociates from reality. The Biblical term, double-minded means *two-souled* or *twice a soul*. Our soul contains our conscious mind, the spirit of our mind (unconscious and subconscious mind) and heart, and our heart is the seat of our emotions. Another aspect of doubled mindedness is that the personal spirit can be wounded, broken and even crushed, in some cases crushed in pieces. (See James 4:1-10; Ephesians 4:22-24; Romans 12:1,2; Proverbs 15:4,13; 17:22; 18:14; 20:27).

Thus, being doubled-minded means, one suffers from divisions within and between the mind, heart and spirit. Peter was double-minded and in denial of his condition. Satan demanded to sift Peter because of his arrogant denial. Jesus warned Peter of his condition and Peter denied that any kind of flawed character existed inside him. Therefore, Jesus allowed Satan to sift Peter. The Lord did pray for Peter's faith that it would not fail; so, when Peter hit bottom and woke up to the truth, he then would have answers for his brethren. Jesus allowed Satan to sift Peter to a point. This forced Peter to see the (Simon) part within; this was a hidden, divided part of Peter.

This is the case with millions of Christians today. From severe schizophrenia to mild dissociative disorders, God's people suffer from different degrees of wounds to the spirit, mind and emotions. There is healing and wholeness for God's people who suffer such and who want to go all the way with Christ.

Most Christians, when confronted with the truth choose to stay wounded and unstable, which only allows Satan to continue to harass and torment. Each Christian is tempted and lured into vices and sin through his own hidden desires. (See James 1:12-15). Study the book of James, especially chapters three and four. One must count the cost to go all the way with Jesus. In other words, work out your own inner salvation in fear and trembling. I will be quite frank, as I share from my own healing and sanctification work; it is not easy! Remember, God is faithful, and He will lead and guide you, but it is up to you, for faith without works is dead.

BITTER JEALOUSY AND SELFISH AMBITION
RUNNING RAMPANT IN THE BODY OF CHRIST

Just as Peter was in denial of his duality, so are many Christians. These Christians avoid the reality of their inner, sick, and divided self, which stems from past defilements from childhood wounds and from sinful lifestyles as adults. One of the most prevalent maladies within many Christian families and fellowships is bitter jealousy and selfish ambition.

Many Christians in this condition live an aggressive, pushy Christian lifestyle. They deny the truth about their inner motives for Christian service and ministry. Self-pity, jealous outbursts, subtle manipulation of other Christians, and hunger for leadership and recognition, drive these wounded Christians into religious works. As it says in James, wherever this condition exists and is not dealt with, all manner of disorder and vile practices will take place. (Paraphrased from James 3:15,16). This condition and the results of it are not of God, but rather earthly, unspiritual, and devilish.

Many pastors and Christian leaders suffer from this condition themselves, and many in leadership enlist and release Christian workers motivated by bitter jealousy and selfish ambition. This spiritual state is prevalent throughout the body of Christ and this condition gives Satan a right to attack and bring disorder. In some cases, it can destroy whole fellowships and families. The teachings that help motivate Christians for service by identifying the so-called personality types are in reality false teachings that harness carnal personalities stemming from dividedness of soul and personal spirit.

As stated earlier, the common surface symptom of being double-minded is passivity. Divided Christians are passive in mind, allowing outside influences to break and lose train of thought. Their inner carnal desires derail any truthful examination of motives and intentions of the heart; thus, these divided Christians seem active but are very passive in mind. They are unstable, emotionally volatile, and very moody. They have extreme emotional highs allowing them to accomplish much in an obsessive manner, especially if they get acknowledgment. Then, they often burnout, become depressed and suffer basic lack of motivation for doing the mundane task of everyday living.

These symptoms, as well as others, are the results of their natural, carnal defense and survival mechanisms that allow hidden pain from past abuse to stay suppressed.

This and other characteristics discussed later in this book and in more detail in our next volume are why double-minded Christians fall prey to the false teachings and empty spiritual encounters. These meetings give mesmerizing and soothing feelings to the wounded spirit and divided soul facilitated by demonic spirits counterfeiting as the presence of God. These double-minded Christians indeed lust after a dose of spiritual Prozac to help suppress the pain and conviction of the true Holy Spirit; and like King Saul, find comfort from the tormenting spirits allowed by God to break them of their denial. Their minds are passive or lazy as they seek spiritual experiences that continue to numb inner warnings given by God. At the root of their passivity and lusts, are issues of bitter jealousy and selfish ambition, which should be exposed, cleansed, and healed. Instead, many leaders serve up carnal, fanatical dance and chant meetings mixed with various carnal methods to stir the personal spirit and soul into a hyper-euphoric state—another dose of spiritual Prozac.

SATAN USES JEALOUS CHRISTIANS TO SPIRITUALLY ATTACK OTHERS

One of the most insidious works of Satan is using double-minded carnal Christians to attack others by the use of their own personal spirit. Satan tried to use Peter to oppose Christ. Peter's words were not his own but were Satan's thoughts working through Peter's dividedness.

"Now when Jesus came into the district of Caesarea Philippi, he asked his disciples, 'Who do men say that the Son of man is?' And they said, 'Some say John the Baptist, others say Elijah, and others Jeremiah or one of the prophets.' He said to them, 'But who do you say that I am?' Simon Peter replied, 'You are the Christ, the Son of the living God.' And Jesus answered him, 'Blessed are you, Simon Bar-Jona! For flesh and blood has not revealed this to you, but my Father who is in heaven. And I tell you, you are Peter, and on this rock I will build my church, and the powers of death shall not prevail against it. I will give you the keys of the kingdom of heaven, and whatever you bind on earth shall be bound in heaven, and whatever you loose on earth shall be loosed in heaven.' Then he strictly charged the disciples to tell no one that he was the Christ. From that time Jesus began to show his disciples that he must go to Jerusalem and suffer many things from the elders and chief priests and scribes, and be killed, and on the third day be raised. And Peter took him and began to rebuke him, saying, 'God forbid, Lord! This shall never happen to you.' But he turned and said to Peter, 'Get behind me, Satan! You are a hindrance to me; for you are not on the side of God, but of men'" (Matthew 16:13-23).

Not too many Christians understand why Jesus turned to Peter and addressed Satan. In one moment, Peter has divine insight concerning the Christ, then the next moment Satan is channeling through Peter in opposing the Lord. How can this be?

Satan used a part of Peter's inner being (spirit) because Peter was double-minded or *twice a soul* (divided). This kind of divided condition exists within many Christians today. Divided in heart, mind and/or spirit, Christians are vulnerable to satanic influences that can channel and even enlist their personal spirit to oppose God's will in the lives of others. These divided Christians can have their divided spirit intertwined with demonic powers. One part of the Christian has faith, but deeper inner parts are still hanging onto the world, suffering from jealousy, insecurities, wounds, bitterness, envy, or selfish ambitions. They are ready to glorify self, usually at the expense of others. Divided Christians are very competitive for recognition and praise. These defiling issues of heart and spirit can often have a spirit of witchcraft intertwined within their fragmented spirits.

Contrary to false doctrine, when one is born again, a divided state can exist in the old sin nature, soul and personal spirit. In addition, this divided condition is not magically swept away instantly at the born-again experience. A divided heart is the most severe issue for the divided Christian. Like king Saul in the Old Testament, the Christian with a divided or double heart can become very obsessive and even murderous. Overcoming this condition is paramount to a healthy and fulfilled life in Christ.

In Peter's case we find that when Jesus warned Peter about Satan's desire to sift him, Jesus addressed Peter in a very enlightening way.

Jesus said, *"Simon, Simon, behold, Satan demanded to have you, that he might sift you like wheat, but I have prayed for you that your faith may not fail; and when you have turned again, strengthen your brethren"* (Luke 22:31,32).

The Greek word Christ used in this passage for the word **you**, in saying *Satan demanded to have **you***, and further on in this verse, to *sift **you** like wheat* is in this case plural, not singular, meaning the ***two of you***—or, ***both of you***.

But where Christ says, *but I have prayed for **you***, this use for the word **you** in the Greek is singular, that is, ***one of you***.

This helps us understand how the double-minded condition can have true dividedness of personality and character.

Further, the Christian human spirit, when divided and defiled, has a potential spiritual power that can touch others, having distinct symptoms and harmful results. The demonic can use an unregenerate and defiled part of a divided human spirit to spiritually attack others. When a human spirit attacks another under a demonic influence, the results can be serious, and sometimes even fatal. This is a major area of satanic work—to use a human spirit in a so-called out-of-body spiritual experience.

SIFTING IS COMING TO THIS GENERATION OF CHRISTIANS

Peter was in denial of his double-minded condition and his inner character flaws that needed changing. Satan saw Peter's potential for the kingdom of God, but also saw his divided condition as an opportunity to destroy this disciple of Christ. Satan demanded to sift Peter and cause him to deny the Lord, to run Peter through a series of attacks and trials in hopes that Peter would fall away from the Lord for good. If Satan could incite Peter with self-condemnation and fill his heart with self-pity, he might get Peter to give up. If Satan could get Peter to believe that he should have been able to die with Christ, which might get Peter to believe that he was no different from Judas, and we all know what happened to that son of perdition.

Literally, thousands upon thousands of Christians are in this sick spiritual condition. In these coming days, some who are in this condition will choose suicide to escape the torments of Satan, while the majority will just fall away, denying they ever knew Jesus.

However, Jesus prayed for Peter's faith. Jesus did not pray for his self-righteousness and false courage, which needed to die on the cross. As long as Christians are in denial of a divided condition, the work of the cross becomes ineffective in crucifying the works of the flesh. They deny Christ yet proclaim Him, becoming enemies of the cross. (See Galatians 5:13-25 Philippians 3:17-19) The divided believer must die to inner selfish agendas. Each divided part will have contradictory beliefs, which will require change or transformation to the new life in Christ. Christ allowed Satan to sift Peter in order to expose his doublemindedness. In reality, Satan became a pawn in the hand of Christ in exposing Peter's inner problems.

Persecution and possible death ignited Peter's sifting. This generation of Christians will soon know what it means to suffer persecution. God will allow Satan to drive lukewarm and carnal Christians into turmoil and confusion to awaken as many as possible to the truth.

Society is about to heave hatred, rejection and intimidation toward every Christian who professes Christ. Satan is asking permission to terrorize Christians, especially those who pridefully flaunt Christ on bumper stickers, practice in-your-face witnessing, being misled to believe this is true witnessing for Christ. For those who sanctimoniously protest immorality while denying their own sins, hate and persecution will increase even more.

The stir over Mel Gibson's movie, *The Passion of the Christ*, is helping fuel a deep distaste for Christians. Few Christians understand the evils inflicted upon Jews and Muslims by Christianity during the crusades of the middle ages. Indeed, during these last days Satan will resurrect old world religious conflicts to pit an apostate church against its religious rivals in a mighty war over souls.

The Passion depicts Christ's last 12 hours of life leading up to His death on the cross. Indeed, this movie leaves out important aspects of God's plan of redemption and is rooted in carnal religious Christianity that brazenly talks Christ but has not the true character of Christ. I will share more about this movie in the following chapter, *Doctrines of Men and Demons*.

In 2002, during one of the most critical elections of our lives, I watched a popular Christian TV network run their "praise-a-thon," attempting to raise millions of dollars to finish another end-time movie that quite frankly is irrelevant, theologically wrong and later, was to be clouded with accusations of plagiarism. Instead of calling Christian listeners to prayer and fasting during this time, they begged for money, sang, and preached the message of "give to get." They laid upon their supporters a false responsibility to maintain 15 broadcast satellites at $700,000 per month. This, along with their other fleshly projects and extravagant facilities, bleeds their supporters dry. What is so disheartening is most ministry programs tend to make viewers hardened to the true Gospel and arrogantly embrace a shallow compromised Gospel.

These, and most national ministries, have not a clue concerning the trouble that is in store for the body of Christ. Like many, these Christian ministries, along with their leaders and supporters, have little time left to repent. Many are at risk of being "left behind" or barred from the marriage feast, and justly so!

Persecution toward Christians will increase from the far-left liberals. Secretly organized hate campaigns will spew poison against the outspoken far-right Christian conservatives. This began as part of the effort to get President George W. Bush out of the White House. The fires of the last-day persecution that Jesus prophesied are igniting. *"Then they will deliver you up to tribulation, and put you to death; and you will be hated by all nations for my name's sake"* (Matthew 24:9).

This type of attack has always been in the devil's arsenal, but soon thousands and thousands of churchgoing, believing Christians are going to be run through the most horrific sifting that has ever been experienced. Literally, thousands of Christians will weep bitterly and find themselves in the pit of despair. They will writhe in agony over the troubles and temptations that have overtaken them. They will cry out, but they will get only silence from God. God will allow everything that they hold dear and have made an idol become crushed and ruined. There will be no hope in any program, fellowship, or so-called counsel in and of itself. Many will hear the truth but reject it, due to their watered-down-gospel-hardened hearts. When the sifting is at its peak, those who cry out to God and repent will see the light. Jesus Himself will come to the rescue and call them back to Himself. These broken and cleansed saints will the false, the lust of the flesh and pride of life, and let go of the love of the world, never to leave His side again. True humility will result from this sifting discipline.

As for many double-minded Christians, who rejected conscience and allowed their faith to shipwreck, **the party will be over.** (See 1 Timothy 1:19) These Christians, who foolishly shunned sanctification and death to self, will find themselves left behind. Jesus will have His Church without spot, wrinkle or blemish. That means the false and carnal will not enter into the coming kingdom of God! (See the parable of the wise and foolish maidens found in Matthew 25:1-13).

Jesus wants disciples and workers who are truly faithful and loyal unto death—not pretending they are. He knows who is true and who is phony. The sifting is coming, and if you think you are exempt, you had better take heed. *"Therefore let anyone who thinks that he stands take heed lest he fall"* (1 Corinthians 10:12). Part of the sifting of this generation of Christians has been with prosperity, knowledge, and licentiousness. This flood of filth and persecution will challenge all Christians and wake up many, forcing them to truly seek God. Unfortunately, many Christians will not leave (in their secret heart) the curiosity, lust and greed of the world. Remember, Jesus warned of this end-time sifting when He said, *"Remember Lot's wife!"*

This economic prosperity, persecution and avalanche of filth will pull in insincere and phony Christians all the way. No more straddling the fence and lingering over a society turned Sodom; millions of Christians will be in the valley of decision. Those ministers and pillow prophets who watered down the Gospel and lightened up God's tough-love messages of repentance and judgment will suffer grave consequences. Leaders who taught Christians to cover up past defilements and placate the uncrucified sin nature and double mindedness will find themselves in deep trouble with God.

When the economic crash comes—and it will come soon—these game-playing Christians will want back into God's fold, but for many it will be too late! However, Christians who cleanse themselves and endure to the end, as Jesus said, *will be saved*! They will stand in the coming flood because they dug deep and built their life on the solid rock! (See Luke 6:45-49 and 2 Corinthians 6:14–7:1).

THE SIGN OF JONAH—FOR THE CHURCH

Nineveh, the ancient capital city of the Assyrian Empire, was evil and epitomized Israel's oppression. The Lord called the prophet Jonah to go to this city and declare an irrevocable judgment upon the city and its people. Most are familiar with Jonah boarding a ship to flee from the Lord's presence. *If you are not familiar with this story, read the short book of Jonah for background.*

Now God has Jonah's attention and tells Jonah to pronounce an immediate and irrevocable judgment coming upon Nineveh and all its inhabitants at the hand of God. *"Yet 40 days, and Nineveh shall be overthrown!"*

Jonah enters the city and repeatedly announces this message. Within a day's journey into this large city, the people believed God and started fasting and humbling themselves. Word of this spread and the king, hearing the news, also humbled himself and published a proclamation throughout Nineveh that everyone was not to eat or drink; and all were to be covered with sackcloth and cry out to God. In addition, everyone was to turn from all evil and violence. The king ended the proclamation, stating, *"Who knows, God may yet repent and turn from his fierce anger, so that we perish not?"* (Jonah 3:9).

God saw this turning from sin with contrition, changed His mind, and chose not to allow destruction to come upon Nineveh. Jonah was not happy about this and became angry. Jonah told God, *"I pray thee, Lord, is not this what I said when I was yet in my country? That is why I made haste to flee to Tarshish; for I knew that thou art a gracious God and merciful, slow to anger, and abounding in steadfast love, and repentest of evil. Therefore now, O Lord, take my life from me, I beseech thee, for it is better for me to die than to live"* (Jonah 4:2,3).

Israel expected God to deliver them from the Assyrian rule, yet Israel was still oppressed, due to wickedness covered by national self-righteousness. As God's people, they had not repented of their own wickedness and false worship of God.

So when Jonah first heard from God, he knew that if Nineveh repented, most likely God would stay judgment. The type of warning Jonah was to give was irrevocable. This meant it did not matter what Nineveh did; it would come to pass regardless—in 40 days!

One must understand; God gave Israel a rule in determining a false prophet. If the prophecy does not come to pass, then the prophet is false. Now we can truly understand Jonah's reluctance and disobedience, as well as his wanting to die when God relented. As far as Israel was concerned, Jonah was a false prophet. Nevertheless, because Jonah delivered this terrifying, end-of-Nineveh message, all of Nineveh turned from their evil ways. God's answer to Jonah's complaint was, *"And should not I pity Nineveh, that great city, in which there are more than a hundred and twenty thousand persons who do not know their right hand from their left, and also much cattle?"* (Jonah 4:11).

When Christ came to Israel—God's chosen people—they did not believe Him and thus looked for a sign in order to believe. Jesus said the only sign they would receive from Him concerning God's work was the sign of Jonah. Again, Israel, as God's people, was under rule of the Roman Empire due to their own sinfulness and disobedience. They were looking for a prophet, or even the promised Messiah, to deliver them from the Roman oppression.

As God's people, they had great disdain for their Gentile-pagan oppressors. They looked for deliverance from the evil Roman occupation, not willing to see that Christ came to deliver Israel and the world from the evil human sin nature.

"When the crowds were increasing, He began to say, *"This generation is an evil generation; it seeks a sign, but no sign shall be given to it except the sign of Jonah. For as Jonah became a sign to the men of Nineveh, so will the Son of man be to this generation. The queen of the South will arise at the judgment with the men of this generation and condemn them; for she came from the ends of the earth to hear the wisdom of Solomon, and behold, something greater than Solomon is here. The men of Nineveh will arise at the judgment with this generation and condemn it; for they repented at the preaching of Jonah, and behold, something greater than Jonah is here. No one after lighting a lamp puts it in a cellar or under a bushel, but on a stand, that those who enter may see the light. Your eye is the lamp of your body; when your eye is sound, your whole body is full of light; but when it is not sound, your body is full of darkness. Therefore be careful lest the light in you be darkness. If then your whole body is full of light, having no part dark, it will be wholly bright, as when a lamp with its rays gives you light"* (Luke 11:29-36).

Millions of Christians are looking to the signs of Christ coming. They are eager for the rapture (caught up to the clouds to be with Christ) before the Great Tribulation starts. Most Christians refuse to embrace the truth found in Scripture concerning the Second Coming. They believe lies that put them at ease, thinking they walk in the light as Israel did, declaring to be right with God by comparison to the lost and the wicked. The light of the truth concerning Christ's return has been darkened by believing false doctrine excusing them from the tough work God requires His people to endure. They are not ready to endure trouble for God and be a witness to the lost when the Great Tribulation comes and awakens millions to the truth.

Instead, they point the finger at the wicked; saying, *"Christ is going to rapture us to safety and you will be in terrible trouble, you horrible sinners."* They are like malingerers in the military, looking for excused duty in the heat of battle. They are running from God's call to holiness and sacrificial living for Christ. Millions are asleep to the truth, like Jonah in the bottom of the boat as the storm rages. They truly think Christ will rapture them to safety, not requiring them to be light to millions of terrified souls who finally believe in Christ and His soon return.

Millions of lost souls are at risk, turned off to the self-serving gospel presented by the majority of Christianity. Most of God's people live self-righteously and arrogantly, expecting God to crush these lost sinners along with the wicked. To the contrary, God is saying to His people today, *Should I not pity the lost sinner who is confused by your deplorable witness and have mercy on the wayward Christian who finally awakens to the truth by way of the Great Tribulation?*

If God's people are missing, who will be a witness and help those who do not know their right hand from their left concerning the truth of God's plan of salvation and Christ's return?

As it was for Israel, so it is for the arrogant, self-righteous last generation Christian, the sign of Jonah. The last-day Christian will see a mighty army of true believers arise. Yes, the Great Tribulation will have started, the Antichrist will appear and the world will cringe in terror for the trouble coming upon all—a magnitude of trouble never seen before.

This is the true sign for this wayward, last-day lukewarm church. Many deceived and lukewarm Christians will wake up due to intense suffering during this time. Even then, millions of unprepared Christians will be shut out, unable to see clearly in the coming dark days that overshadow Christ's coming.

We must take heed now, get ready, and walk in the light, having not one-part dark. Let us not allow false teachings to lull us to sleep. Let us not be named among the foolish maidens spoken of by Christ who could not trim their lamps for lack of oil. *"And the foolish said to the wise, 'Give us some of your oil, for our lamps are going out.' But the wise replied, 'Perhaps there will not be enough for us and for you; go rather to the dealers and buy for yourselves.' And while they went to buy, the bridegroom came, and those who were ready went in with him to the marriage feast; and the door was shut"* (Matthew 25:8-10).

CHAPTER 3

Doctrines of Men and Demons

MISHANDLING THE WORD OF TRUTH

Far too many ministers of the Gospel mishandle the Word of God. They jump on a scriptural principle and make a virtually exclusive teaching or doctrine. These teachings often accompany supernatural signs and wonders that give the teachings credence to the hearer. Often, false Christian leaders who have counterfeit faith are empowered by demonic spirits deceiving them, as well as those who follow them. These imposters often persecute those who desire to live godly lives in Christ Jesus.

"Now the Spirit expressly says that in later times some will depart from the faith by giving heed to deceitful spirits and doctrines of demons, through the pretensions of liars whose consciences are seared, who forbid marriage and enjoin abstinence from foods which God created to be received with thanksgiving by those who believe and know the truth" (1 Timothy 4:1-3). (See also 2 Timothy 3:1–4:5 as well as all of 2 Peter 2).

The apostle Paul wrote to Timothy, *"Do your best to present yourself to God as one approved, a workman who has no need to be ashamed, rightly handling the word of truth"* (2 Timothy 2: 1). Contrary to this sound advice, these false teachers go from bad to worse, exploiting God's people who are already deceived, all for ill gain. These activities incite an outsider to revile the Gospel.

SCRIPTURAL GIMMICKS: SCRIPTURE TAKEN OUT OF CONTEXT

These teachers lift Scripture out of context and make an aspect of a biblical principle into self-contained religion or into spiritual gimmicks or methods. These methods are then empowered by the soul of man (arm of the flesh), not the Spirit of God.

Some of these teachers have been caught in fraud. One in particular presented a teaching to acquire the gift of faith by sending in money. The amount for the "gift of faith" had to be at least $1,000. Many Christians were caught up in this gimmick and sent in the money. One young woman sent in $1,000 and this false teacher sent back a letter of thanks and confirmation that she now had the "gift of faith" that moved mountains. This naïve Christian became a victim of this false teacher. She became distraught and nearly completely lost faith in God when she commanded—by "the word of faith"—that two of her ducks return to shore immediately. They were in danger while out in the middle of a large pond. Of course, the ducks kept swimming away and were lost. This crushed what faith she did have. By the way, this particular false teacher was exposed nationally, but is back in operation.

Surfing the Christian TV channels is an *eye opener*, or at least it should be. There are plenty of ministries one can observe practicing deceitful, cunning or underhanded schemes to raise money. One promotes a "get out of debt" ministry where the indebted Christian sends in a list of bills, along with a healthy financial gift as a "seed" offering. This TV ministry sets a date when an enormous pile of these lists of bills from deceived Christians are burned in a special, anointed ceremony, breaking the bonds of indebtedness. Come on, brothers and sisters. How gullible can we get?

There are many scriptural examples of believers led by the Lord to take risky action. Making a method out of what God did, under a certain circumstance and for certain persons, creates situations in which the Christian can become willful and presume upon the Will of God. Any doctrine that puts emphasis on God working in a certain way that the believer can manipulate is not faith, but fanaticism that puts God to the test. This type of carnal faith is like the infamous "snake handling cult" that constantly tempts the Lord. These false faith ministries *hype* up a believer to mislead them into "having faith in their own faith," which is tantamount to tempting God. *"But who can discern his errors? Clear thou me from hidden faults. Keep back thy servant also from presumptuous sins; let them not have dominion over me! Then I shall be blameless, and innocent of great transgression"* (Proverbs 19:12,13).

In Colorado Springs, the World Prayer Center is supported nationally and partially by a megachurch of over 11,000 members. I joined in on one of their "concerts of prayer," only to be horrified at what I saw. In 1989 a similar concert of prayer movement came to the Pacific Northwest with the intention of praying and beseeching God for revival and restoration of America. I preached in some of these concerts. I bowed out after it turned into another church meeting full of entertainment. In this recent visit, some 15 years later, I saw how this carnal activity has evolved into a warped and nightmarish dance and chant ritual, not unlike voodoo gatherings.

One meeting had a band blasting away under a giant spinning globe. Young and old alike began to walk around the chairs, praying, which soon turned into speaking in tongues, yelling, and dancing. My associate in ministry, Mark, attended with me and both of us were disgusted. He commented that he never saw anything so appalling and erotic, other than when he was unsaved, went to dance clubs and joined in sensuous slam-dancing *mosh-pit* revelry.

Those involved in these carnal escapades pray in their spirit with no understanding. Many have unclean issues in spirit and heart causing their so-called prayer language to spew out poisonous *human spirit prayer vibes* that do not align with God's Will. This prayer center and other movements practicing carnality in prayer have an effect in promoting man's will and Satan's purposes, not the Will of God.

The World Prayer Center in Colorado Springs contains several sick, humanistic depictions of the Holy Spirit and Christ. One picture in the main hallway is of a bald, muscular, bare-chested man kneeling behind a giant cup. There is liquid flowing down over his head and upper naked torso into this cup, with the cup overflowing. As one's eyes follow up the liquid flow, one can see it is coming from a giant tipped vase. Two women on each side, clad in scanty robes with their breasts about 70 % exposed, hold this vase. The caption for the picture refers to how the Holy Spirit fills our cup to overflowing.

This revolting depiction of the Holy Spirit, along with other pictures and artwork, line this prayer center. Instead of a place to meet a Holy God in reverence and prayer, this megachurch program has pushed carnality into humanism, like the way the Greeks and Romans worshipped their gods of human form.

This meeting, we attended was so obnoxious and loud, we could not concentrate on hearing from the Lord in sincere prayer and intercession.

At the end, the leaders of this meeting released the attendees out into the world to convert lost sinners and continue the effort to bring revival to the city. These deceived Christians have no idea what they are up against in praying for revival. Unfortunately, they really believe they experienced revival themselves and expect the lost to accept this kind of example and display as the infilling of the Holy Spirit. This is false revival, inspired by Satan to hamper the true work of the Holy Spirit and true revival.

This hyped-up form of worship and prayer activates a false or counterfeit faith in the power of the human spirit. The soul or emotions of the participant is worked into an emotional-spiritual state in the belief that this is how one connects with the Spirit of God. They do experience a spiritual feeling of peace and satisfaction, but this is worked up from their own personal spirit.

This is humanistic spiritualism practiced in the name of Christ. Therefore this prayer center's décor and pictures of the works of God and the Holy Spirit are depicted in such common and humanistic art form. These Christians are deceived, wounded and under a self-mesmerizing worship form that, as I explained earlier, make these deceived followers of Christ vulnerable. The time is coming when Satan will demand to sift these lukewarm carnal babes in Christ.

These are just a few dangerous teachings and false worship form in the body of Christ that lead many young and naïve Christians into error. Do not misunderstand me, our ministry practices the gifts of the Holy Spirit, but we are constantly on guard not to practice the gifts of the Holy Spirit in the flesh!

Some examples of false teachings that produce false gifts are:

- Conjuring up a *hyper-faith* spiritual state of being.
- Pleading the blood of Jesus instead of examining issues of the heart when attacked spiritually.
- Speaking a presumed word from God to bring to pass a desired need or blessing.
- Singing praise verses repetitiously until a spiritual state exists that will allow inner peace and a special feeling of "closeness" to God.
- Financial seed sowing to reap larger financial blessings.
- Speaking in an unknown language in order to reach a higher level of spirituality, which often solicits a counterfeit tongue.
- Being slain in the spirit in order to receive instant spiritual blessings, a healing, demonic deliverance, inner emotional feeling of *well-being* while blanked-out or without understanding. Most need to deal with bitter issues that require purifying the heart often characterized with weeping and mourning.
- Attempting to obtain an inner voice communication that is supposedly the Holy Spirit without embracing sound doctrine and teachings that enable discernment to test for the counterfeit spirits that might be operating upon the believer's own spirit.

Again, God does heal. Christians are to walk in the gifts, as the Holy Spirit apportions, but few seek to understand and discern between what is counterfeit and what is true. Many lust after the gifts with self-edifying motives—seeking recognition and making a living off the work of the Holy Spirit.

ENEMIES OF THE CROSS: TEACHING ANTI-PAIN AND ANTI-SUFFERING GOSPEL

The main theme within every one of these false teachings is the lack of balance with the *message of the cross*. These teachings oppose letting God, by way of circumstantial discipline, expose the selfish motives, thoughts and intentions of the heart. The main characteristic of these false doctrines is avoidance of the sufferings of Christ for the believer. In fact, much of the New Testament warns us of these teachers and their teachings.

The apostle Paul wrote to the Philippians, *"But whatever gain I had, I counted as loss for the sake of Christ. Indeed I count everything as loss because of the surpassing worth of knowing Christ Jesus my Lord. For his sake I have suffered the loss of all things, and count them as refuse, in order that I may gain Christ and be found in him, not having a righteousness of my own, based on law, but that which is through faith in Christ, the righteousness from God that depends on faith; that I may know him and the power of his resurrection, and may share his sufferings, becoming like him in his death, that if possible I may attain the resurrection from the dead. Not that I have already obtained this or am already perfect; but I press on to make it my own, because Christ Jesus has made me his own. Brethren, I do not consider that I have made it my own; but one thing I do, forgetting what lies behind and straining forward to what lies ahead, I press on toward the goal for the prize of the upward call of God in Christ Jesus. Let those of us who are mature be thus minded; and if in anything you are otherwise minded, God will reveal that also to you. Only let us hold true to what we have attained. Brethren, join in imitating me, and mark those who so live as you have an example in us. For many, of whom I have often told you and now tell you even with tears, live as enemies of the cross of Christ. Their end is destruction, their god is the belly, and they glory in their shame, with minds set on earthly things. But our commonwealth is in heaven, and from it we await a Savior, the Lord Jesus Christ, who will change our lowly body to be like his glorious body, by the power which enables him even to subject all things to himself"* (Philippians 3:7-21).

Far too many in the pulpit remove the message of the cross and its needful work in the believer's life. They do this to keep the lukewarm and self-centered Christian coming to church and to attract the spiritually inquisitive. The offense of the cross and the stumbling block to the phony is removed.

These Christians and weak leaders become enemies of the cross and spew out quick-fix teachings that avoid the pain and suffering involved in true and full sanctification. The work of the cross produces death to the old sin nature. Much of the body of Christ has bought into the world's lust for quick and easy success. We want truth, as long as it does not hurt us. The Lord's truth penetrates our hypocrisy and denial of hidden and unhealed wounds, which is often very painful, but later yields the peaceful fruit of righteousness and wholeness. Our spiritual, mental and emotional sickness are deep because we as a nation and as Christians have developed an ability to instantly lie to ourselves, cover it up and pretend we are all right. We learn to pretend before we learn to walk.

More than ever, Christians are lusting after magical, quick-fix and painless formulas full of cheap grace, false peace, and false security. Hearing repeatedly a compromised Gospel has created hardhearted Christians; gospel-hardened Christians who do not want to be truly set free by hearing the painful truth about self, others, and a sick relationship with God! We treat God as if He is our servant, like a magic slot machine—a slot machine that always turns up cherries for a quarter's worth of prayer.

MAGIC FORMULAS, CHEAP GRACE AND FALSE ETERNAL SECURITY

The *gospel* message presented today is loaded with magic tricks and quick-fix formulas. Satan loves to get his servants to appear as workers of righteousness to deceive as many naïve Christians as possible. Gullible and ignorant by choice are probably the best terms to describe the masses of believers who run from one *easy road gospel* doctrine to the next. They are *"ever learning, but never arriving at the truth"* (See 2 Timothy 3:1-9).

These teachings avoid the message of the cross for the believer. The cross of Jesus is held up high and glorified, and rightly so, but the other side of the cross is ignored—that is, the believers' cross. At the core of these false teachings is the absence of *the work of the cross in the believer's life*. These teachings put it all on the back of Jesus. He did it all! Enter the kingdom of God freely. All may come and follow the *easy road gospel*. Recall Peter's resistance to the cross. Jesus told Peter that he was not on God's side, but on man's. Let us continue the account. *"But he turned and said to Peter, 'Get behind me, Satan! You are a hindrance to me; for you are not on the side of God, but of men.' Then Jesus told his disciples, 'If any man would come after me, let him deny himself and take up his cross and follow me. For whoever would save his life will lose it, and whoever loses his life for my sake will find it. For what will it profit a man, if he gains the whole world and forfeits his life? Or what shall a man give in return for his life? For the Son of man is to come with his angels in the glory of his Father, and then he will repay every man for what he has done. Truly, I say to you, there are some standing here who will not taste death before they see the Son of man coming in his kingdom'"* (Matthew 16:23-28).

Paul wrote in Philippians 3:17-19 about enemies of the cross of Christ. Peter wrote about the false teachers coming that would appear among us and secretly bring in false teachings. Peter wrote, *"… who will secretly bring destructive heresies … And many will follow their licentiousness, and because of them the way of truth will be reviled. And in their greed they will exploit you with false words; from of old their condemnation has not been idle, and their destruction has not been asleep"* (2 Peter 2:1-3).

In 1995, a TV documentary with ABC anchor Peter Jennings entitled *"In The Name of God"* showed some of the most bizarre behavior ever demonstrated by Christians. They acted not much differently from those involved in cult spiritualistic meetings. The Gospel, Christ, and His truth are more than ever maligned, ridiculed, and reviled by the wicked. The lost sinner is now confused more than ever, due to this and other wicked and deranged behavior that is taking place throughout the body of Christ. Christian leaders from a national level down to the small-town congregation are exposed. Affairs, fraud, deception, exploitation of supporters and just plain extravagant and lustful lifestyles are headlines. The apostle Peter's prophetic words have *come to pass* for this generation of Christians.

Many of these errant teachings are dispensing false security to the so-called born-again and the so-called baptized-in-the-Spirit believers. There are wrong messages of eternal security for Christians, which imply that a Christian cannot lose their eternal salvation or their ticket to ride in the rapture. This is a lie devised in hell! Yes, a Christian can lose their eternal salvation. They can also become foolish and be left behind when Christ calls the saint unto Himself in the rapture.

Jesus said, *"Enter by the narrow gate; for the gate is wide and the way is easy, that leads to destruction, and those who enter by it are many. For the gate is narrow and the way is hard, that leads to life, and those who find it are few"* (Matthew 7:13-14).

In Luke, Jesus taught, *"He went on his way through towns and villages, teaching, and journeying toward Jerusalem. And some one said to him, 'Lord, will those who are saved be few?' And he said to them, 'Strive to enter by the narrow door; for many, I tell you, will seek to enter and will not be able. When once the householder has risen up and shut the door, you will begin to stand outside and to knock at the door, saying, 'Lord, open to us.' He will answer you, 'I do not know where you come from.' Then you will begin to say, 'We ate and drank in your presence, and you taught in our streets.' But he will say, 'I tell you, I do not know where you come from; depart from me, all you workers of iniquity!' There you will weep and gnash your teeth, when you see Abraham and Isaac and Jacob and all the prophets in the kingdom of God and you yourselves thrust out. And men will come from east and west, and from north and south, and sit at table in the kingdom of God. And behold, some are last who will be first, and some are first who will be last'"* (Luke 13:22-30).

Many false teachers have taught God's people to enter by the wide gate and follow the easy path. Right now, millions of Christians are following the *easy road gospel* that leads straight to destruction. Many have made a shipwreck of their faith, believing that they can sin deliberately, cover it up and continue going to church with a form of godliness that will bless them and be a means to financial gain. (See 2 Timothy 6:1-10).

There is one very terrible effect these false teachings of a painless salvation have on Christians. These doctrines of demons are aimed at nullifying the work of the believer's conscience. Christians sitting under the false do not learn how to work with the Holy Spirit and their consciences properly.

A properly working conscience is vital for the believer. The Holy Spirit uses our conscience to warn of ill motives, sinful behavior and bad thoughts. We can suffer from a wounded and weakened conscience, thus condemning us in doing what is right or pulling us into paranoid legalism. The spiritual work wrought by Christ's shed blood and broken body is blocked when Christians return to legalism because of a weak conscience.

Few Christians are taught how to discern condemning thoughts that are from self, others or Satan—versus the conviction of sin brought on by the Holy Spirit and the word of God.

Many Christians are wounded, double-minded and narcissistic. These false teachings cater to millions of self-centered Christians who reject the work of the cross for the believer. Instead of helping the Christian sort out their internal wounds and foul thoughts for proper cleansing, and learning how to die to carnal personalities, these teachers serve up false doctrine to soothe the conscience from self-condemnation, but also nullify the convicting work of the Holy Spirit.

These deceived Christians are taught to reject the pain of conscience. Paul wrote, *"This charge I commit to you, Timothy, my son, in accordance with the prophetic utterances which pointed to you, that inspired by them you may wage the good warfare, holding faith and a good conscience. By rejecting conscience, certain persons have made shipwreck of their faith, among them Hymenaeus and Alexander, whom I have delivered to Satan that they may learn not to blaspheme"* (1 Timothy 1:18-20).

Every child of God must understand the teaching of true and full sanctification and the grace of God. The process of working out our salvation must be understood, embraced, and completed in order to obtain eternal security. Many of God's people have not dealt with their evil and unbelieving hearts. Times of prosperity have not exposed the true condition of the heart, but when trouble comes, many will fall away from God and many will lose their salvation; others will wake up and grow up into salvation and eternal security.

The parable of the sower (Luke 8:5-18) and the parable of the ten maidens (Matthew 25:1-13) are two examples Jesus used in teaching about cheap grace, false Christianity and phony Christians. The following additional Scriptures will help us understand the seriousness of falling from grace and losing one's salvation. Far too many believers have made a shipwreck of their faith, ending up neglecting God's great plan of salvation.

"Therefore we must pay the closer attention to what we have heard, lest we drift away from it. For if the message declared by angels was valid and every transgression or disobedience received a just retribution, how shall we escape if we neglect such a great salvation? It was declared at first by the Lord, and it was attested to us by those who heard him, while God also bore witness by signs and wonders and various miracles and by gifts of the Holy Spirit distributed according to his own will" (Hebrews 2:1-4).

The following passages help us understand that the process of sanctification, when complete brings the guarantee of eternal life.

"But now that you have been set free from sin and have become slaves of God, the return you get is sanctification and its end, eternal life" (Romans 6:22).

"But we are bound to give thanks to God always for you, brethren beloved by the Lord, because God chose you from the beginning to be saved, through sanctification by the Spirit and belief in the truth" (2 Thessalonians 2:13).

"May the God of peace himself sanctify you wholly; and may your spirit and soul and body be kept sound and blameless at the coming of our Lord Jesus Christ" (1 Thessalonians 5:23).

New Christians must get a steady diet of encouragement and sound doctrine to learn to deal with any bitterness that produces a mean spirit. Many new Christians walk in guile or self-deception. They are naïve and vulnerable to their own hidden issues and false deceitful people and false Christians. Maintaining sincerity of faith allows growth in Christ, which means avoiding religious hypocrisy and avoiding taking an inner self-righteous stance in our relationship with God and in dealing with others.

"So put away all malice and all guile and insincerity and envy and all slander. Like newborn babes, long for the pure spiritual milk, that by it you may grow up to salvation; for you have tasted the kindness of the Lord. Come to him, to that living stone, rejected by men but in God's sight chosen and precious; and like living stones be yourselves built into a spiritual house, to be a holy priesthood, to offer spiritual sacrifices acceptable to God through Jesus Christ" (1 Peter 2:1-5).

Many new converts come to Christ with a divided heart that carries evil tendencies. It was said Jesus could not do many miracles within His own town and other certain cities because of their unbelief.

Christians should be continually exposed to sound teaching and exhortation that helps the sincere believer detect hidden unbelief and sinful alliances with bad attitudes, bitter judgments and inner jealousies.

"Take care, brethren, lest there be in any of you an evil, unbelieving heart, leading you to fall away from the living God. But exhort one another every day, as long as it is called 'today,' that none of you may be hardened by the deceitfulness of sin. For we share in Christ, if only we hold our first confidence firm to the end, while it is said, 'Today, when you hear his voice, do not harden your hearts as in the rebellion'" (Hebrews 3:12-15).

Few Christians are taught the difference between sinning deliberately and being overtaken in a trespass. Recently, a somewhat famous prophet was exposed as an alcoholic and homosexual. This supposed man of God hid these sinful behaviors from his closest ministry associates. Finally, his associates found out, confronted him and tried to restore him, but admittedly failed. This prophet along with his associates did not understand how God treats those who are overtaken by a trespass as compared to one who sins deliberately. If there is any hope for this habitually sinning Christian, it is falling into the fiery judgments of the Lord; and if necessary being turned over to Satan, even to the point of death, in hopes his spirit may be saved in the day of Christ.

"For if we sin deliberately after receiving the knowledge of the truth, there no longer remains a sacrifice for sins, but a fearful prospect of judgment, and a fury of fire which will consume the adversaries. A man who has violated the law of Moses dies without mercy at the testimony of two or three witnesses. How much worse punishment do you think will be deserved by the man who has spurned the Son of God, and profaned the blood of the covenant by which he was sanctified, and outraged the Spirit of grace? For we know him who said, 'Vengeance is mine, I will repay.' And again, 'The Lord will judge his people.' It is a fearful thing to fall into the hands of the living God" (Hebrews 10:26-31).

"It is actually reported that there is immorality among you, and of a kind that is not found even among pagans; for a man is living with his father's wife. And you are arrogant! Ought you not rather to mourn? Let him who has done this be removed from among you. For though absent in body I am present in spirit, and as if present, I have already pronounced judgment in the name of the Lord Jesus on the man who has done such a thing. When you are assembled, and my spirit is present, with the power of our Lord Jesus, you are to deliver this man to Satan for the destruction of the flesh, that his spirit may be saved in the day of the Lord Jesus" (1 Corinthians 5:1-5).

This easy road gospel saturating the body of Christ has made many Christians and lost sinners hardened to the Gospel. We have heard the Gospel in every way imaginable. We have gained knowledge and understanding; we have asked God for blessing upon blessing, only to become lazy and complacent with what the word of God says to us personally. We have accumulated teachers for ourselves that will assure us that our relationship with God is wonderful. They tickle the ears of naïve Christians while robbing their pocketbooks, leaving the hearers alienated from the life of God, due to hardness of heart.

Millions of Christians' love for God has grown cold. A hardened heart has displaced a healthy fear of God. These Christians are full of pride and loaded down with sin and the cares of the world. The *easy road gospel* has become a religious message to sinners presented by self-righteous hypocrites; they are at risk of Christ's rejection at the end of the age.

God allows warnings that seem at first to be attacks by the enemy. The attacks often include perverse personal dreams and troubling situations because of the hidden issues within the heart and mind of the Christian. Yet, instead of humbling themselves, they engage the false teaching that gives them instant relief from the suffering. This is actually a demonstration of lack of true faith and is no different from that of King Saul having David play soothing music or going to the witch of Endor for instant relief. (See 1 Samuel 16:14-23 and 1 Samuel 28:5-20).

EVANGELISM EXPLOSION: A TRAGEDY IN REALITY

Back in the early seventies, church growth swept through the evangelical Christian community like a wildfire. We all thought it was a solid move of God, bringing in souls to the body of Christ. Yes, indeed, there was and still is the call of God on this nation and throughout the world: *a call to repentance, salvation and sanctification!*

However, something has gone wrong. From the "Jesus People" movement to the megachurch growth craze, contemporary evangelical church growth has been ever increasing. Denominations and many ministries have gone after the lost soul with expensive marketing campaigns and fervor that only a Fortune 500 company could match.

The presentation of the Gospel began to take on forms not much different from that of a glitzy Hollywood production. Thousands and thousands of souls have responded to the mega crusades and church outreach programs with Christian celebrities, special speakers, and superstar ministers stirring the audience. Thrilling testimonies, powerful entertainment, and fantastic promises of the abundant life in Christ became so persuasive that perhaps one might think Satan himself could become born again.

This "born again" message became the cure-all for societal ills, as far as the evangelicals were concerned. An obsessive drive to convert the lost has become the main theme for the evangelicals to fulfill the Great Commission in our lifetime.

Let us look at the Great Commission statement made by Jesus.

"All authority in heaven and on earth has been given to me. Go therefore and make disciples of all nations, baptizing them in the name of the Father and of the Son and of the Holy Spirit, teaching them to observe all that I have commanded you; and lo, I am with you always, to the close of the age" (Matthew 28:18-20).

The key phrase to this Scripture is *make disciples of all nations*—meaning all nationalities.

In Acts 2, it states that the Spirit of the Lord added new souls daily to the company of believers. The disciples understood and followed what the Lord was doing and did not get ahead of God's Will and timing. (See Acts 2:46-47). Further, in Acts 13:48 it reads; *"And when the Gentiles heard this, they were glad and glorified the word of God; and as many as were ordained to eternal life believed."*

What went wrong with the evangelism explosion? This work started out by the Spirit of God. Gradually, subversion took place through carnal selfishness, sectarian competition and presumption. Churches became competitive for souls, which drove evangelists to shape the Word of God into enlistment campaigns. These evangelists tampered with the Word of God, making the Gospel attractive to the unrepentant sinner and the spiritually curious—those who wanted to be religious and invest in "fire insurance." The preaching of the Gospel in its original intent, with all the teachings of Christ and letting the Holy Spirit bring salvation to those whom God is calling, has been for the most part pushed aside. The result is false conversions.

Evangelism campaigns have become manipulative soul-winning contests rather than the Holy Spirit drawing souls as He wills! These evangelists present sermons and "born again" slogans tailored to manipulate, trick, and pressure souls into salvation.

In some cases, the pressure becomes so great that these fleshly evangelistic efforts are like a *conscription of souls*. A manipulative pressure takes place to join a church, a denomination, or follow a superlative evangelist, rather than being drawn by the Spirit of God. Few converts receive training in true discipleship and learn to grow up into the kingdom of God. These are victims of greedy church growth programs that avoid Christ's warnings and demands of what will be required of the true Christian.

This opened the door for evil men and women to sneak into thousands of churches and fellowships. A religious atmosphere grew and grew within the so-called *evangelism explosion* movement. False brethren, false teachings, wolves in sheep's clothing, liars, and charlatans were invited into the midst of God's people. To satisfy the needs of these selfish *non-born again converts*, church services became entertainment-oriented to appease. Preaching and teaching on sanctification, the cross, and the discipline of the Lord were minimized, as David Wilkerson, pastor of Manhattan's Times Square Church, puts it, "*Making church 'sinner friendly' and creating a 'comfort zone' for sinners.*"

How many converts, increased membership roles, increased financial budgets and building programs became the measurements for pastoral success? This worldly assessment peaks by touting the pinnacle of success as, *having to build a larger sanctuary that could hold at least a couple of thousand with two to three services each Sunday.*

Instead of being obedient to the Great Commission or making disciples of those whom God called, ministry turned to making converts to the denomination, a pastor, or a beautiful church complex. Many ministries and fellowships grew into an attitude not much different from that of the Pharisees concerning church growth. Jesus warned them, "*Woe to you, scribes and Pharisees, hypocrites! For you traverse sea and land to make a single proselyte, and when he becomes a proselyte, you make him twice as much a child of hell as yourselves*" (Matthew 23:15).

What started out to be a true movement of God, calling lost souls to Christ by the power of God, became an evangelistic tragedy!

STRANGE AND UNHOLY FIRE OFFERED

In examining some of these doctrines of men and demons, I have witnessed what I believe to be one of the most outrageous of all these teachings, "holy laughter," which received prominence within the Toronto Blessing movement and the so-called Brownsville Revival. The hallmark for this sensuous spiritualism purported to be of God is "to get drunk in the Spirit."

In reality, Satan appears as an angel of light and inspires this drunk-in-the-Spirit doctrine. Jesus offered the only acceptable sacrifice, and He leads every true Christian (the royal priesthood) to a sacrificial life such as His. We are to follow His example and mark others who embrace the cross and have crucified the flesh with all its passions and desires. Peter describes a process of suffering so that *fleshly spirituality* can be put to an end for the believer, and then a true servant of the living God will emerge.

"Since therefore Christ suffered in the flesh, arm yourselves with the same thought, for whoever has suffered in the flesh has ceased from sin, so as to live for the rest of the time in the flesh no longer by human passions but by the will of God. Let the time that is past suffice for doing what the Gentiles like to do, living in licentiousness, passions, drunkenness, revels, carousing, and lawless idolatry. They are surprised that you do not now join them in the same wild profligacy, and they abuse you; but they will give account to him who is ready to judge the living and the dead. For this is why the gospel was preached even to the dead, that though judged in the flesh like men, they might live in the spirit like God. The end of all things is at hand; therefore keep sane and sober for your prayers. Above all hold unfailing your love for one another, since love covers a multitude of sins. Practice hospitality ungrudgingly to one another. As each has received a gift, employ it for one another, as good stewards of God's varied grace: whoever speaks, as one who utters oracles of God; whoever renders service, as one who renders it by the strength which God supplies; in order that in everything God may be glorified through Jesus Christ. To him belong glory and dominion forever and ever. Amen. Beloved, do not be surprised at the fiery ordeal which comes upon you to prove you, as though something strange were happening to you. But rejoice in so far as you share Christ's sufferings, that you may also rejoice and be glad when his glory is revealed. If you are reproached for the name of Christ, you are blessed, because the spirit of glory and of God rests upon you. But let none of you suffer as a murderer, or a thief, or a wrongdoer, or a mischief-maker; yet if one suffers as a Christian, let him not be ashamed, but under that name let him glorify God. For the time has come for judgment to begin with the household of God; and if it begins with us, what will be the end of those who do not obey the gospel of God? And 'If the righteous man is scarcely saved, where will the impious and sinner appear?' Therefore let those who suffer according to God's will do right and entrust their souls to a faithful Creator" (1 Peter 4:1-19).

I have quoted a long passage here in order to preserve context. This admonishment by Peter specifies drunkenness as one of many carnal desires that requires death. These popular modern teachings, such as the Toronto Blessing, avoid the sufferings of Christ that believers are to embrace, as well as avoiding the work of the cross for the believer that puts an end to the works of the flesh.

The teacher may acknowledge the process and even declare that they have participated in some kind of death-to-self experience in their walk with God. They usually attribute their death to self as some special one-time moment where they reckoned themselves to <u>now</u> be *dead to self*. These teachings mislead Christians to believe that their individual death to the carnal self was a vicarious inclusion in Christ's experience on the cross.

No, not ever! This is magic thinking. Death to the old carnal nature for the true born-again Christian is not a one-time moment of mental revelation or reckoning, but a period of suffering in the life of the true disciple. For some it takes years of Holy Spirit-led discipline and suffering where every selfish inner motive is destroyed. This is a challenging process to which all-true Christians must submit, where every hidden carnal character structure becomes Christ-like.

These teachings, and much of the charismatic renewal message, also called Second and Third Wave, Toronto Blessing and Brownsville Revival, avoid the painful process of inner death, which is the work of the cross within the believer's life. Much of the so-called Holy Spirit revivals today are counterfeit; a few may be at best just empty manifestations of fleshly *carnal* spiritual activity!

Leadership in these movements is offering "strange and unholy fire" before the Lord. Christian leaders appointed by God are to help God's people present right and acceptable sacrifices and offerings to the Lord. (See Romans 12:1-8 and Hebrews 13:17).

The followers of these current movements are led to practice offerings of insane behavior and become spiritually drunk before the Lord as a kind of sacrificial service that is supposed to be acceptable in the sight of a Holy God. Here is what God really thinks of these abominations:

"And Nadab and Abihu, the sons of Aaron, each took his censer and put fire in it, and put incense on it, and offered strange and unholy fire before the Lord, as He had not commanded them. And there came forth fire from before the Lord and killed them, and they died before the Lord. Then Moses said to Aaron, This is what the Lord meant when He said,' I (and My will, not their own) will be acknowledged as hallowed by those who come near Me, and before all the people I will be honored.' And Aaron said nothing. Moses called Mishael and Elzaphan, sons of Uzziel uncle of Aaron, and said to them, 'Come near, carry your brethren from before the sanctuary out of the camp.' So they drew near and carried them in their under tunics [stripped of their priestly vestments] out of

the camp, as Moses had said. And Moses said to Aaron and Ithamar, his sons (the father and brothers of the two priests whom God had slain for offering false fire), 'Do not uncover your heads or let your hair go loose or tear your clothes, lest you die (also) and lest God's wrath should come upon all the congregation; but let your brethren, the whole house of Israel, bewail the burning which the Lord has kindled. And you shall not go out from the door of the Tent of Meeting, lest you die, for the Lord's anointing oil is upon you.' And they did according to Moses' word. And the Lord said to Aaron, 'Do not drink wine or strong drink, you or your sons, when you go into the Tent of Meeting, lest you die; it shall be a statute forever in all your generations. You shall make distinction and recognize a difference between the holy and the common or unholy, and between the unclean and the clean; And you shall teach the Israelites all the statutes which the Lord has spoken to them by Moses'" (Leviticus 10 verses 1 to 11; Amplified Bible).

These rules that God laid down for the priesthood were to deal with any irreverence toward God and the things of God. We can draw from the account that the reason the Lord killed Aaron's two sons was that they came before the Lord intoxicated, and in that state irreverently offered strange and unholy fire before the Lord. This act mocked God. It was, and still is an irreverent manner of worship. Here is how Jesus walked with God: *"In the days of his flesh, Jesus offered up prayers and supplications, with loud cries and tears, to him who was able to save him from death, and he was heard for his godly fear. Although he was a Son, he learned obedience through what he suffered; and being made perfect he became the source of eternal salvation to all who obey him, being designated by God a high priest after the order of Melchizedek"* (Hebrews 5:7-10).

Holy laughter or getting drunk in the Spirit is carnal spiritualism thought to be a sacrifice of praise and worship but is no different from what Nadab and Abihu did before the Lord.

Paul addressed this type of strange and out of control activity in his letter to the Corinth Christians. (See 1 Corinthians 14:1-40). These believers practiced speaking in an unknown tongue for personal spiritual edification. This activity was getting out of hand and Paul wrote that outsiders would think of them as being mad or insane. He challenged their arrogance in interpreting Scripture to suit themselves and being caught up in a chaotic form of worship. Paul finished his correction stating, *"What! Did the word of God originate with you, or are you the only ones it has reached? If anyone thinks that he is a prophet, or spiritual, he should acknowledge that what I am writing to you is a command of the Lord. If any one does not recognize this, he is not recognized. So, my brethren, earnestly desire to prophesy, and do not forbid speaking in tongues; but all things should be done decently and in order"*(1 Corinthians 14:13-40).

Paul knew about the pagan influence to which Christians in Corinth were subjected. These new Christians lived in a Greek culture that worshiped many gods.

One, Dionysus the god of the vine, supposedly invented wine and spread the art of tending grapes. This god had a dual nature; worshipping this god brought joy and divine ecstasy—but also brutal, unthinking, rage. This reflected both sides of wine's nature, and as the Greeks believed, Dionysus could drive a person mad. The worship of this god required participants to work themselves into a mental, emotional, and spiritual state where the conscience transcended inhibitions or the *inhibition of conscience*. In this state their spirits would be free to experience divine ecstasy. The use of wine helped create this *euphoric inner state of being* and worship included chaotic, maddening activities, loud cries, and often led to sexual orgies.

Part of this idolatrous Greek myth had Dionysus wandering the world actively encouraging his cult, accompanied by the Maenads or Bacchantes. These were wild women, expressing ecstatic devotion to this god, often, flush with wine, shoulders draped with a fawn skin, carrying rods tipped with pinecones. These devoted worshippers were believed to possess occult powers.

While other gods had temples, the followers of Dionysus worshipped him in the woods. Here they might go into mad states where they would rip apart and eat any animal they found—raw.

Dionysus became one of the most important gods in everyday life, the god of wine and cheer where wine miracles were purported to occur in certain festivals. This god was believed to mysteriously induce orgasmic worship. He became associated with several key concepts. One was rebirth after death. This portion of the myth had this god dismembered by the Titans and return to life. This symbolically echoed tending the vines, where the vines must be pruned back sharply, and then become dormant in winter for them to bear fruit. The other is the idea that under the influence of wine, one could feel possessed by a greater power. Unlike the other Greek gods, Dionysus was not only outside his believers but also within them. Under this influence, a man might become greater than himself and do works he otherwise could not.

The festival for Dionysus was in the spring when the leaves begin to ripen on the vine. It became one of the most important events of the year, with theater becoming the main focus in its expressed worship. The most important festival, the Greater Dionysia, was held in Athens for five days each spring. Aeschylus, Sophocles, and Euripides wrote their great Greek tragedies for these festivals.

By 5th century BC, Dionysus also became known as Bacchus to the Greeks, with its forms of festival worship degenerating into occasions for *orgia*, or Dionysiac mysteries, marked with licentiousness, intoxication and sexual orgies. The Roman culture took on this idolatry, which was called Bacchanalia. The celebrations grew in popularity and frequency, culminating into a five-time-per-month ritual, adding to the large Dionysiac annual festivals. The indulgences of Bacchanalia became so extreme that the Roman Senate prohibited its worship and festival celebrations in 186 BC. Nevertheless, the Dionysiac mysteries were still popular in the 1st century AD, as evidenced by Greek-style carvings on Greek and Roman coffins.

The parallel between Dionysus worship and the drunk-in-the-spirit—Toronto Blessing movement is uncanny and mysterious. A Christian brother, Andrew Strom, recently attended a "prophetic" meeting. The following is an excerpt from his newsletter account of how far this movement has gone pagan. This brother, according to his newsletter, left this movement and denounced it for what it is.

"The ON-STAGE DANCING throughout this conference was a good example. Now, I myself am a rock musician, but from the beginning these dance items had a rather 'wild' aspect to them that truly made me uncomfortable in my spirit. There was even one that came across like a sensual 'Harem' dance. Much of it really felt off—and almost anyone who sees the videos will tell you so. Even the worship had a very 'tribal' feel to it at times. And by Day Three they were doing dance items with just loud voodoo-style drums only - and leaping around in a frenzied circle making weird cries to the super-amplified beat. The feeling in the room was so oppressive and 'pagan' during this, that I could hardly even bear to stay in there. Then came one of the most shocking statements of the whole conference—from one of the main prophets. He got up and said that people may feel uncomfortable with such obviously 'pagan' type dancing, but that it was originally God's type of dancing and we were just now 'stealing back' what the pagans had stolen from God!

I have to admit, this was the last straw for me. What could be more blatant? What kind of 'spirits' do they think are being transmitted to people who open themselves up to that music? There is no discernment in this movement at all" (Andrew Strom November 2004).

You may ask, "If these movements are so wrong, why haven't the leaders of these movements been removed by God or died?" It is because most of the followers of these leaders want it so, and God is allowing this to go full-term to finally break this insane counterfeit spiritualism. This work has infiltrated many parts of the body of Christ. Starting back during the Wales revival of 1905, these false manifestations took over this move of God, perverting a true revival into a carnival of *carnally insane spiritualism*. Their end will come soon enough. It is God's people who desire the quick-fix gimmicks and *easy way* gospel. God's people must depart from craving empty manifestations, spiritualistic sensations and renounce embracing these false teachings. God has given them over to these lies, deceived by these imposters for a season. When it all unravels, many will repent and see their own stubborn rebelliousness.

John Wimber considered a prominent co-founder in this movement did depart early, on November 17, 1997 from massive brain hemorrhage. Paul Cain, a noted founder in this movement was recently exposed for being an alcoholic and secretly practicing homosexuality.

Paul wrote, *"As Jannes and Jambres opposed Moses, so these men also oppose the truth, men of corrupt mind and counterfeit faith; but they will not get very far, for their folly will be plain to all, as was that of those two men"* (See 2 Thessalonians 2:9-12 and 2 Timothy 3:1-9; 4:1-5).

Indeed, soon the hand of God will take out other false leaders who persist in this obscene worship.

WILL THE REAL JESUS, SPIRIT AND GOSPEL PLEASE STAND UP?

Paul wrote: *"For if someone comes and preaches another Jesus than the one we preached, or if you receive a different spirit from the one you received, or if you accept a different gospel from the one you accepted, you submit to it readily enough"* (Excerpt from 2 Corinthians chapter 1).

Many Christians are quite gullible and naïve. These teachers compound deception by teaching that Christians are safe from false doctrines and demonic spirits. Christians are convinced that Satan must flee when *told to go*, even though a Christian is in a state of disobedience and rebellious, which is characteristic of being double-minded, or is just plain immature, selfish, and presumptuous. Any teacher, so-called prophet, or a self-proclaimed apostle who comes with signs and wonders and is proclaimed to be an "anointed one of God" is readily accepted by far too many. These teachers push the listener into hyper-faith frenzy and lay acts of fleshly works upon the sheep. A conjured state of blind faith envelops followers, which is analogous to tempting God. Usually finances are the "acts of faith" attached to a "rite of passage" for these hyper-faith believers. These hyper-faith apostles lay a cost on the hearers that is an abomination before the Lord. Many use the seed planting or sowing principles to exhort the believer to give in order to receive an increase.

Again, in this case, as well as any counterfeit work of Satan, a large portion of the teaching is true, but truth implemented for the wrong motives and pushed into carnal method leads to grave error. Teachings founded in part truth lead to counterfeit experiences. Satan's best deception is presenting his lies in a cloak of half-truth. If one looks deeper by using thorough study, it will become apparent that vital parts of the teachings of Christ are missing. The most important truth left out of the counterfeit is the work of the believer's cross, which exposes ill motives and disciplines the Christian in the sufferings of Christ. Most counterfeit teachings are really rooted in the love of money. (See Matthew 6:24-27). The apostle Paul confronted these false teachers and false apostles in his day.

"I wish you would bear with me in a little foolishness. Do bear with me! I feel a divine jealousy for you, for I betrothed you to Christ to present you as a pure bride to her one husband. But I am afraid that as the serpent deceived Eve by his cunning, your thoughts will be led astray from a sincere and pure devotion to Christ. For if someone comes and preaches another Jesus than the one we preached, or if you receive a different spirit from the one you received, or if you accept a different gospel from the one you accepted, you submit to it readily enough. I think that I am not in the least inferior to these superlative apostles. Even if I am unskilled in speaking, I am not in knowledge; in every way we have made this plain to you in all things. Did I commit a sin in abasing myself so that you might be exalted, because I preached God's gospel without cost to you? I robbed other churches by accepting support from them in order to serve you. And when I was with you and was in want, I did not burden any one, for my needs were supplied by the brethren who came from Macedonia. So I refrained and will refrain from burdening you in any way. As the truth of Christ is in me, this boast of mine shall not be silenced in the regions of Achaia. And why? Because I do not love you? God knows I do! And what I do I will continue to do, in order to undermine the claim of those who would like to claim that in their boasted mission they work on the same terms as we do. For such men are false apostles, deceitful workmen, disguising themselves as apostles of Christ. And no wonder, for even Satan disguises himself as an angel of light. So it is not strange if his servants also disguise themselves as servants of righteousness. Their end will correspond to their deeds" (2 Corinthians 11:1-15).

The apostle Paul had a goal concerning these false workmen. He wrote in the above passage, *"And what I do I will continue to do, in order to undermine the claim of those who would like to claim that in their boasted mission they work on the same terms as we do."*

Many pastors see these problems and go along with their wicked deception, afraid of being slandered for confronting their lies. The tendency is to allow the good to flow with the bad, so money and support is not hampered. True leaders must take a clear stand; confront and point out the phony.

Satan sends in his disguised workmen. Most are self-deceived and grow from bad to worse unless true leadership takes a stand. They rob the body of Christ of desperate support needed for valid ministries and the local church. Many well-meaning yet naïve Christians follow them and have embraced a *different Jesus, a different spirit and a different gospel* than that found in Scripture.

LEGALISM THAT VOIDS GRACE AND MAKES CHRIST OF NO USE

The apostle Paul and the other apostles fought against legalism that began to seep into the first century church. Christians began to embrace the ritual of circumcision as well as observing other rituals, special Sabbaths and rules concerning foods. Paul warned that following these practices would actually make Christ of no use or be of no advantage concerning salvation and sanctification. Following these rules would enslave the Christian to legalism and to the men who made up the rules, resulting in the loss of true righteousness and freedom found in Christ.

"For freedom Christ has set us free; stand fast therefore, and do not submit again to a yoke of slavery. Now I, Paul, say to you that if you receive circumcision, Christ will be of no advantage to you. I testify again to every man who receives circumcision that he is bound to keep the whole law. You are severed from Christ, you who would be justified by the law; you have fallen away from grace. For through the Spirit, by faith, we wait for the hope of righteousness. For in Christ Jesus neither circumcision nor uncircumcision is of any avail, but faith working through love. You were running well; who hindered you from obeying the truth? This persuasion is not from him who calls you. A little leaven leavens the whole lump. I have confidence in the Lord that you will take no other view than mine; and he who is troubling you will bear his judgment, whoever he is. But if I, brethren, still preach circumcision, why am I still persecuted? In that case the stumbling block of the cross has been removed. I wish those who unsettle you would mutilate themselves!" (Galatians 5:1-12).

Indeed, we must walk in righteousness and lead an impeccable holy life in Christ. The way to a sanctified life in Christ Jesus, where the sin nature and carnal life dies, is by the work of the cross, not by following outward religious laws, ordinances and special observances.

This problem addressed in the New Testament letters from Paul and others grew even worse over the years. Today, this problem persists with Catholicism and other orthodox sects that promote a pretense of righteousness by outer religious rules and observances. We also see a *self-holiness* movement in certain evangelical denominations as well as charismatic and Pentecostal groups.

Another new movement springing up is turning Christian believers back to legalism by observing the Torah or Old Testament rules and regulations. This movement observes Saturday as the appropriate Sabbath and promotes other Old Testament legalistic observances.

This new heretical insurgence of legalism ensnares many. Beware; the false teachings that emphasize outer appearances to make a religious show will cause many to fall from grace and lose their salvation. As Paul wrote *"These have indeed an appearance of wisdom in promoting rigor of devotion and self-abasement and severity to the body, but they are of no value in checking the indulgence of the flesh"* (Colossians 2:23).

In this passage, Paul warns that those who attempt to justify themselves through Christian legalism will fall from the grace of God. As it states elsewhere, we are saved by grace, *"For by grace you have been saved through faith; and this is not your own doing, it is the gift of God—not because of works, lest any man should boast."*

CHARISMATIC SIDESHOWS AND TABLOID MINISTRIES

Paul challenged the phony leaders who were manipulating the church at Corinth. He wrote, *"We have renounced disgraceful, underhanded ways; we refuse to practice cunning or to tamper with God's word, but by the open statement of the truth we would commend ourselves to every man's conscience in the sight of God. And even if our gospel is veiled, it is veiled only to those who are perishing. In their case the god of this world has blinded the minds of the unbelievers, to keep them from seeing the light of the gospel of the glory of Christ, who is the likeness of God. For what we preach is not ourselves, but Jesus Christ as Lord, with ourselves as your servants for Jesus' sake"* (1 Corinthians 4:2-5).

Much promoted in the church and this nation as the so-called power of God is nothing more than a circus spirit with dozens of sideshow acts. Christian television and large church assemblies present special celebrity entertainment, more phenomenal miracles, testimonies, and extreme scare tactics to move upon the audience, pulling them into financial giving, all inspired by Satan to create scoffing at the Gospel and incite persecution. One major goal of Satan in these *angel-of-light* ministries is to make the real work and power of God look phony. Counterfeiting has three main purposes.

One is to get believers to embrace a false doctrine that will ultimately rob them of a true walk with God, leaving the Christian with a false peace and false joy. The second objective is to get followers dependent on the super-leader: the anointing, teachings and the leader's counterfeit faith. Millions of Christians are dependent on these false ministries, unable to stand on their own two feet of faith. Christians are to grow up into Christ, living by faith in the Son of God—not a superlative apostle on earth.

Another purpose is to get the lost and the outsiders who witness these extreme spiritualistic rituals to scoff and label them as mad or insane in behavior. This will drive people away from the true Gospel. The outer expressions of so-called spiritual ecstatic experiences are out of control and scaring the lost away from Christ. An ulterior motive is to make the true servant of God who walks in the true gifts become suspect.

Paul wrote to the Corinthians to debunk narcissistic spiritual experience and let the mature gifts of the Holy Spirit prevail in the gathering of the believers.

"Brethren, do not be children in your thinking; be babes in evil, but in thinking be mature. In the law it is written, 'By men of strange tongues and by the lips of foreigners will I speak to this people, and even then they will not listen to me,' says the Lord. Thus,

tongues are a sign not for believers but for unbelievers, while prophecy is not for unbelievers but for believers. If, therefore, the whole church assembles and all speak in tongues, and outsiders or unbelievers enter, will they not say that you are mad? But if all prophesy, and an unbeliever or outsider enters, he is convicted by all, he is called to account by all, the secrets of his heart are disclosed; and so, falling on his face, he will worship God and declare that God is really among you" (1 Corinthians 14:20-25).

This passage describes the first century Christians being led away into spiritualism and getting out of control. This generation of Christians has certainly exceeded the error of the Corinthians, carried away with the lust for sensuous humanistic spiritualism.

Many add doctrines of self-righteous and self-manufactured holiness to these counterfeit gifts teachings. The source of this type of spiritual power is in reality a demonic principality hovering over many movements and fellowships. Many Pentecostals pride themselves on an outer qualifying sign, making sure everyone knows that they have "arrived" with God through speaking in tongues and other public ministry gifts.

THE SPIRIT OF SIMON: IDOLATRY OF PENTECOSTAL POWER AND AUTHORITY

These doctrines override the leadership of the Holy Spirit concerning the dispersing of the gifts. They foster a lust for power with an outer expression as a sign. This sign becomes a spiritually prideful *stamp* worn by participating Christians that says, "I have arrived!" This smaller gift has been glorified, abused, and made into a fleshly spiritual experience that leaves many Christians vulnerable to counterfeit experiences. The mature Christian should have grown out of this or probably never should have experienced it in the first place.

The Holy Spirit is to appoint and distribute His gifts as He wills. He does this for those who are ready and mature. The gifts of the Holy Spirit are for the common good of the local fellowship and body of Christ at large, not a sign for the believer to indicate spiritual perfection!

Like Simon the Magician in the book of Acts, many believers lust after power and authority so others will recognize that they have the so-called power of God. Simon had previously practiced magic and amazed many people. The local people said of him, *"This man is that power of God which is called Great"* (Acts 8:10).

Philip preached the Gospel, and many believed; even Simon the Magician believed on the Lord and was baptized. Simon continued with Phillip and was amazed with the great miracles and signs performed. (Acts 8:13).

John and Peter came down to check out this revival in Samaria. Arriving, they prayed that the new believers might receive the Holy Spirit. John and Peter laid hands on these new converts, and by this they received the Holy Spirit.

When Simon saw this demonstration of power and that it was done by the laying on of hands, he offered money to John and Peter saying, *"Give me also this power, that any one on whom I lay my hands may receive the Holy Spirit"* (Acts 8:19).

Fortunately, Peter had courage to confront this evil, and the following is what Peter said in response to Simon the Magician's offer.

"'Your silver perish with you, because you thought you could obtain the gift of God with money! You have neither part nor lot in this matter, for your heart is not right before God. Repent therefore of this wickedness of yours, and pray to the Lord that, if possible, the intent of your heart may be forgiven you. For I see that you are in the gall of bitterness and in the bond of iniquity.' And Simon answered, 'Pray for me to the Lord, that nothing of what you have said may come upon me'" (Acts 8:20-24).

This new believer was not right in his heart towards the things of God and the power of God. Peter saw that he was bitter over the loss of being recognized as the, *"This man is that power of God which is called Great."* Peter exposed Simon's motives and intentions of heart by confronting Simon immediately. Peter could see this new believer was in the bonds of iniquity and his request was wicked. Peter was so incensed with Simon's offer that Peter pronounced that he and his money perish.

These teachings today have created thousands and thousands of believers who, as did Simon, lust after the power of God for the wrong reasons. These insecure believers are full of jealousy, bitterness, and selfish ambition. Money has become central in receiving these so-called gifts and the power of the Holy Spirit. Leadership should be incensed over the many wrong motives involved with those seeking the power of God. Instead, many sell the power of God indirectly though in many cases offers a spiritual gift for a direct donation.

The problem is, those seeking this power are taught to prophesy and practice speaking in tongues through the power of their own spirit, often enhanced by the demonic, not by the Spirit of God. Many are like those in Ezekiel's day, *"The word of the LORD came to me: 'Son of man, prophesy against the prophets of Israel, prophesy and say to those who prophesy out of their own minds: 'Hear the word of the LORD!' Thus says the Lord GOD, Woe to the foolish prophets who follow their own spirit, and have seen nothing! Your prophets have been like foxes among ruins, O Israel. You have not gone up into the breaches, or built up a wall for the house of Israel, that it might stand in battle in the day of the LORD. They have spoken falsehood and divined a lie; they say, 'Says the LORD,' when the LORD has not sent them, and yet they expect him to fulfill their word. Have you not seen a delusive vision, and uttered a lying divination, whenever you have said, 'Says the LORD,' although I have not spoken?' Therefore thus says the Lord God: 'Because you have uttered delusions and seen lies, therefore behold, I am against you, says the Lord GOD'"* (Ezekiel 13:1-8).

FALSE PROPHETS, WOLVES AND WHITEWASHED TOMBS

Jesus warned the disciples and followers about false prophets, wolves in sheep's clothing and so-called godly people who in reality are hypocrites—*actors playing a self-righteous role.*

Here's what He said, *"Beware of false prophets, who come to you in sheep's clothing but inwardly are ravenous wolves. You will know them by their fruits. Are grapes gathered from thorns, or figs from thistles? So, every sound tree bears good fruit, but the bad tree bears evil fruit. A sound tree cannot bear evil fruit, nor can a bad tree bear good fruit. Every tree that does not bear good fruit is cut down and thrown into the fire. Thus you will know them by their fruits. 'Not every one who says to me, 'Lord, Lord,' shall enter the kingdom of heaven, but he who does the will of my Father who is in heaven. On that day many will say to me, 'Lord, Lord, did we not prophesy in your name, and cast out demons in your name, and do many mighty works in your name?' And then will I declare to them, 'I never knew you; depart from me, you evildoer'"* (Matthew 7:16-23).

He called these people evil doers and of the religious phonies Jesus said this: *"Woe to you, scribes and Pharisees, hypocrites! For you are like whitewashed tombs, which outwardly appear beautiful, but within they are full of dead men's bones and all uncleanness. So you also outwardly appear righteous to men, but within you are full of hypocrisy and iniquity"* (Matthew 23:27,28).

Jesus lets us know about this kind of person who appears righteous, but inwardly is wicked and evil. These people ran the show in His day—manipulating and doing great evil to the poor sinner. Today, these false leaders make up rules and teachings that elevate themselves in the eyes of the naïve and manipulate the minds of those who follow to make them dependent on their teaching and ministry. Indeed, it is a subtle form of mind control. Jesus confronted them outright and taught the apostles to do the same. As you read the New Testament, you will see that the apostles were constantly confronting those who would pervert the Gospel of Christ.

"I am astonished that you are so quickly deserting him who called you in the grace of Christ and turning to a different gospel—not that there is another gospel, but there are some who trouble you and want to pervert the gospel of Christ. But even if we, or an angel from heaven, should preach to you a gospel contrary to that which we preached to you, let him be accursed. As we have said before, so now I say again, if anyone is preaching to you a gospel contrary to that which you received, let him be accursed. Am I now seeking the favor of men, or of God? Or am I trying to please men? If I were still pleasing men, I should not be a servant of Christ. For I would have you know, brethren, that the gospel which was preached by me is not man's gospel. For I did not receive it from man, nor was I taught it, but it came through a revelation of Jesus Christ" (Galatians 1:6-12).

"Beloved, being very eager to write to you of our common salvation, I found it necessary to write appealing to you to contend for the faith which was once for all delivered to the saints. For admission has been secretly gained by some who long ago were designated for this condemnation, ungodly persons who pervert the grace of our God into licentiousness and deny our only Master and Lord, Jesus Christ" (Jude 3,4).

These people have secretly gained admission into the body of Christ. They are ungodly people who pervert the Gospel and the grace of God. They are accursed and destined for destruction, but not until they deceive many Christians.

END OF THE AGE FALSE SIGNS AND WONDERS
The spirit of alchemy and the message of instant change

"For false Christs and false prophets will arise and show great signs and wonders, so as to lead astray, if possible, even the elect. Lo, I have told you beforehand" (Matthew 24:24,25).

Christ was very specific about this end of the age deception directed at true Christians. Satan and demons will empower false evangelists and false prophets with demonic signs and wonders. These preach a false gospel backed by great signs and wonders that have a power over the physical.

These deceived men and women oppose the truth concerning Christ's harder teachings such as the work of the cross in the believer's life and true discipleship. They espouse the doctrine of *instant change* with signs and wonders to back up their teachings. Masses are enthralled with their anointing and demonstrated power. This message of instant change is like a magnet pulling wounded and deceived Christians into believing the false promise that Christ will instantly change, deliver, free, save, heal and transform the flesh into Christ likeness.

Paul prophesied concerning certain deceitful men at the end of the age, *"As Jannes and Jambres opposed Moses, so these men also oppose the truth, men of corrupt mind and counterfeit faith; but they will not get very far, for their folly will be plain to all, as was that of those two men."* (2 Timothy 3:8,9).

Who were Jannes and Jambres? These two men opposed Moses, duplicating the miracles God wrought through Moses and Aaron. Their names mean *he who seduces* and he *who is rebellious*. These Egyptian magicians practiced secret arts and walked in demonic power that produced the same miracles that Moses did: turning a stick to a serpent, turning the waters of the Nile to blood and bringing frogs upon the land of Egypt. Finally, when God commanded Moses to have Aaron bring forth gnats upon man and beast, these magicians tried and failed, saying, *"This is the finger of God."* (See Exodus 7:1 – 8:19).

The apostle Paul uses this biblical account to describe the power that these false evangelists and prophets will have at the end of the age.

Signs and wonders are following these peddlers of God's power that magically and instantly change the Christian on the inside. Masses are enthralled and deceived by ministers such as Benny Hinn, Rhinehart Bonke, Oral Roberts, Paula White and Robert Tilton.

Deceived Christians buy into their counterfeit faith that indeed has power. Unfortunately, that power is like that of Jannes and Jambres, only real and effective to a point. Counterfeit faith will have satanic power to counterfeit the Holy Spirit. Miracles, signs and wonders will manifest in many of these meetings. Jesus said false prophets *"will arise and show great signs and wonders."* Few test the spirit manifesting through these flamboyant evangelists and prophets.

I believe in miracles, signs, healings, and the gifts of the Holy Spirit. The issue with God's people in these last days is that few dig deep, develop a relationship with the true Christ and know God's word on the matter of discernment.

Satan will be allowed to perform miracles, signs and wonders through men and women who preach a false gospel to test even the elect. Christians who crave signs and wonders so that life is made easier are subject to the counterfeit. Satan is demanding to sift millions of Christians who lust after the power of God and become enthralled with any false flamboyant leader.

What is the spirit behind the power under which these men and women operate? The principality in charge of this satanic effort can be called the spirit of alchemy, where Alchemy is defined as a medieval chemical science and speculative philosophy aiming for transmutation of the base metals into gold; the discovery of a universal cure for disease, and the discovery of a means of indefinitely prolonging life. Also, alchemy is a power or process (magic) of transforming something common into something precious.

This counterfeit spirit is even invading some churches where gold flakes and other precious stones appear out of thin air. Oh, some of these manifestations are real, just as Jannes and Jambres' sorceries produced real snakes, blood and frogs. Satan, the god of this world has a limited supernatural power, and you will see more great signs and wonders, so compelling that, if possible, the elect of God would be deceived!

Paul prophesied that these last-day charlatans would not get far, like Jannes and Jambres keeping up the demonic miracles with the power of God for just three times. These two did all right for themselves in the court of the Pharaoh until true servants of the Lord came on the scene.

Likewise, these last day counterfeit ministries are doing fine for now, as they mesmerize and deceive the majority. But they will not get far when the true servants of the Lord come on the scene, working miracles in the true power of

God. Many who were deceived will concede and repent, saying the *finger of God is working through His true servants.*

MESMERIZING OF THE MASSES

Today we see more and more attendance records being broken in ministry meetings, conferences, and crusades. It is common for a megachurch to have 3,000 to 5,000 attending any service. Christians and spiritual seekers attend these gigantic rallies led by flamboyant, superlative speakers and ministry leaders who demonstrate signs and wonders. Many declare all this as a renewal or revival—a spiritual awakening.

Indeed, Jesus predicted that a spiritual movement would come at the end of this age. *"Take heed that no one leads you astray. For many will come in my name, saying, 'I am the Christ,' and they will lead many astray"* (Matthew 24:4,5). Also, *"And many false prophets will arise and lead many astray"* (Matthew 24:11). Further, *"Then if any one says to you, 'Lo, here is the Christ!' or 'There he is!' do not believe it. For false Christs and false prophets will arise and show great signs and wonders, so as to lead astray, if possible, even the elect. Lo, I have told you beforehand"* (Matthew 24:23,25).

Yes, there is a spiritual awakening and some of it is a result of the Holy Spirit drawing those called of God to salvation and ministry. There was a reason Christ warned of this false movement at the end of the age. It should be clear to us that Satan will be working a counterfeit movement prior to the real move of God in order to, if it were even possible, derail and even stop the true work of the Holy Spirit. There is coming a final great outpouring of God's Spirit and a final harvest of souls at the end of this age.

The fruit of these mass movements and fads in Christianity today demonstrate shallowness and a self-centered lifestyle with materialism and money at the center of attention. Leaders in these movements appear to have an anointed work, but the fruit of their work draws attention to their ministry and themselves. As Paul warned, *"I know that after my departure fierce wolves will come in among you, not sparing the flock; and from among your own selves will arise men speaking perverse things, to draw away the disciples after them. Therefore be alert, remembering that for three years I did not cease night or day to admonish every one with tears"* (Acts 20:29-31).

What we are witnessing is mostly a false work within these movements. Those attending come with the hope and promise of blessings, healings and quick-fix spiritual touches. Masses of Christians fall prey to deception, held spellbound by the miraculous signs and wonders. When the masses followed Jesus, how did Christ respond to these large crowds?

"After this Jesus went to the other side of the Sea of Galilee, which is the Sea of Tiberias. And a multitude followed him, because they saw the signs which he did on those who were diseased. Jesus went up on the mountain, and there sat down with his disciples. Now the Passover, the feast of the Jews, was at hand. Lifting up his eyes, then, and seeing that a multitude was coming to him, Jesus said to Philip, 'How are we to buy bread, so that these people may eat?' This he said to test him, for he himself knew what he would do. Philip answered him, 'Two hundred denarii would not buy enough bread for each of them to get a little.' One of his disciples, Andrew, Simon Peter's brother, said to him, 'There is a lad here who has five barley loaves and two fish; but what are they among so many?' Jesus said, 'Make the people sit down.' Now there was much grass in the place; so the men sat down, in number about five thousand. Jesus then took the loaves, and when he had given thanks, he distributed them to those who were seated; so also the fish, as much as they wanted. And when they had eaten their fill, he told his disciples, 'Gather up the fragments left over, that nothing may be lost.' So they gathered them up and filled twelve baskets with fragments from the five barley loaves, left by those who had eaten. When the people saw the sign which he had done, they said, 'This is indeed the prophet who is to come into the world!' Perceiving then that they were about to come and take him by force to make him king, Jesus withdrew again to the mountain by himself" (John 6:1-15).

Jesus would not allow the multitude to manipulate and control Him nor allow them to make Him an earthly king. Jesus knew they were only interested in having their stomachs full and life's troubles made easier. This is the message today for the masses that follow these *extraordinary* prophets, national TV evangelists and megachurch leaders. Jesus warned that an evil and adulterous generation seeks after signs and wonders. Many in these meetings refuse to believe in the Word of God. Jesus said to many, "Why do you call me 'Lord, Lord,' and not do what I tell you?" (Luke 6:46). They do not obey Christ's commands. Their faith is in the faith and the works of leadership; indeed, many leading these movements are making themselves indispensable. The masses keep coming back for more, being made dependent on the false leader rather than standing on their own two feet of faith and obeying Christ and growing up into Christ, where He is all and in all.

When Christ performed the miracle of the barley loaves and fish, the masses following Jesus, ate their fill and declared, *"This is indeed the prophet who is to come into the world!"* (John 6:14). Jesus left this crowd with His disciples and withdrew to Capernaum across the sea. The people saw Christ had left and they got into boats and went across the sea to Capernaum, looking for Jesus. *"When they found him on the other side of the sea, they said to him, 'Rabbi, when did you come here?' Jesus answered them, 'Truly, truly, I say to you, you seek me, not because you saw signs, but because you ate your fill of the loaves. Do not labor for the food which perishes, but for the food which endures to eternal life, which the Son of man will give to you; for on him has God the Father set his seal'"* (John 6:25-27).

Jesus challenged their motives for following him. He knew they were elevating Him to become their earthly king; then they could manipulate by giving Him homage to get temporal material blessings.

Again, Jesus warned of false prophets tapping into the masses who seek miracles and financial blessing from God to make life on earth comfortable.

Sound ministries, pastors and ministers will tell those who come and listen, what they need to hear and not pander and cater to carnal desires for miracles that make life easier.

Another Gospel account reads, *"Now great multitudes accompanied him; and he turned and said to them, 'If any one comes to me and does not hate his own father and mother and wife and children and brothers and sisters, yes, and even his own life, he cannot be my disciple. Whoever does not bear his own cross and come after me, cannot be my disciple. For which of you, desiring to build a tower, does not first sit down and count the cost, whether he has enough to complete it? Otherwise, when he has laid a foundation, and is not able to finish, all who see it begin to mock him, saying, 'This man began to build, and was not able to finish.' Or what king, going to encounter another king in war, will not sit down first and take counsel whether he is able with ten thousand to meet him who comes against him with twenty thousand? And if not, while the other is yet a great way off, he sends an embassy and asks terms of peace. So therefore, whoever of you does not renounce all that he has cannot be my disciple. 'Salt is good; but if salt has lost its taste, how shall its saltness be restored? It is fit neither for the land nor for the dunghill; men throw it away. He who has ears to hear, let him hear'"* (Luke 14:25-35).

Clearly, Christ tells those who follow Him that there was something more than just becoming a follower. The call was to become disciples and He let them know what is expected. He did not pander pity or cater to the masses. He told them the truth!

EVANGELICAL ERASING OF THE TRUE POWER OF GOD

Since many doctrines practiced by Charismatic and Pentecostal churches abuse the truth found in the Gospel, many evangelical Christians embrace doctrines that counteract these heresies but end up being just as wrong. In reacting to the madness expressed by many charismatic and Pentecostal brothers and sisters who practice false gifts, the evangelical teachings throw out the gifts and the offices of apostle and prophet entirely. Yet all that the first century Christians and apostles experienced was never meant to stop. Teachings that say otherwise are not scriptural. The true gifts are for today, just as they were in the days of the first apostles. I will discuss the functions and characteristics of the gifts and offices of apostle and prophet later.

TRUE PROPHETIC MINISTRIES REJECTED AND THE TRUE GIFTS OF THE HOLY SPIRIT ARE AVOIDED

Due to the radical and fleshly false movements by some charismatic and Pentecostal Christians, a very damaging reaction has swept through the body of Christ. Evangelicals and other Christians reject the true gifts and true prophetic ministries that God is currently reestablishing.

In 1973, David Wilkerson wrote a very disturbing message concerning things he saw coming to America and to the church. His book, *The Vision,* received little support or acceptance by the body of Christ. Wilkerson and his family took a lot of rejection, criticism and persecution for being obedient.

The body of Christ said then and is still saying; *we don't want to hear anything bad, just preach and prophesy about good and pleasant things.* Israel demanded the same things the church is demanding today—pleasant prophecies, peace, and prosperity; and the church is only listening to those who preach and teach such.

Most of God's people choose to hear these lies. They accumulate for themselves teachers that suit their own liking. Not too many true prophets last long in the body of Christ; they refuse to soften the message even in the face of rejection. These men and women of God refuse to practice cunning or underhanded methods to keep financial support coming in. They resist the temptation to teach and preach, as do many of the false prophets and teachers today; running from coast to coast, spewing out deceit, and selling their wares like door-to-door vacuum salesmen. Indeed, they sell and compete with one another using flattery to gain advantage.

These imposters speak visions and soothing words that are lies from their own spirit. For ill gain, they have daubed the "crumbling wall of protection" with whitewash (pretty paint), selling God's people a bill of goods. What is so terrible is that far too many of God's people want it so and buy into it, wholeheartedly.

Paul prophesied, *"Indeed all who desire to live a godly life in Christ Jesus will be persecuted, while evil men and impostors will go on from bad to worse, deceivers and deceived"* (2 Timothy 3:12-13).

God's people are deceived into thinking their wall of protection is secure. In reality, it is like a homebuyer who bought a house full of dry rot. The seller lied and covered up the rotten condition of the foundation and main supporting timbers with paint. It looks good on the outside, but when the storm comes, it will crumble. (See Ezekiel 13:1-16).

We must all take heed. And as for those who rejected inner cleansing and sanctification, for those who practiced false gifts and gave ear tickling sermons, for those pillow prophets that daub with whitewash—they will be cut off!

The true gifts that expose evil in the midst of the church do not operate in most fellowships. The self-edifying gifts, along with words of knowledge that do not challenge unbelief, sin or ill motives, receive center attention. Most of God's people who believe in the gifts of the Holy Spirit seek those who practice false gifts. Lying and deceiving spirits "anoint" these false ministers and deceitful workers who preach a wrong gospel. They dispense a myriad of mystic and prophetic words with supposed demonstrations of power that amaze the immature and naïve Christian. True gifts of the Holy Spirit that expose hidden secrets of the heart, sin, or bitterness become suspect and are declared false.

Paul gave guidelines to the body of Christ in 1 Corinthians 14 that order must prevail in all meetings. He also said that the church needed to no longer be children in their thinking, but rather be mature. He was encouraging the churches at Corinth to become mature concerning the gift of tongues by growing up spiritually, and that all should practice the true gift of prophecy and all learn to prophesy. He warned not to forbid the gift of tongues, but rather ensure this personal and self-edifying gift be managed in such a way as to not cause confusion nor draw attention to the one who practices this particular gift. He emphasized the most important gift to seek is the gift of prophecy, which, when controlled by the Holy Spirit, will expose the root problems in people's lives.

This prophetic gift must be accurate and specific in order to expose the secrets of the heart. (See 1 Corinthians 14:20-25). Paul finally warned to stop letting meetings get out of control. He wrote that the true gifts of the Holy Spirit were under the mental understanding and control of the one who was walking in the gift, and that *"all things should be done decently and in order."*

LATTER-RAIN: ESTABLISHING THE KINGDOM OF GOD IN THE FLESH
Counterfeit Revival and False Movements

For then there will be great tribulation, such as has not been from the beginning of the world until now, no, and never will be. And if those days had not been shortened, no human being would be saved; but for the sake of the elect those days will be shortened. Then if any one says to you, 'Lo, here is the Christ!' or 'There he is!' do not believe it. For false Christs and false prophets will arise and show great signs and wonders, so as to lead astray, if possible, even the elect. Lo, I have told you beforehand. So, if they say to you, 'Lo, he is in the wilderness,' do not go out; if they say, 'Lo, he is in the inner rooms,' do not believe it. For as the lightning comes from the east and shines as far as the west, so will be the coming of the Son of man. Wherever the body is, there the eagles will be gathered together. "Immediately after the tribulation of those days the sun will be darkened, and the moon will not give its light, and the stars will fall from heaven, and the powers of the heavens will be shaken; then will appear the sign of the Son of man in heaven, and then all the tribes of the earth will mourn, and they will see the Son of man coming on the clouds of heaven with power and great glory; and he will send out his angels with a loud trumpet call, and they will gather his elect from the four winds, from one end of heaven to the other" (Matthew 24:21-31).

Over the last 30 years many false apostles and prophets have networked with each other, attempting to bring in the *kingdom of God Now*, that is, God down to earth. Their theology and teachings are in direct contradiction to Christ's warnings about the end of the age, the Great Tribulation, the final harvest of souls and the rapture of the true Christian.

Truth is, these people want to be in control and establish God's kingdom on earth in a supposed power of God, which in reality is the spiritual power of their own flesh. These groups of false servants who appear to be righteousness are like those Paul addressed in 2 Corinthians 11:14,15. They have numerous names that identify their insidious demonic agenda.

Terms that describe this movement are: Dominion Theology; Kingdom Now; and Reconstructionist, having a postmillennial eschatology foundation. Postmillennialists believe that they have a mandate from God to reconstruct society with biblical principles, which will usher in the kingdom of God and the rule of Christ through the church—before Christ returns.

Other false movements similar in message are: Latter-Rain, Toronto Blessing, Holy Laughter, Third Wave, Shepherding Movement, Promise Keepers, Brownsville Revival, and others around the world. *The Purpose Driven Church* book outlines a similar agenda. Many ministries have sprung up preaching variations of this false doctrine where carnal motives drive church growth, contradicting the leadership of the Holy Spirit. (See Romans 8:14 and Galatians 5:18).

These misguided movements push for revival and restoration. Yes, hearts are burdened for the lost and the lukewarm Christian, but those in the movement suffer from an *inner lust driven motive* for power. They lust for a shortcut anointing or baptism of fire by the Holy Spirit to magically implant a Christ-like nature within.

They have become militant warriors for God, trying to grasp the power of God and bring the kingdom of Heaven down to earth. They hold the cross central to their teaching, but their message of the cross does not include the work of the cross in the believer's life that crucifies inner carnal motives, personalities and exposes defilements of spirit. Deceived, they take the easy way by trying to harness the power of their own spirit in the name of Christ. In truth, they serve a different Christ, work with a different spirit and preach a perverted gospel.

The power of the human spirit has an effect. Demonic principalities tap into the inner lust for power of an unclean heart and spirit, and through false teachings, these demonic spirits harness the power of the human spirit. This power is manifested through counterfeit signs, wonders, spiritual gifts and spiritual touches upon the spirit and soul.

The result is that those who follow these errant ministries become dependent on this type of false anointing to anesthetize the pains of the uncrucified carnal self. Demonically boosted carnal spirit touches soothe their inner pain like a *spiritual Prozac*. They call this spiritual Prozac the *anointing*. Ear-tickling messages fill these poor sheep with false hope, leaving them in a carnal state, believing they are spiritual. Christians who continue to embrace these lies will not become ready to endure the coming trouble, stand at Christ's appearance, and ascend with the last trumpet call.

Leaders in this movement use revival as the vehicle to restore God's justice and divine influence upon society, where the supposed power of God will come and convert the whole world. Again, this is a carnal, drummed-up revival drawing converts by the power of their personal spirit, harnessed by the demonic.

Those involved in this movement do not learn how to die to their carnal personalities and become truly cleansed in heart and spirit, growing up into Christ and standing on their own two feet of faith. Paul Cain, a key leader-founder in an arm of this movement was just recently exposed as an alcoholic and homosexual. When first confronted, he resisted counsel, lacked repentance, and continued to minister—even though he was ousted from this portion of the apostle-prophet movement.

The movement leaders attempt to govern with tight control through a hierarchy of leadership based upon the five-fold ministry model of apostle, prophet, evangelist, pastor and teacher. By force, they attempt to restore the gifts of the Holy Spirit to the church, and to re-assert the office of apostle and prophet. The founders within these movements presumed to "take heaven forcefully" and build a network of apostles and prophets as overseers, ruling those churches and ministries lured into their scheme. The Scripture they often use to justify this militant-zealot approach is Matthew 11:12-15 where Jesus was speaking of violent men taking the kingdom of Heaven by force during His earthly ministry.

The masses followed Christ looking for the kingdom of Heaven to be made manifest on earth, bringing God's justice, throwing off the Roman occupation, and expecting a heavenly life come to earth. At one point the crowds tried to seize Jesus by force and make Him king.

Taking the kingdom of God by force is a carnal, earthly attempt to make life on earth *heavenly*. This coincides with their doctrine that a unified holy Christian church will establish a big portion of the kingdom of God on earth and then Christ will return. That is the postmillennial position they preach.

Jesus taught the opposite, both in His earthly ministry and concerning His second coming.

Christ warned, *"Lo, I have told you beforehand. So, if they say to you, 'Lo, he is in the wilderness,' do not go out; if they say, 'Lo, he is in the inner rooms,' do not believe it. For as the lightning comes from the east and shines as far as the west, so will be the coming of the Son of man"* (Matthew 24:25-27).

God's people will not establish the kingdom of God on earth and usher in Christ's return. God's people are to walk in a kingdom that is not of this earth, to become separate from the world's influence and false Christianity. They are to abide in Christ until death or through the gathering of the saints into the air upon His appearance.

Paul exhorted those under his care that they should, *"... continue in the faith, and saying that through many tribulations we must enter the kingdom of God"* (Acts 13:22). In the letter to the Christians at Galatia he wrote, *"Now the works of the flesh are plain: fornication, impurity, licentiousness, idolatry, sorcery, enmity, strife, jealousy, anger, selfishness, dissension, party spirit, envy, drunkenness, carousing, and the like. I warn you, as I warned you before, that those who do such things shall not inherit the kingdom of God. But the fruit of the Spirit is love, joy, peace, patience, kindness, goodness, faithfulness, gentleness, self-control; against such there is no law. And those who belong to Christ Jesus have crucified the flesh with its passions and desires. If we live by the Spirit, let us also walk by the Spirit"* (Galatians 5:19-25).

Notice that these passages indicate the kingdom of God is available now, for the true and pure disciple to enter into or inherit. We abide in Christ where His presence within us brings the kingdom of God to others in the world. This kingdom is the true walk with God and fellowship of the saints in the Holy Spirit. *"For the kingdom of God is not food and drink but righteousness and peace and joy in the Holy Spirit; he who thus serves Christ is acceptable to God and approved by men"* (Romans 14:17,18).

At the end of this age, a great harvest of souls will become clean on the inside, changed into a Christ-like nature through a baptism of fiery trials. These are they who come through the Great Tribulation and are raptured just as God ends this terrible time. They will leave the world to the wrath of God and Christ's return. After this, the kingdom of God will be established on earth.

Please understand the true gifts of the Holy Spirit are for today. The office of apostle and prophet are for today. God wants to restore the church to its first century power and witness. Unfortunately, true restoration has been a long, arduous process. When the government of Rome declared Christianity to be its state religion, the Church of Rome became institutionalized, paganized, corrupt, political, and finally, apostate.

For 1,000 years Western civilization fell into the dark ages as Catholicism hijacked the truth of the Gospel. True Christianity was virtually destroyed. Then the Reformation occurred where courageous men and women stood up to the institutionalized and politically powerful false church, with Martin Luther re-establishing the doctrine of salvation by God's unmerited grace through the believer's faith. Luther held the office of apostle, as a sent messenger used by God to restore truth. Slowly we see other sound biblical doctrine restored.

Reputations were given up. Even death occurred in order to restore truth to the body of Christ. Cessationists who preach that God does not call, discipline, train, and make apostles and prophets as a gift to the church are in error! These, like the pastors, evangelists, and teachers, are to help equip the saints for the work of the ministry. Those who teach that the gifts of the Holy Spirit ceased at the end of the apostolic age are also in error.

Historically, false apostles have invaded any true move of God, as seen in the first century church. So the restoration of the true gifts of the Holy Spirit, true revival and the true apostle and prophet will be counterfeited at the end of the age, just as Jesus warned.

These false workers have always attempted to hijack the true work and gifts of the Holy Spirit. The Latter-Rain teachings set-up many deceived Christians to expect that the kingdom of God will be ushered in by the reconstruction of society through the influence of the church. Jesus said His kingdom was not of this world and He warned that the kingdom of God for the Christian is also not of this world; nor can it be brought down by the power of the flesh. Christ will return, and then the kingdom of God will be established on earth!

The true shepherd must exhort the saints to set their minds in heavenly places, where Christ is, seated at the right hand of the Father. Paul preached and ministered by, *"strengthening the souls of the disciples, exhorting them to continue in the faith, and saying that through many tribulations we must enter the kingdom of God"* (Acts 14:22).

Indeed, we must enter the kingdom of God—not bring it down!

HIJACKING THE TRUE MOVE OF GOD

Through the years there have been mighty moves of God upon various peoples all around the world. I have studied some revivals and been involved and gotten out of the current false revival movement. I have worked with troubled Christians for over 18 years and been involved in ministry over 20 years. I came to Christ in 1973 and was miraculously discharged in 1974 from the Marines, five years early, to prepare for full-time ministry. I worked in full-time ministry, attended Bible College, and studied great men of God while working in a Christian bookstore to help make ends meet.

The nagging problem is discerning what false revival is and what true revival is, and how to prepare for revival and keep true revival pure.

We see a false, liberal church completely dead, or a lukewarm church that may as well be dead. We see a carnal church that is tossed about by deceitful men with demonic doctrines; and we also have an almost completely invisible church that is sincere, being disciplined by Christ and about to spring forward to lead the body of Christ in a mighty move of God.

The most qualifying experience I have is my own recovery and steady walk with Christ. Indeed, my life has been revived as I press on to the high call of God in Christ. As a young born-again Christian called to ministry, there was little help, with no sound doctrine or sound fellowship to guide me.

In my search for answers, I attended evangelical, charismatic and Pentecostal fellowships. I attended an evangelical Bible College and was appointed assistant pastor, expecting tutelage and discipleship, which did not happen. I fell prey to the abusive shepherding movement and sat under false spirit manifestations. I was told to speak in tongues and prophesy only to find later it was false and originated from my own spirit, not the Holy Spirit.

I read one Christian book after another, only to find few authors alluding to the process of true sanctification, that is, sound doctrine allowing one to grow up into salvation, having Christ formed within.

Totally confused, aggravated and near hopeless, all I could think of doing was throw myself into the hands of Christ, making a covenant by giving Him permission to do whatever it took to change me into the person he called me to be — on the inside. I expected trouble, but not the fiery trials that came.

After this prayer, all hell broke loose and in total discouragement I eventually slid away from the pursuit of ministry. For 12 years I wandered in a wilderness full of trouble, heartache, and failure. I occasionally found some study for ministry, but I concentrated on my education, occupation and running my own corporation.

Near the pinnacle of success, I lost everything; then at the bottom of it all, God began to lead, revive me, and bring me into a full rest in him. In 1988, I returned to work in a full-time faith ministry as a counseling pastor. That was when my real training in ministry and recovery began.

When I was the counseling pastor of a 400-member Foursquare church, my appointment schedule was booked three months in advance to counsel devastated, unstable, double-minded Christians. I was involved in the beginnings of the current charismatic-revival movement long before the Toronto Blessing sprang up. I learned the truth of what counterfeit revival could do to individual Christians and fellowship.

In this, the Lord led me through a ministry training program that gave me great insight concerning the work of God, the gifts of the Holy Spirit, true discipleship in the Lord, true revival, and church administration.

What I have learned by experience and study is: men and women of God do not know how to prepare for true revival nor how to make certain true revival is not taken over by a false spirit.

In 1904-1905 the Wales revival started with the true move of the Holy Spirit. Ignorant carnal Christians and impostors eventually turned God's work into empty manifestations and error, hijacking this true move of God. Leaders in the Wales revival began to see how the counterfeit took over the pure move of God through the carnal human spirit. Many of the participants allowed deceiving demonic spirits to infiltrate the meetings. Jessie Penn-Lewis worked in the Wales revival with Evan Roberts, and she observed,

"Now as to the perils of Revival: These again primarily may be briefly defined as, (1) the danger of acting or living by 'feeling', or the sensuous life, instead of the spirit-life; and (2) the peril arising from the spirits of evil counterfeiting the workings of the Holy Spirit. Alongside of the danger of becoming dominated by 'feelings' and emotions, the perils of Revival come mainly from the invisible world of spirits. The Counterfeiter is watching to counterfeit, and to insert his workings in the place of God's workings. The fact became clear again and again in Wales, during the height of the 1905 Revival, that it was possible for God to begin with a pure work of the Holy Spirit, and for the counterfeiting spirits to insert a 'counterfeit' which the soul ignorantly accepted. In this way the same manifestations appeared, but the source was changed without it being detected. The changing of the source of the supernatural manifestations without the believer's cognizance is therefore the main peril. A very small inserted 'stream', or 'tincture' from the enemy, causes mixture which may not be discerned at first, but which sooner or later produces fruit in confusion and trouble" (The Cross and Revival, Jessie Penn-Lewis).

Word of the Welsh revival spread to various areas of the world. Other Christian leaders in the United Sates had been seeking a last-day outpouring of the Holy Spirit, looking to the accounts in the book of Acts for inspiration and direction. Believing that the end of the age was near, these leaders were convinced an outpouring of the Holy Spirit for revival would come before the rapture of the true Christian. News of the Wales Revival inspired a Baptist preacher, Joseph Smale of Los Angeles, to take to heart the need for revival, as experienced in Wales. He began to preach and teach about the need of God to move upon Los Angeles and throughout the United States.

William J. Seymour, an African American minister, sought understanding of these issues and after sitting under Charles F. Parham's teachings, came to the conclusion that receiving the fullness of the Holy Spirit was evidenced by the speaking of intelligible languages, especially for missionary evangelism. Parham led the Apostolic Faith movement originating in Topeka, Kansas in 1901. Apostolic Faith was the original name of the modern Pentecostal movement.

Early 1906, William J. Seymour took a ministerial position in Los Angeles, preaching on this doctrine. He was not well received and was locked out of his church. Seymour continued to preach in home meetings. Soon, a participant in these meetings spoke in a tongue and this experience began to spread to others. Extreme emotionalism began to grow within the meetings. This movement became known as the Azusa Street Revival. Parham came to Azusa Street to consolidate the revival into a larger network within the Apostolic Faith movement that he was leading. Upon arrival, Seymour's lack of control over the emotionalism and the mix of black and white Christians within the meetings disturbed Parham. He left, took some people with him and started his rival mission in the Los Angeles area. Most stayed with Seymour. Later, prejudice took over Seymour's leadership as well, appointing blacks only in leadership. In the end, Seymour taught that the Baptism of the Holy Spirit did not have to be evidenced by the speaking in tongues.

This brief history gives us foundational insight on what went wrong with the modern Latter-Rain Revival and Pentecostal movement. The deep desire for revival is commendable in the church, whether it is Latter-Rain, Pentecostal, and Third Wave, or however one would describe a sincere desire to see people come to Christ and walk in His fullness.

It is apparent that carnality, lack of wisdom and lack of trained leadership allowed what started as a true move of God to become hijacked by a counterfeit spirit. What was missing was the preaching of the cross and how believers must learn to embrace the work of the cross themselves, destroying the works of the flesh.

Leaders were awestruck by the outer manifestation of weeping, repentance, confession and sincere, heart-felt praise and worship. They became caught up in the enormous number of souls who responded to the move of God. They did not know how to consolidate a move of God into true discipleship, with the preaching and teaching of sound doctrine. They did not understand that the demonic could counterfeit the outer emotional expressions. Leadership did not understand that the comforting presence of God that assures salvation and peace, also convicts of sin, judgment and of righteousness, is a small part of revival. The deep work of sanctification and crucifying the works of the flesh; the work of exposing the deeply hidden, defiled character structures for the double-minded believers; the teaching of how the spirit must be separated from the soul with the exposure of the true thoughts and intentions of the heart—all this and more was not taught.

Leaders allowed the masses touched by God to become a spontaneous movement. Fearful of stopping revival, they allowed the counterfeiting of Satan to take over true revival.

Sadly, the excitement, the glory and the attention became an enthralling aspect for leaders. They did not understand that the Wales revival needed to be guided into a true discipleship consolidation, just as the disciples experienced in the book of Acts.

Remember Jesus drew enormous crowds; they swarmed all around Him and the disciples. Jesus knew that a move of God upon so many people would require trained disciples and workers to be available to work with these new believers and followers. These trained disciples and workers would produce like kind. He saw the masses to be very vulnerable. *"When he saw the crowds, he had compassion for them, because they were harassed and helpless, like sheep without a shepherd. Then he said to his disciples, 'The harvest is plentiful, but the laborers are few; therefore ask the Lord of the harvest to send out laborers into his harvest"* (Matthew 9:36-38).

True disciples embrace the work of the cross and grow up into Christ standing on their own two feet of faith. They produce other disciples, which is Christ's commission given to the first disciples. The true disciple applies sound doctrine to bring those in their care to a full faith in God, not faith and dependence on the worker doing the *teaching and disciplining*.

Wolves desiring to control and manipulate came from within and from the outside, pouncing on the Wales revival converting it into a carnal movement and making a name for themselves. (See Acts 20:29-31).

We see true revival short-circuited, never reaching God's intended goal—making true disciples. The power of God that draws men and women to Him became the enthralling goal. Leaders became enamored, awestruck and held spellbound by the outpouring. They did not know what to do with the many coming to Christ or how to assure they were given into the care of true shepherds and disciples for the completion of the work.

Look carefully in the Acts of the Apostles; you will note how the move of God was consolidated into solid discipleship, how the counterfeit was avoided and how the power hungry were stopped dead in their tracks.

In the Wales Revival and ensuing Azusa Street Revival, the hard work of discipleship was abandoned to false shepherds. Eventually ignorant and false leaders pushed for the counterfeit, preying on seekers who came wanting the fullness of God.

Here is the real issue. All who seek revival look to the different accounts found in the book of Acts as a guide and biblical pattern to mimic. They do not take into account and follow Christ's teachings and example on how He prepared the disciples to handle the coming revival that God had planned to come on the day of Pentecost.

The outpouring of the Holy Spirit came because the Father had earthen vessels, disciplined and changed by the person of Christ. The main instrument Christ used to prepare his apostles was the work on the cross that He accomplished—and the work of the cross within each of their lives.

The best study on true revival is Christ's call, teaching and training of the apostles for their commissioned work in making disciples, which is the foundation that facilitates true revival. Jesus commanded believers to make disciples—not make revivals.

"And Jesus came and said to them, 'All authority in heaven and on earth has been given to me. Go therefore and make disciples of all nations, baptizing them in the name of the Father and of the Son and of the Holy Spirit, teaching them to observe all that I have commanded you; and lo, I am with you always, to the close of the age'" (Matthew 28:18-20).

The grave mistake made by many in leadership is not preparing for the true outpouring of the Holy Spirit. Christ took His disciples through training and discipline that eradicated self-centeredness, competition, ego-building desires, greed for power and money, naïveté, and the fear of men—especially the fear of the false leaders within the temple of God.

They had an example of truth and had truth worked into them and learned how to avoid hypocrisy—the most deceptive and destructive aspect of false religion.

By the time the day of Pentecost came the apostles had been dealt one deathblow after another concerning their hidden character flaws, dividedness and fears. Christ by His Word and the tough training made His disciples pure in heart. They were ready to receive the Holy Spirit before the day of Pentecost.

Remember, soon after Christ's first appearance after His resurrection, He imparted the Holy Spirit to each of them. They now had the Spirit of Truth, the Counselor, the Comforter and peace and joy of His presence. They were one with Christ and the Father through the Holy Spirit.

During Christ's ministry with the disciples, they were given the power of God. This power came upon them during those first years of ministry with Christ. After the passion and resurrection of our Lord, they now were ready to receive the indwelling Holy Spirit.

After the ascension of Christ, as those disciples met in true fellowship in the upper room, they ministered to the Lord in prayer, and ministered the word of God to each other in the Holy Spirit. They were one in spirit, bound in true love — love of the Father, Son and Holy Spirit.

They waited for God's timing to receive power like the power they had upon them during Christ's earthly ministry. Again, this power was to come upon them — not within them; they had already received the Holy Spirit.

They did not lust after the outer visible power of God to fill any void of character or suppress any pain from carnal inner personalities. The issues of flesh had been dealt with already through Christ's school of discipleship and the work of the cross within each of their lives. They were ready to have the power of God fall about them to draw attention to the message of the Gospel — that had been worked within them!

As we see this revival start, as recorded in Scripture, these disciples were full of discernment, wisdom and insight. They followed the Holy Spirit directives in carrying out their leadership responsibilities in keeping the move of God pure and on course.

You know the accounts: Ananias and Sapphira, Simon the Magician, and how the disciples stood up to the Pharisees!

The movements of today are a far cry from the example we have in Scripture. The disciples did not manipulate, conjure, cajole, bribe, blackmail, sell trinkets or shear the sheep of money and possessions, nor glorify themselves. They did not network to manipulate and control, nor did they form rules to oppress or to exalt themselves. They certainly did not compete with one another. They learned not to attack those who did not work directly with them and yet were preaching the true Gospel. (See Luke 9:46-50). They walked with integrity, boldness; they were courageous and confronted evil outright, yet were compassionate, long-suffering, demonstrating patience, and led by wisdom from above. The Holy Spirit revealed to them inner hidden issues of the heart. They enjoyed harmonious leadership where no one exalted himself over the other. Again, there was no glory-seeking and leadership exaltation. The disciples fed the sheep, not themselves.

Today, God is trying to build true disciples who will walk as the original apostles. Instead, we have carnal Christians asserting themselves into leadership and prophesying from their own spirit. We see imposters and deceivers going from bad to worse slaughtering the sheep for ill gain. Anytime there is even a hint of a true movement of God brewing, these phonies and wayward Christians jump on the bandwagon, build on another man's work, and hijack the true move of God.

In the coming end of the age revival, God will have a pure people. A multitude of desperate people will turn to this true church and be told how to prepare to meet the coming Christ!

FALSE ECUMENICAL MOVEMENT

The unity movement in the body of Christ has gotten out of hand. For the sake of unity, *scriptural truth and integrity go out the window*. On the other hand, the working together of *Christ-centered—cross-embracing* fellowships, regardless of denomination, is God's deep desire. It is God's desire that unity and harmony prevail within the body of Christ, which is comprised of genuine and sincere believers. This unity is not to include the false, deceived, and lukewarm believers. Just because someone calls himself a Christian does not mean one should be embraced as a sold-out, like-minded believer who loves Christ above all else.

True unity will come, but not by watering down the Gospel. Some liberal denominations, many evangelical, charismatic, and Pentecostal denominations are uniting with the Roman Catholic Church. A spirit of unity has swept into Christianity, deceiving many, pulling weak but genuine Christians away from the true body of Christ toward a unified worldly Christian religion. The practice of gifts within Catholicism and in the charismatic movement (these are often false gifts) is helping to bring about unity that is not of God!

For the most part, the current ecumenical movement is counterfeit! However, true unity of faith is the goal for the body of Christ, as mentioned previously. Part of the great falling away at the end of the age is the unified false church and false Christianity that will have its own spiritual power, giving false spiritual satisfaction.

There is a hunger for a full relationship with God throughout Christianity, regardless of denominational ties or worship preference. This common hunger for a closer walk with God brings a sense of family or kinship among all Christians. This same spiritual hunger is present in most human beings, leading one to find God in Mormonism, Buddhism or any other worship form. It is a *carnal spiritual desire to be close to God on our terms,* instead of the way of the true Gospel and the lordship of Christ.

Faced with growing persecution from atheists, the far liberal left, and radical world religions such as Islam, those of the Christian faith are drawing together in growing numbers. This rise of immorality and mild persecution is adding more spiritual magnetism to the growing false Christian unity. A common ground for the defense of the Christian faith and way of life on earth becomes a rally cry. This is one of several satanic end-time ploys to deceive, if possible, even the elect, and it will draw more and more Christians and even whole denominations into a *global-universal* unified Christian church.

Mel Gibson's movie, *The Passion of the Christ* is an excellent case in point. The idea for this movie was taken from the book *The Dolorous Passion of our Lord Jesus Christ*, written by Anne Catherine Emmerich. She was of the Catholic order Augustinian Canonesses at Agnietenberg, a convent where eventually she became very mystical and developed the supposed marks of Christ's passion, or stigmata.

Dolorous means sorrowful, tearful, weeping. Stigmata refer to marks on a person's body, resembling the wounds suffered by Jesus Christ in the crucifixion and inflicted presumably by a supernatural force. Observations of stigmata have included not only wounds of the hands and feet and of the side, such as those received in the crucifixion, but also those impressed by the crown of thorns and by the scourging. These manifestations will occasionally occur during religious ecstasy or hysteria.

The movie is rooted in the Catholic preoccupation with the brutal aspects of Christ's death that subtly de-emphasizes His resurrection, His sacrifice for the entire world, the Christian's promise of Christ formed within the true Christian. This diverts attention from the return of Christ.

Such preoccupation with His death leads to Christian mysticism that arouses carnal emotions and pity for Christ, similar to the pity aroused in Peter that motivated his opposition to Christ's death. As you recall, Satan inspired this opposition.

This approach to Christ's passion often stirs carnal sentiment to Christ's sacrifice and inspires morbid sentimentality. It can also inspire mysticism, self-abasement and self-flagellation that produce the appearance of holiness but have no value in checking the indulgence of the flesh. (See Colossians 2:16-23).

In addition, the movie is inspiring more Jewish and Islamic resentment toward Christians. Church history informs us that this Catholic-Christian morbid pity for Christ's passion often incited the Crusades and persecution toward Jews. Catholicism's worldly religious view of why and how Christ died for the lost sinner—Gentile and Jew alike—keeps Christ in the minds of many Christians as still hanging on the cross.

Beware of embracing all of Christianity at the expense of essential truth found in Scripture! There was a reason the Reformation began, and Martin Luther nailed 95 good reasons to the Catholic Church door.

At the end of the age, Christianity will be like any other world religion, where the resurrected and living Christ is crucified afresh by an apostate church. This carnal ecumenicalism is part of the end-time false church. Jesus warned of this. (See Matthew 24:9-14).

Gibson's intent was supposedly a demonstration of Christ's sacrificial death for all of mankind, including the Jew and the Gentile. As mentioned earlier, the preoccupation with the brutality of Christ's death is error and is rooted in Catholicism.

The end of the movie shows an empty tomb—a quick inference of the resurrection of Christ. There are no scenes depicting Christ appearing to the disciples after the resurrection or the ascension of Christ.

Most Christian leaders raved about the movie. Few saw the deception woven within the movie and the telltale issue surrounding its production. These leaders were mesmerized by passion madness, blinding any doctrinal and spiritual objectivity for proper discernment.

Yes, Gibson's movie, *The Passion of the Christ*, was a record-breaking box office hit. Millions of Christians have witnessed a twisted depiction of Christ's death rooted in Gibson's own interpretation of the Gospel accounts. After viewing the movie and doing research, it was astoundingly obvious Satan inspired this movie. What is truly an indictment against most evangelical Christians and the majority in leadership is how deceived and gullible Protestant Christians have become.

Gibson's so-called artistic freedom was really inspired and influenced by the heretical teachings found in Catholicism and Emmerich's delusional memoirs and writings. These were meant to inject subtle messages that de-emphasized Christ's divinity and venerated Mary. There were clever innuendos injected to incite aversion toward Jews such as the slanderous phrase, "you Jews", and the depiction of Hebrew children morphing into demons. It is interesting that Iran, an Islamic nation, allowed the showing of Gibson's movie to Iranians. The reason cited for this special consent was that the movie depicts the Jews as evil and responsible for Christ's death.

Christ's passion was portrayed as a torturous carnage rather than a sacrifice given by God for the sins of mankind by way of divine plan. Interwoven were scenes meant to horrify, shock and defile viewers with vile and demonic imagery that was grotesque and repulsive. One scene depicted a crow plucking out an eye of one of the thieves, crucified with Christ, who railed at Christ.

A diabolical aspect of this film was Gibson's depiction of the earthquake that Gospel accounts record as occurring the very moment Christ died. Gibson directed a scene deceptively depicting the Jewish temple split in half by this earthquake, rather than truthfully depicting the inner veil of the temple torn in two from top to bottom. Whether the temple was split by this earthquake could be debated, but leaving out the rending of the veil is deliberately ignoring a very profound and divine act of God.

The rending of the veil was an act of God that signified the end to the Old Covenant between man and God. In the Old Covenant (Old Testament), the believer approached God through worship at the temple and intermediary priests with the high priest performing various ritualistic sacrifices to God on behalf of the people of God.

Christ's teachings, life, death, resurrection, ascension, and commission of the body of Christ (all true believers in Christ) represent the New Covenant between God and the believer. The living ascended Christ has become our High Priest and now is the only intermediary between the believer and God the Father.

Gibson has injected the Roman Catholic lie that the Pope, Mary, the Catholic priesthood, Roman Catholic sacraments, and especially the sacrament of the Eucharist (communion), are the new intermediaries required by God, which is the only way one can be saved or have eternal life.

The outrageous reality of this so-called "Christian epic film," revered by many as "the greatest evangelistic tool in 2000 years" is that the shepherds over God's people have led millions of Christians and the curious unsaved person into deception.

No, the greatest evangelical event is the ongoing work of Christ's commission to His church, which is to make disciples of all peoples and have Holy Spirit empowerment in all true believers whose hearts and lives witness to the living Christ. We, as true disciples of Christ, are to be tools in the hand of God who are conformed to Christ's character, who present the living Christ to the world—not by some distorted, grotesque movie!

I also question Gibson's employment of several actresses with dubious biographies. Monica Bellucci, who played Mary Magdalene, has portrayed leading roles in violent and sexually explicate films. Rosalinda Celentano, who played Satan in the *Passion*, starred in the movie, *Diary of a Porn Star*, as a gay porn star. Maia Morgenstern, who played Mary the mother of Jesus, starred in *The Whitman Boys (Brothers)*, a film with prostitution, violence, animal sacrifice and nudity. Claudia Gerini, who played Pilate's wife, as with the aforementioned actresses can be found on the internet search engines where porn sites fill the monitor screen. How many teenage Christians, enamored by this perverted depiction of Christ's passion, will do an Internet Google search to find filth and perversion beyond their imagination? I believe God allowed this movie to be released as a judgment and indictment upon a lukewarm and apostate Christian church. Satan was allowed to pull Christian leaders into this deception so that eventually all will see how selfish, wayward and greedy leadership in the body of Christ has become. Indeed, Satan has begun to sift the unprepared, ignorant and deceived Christian as the end of this age falls upon us. Few Christians understand what Jesus warned about concerning false leaders, false doctrine, end-time persecution, the Great Tribulation and how Christians must endure a great portion of these terrible troubles.

The coming deception will be so great that even those soundly rooted in Christ, rightly understanding Scripture, will be challenged to discern what is true and what is false. How easily this film deceives leadership and sheep alike. How defensive many become when one challenges these lies portrayed in Gibson's movie.

Gibson's character as a so-called devout Catholic and the following teachings of Christ should have guided most Christians and all Christian leaders to instantly disqualify this movie.

"Beware of false prophets, who come to you in sheep's clothing but inwardly are ravenous wolves. You will know them by their fruits. Are grapes gathered from thorns, or figs from thistles? So, every sound tree bears good fruit, but the bad tree bears evil fruit. A sound tree cannot bear evil fruit, nor can a bad tree bear good fruit. Every tree that does not bear good fruit is cut down and thrown into the fire. Thus, you will know them by their fruits. "Not every one who says to me, 'Lord, Lord,' shall enter the kingdom of heaven, but he who does the will of my Father who is in heaven. On that day many will say to me, 'Lord, Lord, did we not prophesy in your name, and cast out demons in your name, and do many mighty works in your name?' And then will I declare to them, 'I never knew you; depart from me, you evildoers'" (Matthew 7:15-23).

"Either make the tree good, and its fruit good; or make the tree bad, and its fruit bad; for the tree is known by its fruit. You brood of vipers! how can you speak good, when you are evil? For out of the abundance of the heart the mouth speaks. The good man out of his good treasure brings forth good, and the evil man out of his evil treasure brings forth evil. I tell you, on the day of judgment men will render account for every careless word they utter; for by your words you will be justified, and by your words you will be condemned" (Mathew 12:33-37).

And he said, *"What comes out of a man is what defiles a man. For from within, out of the heart of man, come evil thoughts, fornication, theft, murder, adultery, coveting, wickedness, deceit, licentiousness, envy, slander, pride, foolishness. All these evil things come from within, and they defile a man"* (Mark 7:20-23).

Most characters portrayed by Gibson in his many movie roles do not reflect Christ's standard of "good fruit." TV journalist Diane Sawyer interviewed Gibson on the making of his *Passion* movie. Sawyer asked Gibson to confirm the rumor concerning his angry outburst directed at the *Time* magazine columnist Frank Rich who criticized the *Passion*. Gibson admitted saying, "I want to kill him ... I want his intestines on a stick ... I want to kill his dog."

Christians and Christian leaders—do you have any discernment? Jesus said you would know them by their fruit and you would be able to know what was in a man's heart by what proceeds out of his mouth.

Gibson downplayed this murderous expression by telling Sawyer he was just venting. Again, Gibson supposedly lives by the teachings of Christ, but these very teachings judge the fruit of Mel's life and that of his words as evil!

As a minister of the Gospel, I admonish Gibson to *"Either make the tree good, and its fruit good; or make the tree bad, and its fruit bad; for the tree is known by its fruit. You brood of vipers! how can you speak good, when you are evil?"*

Ted Haggard, Pastor of New Life Church in Colorado Springs and President of the National Association of Evangelicals, when asked on a radio interview, downplayed Gibson's murderous expressions, implying that God will use *"not so perfect people"* for the Gospel.

Chuck Swindoll, Billy Graham, and leader after leader praised this movie— Jesus said of the deceived leaders of His day, *"they are blind guides. And if a blind man leads a blind man, both will fall into a pit."*

Gospel writers did not inject this kind of graphic description of Christ's death. Even Isaiah's prophecy of Christ's suffering was not graphic. The Holy Spirit-inspired words of this prophecy— "bruised," "rejected," "despised," "wounded," "chastisement," "oppressed," "afflicted," "a lamb led to the slaughter," "a man of sorrows acquainted with grief" were a sufficient description of Christ's passion. (See Isaiah 53). This was deliberate. Christianity's roots are in a Jewish remnant that believed in God and responded to Christ and His Gospel.

Recreating a graphic depiction of Christ's death, without the same attention to His resurrection and ascension, mocks God's work and holds up Christ to the world in contempt. It brings Christ down from His ascension; that is, it diminishes His Divinity. Apostate Christianity brings Christ down and turns the Gospel into a world religion, no different than worshipping Allah and following Mohammed.

It is interesting to note Gibson is getting a taste of Catholicism's game-playing politics with the Vatican's denial that the Pope gave the film approval. Pray that Gibson awakens to truth and makes Christ his all and in all and leaves false Christianity behind.

The test for Gibson and other celebrity Christians is their true commitment to Christ that allows God to bring circumstances and trials that validate sincerity and purify faith. A true disciple of Christ will, sooner or later, flee false doctrine and fellowship with like-minded disciples, and allow Christ's death to be theirs.

God is allowing most of Christianity to become enthralled with the film and witness afresh a graphic depiction of Christ's brutal death. Most denominations are using this film as a great evangelistic outreach. Multitudes of Christians will view Christ's death as if they were personally there some 2000 years ago.

"And there followed him a great multitude of the people, and of women who bewailed and lamented him. But Jesus turning to them said, 'Daughters of Jerusalem, do not weep for me, but weep for yourselves and for your children. For behold, the days are coming when they will say, 'Blessed are the barren, and the wombs that never bore, and the breasts that never gave suck!' Then they will begin to say to the mountains, 'Fall on us'; and to the hills, 'Cover us.' For if they do this when the wood is green, what will happen when it is dry?" (Luke 23:27-31).

Jesus was referring to the coming abuse, destruction and disbursing of the Jewish nation at the hands of the Romans. The Jews rejected Christ as their Savior, and forfeited God's blessing of protection. Although the apostate Jewish people who believed in God rejected God's plan of salvation, this was a benefit to the whole world that all might be saved through Christ—Jew and Gentile alike. (See Romans chapters 9 and 10). "But of Israel He says, *'All day long I have held out my hands to a disobedient and contrary people'* (Romans 10:21). Here we see God working with His people Israel, but they rejected his correction and protection.

This is the condition of God's people today, as it was with Israel at Christ's passion. Most of Christianity is lukewarm, disobedient and apostate, rejecting the Lordship of Christ! Christianity has turned apostate and competes for souls like any other world religion. (See Matthew 24).

Millions of Christians wept and mourned as they witnessed this depiction of Christ's death and yet reject Christ's discipline and refuse obedience to all that Christ taught. Jesus is saying to this last generation of Christians who are lukewarm, carnal and apostate, paraphrased: *don't weep for me; weep for yourselves and for your children, for you have rejected my cleansing discipline, therefore you have forfeited my protection from the coming persecution and tribulation.*

This movie, along with other carnal Christian religious pressures, fuels what can be termed a "spiritual carnal yearning" for God—approaching God on our terms religiously, not on God's terms. This creates a strong demonic influence to push millions of unsuspecting Christians into a false unity where many hold the form of religion but deny the true power of God. (See 2 Timothy 3:1-9). Jesus said, *"Then if any one says to you, 'Lo, here is the Christ!' or 'There he is!' do not believe it. For false Christs and false prophets will arise and show great signs and wonders, so as to lead astray, if possible, even the elect. Lo, I have told you beforehand. So, if they say to you, 'Lo, he is in the wilderness,' do not go out; if they say, 'Lo, he is in the inner rooms,' do not believe it"* (Matthew 24:23-26).

CATHOLICISM: THE MOST POWERFUL CULT OF ALL

Today, as great darkness and confusion increase throughout the body of Christ, the devil will serve up more counterfeit powers, propagate the "spirit of unity," and deceive many. One of the most powerful cults that Christians are accepting through this false ecumenical movement is Roman Catholicism; it is perhaps the most deceitful and satanic work of all.

I know many readers will be outraged and attack what I have to say on this subject, but regardless—I am compelled to warn you. I have some very dear friends who practice Catholicism, and that is even more reason to speak out this warning.

I am not against Catholic Christians who desire to truly know and obey Christ. I oppose Catholicism's poisonous deceptive doctrines. Many Protestant leaders describe Roman Catholicism as mainline Christianity because this sect believes in all the basic tenets of Christianity. However, the added heresy to the basic teachings of Christ is a dogma that is straight from the devil himself.

Naïve and deceived Catholics are taught to pray to the dead, taught to believe that the religious ceremony of "communion" is a Holy Sacrament (transubstantiation) that mysteriously becomes the literal presence of Christ in His whole divinity. This in reality is superstitious worship of an act performed by the priest.

Roman Catholic teachings elevate Mary, the Lord's mother, to a position equal with God. They let the church tell them what to believe and very few Catholics open the written Word of God and search the Scriptures for themselves. This sect in reality is the worst of all cults because it carries the basic tenets of true Christianity, but what they believe in is a different Jesus, a different gospel, and a different spirit. They practice praying to the dead saints to solicit their help. (See Deuteronomy 18:9-14). Catholics are unwilling to acknowledge that this is an abomination unto the Lord and that this practice is no different from that of the occult. They are communicating with demons! This activity has spiritual influences that sometimes bring answers to their prayers. This is a very powerful form of witchcraft, and those who continue to practice this abomination will come to ruin. Unless they turn from this deception, they will be rejected by Christ and lose eternal life.

Satan protects his worshippers, and most Catholics worship Satan indirectly. Lucifer goes to great lengths to legitimize these evil and forbidden practices. Catholicism is loaded with these foul practices, just as Israel incorporated Baal and Asherah worship with the worship of God, right in the temple. This led to Israel's downfall and judgment.

Men and women who enter full-time service in Catholicism must take vows of celibacy. If they choose to marry, they must give up ministering the Gospel under the auspices of the church. I personally know several Roman Catholic priests who have secret "marriage partners," ignoring this heretical man-made rule. Their live-in wives suffer shame, since neither the church nor the state recognizes their marriage.

Read a prophetic message about the Catholic Church written by Paul. *"Now the Spirit expressly says that in later times some will depart from the faith by giving heed to deceitful spirits and doctrines of demons, through the pretensions of liars whose consciences are seared, who forbid marriage and enjoin abstinence from foods which God created to be received with thanksgiving by those who believe and know the truth. For everything created by God is good, and nothing is to be rejected if it is received with thanksgiving; for then it is consecrated by the word of God and prayer. If you put these instructions before the brethren, you will be a good minister of Christ Jesus, nourished on the words of the faith and of the good doctrine which you have followed"* (1 Timothy 4:1-6).

This warning by Paul leaves no room for doubt concerning the demonic influence in Roman Catholicism. It should be clear that most of those in leadership within the Catholic Church have embraced lies and suffer from a seared conscience. Many of the practices within this cult conjure up demonic influences in the lives of the innocent victims caught in the snare of Catholicism. Some of the rituals involve the hiring of nuns and priests to pray for fleshly and sometimes evil desires requested by those who seek prayerful help. One such ritual, novenas, involves participants offering a financial gift with their prayer request. There is very little discernment concerning the prayer request, and essentially these so-called ministers of the Gospel become hired *"spiritual gangsters and thugs."* If you ever have a conflict with a Catholic who uses these services, you will experience the demonic power coming from these prayers, and you will know what I mean, firsthand.

We have helped a few Christians recover from the evils of Catholicism, which is not an easy ministry. These people suffered great harm by evil teachers, nuns and priests who molested or abused, or where harsh authoritarians' cruelty characterized *occult practices*.

The whole world has been shown the wickedness of Catholicism as one appalling revelation after another has come to light. Jesus warned, *"Beware of the leaven of the Pharisees, which is hypocrisy. Nothing is covered up that will not be revealed, or hidden that will not be known. Therefore whatever you have said in the dark shall be heard in the light, and what you have whispered in private rooms shall be proclaimed upon the housetops"* (Luke 12:1-3).

Stories about vast numbers of victims of molestation, rape, secret abortions by impregnated nuns, and even slave labor convents, have surfaced.

Yes, there were slave labor camps run by the Roman Catholic Church. One in Ireland, the Sisters of the Magdalene Order, finally closed down in 1996. Catholic parishioners sent thousands of girls, sisters, daughters and orphans and illegitimate girls to a slave labor work camp run by the convent. This slavery lasted over 150 years. These labor camps had an estimated 30,000 women who were forced to work out brutal penance, all in secret behind the convent walls. Women who became pregnant, even from rape, or girls who were illegitimate, orphans, simple-minded or even too pretty (considered a moral danger) went to these convents.

These women were stripped of their identities and given numbers instead of names and were forbidden to speak except to pray. They were forced to do laundry as slave labor for the Order's profit. If they broke any rule or tried to escape, they went to solitary confinement or were sent to a mental hospital. Those who were still alive when finally released received neither reparations nor an apology. Few Catholics comment on this scandal. According to the ABC News website, the Reverend Patrick O'Donovan did comment, *"It's an appalling scandal; you could compare them to concentration camps."*

The Pope and the Vatican are still minimizing these despicable and heinous evil abuses. A 40-year-old Vatican document recently discovered instructed dioceses all over the world to keep any sexual misconduct hidden from the public. Still, the Roman Catholic Church is trying its best to minimize the repercussions and retribution payments towards the victims. How evil and despicable!

Satan sends evil people to hide out in undiscerning churches. Roman Catholicism and many of the liberal Protestant churches have become part of the harlot false church of the end times. They have amongst them evil people spewing out poison and secretly practicing wickedness. There are many of God's people who still have a portion of their faith left. They are not evil, but are members of the Roman Catholic Church and other false or apostate churches. May God open their eyes and give them courage to flee these false and evil so-called Christian religions. *Note: Many theologians consider the Roman Catholic Church in conjunction with the liberal Protestant and the great Anglican Church, as the mysterious "Babylon the great, mother of harlots and of earth's abominations," mentioned in Revelation. One cannot deny that these false Christian religious powers carry much political weight and influence throughout the world.*

EVIL PEOPLE HIDDEN IN THE CHURCH

Jesus warned of wolves in sheep's clothing coming into the fold with nothing but destruction on their minds. Paul, Peter, and Jude wrote some very poignant letters exposing evil in the midst of God's people. The evil in the previous section concerned evil and false organizations. This section addresses evil hidden within doctrinally sound denominations, congregations, and fellowships. Seldom does one hear the following Scriptures expounded from the pulpit.

Jude 4 and 10-21 state, *"For admission has been secretly gained by some who long ago were designated for this condemnation, ungodly persons who pervert the grace of our God into licentiousness and deny our only Master and Lord, Jesus Christ. ...But these men revile whatever they do not understand, and by those things that they know by instinct as irrational animals do, they are destroyed. Woe to them! For they walk in the way of Cain, and abandon themselves for the sake of gain to Balaam's error, and perish in Korah's rebellion. These are blemishes on your love feasts, as they boldly carouse together, looking after themselves; waterless clouds, carried along by winds; fruitless trees in late autumn, twice dead, uprooted; wild waves of the sea, casting up the foam of their own shame; wandering stars for whom the nether gloom of darkness has been reserved for ever. It was of these also that Enoch in the seventh generation from Adam prophesied, saying, 'Behold, the Lord came with his holy myriads, to execute judgment on all, and to convict all the ungodly of all their deeds of ungodliness which they have committed in such an ungodly way, and of all the harsh things which ungodly sinners have spoken against him.' These are grumblers, malcontents, following their own passions, loud-mouthed boasters, flattering people to gain advantage. But you must remember, beloved, the predictions of the apostles of our Lord Jesus Christ; they said to you, 'In the last time there will be scoffers, following their own ungodly passions.' It is these who set up divisions, worldly people, devoid of the Spirit. But you, beloved, build yourselves up on your most holy faith; pray in the Holy Spirit; keep yourselves in the love of God; wait for the mercy of our Lord Jesus Christ unto eternal life."*

Paul wrote to the Christians in Rome about evil people in the midst of the church. *"I appeal to you, brethren, to take note of those who create dissensions and difficulties, in opposition to the doctrine which you have been taught; avoid them. For such persons do not serve our Lord Christ, but their own appetites, and by fair and flattering words they deceive the hearts of the simple-minded. For while your obedience is known to all, so that I rejoice over you, I would have you wise as to what is good and guileless as to what is evil; then the God of peace will soon crush Satan under your feet. The grace of our Lord Jesus Christ be with you"* (Romans 16:17-20).

One of the teachings that naïve Christians embrace is the lie that *"there is good in everyone,"* therefore everyone is redeemable. On the contrary, these passages—as well as other Scriptures, instruct that there are evil men and women who have no faith. These people cause trouble and bring shame on the church. Paul warns that we are to avoid these liars and hypocrites. The problem is that this type of person will deceive the naïve and draw many well-meaning Christians into harm's way.

These "evil people" sent by Satan have a counterfeit faith and snare the innocent and naïve into being involved with them. Their ensuing relationship becomes sick and troublesome. Wounded Christians who still have faith are often misled to marry "evil people." The naïve Christian in such marriages will have a fight on their hands to keep even a portion of their faith and stay true to Christ. A few escape the clutches of the evil partner, but not without trouble, destruction and shame. Many who do break away end up looking like the offender, as the evil spouse is able to lie, put on a false front and get away with the deception. The evil spouses within these marriages have an ability to make the spiritually weaker partner act out wickedness. Most evil lives in a powerful self-righteous pretense that continually picks the significant other to pieces under the guise of helping.

Evil people drain church resources, and they attack true faith and those undiscerning Christians who have life in Christ but are naïve. They suck the goodness from the fellowships they attend and deposit their filth onto the weak, struggling and naïve within the congregation. Many of these evil people come asking for help but will never arrive at the truth or establish a faith-based relationship in Christ. They always stay dependent and burdensome, preying on Christian good will and charity.

They have a welfare mentality and often victimize others with an inner subtle attitude of: *"You owe me!"* Again, they appear to be the poor victims as they wallow in self-pity and hide behind a self-righteous veneer that deceives many, even as they enlist help to attack their victims. Christians run to the rescue of these wounded, narcissistic and more often than not, false Christians. They can be characterized as *"waterless springs, lacking substance as mist driven by a storm."* This may seem to be a harsh judgmental attitude and stance. On the contrary, read the following passage.

"Bold and willful, they are not afraid to revile the glorious ones, whereas angels, though greater in might and power, do not pronounce a reviling judgment upon them before the Lord. But these, like irrational animals, creatures of instinct, born to be caught and killed, reviling in matters of which they are ignorant, will be destroyed in the same destruction with them, suffering wrong for their wrongdoing. They count it pleasure to revel in the daytime. They are blots and blemishes, reveling in their dissipation, carousing with you. They have eyes full of adultery, insatiable for sin. They entice unsteady souls. They have hearts trained in greed. Accursed children! Forsaking the right way they have gone astray; they have followed the way of Balaam, the son of Beor, who loved gain from wrongdoing, but was rebuked for his own transgression; a dumb ass spoke with human voice and restrained the prophet's madness. These are waterless springs and mists driven by a storm; for them the nether gloom of darkness has been reserved. For, uttering loud

boasts of folly, they entice with licentious passions of the flesh men who have barely escaped from those who live in error. They promise them freedom, but they themselves are slaves of corruption; for whatever overcomes a man, to that he is enslaved. For if, after they have escaped the defilements of the world through the knowledge of our Lord and Savior Jesus Christ, they are again entangled in them and overpowered, the last state has become worse for them than the first. For it would have been better for them never to have known the way of righteousness than after knowing it to turn back from the holy commandment delivered to them. It has happened to them according to the true proverb, The dog turns back to his own vomit, and the sow is washed only to wallow in the mire" (2 Peter 2:10-22). (See also Romans 16:17-20, 1 Timothy 5:20-22, Titus 1:10-16, 3:9-11, 2 Peter 2:10b-22, and Jude 5-16).

Those who attempt to help a *"waterless spring,"* false Christian without discerning the true issues find themselves spiraling down into impossible situations where the only way out is to completely sever the connection with such a person. Again, these so-called believers live in narcissistic self-pity and deny that they have inner defilements. They practice secret sin, defile and entice others to sin, flatter Christians who have life in Christ to gain an advantage, work from inner jealous motives, and if allowed to continue will bring trouble and destruction to fellowships, friends and family.

There is another brand of "evil people" that Satan sends to war against the saints. These people oppose the true Gospel and are very influential in the community or family systems. They appear to be successful and use flattery to gain an advantage. They walk in spiritual power that comes from making an indirect deal with Satan. They are selfish cowards who attack the weak and wounded. They can even appear to be godly. Again, identify and avoid this type of person; do this for your own protection, your family's safety; and encourage others in your fellowship that may be in your charge.

The church has embraced this type of person, appointed them to boards, hired them as pastors, and in general believed their lies. Why has the church allowed these people into the ranks of the saints? This type of evil person uses money with its power to buy recognition and leadership.

On the other hand, some evil people are poor and needy, but use learned helplessness (a form of laziness) to enlist well-meaning Christians for help.

There is another area of satanic influence within the life of many fellowships and congregations: the single, divorced or widowed woman who is in search for the perfect Christian man. First Timothy 5:3-16 is our scriptural reference.

Paul recognized an issue with single women who enter into the work of the Lord but who were self-indulgent. These single, divorced or widowed women violated their first pledge to Christ by wantonness (immoral, unchaste, lewd behavior) and desired to marry. Paul emphasized the seriousness of this issue by stating this moral decline among younger single or widowed women led some to actually stray after Satan. The characteristics among these pleasure-seeking Christian women were idleness, gossiping, and meddling in others affairs.

This issue is prevalent in most Christian congregations today. Very little is taught on how to help the wounded and angry Christian woman overcome the belief that she cannot make it without having the man of her dreams who, when snared will give the woman vicarious success and material blessings. This serious problem has progressed into a form of relationship idolatry and has created much trouble. These carnal desires increase the works of the flesh—especially fornication, sorcery, selfishness, envy, strife, and jealousy.

Men can also become idolatrous toward the opposite sex. Teachings that allow men to dominate their spouse are error. There is neither male nor female in Christ Jesus, but some denominations treat women as a *second-class creation*.

Unless those who married out of lust and inner idolatry become cleansed, they will never become satisfied with their Christian mate. This is a major reason why so many Christian marriages experience adultery and divorce. Paul confronted the *idolatry of marriage* by encouraging husbands and wives in Christ to promote good order in the Christian marriage. Good order in a Christian marriage is accomplished when each partner secures an undivided devotion to the Lord. They trust God for one another and do not anxiously pursue worldliness or material wealth to please each other. (See 1 Corinthians 7:25-40).

Evil and carnality (lust for the temporal, sexual or self-gratifying activities and recognition) infiltrate far too many churches because only the attractive aspects of the Gospel are preached. The harder teachings of Christ are avoided. The Gospel is presented as a panacea or cure-all remedy for everything that is troubling for the lost sinner or backslidden Christian. Christ warned that this approach to God was a wide gate and easy road that leads to destruction. Many lost sinners do give their hearts totally to Christ. Unfortunately, evil people do not give their hearts totally to Christ as they come straggling into church. They immediately put on a false front and learn to mimic Christian social norms to gain access to leadership positions.

The fall of Adam and Eve with Satan's influence has created a fallen world where male and female innately have an adversarial relationship that extends to husband and wife. Christ came to heal and resolve this destructive aspect between men and women. This *can be accomplished* if sound doctrine and all that Christ taught is presented from the pulpit. There is neither male nor female in Christ, which means true equality between the sexes *should be established* in Christian fellowship and in all Christian relationships. To do this, inner judgments, past wounds that formed resentment and competition must be cleansed from the heart. Christian men and women must submit to the work of the cross and die to these hidden old-nature and worldly attitudes of heart.

Women's oppression has a long history. Finally, during this last century, civil laws and societal norms began to change, giving aid to the cry of the suffragettes. Resentment within women, handed down from generation to generation, hinders and destroys relationships. Now there is a backlash toward the subtle oppression of men by wounded and angry women. Some women come to Christ but never address this revengeful inner desire.

Men and women who harbor prejudice of the opposite sex have ambivalent feelings where their emotions of love are no more than *surface-felt affections that cover inner hatred* deep within the secret heart.

Some who are severely double minded in this matter come into Christianity and instinctively carry out an inner hidden agenda of hate. There are biblical people who accentuate these male and female dual personas. King Saul loved and hated David. Jezebel loved Ahab but undermined his position and pretended to be a believer in the God of Israel while she also worshipped the Canaanite idols, Baal and Asherah. In fact, the Jezebel personality is specifically addressed in Revelation 2:18-29. This woman was a self-proclaimed prophetess who practiced the deeper things of Satan, influenced others, and even taught within the church at Thyatira.

Church leadership at Thyatira tolerated this woman. This incited Christ to warn and pronounce judgment to all concerned within the fellowship, including Jezebel. In this passage, the apostle John prophesied that she would be thrown on her sickbed.

We have insecure males in leadership who abuse and deceive, just as king Saul abused his authority. Evil people have indeed seeped into the church and been left to their own devices as they work wickedness and deceit.

Judas, Simon the Magician, Ananias and Sapphira, Elymas the Magician, Alexander the coppersmith, Hymenaeus, and many others who tried to enter the church or oppose God's work were stopped by sound doctrine and courageous and obedient leadership.

Now, more than ever, the modern-day *evil person* infiltrates the body of Christ. Satan's strategy is, *if you can't beat them, then join them.* This plan works! That is why Christ and the apostles warned repeatedly that evil and evil people are real and they cause much destruction.

Every true fellowship must pray for the exposure of hidden evil; and take courage, counsel and obtain wisdom to drive out the wicked and evil person. Satan has programmed evil people to cause destruction. Often a vicious battle will be required to expunge them because they have become so entrenched. (See 1 Corinthians 5:9-13; 2 Thessalonians 3:1-3; 2 Timothy 3:1-13; Titus 1:10-16; 3: 9-11; 2 Peter 2:1-22 and lastly Jude verses 3 to 16).

There is a day coming when a pure people of God will rise up. All will see the difference between one who serves God and one who is a wicked hypocrite. Paul wrote to the church at Corinth not to judge the outsider, but rather to judge those who proclaim to be Christians but practice evil and/or try to hide their immorality and wickedness. Now more than ever Paul's admonition must be acted upon—*"Drive out the wicked person from among you"* (See 1 Corinthians 5:9-13).

MILLENNIAL DOCTRINES—WHICH ONE IS TRUE?

When will Christ return? There are four basic doctrines about Christ's return.

A Premillennial view purports the Great Tribulation marks the end of this age. Christ rescues the true Christian to safety, and then the wrath of God falls on the world. Only then does Christ physically return to rule the world for 1,000 years.

Postmillennial, or progressive millennialism, holds that through a process of reconstruction and revival, the Christian church converts and influences the world in such a way as to bring the kingdom of Heaven to earth. A 1,000-year reign of Christian ideals will culminate in Christ's return.

A preterist view is that the tribulation and wrath found in Revelation occurred during the Roman rule over Israel, culminating in the destruction of the Jewish temple and persecution of the Christians around 70AD. A new book entitled *The Last Disciple* by Hank Hanegraaff pushes this false doctrine.

Amillenialists believe that references to the millennium are figurative, that where there is no earthly millennium. Some amillenialists believe that the millennium in Revelation refers to Christ's reign in the kingdom of Heaven, not on earth.

Within the premillennial doctrine is the belief that Christ will rapture or rescue Christians to safety before the predicted tribulation and the wrath of God falls upon earth.

Premillennialists, where Christ comes to usher in the kingdom of God on earth, believe in three basic doctrines concerning the rapture (rescue) of the Christian.

Christ will rapture Christians to safety before the Great Tribulation period (seven years) begins. The popular *Left Behind* series of books espouses this doctrine. This is called pre-tribulation rapture.

The rapture of Christians takes place halfway through the Great Tribulation. This is called mid-tribulation rapture.

The rapture of Christians takes place at the end of the Great Tribulation Period. This is what Christ taught. This is called post-tribulation rapture.

Which doctrine concerning the end of this age should you believe? People who promote false teachings are deceived, and in turn they deceive many. Paul warned concerning the end of the age, *"while evil men and impostors will go on from bad to worse, deceivers and deceived"* (2 Timothy 3:13).

Why are so many deceived? Frankly, these doctrines that excuse Christians from tribulation and trouble put Christians at ease and allow for sin and laziness to prevail. Prosperity and love of this world breed a lukewarm love toward Christ. Indeed, this is the sad condition for most of God's people in America and other prosperous countries.

The question that must be answered is, "What did Jesus say about the end of the age?"

Jesus taught that the true believer would have to endure a terrible period of time prior to His appearance, that is, His coming in the clouds. This period of time would be cut short for the sake of the true Christian, if not, no person would be left alive on earth. Jesus said that the elect, or the true saint, would be called up into the air to safety at the last angelic trumpet call. This is called the rapture of the saints, of which no one would know the day or hour—only Father God.

This troubling period just prior to Christ's return is known as the Great Tribulation, which will be marked by catastrophic destruction, death and mayhem. Christians will be required to endure much of this period, as they minister and preach the Gospel. A total breakdown in society will occur where anarchy, starvation and death will occur on a pandemic level. The world, in terror and disarray, will embrace a leader to straighten out the mess and bring peace to the world. This world leader is biblically known as the Antichrist and will bring a tyrannical socialistic order to the world.

The Antichrist, also known as the son of perdition or lawless one, will declare himself god and bring a false peace to the world and Israel. Jesus warned that this would be the detestable sacrilege Daniel wrote about.

These events, though terrible, are what Jesus predicted and are found in the gospels of Matthew, Luke and Mark. Carefully read Matthew chapters 24 and 25. You will find in Matthew 24 that Christ refers to the elect or the true Christian throughout this chapter. Here are highlights of how the Christian will be required to endure these troubles, through the Great Tribulation:

- Birth pangs would increase as a prelude to the Great Tribulation—Christians are not to be alarmed, yet. (Verses 4-8).
- Persecution after the birth pangs; Jesus warns the Christian—*"then they will deliver you up to tribulation and put you to death; and you will be hated by all nations*

for my name sake." This will cause many Christians who were not ready, to fall away from the Lord. There will be hatred between Christians and betrayal. Hard to tell how one Christian will betray another, other than through political or a government situation. Remember Judas. There will be an increase in false prophets and great wickedness with a callous attitude prevailing in society. Jesus finishes this part of the end-of-the-age sequence, warning the Christian, *"But he who endures to the end will be saved"* (Verses 9-13).

- At the peak of this time of persecution, the true Gospel of Christ will be preached throughout the world. This must be accomplished before the end comes. Note that Jesus said, *"And this gospel of the kingdom will be preached,"* this will be the true plan of salvation, which includes sanctification and how the kingdom of God will come after the Great Tribulation. You see there are many gospels being preached right now, many interpretations of how the kingdom of God will come—but there is only one true version, that is why Jesus states, *"this gospel of the kingdom"* (Verse 14).
- Next, Jesus warns the Christian, *"when you see the desolating sacrilege,"* referring to when the Antichrist or son of perdition declares himself to be god and brings peace to the world and the Middle East, then those who live in Judea had better flee. Jesus is warning believers who understand what all this means to get away to a safe place, at least for those living in and around Judea. Again, Christians are still here on earth enduring these difficult times. (Verses 15-20).
- Now comes the tribulation period that comes after the Antichrist leader makes his move. This period is called the Great Tribulation and it will be terrible, full of destruction. These days will be shortened for the sake of the elect (the true Christian) and if they were not stopped no human being would be spared. (Verses 21,22).
- During this Great Tribulation Jesus warns that more false prophets and false Christian leaders will mislead many Christians, causing many to think Christ has come back already or that the kingdom of God is already on earth. Jesus warns that these lies will be powerful, having signs and wonders to persuade many not to look for the Christ to appear in the air, coming on the clouds as he originally ascended to heaven. (See Acts 1:10,11). The deception by these false Christian leaders would be so convincing that the elect of God or true Christians could easily be swayed to believe these lies, if it were not for the fact that true Christians had prepared themselves and understood exactly what Jesus had said about these terrible times. (Verses 23-28).
- The very next event in Christ's warnings is, *"Immediately after the tribulation of those days the sun will be darkened, and the moon will not give its light, and the stars*

will fall from heaven, and the powers of the heavens will be shaken" — here Jesus is very clear as to when He will appear to the whole world as a sign, at the end of the Great Tribulation. Not before or in the middle, but *immediately after*. Christ's appearance is in the clouds and the whole world will mourn. The whole world will know that they missed the time of their visitation and that the wrath of God is ready to fall upon them. Revelation chapter six says concerning this moment in the end of this age, *"When he opened the sixth seal, I looked, and behold, there was a great earthquake; and the sun became black as sackcloth, the full moon became like blood, and the stars of the sky fell to the earth as the fig tree sheds its winter fruit when shaken by a gale; the sky vanished like a scroll that is rolled up, and every mountain and island was removed from its place. Then the kings of the earth and the great men and the generals and the rich and the strong, and every one, slave and free, hid in the caves and among the rocks of the mountains, calling to the mountains and rocks, 'Fall on us and hide us from the face of him who is seated on the throne, and from the wrath of the Lamb; for the great day of their wrath has come, and who can stand before it?'"* (Revelation 6:12-17). This is Christ's appearance in the clouds, but He has not yet set His feet upon the earth. Therefore it is important to be ready and endure to the end of these terrible events in order to not be led astray and miss what happens next.

- The rapture occurs — at the end of the Great Tribulation period, just as God's wrath is ready to be poured out on the world with earthquakes and asteroids bringing destruction to the earth. Those who were not raptured to safety will be terrified. Jesus said, *"Then will appear the sign of the Son of man in heaven with power and great glory; and he will send out his angels with a loud trumpet call, and they will gather his elect (true Christians) from the four winds, from one end of heaven to the other"* (Verse 30,31).

These are not the predictions by Hal Lindsey, or Tim LaHaye and Jerry Jenkins with their blockbuster fictional *Left Behind* series of misleading books, or the Latter Rain postmillennialists. Neither are Hank Hanegraaff's, whose preterist views suggest all these terrible events already took place around 70AD. These are not the predictions of Nostradamus, Edgar Cayce, or any so-called doom's day cult. Nor does one need to follow Paul Crouch of TBN and try to decipher his strange Bible code system to get dates and times. These are not my predictions as a pastor; <u>these are Christ's warnings, plain and simple.</u>

Jesus, the Good Shepherd has left clear instructions and warnings as to the sequence of events and the promise to send His angels to catch the true Christian to safety, before He returns to earth and sets up the kingdom of heaven. They are laid out in a straightforward manner, so that any true and sincere Christian can understand. Now, looking carefully at Christ's words, you will see clearly that

Christ's doctrine of the end of the age is premillennial with post-tribulation rapture. End of debate and speculation!

One very special note: Jesus said, *"But that day and hour no one knows, not even the angels of heaven, nor the Son, but the Father only"* (Verse 36).

What does this warning mean to you and me? Well, if you continue to read the rest of Matthew 24 and all of Matthew chapter 25, you will get a picture of how Christians will not be ready for this terrible time and its glorious end. Jesus warned of many last day Christians being lazy, complacent and allowing the cares of this life to weigh down their hearts. The sudden end-of-the-age trouble and the instant rapture of the saints will leave many lukewarm and backslidden Christians behind, to suffer the wrath of God. (Again, read Matthew chapters 24 and 25; 1 Thessalonians 4:13; 5:11 and Revelation chapter six).

MISLEADING RAPTURE THEOLOGY
Son of Perdition Revealed First

In review of the previous section, Jesus laid out the conditions that most Christians would be in: seeing the rise of many false brethren, false Christs, false teachers and prophets pointing to a wrong Christ; persecution of true Christians; manifold increases in wickedness and a call for endurance for the true Christian. He also referred to the man of perdition declaring himself god in the holy place to be the major sign of the end and the beginning of terrible trouble preceding the rapture, His return and the end of this age.

"For then there will be great tribulation, such as has not been from the beginning of the world until now, no, and never will be. And if those days had not been shortened, no human being would be saved; but for the sake of the elect those days will be shortened" (Matthew 24:21,22).

Jesus continued saying, *"...when you see all these things, you know that he is near, at the very gates."* Again, as a reminder, Christ concludes with a final warning, *"But of that day and hour no one knows, not even the angels of heaven, nor the Son, but the Father only"* (Matthew 24:33,36).

This outline by Christ clearly indicates that true born-again, sanctified Christians can expect to endure the Great Tribulation up to a point, for Christ said that for the sake of the true Christian, these terrible days will be shortened.

Paul wrote, *"Now concerning the coming of our Lord Jesus Christ and our assembling to meet him, we beg you, brethren, not to be quickly shaken in mind or excited, either by spirit or by word, or by letter purporting to be from us, to the effect that the day of the Lord has come. Let no one deceive you in any way; for that day will not come, unless the rebellion comes first, and the man of lawlessness is revealed, the son of perdition, who opposes and exalts himself against every so-called god or object of worship, so that he takes his seat in the temple of God, proclaiming himself to be God"* (2 Thessalonians 2:1-4).

The rapture will occur at the end of this terrible time, as multitudes come to a true saving relationship with Christ. This final time of terrible trouble will awaken millions of lost sinners, backslidden believers, and lukewarm Christians. *"...These are they who have come out of the great tribulation; they have washed their robes and made them white in the blood of the Lamb"* (Revelation 7:14).

To the lukewarm Christian and backslidden believer, hearing the truth about the Great Tribulation is terrifying. They know instinctively that they are not ready. It is no wonder so many false teachings about the rapture become popular, especially the *Left Behind* books.

The *Left Behind* series of books, written by Tim LaHaye and Jerry Jenkins, is very popular and very misleading. Hal Lindsey's pre-tribulation position has put millions of Christians at ease. LaHaye, Jenkins, Lindsey and other proponents of pre-tribulation, mid-tribulation or postmillennial doctrines will have blood on their hands if they do not turn from these deceptive teachings.

These books purport that the rapture of all Christians occurs at the beginning of the Great Tribulation. To the contrary, as described in Matthew 24, the true Christian will not escape before the tribulation begins, with the rapture of the true believer taking place sometime during the Great Tribulation, most distinctly near the end of this period.

In Joel 3:13-15 we read, *"Put in the sickle, for the harvest is ripe. Go in, tread, for the wine press is full. The vats overflow, for their wickedness is great. Multitudes, multitudes, in the valley of decision! For the day of the LORD is near in the valley of decision. The sun and the moon are darkened, and the stars withdraw their shining."*

Yes, multitudes must decide whether to choose the world system and the lies of the Antichrist or the true Gospel, preached by a pure, holy and powerful people during the Great Tribulation.

You and I must be ready to endure this coming time in purity and total obedience to Christ. He will protect and guide His own. Those who played church and listened to lies will follow the ultimate lie of Satan through false signs and wonders performed by the man of perdition.

"The coming of the lawless one by the activity of Satan will be with all power and with pretended signs and wonders, and with all wicked deception for those who are to perish, because they refused to love the truth and so be saved. Therefore God sends upon them a strong delusion, to make them believe what is false, so that all may be condemned who did not believe the truth but had pleasure in unrighteousness" (2 Thessalonians 2:9-12).

Among those deceived will be many Christians who were foolish and did not take to heart the warnings and sound doctrine that dealt with their love of the world, secret sins, pride and lust for recognition in this age. Matthew 25 has many challenging parables concerning foolish Christians, wicked servants, false shepherds and cowardly Christian hypocrites.

Do not believe a lie and take the easy way in preparing for Christ's return, for if you do, indeed you will be left behind!

Now is the time to choose whom you will serve, the true Christ or a different Jesus, spirit and gospel preached by so many false and weak shepherds. You are accountable to discern the truth, there will be no one else to blame, for Jesus said, *"Ask, and it will be given you; seek, and you will find; knock, and it will be opened to you. For every one who asks receives, and he who seeks finds, and to him who knocks it will be opened"* (Matthew 7:6,8).

Do not follow me, or believe what I write merely because you read what I teach in this book. You, as a Christian, have the written word of God. Open it up and read. Cry out to God until you know the true Christ intimately and understand the truth.

I know why I believe. I know how and what I learned concerning the false. All this came from following what Jesus taught. I sought the Lord; I searched and cried out; I prayed and read what others wrote with a grain of salt, seeking confirmation from the true Holy Spirit and the written word of God.

None of us will have an excuse if we end up deceived and choose to follow the wrong Christ, embrace the wrong Gospel, and allow a demonic spirit to counterfeit the Holy Spirit.

My advice is, do not play church, and pretend that you are OK, when you know you are not. If your pastor, church or denomination offers teachings that don't align with all that Jesus taught, then ...

GET OUT OF A MUDDLED CHRISTIANITY AND GET INTO CHRIST

Yes, there is much confusion and misunderstanding in Christianity. Very few see true Christianity in action. The discernment of the carnal and the false is almost impossible. Nevertheless, Christ will open your eyes if you are willing to see the truth. Don't be fooled and become satisfied spiritually by the false.

Just as the false ecumenical movement gives spiritual satisfaction, so, too, there is a false spiritual satisfaction by *just* attending church, worshipping together and listening to sermons, reading one more power-building book, watching Christian TV or listening to Christian radio. These activities in and by themselves cannot achieve an unwavering and abiding walk with God. This type of Christian finds a false spiritual satisfaction in church activity—or *Churchianity,* which produces lukewarm Christians.

Even more deceptive is how the Christian masses make *mecca*-type journeys to superstar ministries and revival meetings to get closer to God. These subtle deceptions actually draw Christians away from a genuine relationship with the living God by producing false spiritual satisfaction through these activities and *spiritually sensuous experiences.*

A genuine relationship with Christ is the only true way to satisfy our spiritual hunger. This genuine relationship is through a personal relationship with the resurrected Christ and by embracing His discipline and leadership in all of life.

Demonic activity drives the false ecumenical movement and lukewarm *Churchianity* by tapping into mankind's common spiritual hunger. The lust for spiritual power and sense of belonging found in false unity and false fellowship charms many Christians into relinquishing their individual call to be a true disciple of Christ. A lemming is a small rodent known for periodic mass migrations that sometimes end in rushing over a cliff and drowning. Don't be a spiritual lemming!

Those who are truly sanctified by the Holy Spirit are no longer confused and cease their lusting after the power of God by embracing false unity or sitting under a false shepherd trying to fill their lack of inner character, courage and strength. In a true disciple, Christ will have a free hand to work the cross that crucifies the carnal and transform the genuine believer to be Christ-like in nature.

The counterfeiting by Satan has seeped into all areas of the church in these last days. We see that Pentecostalism, charismatic-ism, Baptist-ism, Methodist-ism, Lutheran-ism Third Wave-ism, and Latter Rain-ism, can be as destructive as Mormonism, Catholicism or Jehovah Witness-ism. These "isms" and factions have created confusion and schisms, snaring many in sectarian religious pride. Eventually, many who hang onto this pride will slide into a type of fanaticism, living a self-righteous and carnal-holy life that nullify God's grace and takes away the salvation found in Christ. (See Galatians 2:18-21 and 5:1-12).

Oswald Chambers wrote, *"There is only one thing as futile as the Roman Catholic Church and that is Protestantism. In Roman Catholicism the great dominating authority is Churchianity, the Church is vested with all authority. In Protestantism it is what the Book says that is supreme authority, and a man gets rest when he decides for either. I am going to give up all the turmoil and let my Church do my thinking for me."*

Beware of self-proclaimed prophets, apostles, evangelists, teachers and controlling pastors who manipulate and preach idolatry of leadership. Beware of the institutionalized denominations that brainwash with sectarian pride. Flee the apostate Christian cults and sects that are in love with this world! Find a likeminded fellowship and a leader who has paid the price, and who is not a man-pleaser but a true servant of our Lord Jesus Christ.

There must be a *coming out* from the foolish and false church and a return to local fellowships, regardless of denominational affiliation, which go all the way with Christ and His entire teachings.

Jesus said of many, *"Why do you call me 'Lord, Lord,' and not do what I tell you? Everyone who comes to me and hears my words and does them, I will show you what he is like: he is like a man building a house, who dug deep, and laid the foundation upon rock; and when a flood arose, the stream broke against that house, and could not shake it, because it had been well built. But he who hears and does not do them is like a man who built a house on the ground without a foundation; against which the stream broke, and immediately it fell, and the ruin of that house was great"* (Luke 6:46-49).

These fellowships will not care for denominational ties with pet doctrines or get hung up on public religious acts that encourage prideful distinction, but rather wholeheartedly embrace the cross and have the true Christ formed within. They will learn to embrace all that Jesus taught, including the hard teachings and commands. They will enter at the narrow gate and follow the hard path that leads to life.

Persecution will drive these true fellowships together and the "religious" barriers will crumble. This godly remnant will be on fire for the Lord and put aside petty man-made rules. On the other hand, they will not tolerate the wicked phonies and will avoid the false and hypocritical churches and denominations. They will let go of the world and not look back. This mighty warring body of believers will awaken soon, as the return of Christ approaches. These Christians will unite and do what it takes to be ready. True unity will grow, regardless of worship preferences and differing church governments. Jesus will have a people who indeed love one another, even unto death. They will embrace the cleansing baptism of fire by Christ and live in holiness and the fear of God. They will also die to self-righteous arrogance that makes the lost sinner feel condemned when in their presence.

One other important characteristic of the unity of this true army of Christ is its rejection of the false gifts and empty manifestations deemed as the so-called power of God.

These false gifts and empty manifestations are part of the counterfeit movements. Satan will try to take over ministries and churches that embrace the true work and power of the Holy Spirit. God will not allow this to happen. You will see soon a horrible sifting and judgment fall on those who push this counterfeit gifting and out-of-control empty manifestations.

The election of 2004, where a Christian President is in office has become the catalyst to start a terrible *"hate Christian and bash Christian"* campaign. The coming great persecution has indeed started. This persecution is spreading throughout the world, as the United States becomes hated for its national stance, which will be perceived as being based on Christian principles. *"Then they will deliver you up to tribulation, and put you to death; and you will be hated by all nations for my name's sake... But who endures to the end will be saved"* (Matthew 24:9-13).

CHAPTER 4

Tossed About and Carried Away

CHRISTIAN OSTRICH SYNDROME
The Most Damning Shortcuts of All

The ostrich is a large bird that cannot fly. It can run fast and is very strong. Contrary to myth, the ostrich does not bury its head in the sand when hiding from a predator, though that is part of the ostrich metaphor I have chosen to help describe a very damning set of shortcuts many Christian are taught to take. Indeed, many Christians bury their mind in the sand, become deceived concerning their true condition of heart and learn to ignore how weak they really are in overcoming their sin nature, the works of the flesh, and carnality. They are taught to ignore symptoms and indicators allowed by God to shake them awake before it's too late.

As the ostrich is a bird that cannot fly, this is an excellent picture of the Christian caught in a web of half-truths and lies in their effort to deal with the power of their sin nature. They learn to fight hard, run hard, and work feverishly at attempting to enter into the *rest of God*. They are in a constant struggle trying to walk in His grace and power and overcome the sin nature. They are taught to magically pretend their carnal ways are dead. Eventually these ostrich Christians tire out from sheer exhaustion, unable to escape the gravitational pull of the sin nature.

A biblical metaphor used by the Lord to describe the true saint who has learned to rise above the power of the sin nature is the eagle. *"Have you not known? Have you not heard? The LORD is the everlasting God, the Creator of the ends of the earth. He does not faint or grow weary, his understanding is unsearchable. He gives power to the faint, and to him who has no might he increases strength. Even youths shall faint and be weary, and young men shall fall exhausted; but they who wait for the LORD shall renew their strength, they shall mount up with wings like eagles, they shall run and not be weary, they shall walk and not faint"* (Isaiah 40:28-31).

These "ostrich' teachings mislead thousands of Christians into trouble, frustration, and depression. An exodus of new and struggling converts leaves Christianity daily, some overpowered by their hidden issues of heart, sinful desires and inability to fight temptations—many quit God altogether.

Still others learn how to create an outer Christian facade by emulating Christian leaders who teach these shortcuts and manmade rules. Some become so enamored and brainwashed, they arrive at a state of hypocrisy that completely alienates their hearts from God. Jesus said of those hypocrites of his day, *"You hypocrites! Well did Isaiah prophesy of you, when he said: 'This people honors me with their lips, but their heart is far from me; in vain do they worship me, teaching as doctrines the precepts of men"* (Matthew 15:7-9).

Remember, Jesus taught that we are to take the *narrow gate and the hard path that leads to life.* There are no shortcuts for the true Christian.

Let's examine some very destructive shortcut teachings that have caused many Christians to stumble, fall back into sin and flounder in despair. We will examine some Scriptures normally taken out of context in the previously mentioned teachings inflicted on the body of Christ. Have your Bible ready to study the referenced contextual Scriptures, as we dismantle these damning shortcuts that keep Christians from dealing with their hidden issues and carnal nature.

ALL THINGS BECOME NEW?

"Therefore, if anyone is in Christ, he is a new creation; the old has passed away, behold, the new has come" (2 Corinthians 5:17).

The misinterpreted shortcut: *"I must always remember that, I am a new creature in Christ, all things have already become new, old things have passed away—including the old sin nature and carnal personalities. These have instantly disappeared, magically! If I continue to tell myself and believe it then it will finally be this way in life."*

This is a terrible misconception of the initial born-again experience and bypasses growing up into Christ, which is the cleansing and dying process of our spirit and old nature.

The key to this Scripture is, *"if anyone is in Christ."* Paul is writing this profound theological point to the church at Corinth, citing its carnal problems. In a previous letter to the Corinthians Paul writes, *"But I, brethren, could not address you as spiritual men, but as men of the flesh, as babes in Christ. I fed you with milk, not solid food; for you were not ready for it; and even yet you are not ready, for you are still of the flesh. For while there is jealousy and strife among you, are you not of the flesh, and behaving like ordinary men?"* (1 Corinthians 3:1-3).

These Christians were not grown up into Christ. (See Ephesians 4:11-15). They were carnal and at risk. Indeed, they are not yet in Christ, rather still on their way in the sanctification process. Elsewhere Paul writes to the Christians at Galatia, *"They make much of you, but for no good purpose; they want to shut you out, that you may make much of them. For a good purpose it is always good to be made much of, and not only when I am present with you. My little children, with whom I am again in travail until Christ be formed in you!"* (Galatians 4:17-19).

Yes, we have a new nature planted within when we experience the true touch from God that creates the rebirth of our spirit in Christ. That rebirth is the beginning point where a portion of our inner spirit has been regenerated. After this, comes the work of maturing in Christ and the death and resurrection process where our carnal nature is transformed. Paraphrasing another passage written by Paul, *We are to cleanse ourselves of all defilements of body and spirit, making holiness perfect in the fear of God.* (See 2 Corinthians 7:1). As Peter put it, *"Like newborn babes, long for the pure spiritual milk, that by it you may grow up to salvation; for you have tasted the kindness of the Lord"* (1 Peter 2:2,3).

When we reach this goal, we have obtained the full grace of God. We have eternal security, having the old nature put to death and the carnal personalities ever changing into Christ-like nature. We press on from a victorious position in Christ, having crucified the flesh with all its passions and desires. We have succeeded in entering into the rest of God. Indeed, we abide in Christ—that is, we are in Christ and all things are new and the old has passed away.

We grow up into Christ through a process, not in an instant change. Christians are deceived in the shortcut of instant change when accepting Christ, they then learn to play a pretend game that everything is all right when the carnal issues surface. Those who embrace this shortcut are vulnerable to backsliding, carnal behavior, holding on to roots of bitterness, and defiling those around them, having double-minded problems; and even worse, many let an impure and evil heart lead them to fall away from the living God.

Embracing this and the other shortcuts helps create a superficial religious personality. When this happens, our inward being and secret heart is walled off by a self-righteous character structure. The Holy Spirit has a difficult time penetrating this self-made, self-righteous religious persona. Some end up like the Pharisees of Christ's day—rejecting the work and convicting presence of the Holy Spirit.

An anecdote to this shortcut is taken from a ministry case involving a pastor, his wife and a false prophet. Embracing this lie brought terrible consequences.

Ministry case: Angel of Light Ministries and the Rebellious Pastor

"There are those who are pure in their own eyes but are not cleansed of their filth" (Proverbs 30:12).

I had worked for some time as the counseling pastor at a charismatic fellowship of about 400 members. I became uneasy with some of the traveling evangelists and so-called prophets that the senior pastor had invited to preach. These evangelists walked in the supposed gifts and many Christians in these meetings were slain in the spirit. I noticed little difference in changed character with those slain in these meetings. Many continued in counseling and struggled with their walk. Others felt deliverance and went merrily on their way, only to later complain of other troubling issues.

There was a revival prayer meeting during this time, and the senior pastor received a very powerful directive prophecy by the person leading this meeting. He was to prepare the congregation for revival through sanctification. He ignored this sound exhortation. Finally, one evening the Lord gave us insight on the condition of the church relating to what had been transpiring in these meetings. Late that night, while asleep, I was half awakened by a vision of a person who looked like the Lord walking toward me. For a moment I was excited. Then I noticed that the robe worn by this figure was dingy gray, not white. Just as I noticed the coloration, I knew it was not the Lord, but something devilish and demonic. Then this entity started choking me. I commanded it to leave, and after a moment or two it left, and I awoke fully.

After prayer, Scripture study and discussion, it became clear this experience was a demonic attack allowed by the Lord. We identified this as *angel of light* demonic deception, in which these evangelists and so-called prophets moved. This is a powerful principality deceiving many in the body of Christ. This senior pastor at one point even expressed concerns but continued to promote this type of false spirit manifestation.

Relationship trouble began to be exposed in some marriages in the fellowship. The wife of an elder revealed her husband was abusing his family and she had him temporarily removed from the home. The senior pastor and I had a discussion over this situation. He felt the treatment was too harsh for an elder, though he condoned such treatment for another abusive man in the congregation just a week prior. The pastor even condoned manhandling women, as he admitted throwing his wife onto their bed occasionally to "put her in her place."

I took exception to this abuse, confronted him, and warned that such action is cowardly and abusive. This pastor had confessed earlier of sexual temptations that often pushed him to almost committing sexual immorality. I had counseled him to allow God to do whatever it takes to get at these issues. The account of the counsel I gave him is in Chapter 8, "*Standing in the Gap*," and in the section, "*Christ-like Character Created by Enduring Fiery Trials.*"

His wife also refused the sound counsel I gave her, and instead took the advice of one of these traveling evangelists. This false teacher told her not to deal with inner issues; they are all gone, all things have become new, the old is passed away and under the blood of Christ. He instructed both of them to continue to praise God, plead the blood of Christ, seek deliverance from any demonic oppression (his type of ministry) and continue to believe the old self is dead and gone.

This issue, and a couple of other situations, convinced this senior pastor to no longer have me continue as the counseling pastor. Knowing in my spirit that this was about to happen, the Lord gave me a prophetic declaration for this man, which follows:

"Since you did not obey the Lord in sanctifying the congregation: Your anointing has been lifted and the lamp stand for *'NAME OF THE FELLOWSHIP'* has been removed."

The senior pastor conferred with the district superintendent and a few other elders. They determined that the prophecy was false.

A year and a half later, this same senior pastor was attending a Foursquare leadership conference led by Jack Hayford in California, and upon returning home, out of guilt, confessed before the congregation that while at the conference he had a sexual encounter with a call girl. His discipline was in the form of a five-year sabbatical from ministry. One year later, he was back in the ministry.

Two years later, the church relocated across town, went through a split and changed its name.

This is one of many examples where Christians, ministries, pastors, and whole congregations fall into sin and trouble because of false doctrine and false spirits, which are embraced as true manifestations of the Spirit of God.

The truth that *all things become new and the old is passed away* is for those who have embraced the cross, become cleansed in the process of sanctification with salvation and the grace of God as the end results. Taking the shortcut by pretending all is new and the old is gone, when it is not, can lead to destruction.

FORGET THE PAST?

"Brethren, I do not consider that I have made it my own; but one thing I do, forgetting what lies behind and straining forward to what lies ahead, I press on toward the goal for the prize of the upward call of God in Christ Jesus" (Philippians 3:13,14).

The misinterpreted shortcut: *"I must forget the past, including bad memories, sins and failures. I must believe I am a new creature in Christ, the new has come and the old has passed away"* (Read Philippians 3:1-16).

This false doctrine comes from twisting Paul's writings to the Philippians. In an effort to get troubled Christians out from under guilt from past sins and failures, this teaching tries to get Christians to forget past memories by focusing on Christ and the future. Christians hampered with past issues, failures and sins have a deeper problem to deal with. This issue is more than just not understanding Christ's forgiveness.

First, let's take a contextual look at Paul's passage in Philippians. It addresses his accomplishments as a Pharisee and as a Christian. He learned to count all his accomplishments under the law as trash because those efforts produced self-righteousness. As a Christian, those things that Christ did through him in the past were forgotten. He learned not to count on past achievements that puff up. Many Christians become carnal and self-righteous standing on what they did for Christ or even what Christ accomplished through them. He concludes that he must press on to the high call of God in Christ, dying to self-effort and religiosity.

You may think, okay, how does a Christian deal with past memories of failure, sin and disappointment?

First we must understand the doctrine of sanctification, cleansing and purification of the heart for Christians. Another false teaching that goes hand-in-hand with forgetting the past is *you are completely changed on the inside* when you accept Christ. This is not true as we discussed earlier. James, John and Paul gave instruction for Christians to become purified in the heart, cleansed of body and spirit, and renewed in the spirit of the mind. As a Christian, the heart, spirit and spirit of the mind make up the inner man. (James 4:8, Ephesians 3:14-21, 4:22-24, and 2 Corinthians 7:1).

Thus, the Christian must allow the Lord to strengthen the inner man, renew the spirit of the mind, and cleanse the heart and spirit in order to walk in victory and put off the old nature.

Many people come to the Lord who are brokenhearted and suffer from a crushed spirit and double-mindedness, a (*two-souled, or twice a soul*) condition. Depending on childhood abuse and sinful lifestyle, new Christians can, in various degrees be crushed in spirit. The following Proverb clearly indicates some of the symptoms, *"A gentle tongue is a tree of life, but perverseness in it breaks the spirit"* (Proverbs 15:4). *"A glad heart makes a cheerful countenance, but by sorrow of heart the spirit is broken"* (Proverbs 15:13). *"A cheerful heart is a good medicine, but a downcast spirit dries up the bones"* (Proverbs 17:22). *"A man's spirit will endure sickness; but a broken spirit who can bear?"* (Proverbs 18:14). *"The spirit of man is the lamp of the LORD, searching all his innermost parts"* (Proverbs 20:27).

Many suffer from all types of abuse. Children especially are targets of abuse, leaving millions suffering from some form of harm. The memory and defilements from these wounds are not resolved properly until one comes to Christ and allows the Holy Spirit to bring those issues to the light for cleansing and healing. Many Christians who suffer from a broken spirit and a divided soul have a tremendous amount of unbelief, even though they have faith in God.

All of Israel was subject to abuse and slavery. In Exodus, the Scriptures indicate when Moses spoke to Israel about God's deliverance, *"but they did not listen to Moses, because of their broken spirit and their cruel bondage"* (Exodus 6:9). These people suffered and rebelled against God and the leadership of Moses. *"They angered him at the waters of Meribah, and it went ill with Moses on their account; for they made his spirit bitter, and he spoke words that were rash"* (Psalm 106:32,33).

Christ as Savior and Healer is close to the brokenhearted and those crushed in spirit, but few understand how Christ deals with these hidden issues within the new child of God. (Psalm 34:18). Indeed, He allows pressures of life and troubles to come our way to make us look at what we do not want to see. When things go well, we do not often look at our wayward life and carnal ways.

In Psalms, Asaph wrote, *"In the day of my trouble I seek the Lord; in the night my hand is stretched out without wearying; my soul refuses to be comforted. I think of God, and I moan; I meditate, and my spirit faints. Selah Thou dost hold my eyelids from closing; I am so troubled that I cannot speak. I consider the days of old, I remember the years long ago. I commune with my heart in the night; I meditate and search my spirit"* (Psalm 77:2-6).

Here we have a clear directive in Scripture to reflect on our past ways and search our spirit to determine what the Lord is trying to get us to see.

In the New Testament we see additional Scripture directing us to examine ourselves and purify our hearts. Our next work, *"Can Christ Heal the Divided?"* will go into specifics on God's principles for healing and recovery. For now, an example from ministry will help you understand how forgotten memories can be powerful and how they can drive unwanted behavior and cause defiling attitudes for the Christian who suffers from a broken spirit and divided soul.

Ministry case: The Lawnmower Incident.

"Behold, I was brought forth in iniquity, and in sin did my mother conceive me. Behold, thou desirest truth in the inward being; therefore teach me wisdom in my secret heart. Purge me with hyssop, and I shall be clean; wash me, and I shall be whiter than snow. Fill me with joy and gladness; let the bones which thou hast broken rejoice. Hide thy face from my sins, and blot out all my iniquities. Create in me a clean heart, O God, and put a new and right spirit within me" (Psalm 51:5-10).

This is an account of a counselee working on relationship issues with which both he and his wife were struggling. It is an excellent example of how memories in the past are like doors that must be opened to get at the roots of bitterness, before they spring up and cause trouble.

This Christian couple was in an argument over something minor. The man decided to go outside and mow the lawn, emanating a self-righteous attitude. As he was mowing the lawn, he saw his wife sitting at the front room window sticking her tongue out at him as he made a pass with the lawn mower.

He had learned to catch his thoughts, take them captive to Christ and examine attitudes and motives. When he saw his wife make this face at him, he heard his inner self say, *"Why doesn't she get up and do something... ah, she's just lazy, she's lazy like NAME OF FIRST WIFE, and she was lazy like my mother!"*

At that point he caught this line of thought and asked God to forgive him. He then heard the Holy Spirit reveal, *Yes, son, you've made a judgment that all women are lazy.* He had understood through counseling and sound doctrine concerning wounds from the past and associated memories often surface to one's awareness as inner self-talk that reflect issues in his heart.

Indeed, Jesus said, *"Judge not for the same judgment you judge shall be given unto you and the same measure you measure out shall be given unto you"* (This verse is paraphrased, see Matthew 7:1). As well as *"For out of the heart come evil thoughts, ... These are what defile a man"* (Matthew 15:19,20).

He asked the Lord to show him any memory from the past that embittered his spirit concerning women. Immediately a memory came.

As a young man, during his junior year in high school he and his brother had to do the dishes all the time, while their sister, who was old enough to help, sat in the living room with their mother watching TV. He turned to his younger brother, shaking his fist and saying, *"I hate them, they're lazy."*

His parents were wrong in preferential treatment. As it turned out, his sister became a chronic drug user and thief. Nevertheless, he had to immediately, while mowing the lawn, forgive his mother, father and sister and even forgive himself for the years of deep-seated bitter hatred toward women.

He prayed for his wife and former wife, that they be released from his bitter expectation.

Paul wrote, *"Since we have these promises, beloved, let us cleanse ourselves from every defilement of body and spirit, and make holiness perfect in the fear of God"* (2 Corinthians 7:1), and also, *"Put off your old nature which belongs to your former manner of life and is corrupt through deceitful lusts, and be renewed in the spirit of your minds, and put on the new nature, created after the likeness of God in true righteousness and holiness"* (Ephesians 4:22-24).

This was an old memory that was a *tip of the iceberg* so-to-speak, pointing to a deep bitter root full of hate, anger and unforgiveness.

Of course, there are memories of abuse that are full of emotional pain and spiritual trauma. The above example is mild compared to other cases. Other memories can carry deep pain where the side-effects of cleansing are as those described by James, "weeping and mourning," until the pain and roots of bitterness are gone. In this inner work, memories are healed and the divided part of the soul is cleansed, healed, changed into Christ-like attitude and finally fused with the inner faith person, in righteousness and holiness. (See James 4:7-10).

WHOSE THOUGHTS ARE THEY ANYWAY?
Mine or the Devil's

"For out of the heart come evil thoughts, murder, adultery, fornication, theft, false witness, slander. These are what defile a man; but to eat with unwashed hands does not defile a man" (Matthew 15:19,20).

<u>The misinterpreted shortcut:</u> *"I am a new creature in Christ, I have a new heart and Christ-like nature, the old is gone; therefore, if I have any bad thoughts they are not mine; they are from the devil and any oppression is from the devil and any trouble is from generational curses."*

The previous ministry account, "The Lawnmower Incident," also shows how the majority of our bad thoughts come from within our heart and spirit of our mind.

In 1975, while attending Bible College, one of our professors of religion made a comment about thoughts. He said, *"They are like birds that come and go; if they land don't let them make a nest."* He was implying that the thoughts don't matter; just don't let them drive behavior. They are just tempting thoughts from Satan, not from yourself. As a born-again Christian who has automatically received a new and clean heart, bad thoughts will always come from the devil.

Again, this is error, for Jesus taught, *"Out of the heart come evil thoughts."*

Temptations will come with wicked thoughts, but not all thoughts are from our heart. Satan can implant evil thoughts looking to find place in our heart through hidden defilements. Unfortunately, few know how to discern their own thoughts that are evil, from the thoughts that come from the evil one.

We can train our minds to dwell on what is pleasing to the Lord, what is lovely and good, but we must also learn to take every thought captive and examine the intent and look for sources of bitterness, hate, fear, jealousy, insecurity, unbelief, anxiety and other feelings. Track them down and get to the root.

Some double-minded Christians have no feelings when bad thoughts are activated. In fact, they have a hard time catching their thoughts. They often just blurt out words that are out of order, hurtful and poisonous. They suffer from severe dividedness with their feelings walled-off from their thoughts. These troubled saints are 'two souled' or divided in spirit and soul. When they have a carnal feeling or desire, it bypasses their cognitive thought process. They usually have no expression at all, with body language that appears to show they are unaffected, but underneath is seething rage, self-pity or revenge.

If we learn to work with the Holy Spirit and the Word of God, we can track down and discern the thoughts and intentions of the heart. This is God's principle for recovery that allows us to avoid severe trials and sifting by Satan to break our denial of having bad thoughts and ill motives of the heart.

"For the word of God is living and active, sharper than any two-edged sword, piercing to the division of soul and spirit, of joints and marrow, and discerning the thoughts and intentions of the heart" (Hebrews 4:12).

If we refuse to examine our thoughts, deny ownership, and avoid the hard work of finding the root of the ill thought, then God will try us more than need be.

We must humble ourselves and agree with God concerning our heart and mind. It is written, *"The heart is deceitful above all things, and desperately corrupt; who can understand it? 'I the LORD search the mind and try the heart, to give to every man according to his ways, according to the fruit of his doings'"* (Jeremiah 17:9,10).

Are things going consistently bad in life? Do you lead an unstable lifestyle? Examine the thoughts of your heart. They will begin to tell you what God is trying to get you to see. They are your thoughts, not from the devil! And they come from your own dark heart.

Remember James wrote, *"Purify your hearts, you men of double mind."* And again, Jesus said, *"Out of the heart come evil thoughts."*

Let me say this, our thoughts can be helpful and kind but still carry wrong motives for self-glory or selfish ambition. What are our true motives in helping others, our work in ministry and making friends in Christ? Sometimes as Christians we have mixed motives in doing God's will, like combining true motives out of obedience, and 'two souled' motives of self-recognition for ego building.

DELIVERANCE FROM THE FLESH?
The Futility of Casting Out the Carnal Personality

"For God speaks in one way, and in two, though man does not perceive it. In a dream, in a vision of the night, when deep sleep falls upon men, while they slumber on their beds, then he opens the ears of men, and terrifies them with warnings, that he may turn man aside from his deed, and cut off pride from man; he keeps back his soul from the Pit, his life from perishing by the sword. 'Man is also chastened with pain upon his bed, and with continual strife in his bones; so that his life loathes bread, and his appetite dainty food. His flesh is so wasted away that it cannot be seen; and his bones which were not seen stick out. His soul draws near the Pit, and his life to those who bring death'" (Job 33:14-22).

<u>The misinterpreted shortcut:</u> *"If I am bothered by besetting thoughts, temptations and sinful behavior; it is the work of a demonic spirit, generational curses and familiar spirits that must be cast out and broken by an anointed ministry that operates in deliverance and powerful manifestations of the Holy Spirit. This will chase the blues away and bring me into victory. My spirit must be touched in order to make these miraculous changes, that means I must go down under the power from someone who has a special anointing."*

The Toronto Blessing, Third Wave, Brownsville Revival, and Latter-Rain revivalists have created profitable enterprises. They buy and sell what they believe to be the power of God to magically deliver the struggling Christian. Though many will denounce this assertion, the main motive is money and to increase followers. These leaders are greedy for recognition, attempting to make a living selling a perverted gospel.

"But false prophets also arose among the people, just as there will be false teachers among you, who will secretly bring in destructive heresies, even denying the Master who bought them, bringing upon themselves swift destruction. And many will follow their licentiousness, and because of them the way of truth will be reviled. And in their greed they will exploit you with false words; from of old their condemnation has not been idle, and their destruction has not been asleep" (2 Peter 2:1-2).

They sell the anointing, making people dependent on their special gifting. Peter's prophesy has, indeed, come to pass, as these people become peddlers of God's word who continually commend themselves. Paul fought these deceitful workmen as well, *"For we are not, like so many, peddlers of God's word; but as men of sincerity, as commissioned by God, in the sight of God we speak in Christ"* (2 Corinthians 2:17).

God did not commission these false prophets, but they are self-appointed, living in a licentious or extravagant manner, making claims about the abundant life and prosperity found in their version of the gospel.

These deceitful ministries prey on the deceived and naïve Christian, bilking them of millions of dollars. They sell a shortcut to the life in Christ. But the life they promulgate is counterfeit and will crumble in the coming trouble.

The *anointing that delivers* is the main product they peddle. Like snake oil sellers of the Old West, they make outrageous claims of instant relief and deliverance from whatever ails the struggling saint. In reality they are either attempting to cast out the carnal self or manipulating a false anointing of spiritual anesthesia to quell the inner pain and torment due to a 'twice a soul' condition.

Participants at these false revival meetings fall over from the power of this counterfeit anointing, thinking they are *slain in the spirit*. Some of the expressions of deliverance and anointing are laughing uncontrollably, barking like dogs, staggering around feeling drunk and falling over in ecstatic hysteria.

Many will challenge such assertions and say, *"Unless you have experienced this power yourself, how do you know this is false?"*

The Scriptures I have shared should be ample insight to help the sincere Christian escape this counterfeit revival movement. Nevertheless, I have experienced these false manifestations and ministered in them starting in 1989 when these maddening demonstrations were just beginning within the charismatic and evangelical churches. All that I saw and experienced did not seem right and I began to seek God for answers.

I was slain in the spirit a couple of times. The last time the Holy Spirit said, *"Chuck, what's happening to your heart?"* I said, *"Nothing."* Prior to this, the Lord had me renounce the false gift of tongues that I practiced, which started back in 1976. After I renounced this false gift, then the true gifts began in ministry and counseling.

Indeed, sensuous spiritual touches will not change the old nature into Christ-like character. They do nothing to expose, confront and cleanse an evil unbelieving heart from which so many Christians suffer. These counterfeit-empty manifestations give false hope, temporal relief to warnings that God allows, and eventually create a weak and dependent outer Christian personality to help cope. In the end, these false doctrines and counterfeit experiences harden the heart of many believers, causing an alienation from the true Holy Spirit of God. These foul addictive experiences grieve God and hijack true revival and derail true discipleship.

The following is an example of how destructive and far reaching these deceitful teachers and counterfeit activities can become.

Ministry case: It happened at a church picnic.

"To the choirmaster. A Psalm of David, the servant of the LORD. Transgression speaks to the wicked deep in his heart; there is no fear of God before his eyes. For he flatters himself in his own eyes that his iniquity cannot be found out and hated. The words of his mouth are mischief and deceit; he has ceased to act wisely and do good. He plots mischief while on his bed; he sets himself in a way that is not good; he spurns not evil" (Psalm 36:1-4).

I had counseled a couple on and off for about a year. The husband resisted any true work in our sessions. When a charismatic evangelist came to his church, he went to a couple of these meetings. He was slain in the spirit and reported to me in our last session that he was now free of any problems and did not need any more counsel.

I knew that there was still a spirit of lust over him and that he was holding back in counseling concerning his secret sexual problems.

About six months later, this man called me and asked for prayer. He announced that two detectives had requested an interview. He was accused of molesting his four-year-old niece and told me emphatically that *he did not do it*.

I asked the Holy Spirit what was the truth and I heard from the Lord right then and there, while on the phone with this man, *"He is lying; he did it!"*

I told him that I would pray that "God's will be done" and that he should call me back and let me know what happened.

After I finished the conversation, I, along with my wife, prayed for additional direction and confirmation. I heard again, from the Lord, that he did it, and so did my wife. We then prayed, asking that *God's Will* be revealed in the matter. The Holy Spirit gave this answer me: *"Pray that the lying spirit be broken over him and that he would go to jail for what he did."* We prayed accordingly.

The next day this person called me, very distraught, saying that he took a lie detector test, failed it, and confessed to molesting his four-year-old niece. He confessed to me also, giving details of when and where it had happened. I told him I would try to help him deal with this and face up to his problems. (Note: Many pedophiles pass lie detector tests because they lie to themselves and believe the lie. Often a lying spirit will enable a pedophile to completely dissociate from truth, sear or reject conscience and lie without flinching).

Child protection services stepped in and had this man removed from his home. He had two daughters who were now at risk. When he realized the full ramifications of his evil deed, he changed his story and denied he had done such a thing.

By the way, he did this while attending a church picnic. This was the same church that brought in false evangelists and prophets who practiced a counterfeit anointing. His sister had asked him to watch her daughter (his niece). While no one was looking, he molested her to the decree of causing physical trauma in which her parents detected bleeding and took her in for an examination. The medical examination determined there had been a sexual assault. They knew he was the only one alone with her during the time this could have happened.

Now, in the state where this happened, if one confesses and goes into treatment—especially for first time offender—jail time is suspended. As stated earlier, this man recanted his confession, insisting that he was innocent and that the detectives had coerced the confession. The case went to trial. The jury found him guilty beyond any doubt, and he received a five-year sentence for his crime.

This was God's will for such a liar and abuser of children. This man had crossed the line. If we had not done what God wanted in prayer and had not been walking in the true gifts, Satan would have protected this man, and most likely he would still be offending.

As it was, he elicited pity at this very same church that he attended, and there was a battle and division of fellowship over this situation. Few, including the pastor, were willing to hold this man accountable. The attitude was one of forgiving the perpetrator and welcoming him into the fold with open arms, as if nothing ever happened. We counseled his wife to hold him accountable, while others wanted her to take him back into the house while awaiting trial. She would not because it was determined their own daughters were at risk. Later, it was determined he previously had inappropriately touched his youngest daughter.

This is an example of the true gifts of the Lord in action. There have been numerous situations, both positive and negative, concerning the exercise of the gifts in the lives of people in and through this ministry.

Remember, the Holy Spirit instructed Peter to prophesy Ananias and his wife's death. (Acts 5:1-16). Also, recall the account of Paul standing up to Elymas the Magician in Acts 13:4-12. When this kind of power of the Lord is exercised, which is only through broken and disciplined men and women of God, then hidden evil in the church can be driven out and a proper fear of the Lord be restored in the sanctuary.

The issue here concerning the false anointing allowed this evil to escape detection. This man thought he was free of his own wicked heart. God was allowing him to be tormented and attacked by Satan to hold him responsible in dealing with his evil, unbelieving heart. Instead, he fell for the lie, thinking he was free.

In reality his deliverance was from his own painful conscience. The consequence was the abuse of his niece; sinful shame upon himself and his family; division of fellowship and unity within the local body of believers; increasing the prison population and state legal expenses. And the most tragic effect was the lifetime scars inflicted upon his niece, sister, wife and two daughters.

In this case, taking the devil's shortcut had a far-reaching ripple effect on many lives. Multiply this across the body of Christ worldwide. These false teachings and movements are allowed to hijack true revival and church housecleaning, creating fellowship incubators for wolves, both male and female. Evil finds a place right in the congregation and grows with stubborn resistance to exposure, correction, and expulsion.

What is the source of this false power? It is the power of the human spirit harnessed by the demonic, which counterfeits the initial stages of true revival.

SATAN CAN'T TOUCH ME!
I'm a born-again Spirit-filled Christian

"Submit yourselves therefore to God. Resist the devil and he will flee from you" (James 4:7). *"Little children, you are of God, and have overcome them; for he who is in you is greater than he who is in the world"* (1 John 4:4).

<u>The misinterpreted shortcut:</u> *"I'm a born-again Christian protected from Satan's power. Satan is not allowed to touch me, I'm under the blood of Christ and baptized in the Holy Spirit. I am immune to the powers of the devil!"*

This is a very *beguiling* shortcut. It is a game of pretend where Satan loves to play possum with those who believe this lie.

Again, Scriptures used to promote this false security and false protection are taken out of context and presented to the duped Christian. The power to believe this shortcut requires the believer to work up a hyper-magical faith.

The teachers of this lie tap into fear and laziness with which most Christians struggle.

Here is the truth. Satan is allowed by God to attack Christians. Peter wrote concerning the devil, *"Resist him, firm in your faith, knowing that the same experience of suffering is required of your brotherhood throughout the world. And after you have suffered a little while, the God of all grace, who has called you to his eternal glory in Christ, will himself restore, establish, and strengthen you. To him be the dominion for ever and ever. Amen"* (1 Peter 5:9-11).

Notice in this passage what we must understand—*the same experience of suffering is required.* This is how God disciplines His children in the ways of true righteousness, humility, and patience. This pressure helps produce Christ-like character. Hebrews speaks of the discipline of the Lord in the following manner; *"For the moment all discipline seems painful rather than pleasant; later it yields the peaceful fruit of righteousness to those who have been trained by it"* (Hebrews 12:11).

The true child of God learns to embrace the trials and discipline of the Lord, knowing that this training validates them as being accepted as a son or daughter. Jesus said that those whom He loves He chastises, and the Lord admonishes us to be zealous in repentance, allowing His discipline to have its full effect. (See James 1:2,3; Revelation 3:19).

True discipleship is embraced in this manner, not in some school or memorized set of teachings. It is in real life experiences where we are required to sincerely seek God, deal with our carnal hidden issues, and learn to stand on our own two feet of faith, being led by the Holy Spirit, not by some shortcut-preaching idolatrous false teacher. *"For all who are led by the Spirit of God are sons of God"* (Romans 8:14).

In the 1970s many Christians fell into an abusive teaching called the Shepherding Movement. A network of pastors started this teaching to help bring a disciplined life to the believer. It ended in disaster. One of the original founders, Bob Mumford, freely admits to its error. It was an authoritarian type leadership under the guise of discipleship.

Some Promise Keepers' teachings and the newer teaching outlined in the book, *The Purpose-Driven Church,* are laced with authoritarian control and false discipleship teachings that ultimately leads to abuse. Christians are to be led by the Holy Spirit in life, not driven by our carnal personalities and fleshly motives in the service of God for church growth. Remember, Jesus said that the flesh profits nothing!

True discipleship must be restored to the body of Christ. Discipleship is accomplished only when individual pastors and leaders embrace the discipline of the Lord and, in turn, they teach others to observe all that Jesus taught which will facilitate Holy Spirit-led discipline. Once a Christian learns how Jesus disciplines in all of life, then the Holy Spirit can lead and orchestrate harmony between leadership and the saint, avoiding abusive control by false or carnal shepherds dominating the sheep. *"Tend the flock of God that is your charge, not by constraint but willingly, not for shameful gain but eagerly, not as domineering over those in your charge but being examples to the flock."* (1 Peter 5:2,3).

It is for discipline that we are to endure. *"My son, do not despise the Lord's discipline or be weary of his reproof, for the LORD reproves him whom he loves, as a father the son in whom he delights"* (Proverbs 3:11,12).

"The iniquities of the wicked ensnare him, and he is caught in the toils of his sin. He dies for lack of discipline, and because of his great folly he is lost" (Proverbs 5:22,23).

I'M SAVED! I CANNOT LOSE MY SALVATION
Born of God or born of the flesh?

Never been a sinner, I've never sinned,
I've got a friend in Jesus.
So you know that when I die,
It's gonna set me up with the Spirit in the sky.

Goin' on up to the Spirit in the sky,
That's where I'm gonna go, when I die.
When I die and they lay me to rest,
I'm gonna go to the place that's the best.

From Spirit in the Sky
By Norman Greenbaum

<u>The misinterpreted shortcut:</u> *"Jesus took all my sins, past, present and future and forgave them. He died for me and so if I become born again I will have eternal life—guaranteed!*

I am forgiven and He is my righteousness. I belong to him and live under his protection. I cannot lose my salvation, even if I sin or backslide. God's grace is bestowed upon me because I am a friend of Jesus."

During the early seventies, a spiritual stir known as the Jesus People Movement drew many out of the hippie-flower children movement into Christianity. Rock bands of this era depicted this movement in many songs. The song quoted above came to me while praying over this section. The lyrics portray a false concept of salvation and eternal security many Christians embrace today.

Thousands responded to the Jesus movement. Evangelical and Pentecostal denominations developed crusades and outreach ministries over the last 35 years to bring in more converts. Church growth campaigns presented the "get saved" message, turning it into the "become born again," message with evangelistic campaigns creating a variety of "instant salvation" and "guaranteed eternal security" promises.

Many converts struggled, as they fought temptations and lived in fear of backsliding, even fearing the loss of salvation. To bolster the faith of these struggling Christians, and not knowing the root problem, the false doctrine of eternal security spewed from pulpits everywhere. God's grace was preached and soothed many, but in reality, the end result was that a false doctrine of *cheap grace* became the holding power from the pulpit to keep attendance up.

Dietrich Bonhoeffer, one of the Christians martyred by Hitler, wrote, *The Cost of Discipleship*. He saw the carnal, weak, and lukewarm condition of the church of Germany leading up to the Nazi takeover. In this volume he penned the term *"cheap grace."*

"Cheap grace is the preaching of forgiveness without requiring repentance, baptism without church discipline, communion without confession, absolution without personal confession. Cheap grace is grace without discipleship, grace without the cross, grace without Jesus Christ, living and incarnate.

Costly grace is the treasure hidden in the field; for the sake of it a man will gladly go and sell all that he has. It is the pearl of great price to buy which the merchant will sell all his goods. It is the kingly rule of Christ, for whose sake a man will pluck out the eye which causes him to stumble, it is the call of Jesus Christ at which the disciple leaves his nets and follows him." (Cost of Discipleship, Bonhoeffer, Collier Books NY, 1961. page 47).

Indeed, the church of Germany was spewed out of Christ's mouth—as we see that whole nation, including Christians, thrown into terrible judgment and destruction.

Like the majority of Christians in Germany who were lukewarm, over these many years, millions of Christians in America have now bought the lie that they are right with God and have eternal security even though they give into temptation, walk in carnal desires and practice secret sins. These people believe they are born of God! But what does Scripture say about this kind of practice?

"Beloved, we are God's children now; it does not yet appear what we shall be, but we know that when he appears we shall be like him, for we shall see him as he is. And every one who thus hopes in him purifies himself as he is pure. Everyone who commits sin is guilty of lawlessness; sin is lawlessness. You know that he appeared to take away sins, and in him there is no sin. No one who abides in him sins; no one who sins has either seen him or known him. Little children, let no one deceive you. He who does right is righteous, as he is righteous. He who commits sin is of the devil; for the devil has sinned from the beginning. The reason the Son of God appeared was to destroy the works of the devil. No one born of God commits sin; for God's nature abides in him, and he cannot sin because he is born of God. By this it may be seen who are the children of God, and who are the children of the devil: whoever does not do right is not of God, nor he who does not love his brother" (1 John 3:2-10).

Many believe they are called of God but have not purified themselves and become fully born of God. These misled saints struggle with past defilements, doubled-mindedness (a twice-souled condition) and deep roots of bitterness. They have not grown up into Christ, become pure and walked as Christ walked.

This false doctrine keeps many Christians in a frustrating limbo, vacillating back and forth: one moment full of peace and joy; the next in terrible anguish from tempting desires, obsessive carnal behaviors or terrible fears of falling away from God.

Christians are not instructed in the process of sanctification that purifies the soul and heals a double-minded condition. They do not understand the work of the cross in the believer's life, the cleansing work of the Holy Spirit, nor how Satan works through hidden desires. Millions of struggling Christians are ignorant of God's true grace, forgiveness, and discipline in the battle to become transformed on the inside.

Scripture informs us that we can come to a place of rest and peace, having power over our old sin nature. The old carnal personalities must become crucified—a painful process where the discipline of the Lord exposes ill motives, bad thoughts, and intentions of the heart. Harder to understand are the Lord's many attempts to draw to our attention to "a twice a soul" condition that so many struggle with.

Through this process we are under an umbrella of grace. John wrote, *"My little children, I am writing this to you so that you may not sin; but if any one does sin, we have an advocate with the Father, Jesus Christ the righteous; and he is the expiation for our sins, and not for ours only but also for the sins of the whole world. And by this we may be sure that we know him, if we keep his commandments. He who says "I know him" but disobeys his commandments is a liar, and the truth is not in him; but whoever keeps his word, in him truly love for God is perfected. By this we may be sure that we are in him: he who says he abides in him ought to walk in the same way in which he walked"* (1 John 2:1-6).

The issue for the struggling Christian in the process of sanctification is that we will stumble and perhaps even become overtaken by sin, but when we confess our sins and carnal self-centered behavior, we have an advocate, our High Priest Jesus Christ who intercedes on our behalf.

Most Christians, when overtaken by a trespass, condemn themselves and cover up the behavior. Some pretend it never happened and go to church acting like a saint. *"If we confess our sins, he is faithful and just, and will forgive our sins and cleanse us from all unrighteousness. If we say we have not sinned, we make him a liar, and his word is not in us"* (1 John 1:9,10).

Paul wrote, *"Brethren, if a man is overtaken in any trespass, you who are spiritual should restore him in a spirit of gentleness. Look to yourself, lest you too be tempted. Bear one another's burdens, and so fulfill the law of Christ. For if anyone thinks he is something, when he is nothing, he deceives himself. But let each one test his own work,* and then his reason to boast will be in himself alone and not in his neighbor. For each man will have to bear his own load" (Galatians 6:1-5).

Again, we are under an umbrella of grace, though we may struggle, fall and even kick against God's discipline—if in this battle we humble ourselves and confess our sins He is faithful and just to forgive our sins and wash us from all unrighteousness. When we cover it up and deliberately sin and deceive, then we grieve the Holy Spirit, harden our hearts, run the risk of falling away from God and become subject to judgment and possible loss of our salvation.

"Be angry but do not sin; do not let the sun go down on your anger, and give no opportunity to the devil. Let the thief no longer steal, but rather let him labor, doing honest work with his hands, so that he may be able to give to those in need. Let no evil talk come out of your mouths, but only such as is good for edifying, as fits the occasion, that it may impart grace to those who hear. And do not grieve the Holy Spirit of God, in whom you were sealed for the day of redemption. Let all bitterness and wrath and anger and clamor and slander be put away from you, with all malice, and be kind to one another, tenderhearted, forgiving one another, as God in Christ forgave you. Therefore be imitators of God, as beloved children. And walk in love, as Christ loved us and gave himself up for us, a fragrant offering and sacrifice to God. But fornication and all impurity or covetousness must not even be named among you, as is fitting among saints. Let there be no filthiness, nor silly talk, nor levity, which are not fitting; but instead let there be thanksgiving. Be sure of this, that no fornicator or impure man, or one who is covetous (that is, an idolater), has any inheritance in the kingdom of Christ and of God. Let no one deceive you with empty words, for it is because of these things that the wrath of God comes upon the sons of disobedience. Therefore do not associate with them, for once you were darkness, but now you are light in the Lord; walk as children of light (for the fruit of light is found in all that is good and right and true), and try to learn what is pleasing to the Lord. Take no part in the unfruitful works of darkness, but instead expose them. For it is a shame even to speak of the things that they do in secret; but when anything is exposed by the light it becomes visible, for anything that becomes visible is light. Therefore it is said, 'Awake, O sleeper, and arise from the dead, and Christ shall give you light.' Look carefully then how you walk, not as unwise men but as wise, making the most of the time, because the days are evil" (Ephesians 4: 26-5:16).

Some really believe they can sin deliberately and expect to be saved in the day of the Lord. This is a terrible lie. In the book of Hebrews, it clearly warns, "For if we sin deliberately after receiving the knowledge of the truth, there no longer remains a sacrifice for sins, but a fearful prospect of judgment, and a fury of fire which will consume the adversaries. A man who has violated the law of Moses dies without mercy at the testimony of two or three witnesses. How much worse punishment do you think will be deserved by the man who has spurned the Son of God, and profaned the blood of the covenant by which he was sanctified, and outraged the Spirit of grace? For we know him who said, 'Vengeance is mine, I will repay' And again, 'The Lord will judge his people.' It is a fearful thing to fall into the hands of the living God" (Hebrews 10:26-31).

"He who is often reproved, yet stiffens his neck will suddenly be broken beyond healing" (Proverbs 29:1).

"Blessed is the man who fears the LORD always; but he who hardens his heart will fall into calamity" (Proverbs 28:14).

Elsewhere in Hebrews it warns, "Take care, brethren, lest there be in any of you an evil, unbelieving heart, leading you to fall away from the living God. But exhort one another every day, as long as it is called 'today,' that none of you may be hardened by the deceitfulness of sin. For we share in Christ, if only we hold our first confidence firm to the end, while it is said, 'Today, when you hear his voice, do not harden your hearts as in the rebellion'" (Hebrews 3:12-15).

You see there is eternal security for those who are completely born of God. "Jesus answered them, 'I told you, and you do not believe. The works that I do in my Father's name, they bear witness to me; but you do not believe, because you do not belong to my sheep. My sheep hear my voice, and I know them, and they follow me; and I give them eternal life, and they shall never perish, and no one shall snatch them out of my hand. My Father, who has given them to me, is greater than all, and no one is able to snatch them out of the Father's hand. I and the Father are one'" (John 10:25-30).

"And I am sure that he who began a good work in you will bring it to completion at the day of Jesus Christ" (Philippians 1:6).

"Now to him who is able to keep you from falling and to present you without blemish before the presence of his glory with rejoicing, to the only God, our Savior through Jesus Christ our Lord, be glory, majesty, dominion, and authority, before all time and now and for ever. Amen" (Jude 1:25,25).

There is eternal security when the true saint, called of God, obtains the grace of God and grows up into salvation, having Christ formed within. As Paul wrote in Romans, *nothing can separate us from the love of God in Christ*; only our lack of faith and an unbelieving impure heart can lead us to fall away. (Paraphrased from Romans 9:35-39).

Many think they are born again, but really have had an initial spiritual touch of God, gone to church, and then are told lies. The most damning lie is: *"You are now saved, born again, never to lose your salvation."*

Some are born of the flesh and have a spiritual touch from a counterfeit spirit. That is, many respond to carnal religion and are converted to the church, a denomination, a pastor, the wonderful amenities, such as the nursery and daycare-baby-sitting, entertaining services and feel-good sermons. Or, they are converted to the anointed leader who mesmerizes and dispenses spiritual Prozac to the embittered. To be completely born of God one must, *"work out your own salvation with fear and trembling; for God is at work in you, both to will and to work for his good pleasure"* (Philippians 2:13).

An excellent study to consider is Christ's teaching on the word of God as seed falling on different conditions of the human heart. This is the parable of the sower found in Luke 8:1-18.

Other Scriptures follow that reinforce the truth of salvation through a sanctification process leading to eternal security, *"But we are bound to give thanks to God always for you, brethren beloved by the Lord, because God chose you from the beginning to be saved, through sanctification by the Spirit and belief in the truth"* (2 Thessalonians 2:13).

"Do not quench the Spirit, do not despise prophesying, but test everything; hold fast what is good, abstain from every form of evil. May the God of peace himself sanctify you wholly; and may your spirit and soul and body be kept sound and blameless at the coming of our Lord Jesus Christ. He who calls you is faithful, and he will do it" (1 Thessalonians 5:20-24).

"Therefore we must pay the closer attention to what we have heard, lest we drift away from it. For if the message declared by angels was valid and every transgression or disobedience received a just retribution, how shall we escape if we neglect such a great salvation?" (Hebrews 2:1-3).

"So put away all malice and all guile and insincerity and envy and all slander. Like newborn babes, long for the pure spiritual milk, that by it you may grow up to salvation; for you have tasted the kindness of the Lord" (1 Peter 2:1-3).

"I am speaking in human terms, because of your natural limitations. For just as you once yielded your members to impurity and to greater and greater iniquity, so now yield your members to righteousness for sanctification. When you were slaves of sin, you were free in regard to righteousness. But then what return did you get from the things of which you are now ashamed? The end of those things is death. But now that you have been set free from sin and have become slaves of God, the return you get is sanctification and its end, eternal life" (Romans 6:19-22).

Few in leadership teach how to cooperate with the Lord in His sanctification process. Again, many are born of the flesh because they were told about Jesus and salvation, but were not taught on the process of growing up into Christ and obtaining the grace of God and salvation.

"Jesus answered, 'Truly, truly, I say to you, unless one is born of water and the Spirit, he cannot enter the kingdom of God. That which is born of the flesh is flesh, and that which is born of the Spirit is spirit. Do not marvel that I said to you, 'You must be born anew.' The wind blows where it wills, and you hear the sound of it, but you do not know whence it comes or whither it goes; so it is with everyone who is born of the Spirit'" (John 3:5-8).

Those who are born of God become God's elect. God does not take away free will, but one cannot come to God unless He calls them and reveals Himself to them, who have faith. Salvation is a gift from God to those who believe and act on that belief. Many want to be saved but were never called of God. Their motives for salvation are selfish. They walk in an attitude of self-righteousness and; *what can God do for me?* True salvation is of God, not of man. *"No one can come to me unless the Father who sent me draws him; and I will raise him up at the last day. It is written in the prophets, 'And they shall all be taught by God.' Everyone who has heard and learned from the Father comes to me"* (John 6:44,45).

Those, whom God foreknew as to having faith and keeping faith, are called of God. God has predestined these to be conformed to the image of Jesus, our example of a son of God. *"We know that in everything God works for good with those who love him, who are called according to his purpose. For those whom he foreknew he also predestined to be conformed to the image of his Son, in order that he might be the first-born among many brethren. And those whom he predestined he also called; and those whom he called he also justified; and those whom he justified he also glorified. What then shall we say to this? If God is for us, who is against us?"* (Romans 8:28-31).

Those who keep faith are given God's power to grow up into Christ and obtain salvation by the grace of God through faith. Often Jesus said to those healed, *your faith made you well.*

Peter wrote, *"Blessed be the God and Father of our Lord Jesus Christ! By his great mercy we have been born anew to a living hope through the resurrection of Jesus Christ from the dead, and to an inheritance which is imperishable, undefiled, and unfading, kept in heaven for you, who by God's power are guarded through faith for a salvation ready to be revealed in the last time. In this you rejoice, though now for a little while you may have to suffer various trials, so that the genuineness of your faith, more precious than gold which though perishable is tested by fire, may redound to praise and glory and honor at the revelation of Jesus Christ. Without having seen him you love him; though you do not now see him you believe in him and rejoice with unutterable and exalted joy. As the outcome of your faith you obtain the salvation of your souls"* (1 Peter 1:3-9).

Again, God gives power to those born of Him to become children of God.

"He came to his own home, and his own people received him not. But to all who received him, who believed in his name, he gave power to become children of God; who were born, not of blood nor of the will of the flesh nor of the will of man, but of God" (John 1:11-13).

Just as many religious people in Christ's day, who came to God through the Temple system, were corrupted, so many Christians today believe they are born again, that is, born of God—but are born of the flesh by the work of carnal Christianity.

It is these carnal Christians *in name only* that attack struggling Christians, who have true faith, yet are misled concerning how to grow up into salvation.

"But the son of the slave was born according to the flesh, the son of the free woman through promise. Now this is an allegory: these women are two covenants. One is from Mount Sinai, bearing children for slavery; she is Hagar. Now Hagar is Mount Sinai in Arabia; she corresponds to the present Jerusalem, for she is in slavery with her children. But the Jerusalem above is free, and she is our mother. For it is written, 'Rejoice, O barren one who does not bear; break forth and shout, you who are not in travail; for the children of the desolate one are many more than the children of her that is married.' Now we, brethren, like Isaac, are children of promise. But as at that time he who was born according to the flesh persecuted him who was born according to the Spirit, so it is now" (Galatians 4:23-29).

Just as Satan tried to kill baby Jesus, and later kill Jesus before His time; and just as Satan tried to stamp out the first church—Satan continues these attempts to destroy those who have true faith, before they become fully born of God.

Many who have faith hear the word of God, are conceived by God through the hearing of the word of God and the Holy Spirit's call but are aborted or become stillborn—dead on delivery through a lukewarm-carnal church that preaches shortcuts and false doctrine. *"My people are destroyed for lack of knowledge; because you have rejected knowledge, I reject you from being a priest to me. And since you have forgotten the law of your God, I also will forget your children"* (Hosea 4:6). Many struggle with sin nature, not understanding how God leads, cleanses and heals their defiled-wounded spirit and restores wholeness to their 'two-souled' inner being.

Another troubling issue is the lack of understanding of the doctrine of predestination and God's election. It is God's will that no one perish, but many believe that one is already predestined to either eternal life or eternal death, thus there is nothing one can do to change either destiny.

This is part of the false security many walk in today. If I am predestined to salvation, I can't lose my salvation. In a sense, those born of God cannot be taken out of God's safety and protection, unless they willingly leave it. On the other hand, those with an overly sensitive conscience and low self-esteem can feel: *"Why bother trying, I must be the one predestined for eternal death."*

As long as we are humbling ourselves and embracing the work of the cross and relying on the Spirit of God and Christ to purify our hearts, minds and spirits—then we are under God's grace until we obtain total rest in the Lord. We learn to be obedient from the heart resulting in our hearts and minds becoming conformed to Christ-like character. Indeed, we obtain the grace of God where we are ever humble before Him, entrusting our souls to our faithful Creator. This is our eternal security—we have ceased from our labors as it says in Hebrews. *"So then, there remains a sabbath rest for the people of God; for whoever enters God's rest* also ceases from his labors as God did from his. Let us therefore strive to enter that rest, that no one fall by the same sort of disobedience. For the word of God is living and active, sharper than any two-edged sword, piercing to the division of soul and spirit, of joints and marrow, and discerning the thoughts and intentions of the heart. And before him no creature is hidden, but all are open and laid bare to the eyes of him with whom we have to do"* (Hebrews 4:9-13).

Until we enter the rest of God, we run the risk of becoming disobedient and fall from grace and lose our eternal security.

We can become disobedient with deliberate sin—openly or secretly. We can become disobedient by relying on our method of worship and religious Christian work for appearance sake.

Many rely on carnal religious works as an assurance of salvation, thus they have left God or fallen from the grace of God, which can lead to the loss of salvation. The Scripture says that they started out in the Spirit but ended in the flesh by falling back into the religion and adherence to the law. This will eventually nullify the grace of God completely. (See Galatians 2:17- 3:3). In this passage Paul asks the Christians at Galatia, *"O foolish Galatians! Who has bewitched you, before whose eyes Jesus Christ was publicly portrayed as crucified?"* (Galatians 3:1). Yes, these false doctrines bewitch many Christians.

Jesus warned that many would stand before Him as Christians and be rejected. These believed they had eternal security based on the law, good works and outer appearances that create an inner self-righteous stance. These have not worked-out their salvation in the fear of God, where Christ becomes all and in all, whom God made to be our righteousness, wisdom, sanctification and redemption. (See 1 Corinthians 1:28-31).

Jesus is our example, for, *"In the days of his flesh, Jesus offered up prayers and supplications, with loud cries and tears, to him who was able to save him from death, and he was heard for his godly fear. Although he was a Son, he learned obedience through what he suffered; and being made perfect he became the source of eternal salvation to all who obey him, being designated by God a high priest after the order of Melchizedek"* (Hebrews 5:7-10). That is the problem with most Christians. They refuse to submit to the discipline of the Lord that roots out inner issues of heart, which brings to death the old carnal self. Few understand His discipline because few had godly fathers who disciplined them lovingly but firmly as children.

Concerning fathers—scripture states, *"For they disciplined us for a short time at their pleasure, but he disciplines us for our good, that we may share his holiness. For the moment all discipline seems painful rather than pleasant; later it yields the peaceful fruit of righteousness to those who have been trained by it. Therefore lift your drooping hands and strengthen your weak knees, and make straight paths for your feet, so that what is lame may not be put out of joint but rather be healed. Strive for peace with all men, and for the holiness without which no one will see the Lord. See to it that no one fail to obtain the grace of God; that no "root of bitterness" spring up and cause trouble, and by it the many become defiled; that no one be immoral or irreligious like Esau, who sold his birthright for a single meal. For you know that afterward, when he desired to inherit the blessing, he was rejected, for he found no chance to repent, though he sought it with tears"* (Hebrews 12:10-17).

So, those who have faith are predestined to be conformed to the image of Christ. Those who throw away their faith are predestined for wrath, by choice. God's election stands and the free will of each person stands. In God's sovereign foreknowledge He preordained those who willingly chose Him, after God revealed Himself to them to have salvation. Those who willfully rejected faith in Christ are preordained to destruction.

God knows already who will believe and who will reject His grace, but God does not take away our free will in the matter. So no one can say truthfully to God: *"Why have you made me in such a way as to reject the plan of salvation?"*

We cannot choose God without His Spirit calling us, and yet Jesus said; *"Many are called but few are chosen"* (See Matthew 22:1-14). Those truly born of God will grow up into salvation—thus God works with those who have faith, but never takes away the free will of anyone. So those who have faith must work out their issues, grow in Christ and obtain the grace of God.

Paul wrote, *"Therefore, my beloved, as you have always obeyed, so now, not only as in my presence but much more in my absence, work out your own salvation with fear and trembling; for God is at work in you, both to will and to work for his good pleasure"* (Philippians 2:12,13).

Many run to an altar call and ask Jesus to be their Lord and Savior, only to fall back into a life of sin, just as Jesus explained in the parable of the sower. Christians are told that even though they may relapse and backslide they are born again and cannot lose their salvation. This is heresy!

God has not predestined some to have faith and others to reject His grace. God knows who has faith and He knows who has given up their faith, as Esau did, which occurred before Esau was even born. (See Romans 9:1-24).

Salvation is God's gift, to those who have faith. Some had faith but gave it up or made shipwreck of their faith. These are destined for the wrath of God. Again, it is by choice.

In God's amazing plan, God knows already who will and who won't choose Him. He works all things to the good for those who will respond in faith when God reveals himself. As for those who won't choose Him, or, if you will, those who are bent on evil, God will use these people as object lessons for those who will.

Often the religious Christian counts on their religion to be their surety of eternal salvation. These are those that the Scripture speaks of as being born of the flesh.

Paul wrote of this, *"This means that it is not the children of the flesh who are the children of God, but the children of the promise are reckoned as descendants. For this is what the promise said, 'About this time I will return and Sarah shall have a son.' And not only so, but also when Rebecca had conceived children by one man, our forefather Isaac, though they were not yet born and had done nothing either good or bad, in order that God's purpose of election might continue, not because of works but because of his call, she was told, 'The elder will serve the younger.' As it is written, 'Jacob I loved, but Esau I hated.' What shall we say then? Is there injustice on God's part? By no means! For he says to Moses, 'I will have mercy on whom I have mercy, and I will have compassion on whom I have compassion.' So it depends not upon man's will or exertion, but upon God's mercy. For the scripture says to Pharaoh, 'I have raised you up for the very purpose of showing my power in you, so that my name may be proclaimed in all the earth.' So then he has mercy upon whomever he wills, and he hardens the heart of whomever he wills. You will say to me then, "Why does he still find fault? For who can resist his will?' But who are you, a man, to answer back to God? Will what is molded say to its molder, 'Why have you made me thus?' Has the potter no right over the clay, to make out of the same lump one vessel for beauty and another for menial use? What if God, desiring to show his wrath and to make known his power, has endured with much patience the vessels of wrath made for destruction, in order to make known the riches of his glory for the vessels of mercy, which he has prepared beforehand for glory, even us whom he has called, not from the Jews only but also from the Gentiles? As indeed he says in Hosea, 'Those who were not my people I will call 'my people,' and her who was not beloved I will call 'my beloved.' And in the very place where it was said to them, 'You are not my people,' they will be called 'sons of the living God'"* (Romans 9:8-26).

So this is still the problem with those who become religious and walk in false security—they exert themselves and try to religiously grasp eternity and grasp the kingdom of God. Their faith ends up in works of the flesh, or they put faith in their initial belief in God and expect a reward. Self-righteousness leads to hypocrisy that is just as deadly as living in open rebellion and sin.

Others struggle with terrible temptations and sin. They are told they can succeed regardless of sinning. This is Satan's lie to catch those who have faith in a trap, where their faith becomes shipwrecked.

Jesus warned that the end-of-the-age deception by Satan would be so pervasive, subtle and tempting that even God's elect would almost fall for it. If he can deceive God's elect—then maybe he can stand before God and say the plan of salvation by grace through faith does not work.

We know different, but to each of us, we must grow up into God's election, being sanctified or set apart, cleansed and walking as Christ walked. When we obtain God's grace we indeed have eternal security and no plan of Satan can take us out of God's hand!

JOHN THE BAPTIST FAITH
Fighting a losing battle in self-power

"From the days of John the Baptist until now the kingdom of heaven has suffered violence, and men of violence take it by force. For all the prophets and the law prophesied until John; and if you are willing to accept it, he is Elijah who is to come. He who has ears to hear, let him hear" (Matthew 11:12-15).

The misinterpreted shortcut: *"Christ has done the work on the cross. We must enter into the kingdom of heaven with all the faith that we can muster. We must subdue our bodies and fight our sin nature from a position of victory, since Christ has already won it. We must fight the devil, the world and the flesh with a militant, forceful even violent faith."*

Many sincere Christians are in a spiritual limbo, having begun their walk with God in a new covenant faith in Christ, only to be taught to walk with God in a mix of the old and the new covenant faith. Some of the aforementioned shortcuts set up this Christian phenomenon, which I believe is best described as a *John-the-Baptist-faith*. These have not allowed the cross to bring to death their self-power in fighting sin.

I chose *John-the-Baptist-faith* to help clarify the subtle and deceiving issues of mixing the faith of two divine dispensations: the former revealed plan of God found in the Old Testament (Covenant) that is replaced by the New, which is revealed in Christ and the word of God found in the New Testament.

To help us see the carnal and troubling aspects of this Old and New Covenant mix of faith, we must understand John the Baptist's ministry. John was a prophet of God with a specific mission and message. In Malachi we get insight as to what this message and mission was. *"Behold, I send my messenger to prepare the way before me, and the Lord whom you seek will suddenly come to his temple; the messenger of the covenant in whom you delight, behold, he is coming, says the LORD of hosts But who can endure the day of his coming, and who can stand when he appears?... Behold, I will send you Elijah the prophet before the great and terrible day of the LORD comes. And he will turn the hearts of fathers to their children and the hearts of children to their fathers, lest I come and smite the land with a curse"* (Malachi 3:1,2 - 4:5,6).

John's message was to stir God's people (Israel) from their deceived, wayward and backslidden state. This was done at an appointed time in history, when God chose to reveal the way of salvation to the whole world, for the Jew and the Gentiles.

John the Baptist was the foretold messenger, who would call God's people back to the faith of the old covenant. In the old covenant the true prophets were raised up by God to correct and restore the constant waywardness of God's people. Somehow, God's people could never keep God's laws from the heart. As it says; *"They always go astray in their hearts; they have not known my ways."*

The first dispensation was the written law of God, or God's divine principles or standards for living *under* God. This written code delivered by Moses was God's major step in progressively revealing Himself to His lost creation.

Revealing His law showed God's people how to attempt to live in righteousness *under* God's approval and protection. Also, in revealing the law of God, it demonstrates that man's nature did not have the ability to maintain that righteous standard, for we see in history how Israel failed time and again.

So Israel lived *under* God's care and protection, where they learned of Him constantly, but never attained a peaceful rest with God. The result of the old covenant of written codes was to show God's people the truth about the sin nature, that the sin nature has a law or unchangeable principle of its own, whereby adherence to the written law of God actually makes things worse, and brings death, not life. This principle is called the law of sin and death.

The law of God delivered by Moses produced the law of sin and death, exposing man's natural and unchangeable propensity to sin and fall away from God.

But the new dispensation of God's principles is grace and truth, which was not delivered, but rather has come through God's only begotten Son, Christ. This new dispensation has a law or principle quite different from the old, and is called the law of Spirit and life in Christ Jesus.

God's people lived *under* God in the old covenant, whereas under the New, God's people can now *live in* Christ with God. This is facilitated by believing, following, and obeying Christ's teachings, adhering to His example of living, and allowing Christ's Spirit to discipline and transform our attitude of heart to be like His.

The main principle to be followed in the new covenant is living in the Spirit of God and dying to self-power, learning to rely on Him and Christ's work. This process brings us into a direct personal relationship with God, and the dying to self-power is accomplished by the work of the cross in the believer's life.

We can now be trained and disciplined by Christ to live in Christ with God, no longer relying on God's written code and the old covenant system of worship that was empowered by self.

"For the law of the Spirit of life in Christ Jesus has set me free from the law of sin and death. For God has done what the law, weakened by the flesh, could not do: sending his own Son in the likeness of sinful flesh and for sin, he condemned sin in the flesh, in order that the just requirement of the law might be fulfilled in us, who walk not according to the flesh but according to the Spirit. For those who live according to the flesh set their minds on the things of the flesh, but those who live according to the Spirit set their minds on the things of the Spirit. To set the mind on the flesh is death, but to set the mind on the Spirit is life and peace. For the mind that is set on the flesh is hostile to God; it does not submit to God's law, indeed it cannot; and those who are in the flesh cannot please God. But you are not in the flesh, you are in the Spirit, if in fact the Spirit of God dwells in you. Any one who does not have the Spirit of Christ does not belong to him. But if Christ is in you, although your bodies are dead because of sin, your spirits are alive because of righteousness. If the Spirit of him who raised Jesus from the dead dwells in you, he who raised Christ Jesus from the dead will give life to your mortal bodies also through his Spirit which dwells in you. So then, brethren, we are debtors, not to the flesh, to live according to the flesh—for if you live according to the flesh you will die, but if by the Spirit you put to death the deeds of the body you will live" (Romans 8:2-13). (Also see Hebrews 4:3-13 and Hebrews 9:8-15).

John the Baptist walked with God in the old covenant faith, but he also knew this was going to change. So John's *message* was to stir the old covenant faith, but his *mission* was to be that of transitioning from the old covenant to the new covenant, pointing to Christ and his work. John prepared the way for Christ by preaching of the coming Christ and baptizing for the repentance of sins. Thus, John the Baptist had a two-fold ministry for God, to stir God's people to a violent militant old covenant faith and then to have that militant faith die!

John the Baptist's ministry was to restore a remnant of true believers in Israel to God's standard of faith under the old covenant. Most Jews expected Elijah to return, since this prophet of old never saw death. Elijah was used of God to restore true faith in God under the old covenant and was last seen ascending to heaven in a whirlwind. Therefore, the Jews thought Elijah would come again and be associated with the coming Messiah, who would throw off foreign rule and oppression of the Jewish nation. Indeed, they believed in a militant faith in God.

But Christ speaks of John the Baptist as the work of Elijah that was prophesied to come. Many thought that Elijah would actually come again, but instead John the Baptist's message and ministry fulfilled this prophecy. Even Christ's disciples did not expect the prophecy of Elijah to come as John the Baptist. Jesus knew this and said: *"And if you are willing to accept it, he is Elijah who is to come. He who has ears to hear, let him hear"* (Matthew 11:14,15).

John the Baptist knew the Messiah was to come and saw that Jesus was the Christ. He began to hand off his work and ministry to Jesus.

"John also was baptizing at Aenon near Salim, because there was much water there; and people came and were baptized. For John had not yet been put in prison. Now a discussion arose between John's disciples and a Jew over purifying. And they came to John, and said to him, 'Rabbi, he who was with you beyond the Jordan, to whom you bore witness, here he is, baptizing, and all are going to him.' John answered, 'No one can receive anything except what is given him from heaven. You yourselves bear me witness, that I said, I am not the Christ, but I have been sent before him. He who has the bride is the bridegroom; the friend of the bridegroom, who stands and hears him, rejoices greatly at the bridegroom's voice; therefore this joy of mine is now full. He must increase, but I must decrease' He who comes from above is above all; he who is of the earth belongs to the earth, and of the earth he speaks; he who comes from heaven is above all. He bears witness to what he has seen and heard, yet no one receives his testimony; he who receives his testimony sets his seal to this, that God is true. For he whom God has sent utters the words of God, for it is not by measure that he gives the Spirit; the Father loves the Son, and has given all things into his hand. He who believes in the Son has eternal life; he who does not obey the Son shall not see life, but the wrath of God rests upon him'" (John 3:23-36).

John the Baptist's ministry had to end. It was solid faith by way of the old covenant where John subdued his carnal sin nature through extreme effort and constantly fighting temptation, suppressing sins.

He lived in the wilderness, wearing garments of camel hair (rough and prickly to the skin), eating locusts and wild honey. He pounded on his wilderness pulpit calling for repentance, which was to prepare the way for Christ's message and work.

John the Baptist's life and old covenant faith represent the brutal enslavement to a constant war against the old sin nature, which is as far as one can go under the old covenant. As to the old covenant: *"According to this arrangement, gifts and sacrifices are offered which cannot perfect the conscience of the worshiper, but deal only with food and drink and various ablutions, regulations for the body imposed until the time of reformation"* (Hebrews 9:9-10).

God *reformed* the old covenant with the new covenant making the old obsolete. *"In speaking of a new covenant he treats the first as obsolete. And what is becoming obsolete and growing old is ready to vanish away"* (Hebrews 8:13).

John was indeed the greatest of all the prophets and even more. But Christ set the record straight about John's faith: *"Truly, I say to you, among those born of women there has risen no one greater than John the Baptist; yet he who is least in the kingdom of heaven is greater than he."*

In saying this, Christ is preparing God's people for a new and improved faith in Him, not faith toward God by adhering to rules, regulations, and a constant battle against sin through repenting over and over—again and again. This old covenant faith must end and make way for the new! *"For all the prophets and the law prophesied until John"* (Matthew 11:13). With John the Baptist, the prophets of the old covenant faith and the law came to an end! These prophesied of Christ and the coming new covenant; their example and teachings must be understood in the light of the new covenant and Christ. We are to teach the law and the prophets for Christ said: *"Think not that I have come to abolish the law and the prophets; I have come not to abolish them but to fulfil them. For truly, I say to you, till heaven and earth pass away, not an iota, not a dot, will pass from the law until all is accomplished. Whoever then relaxes one of the least of these commandments and teaches men so, shall be called least in the kingdom of heaven; but he who does them and teaches them shall be called great in the kingdom of heaven"* (Mathew 5:17-19).

The Law and the prophets are our schoolmaster leading us to discover how morally destitute we are and how impotent we are in obeying God's commandments. The issue is this: we must be obedient, if not, we suffer severe consequences.

So we are in a no-win situation with God, but when we understand that we can obey God through Christ, learning to let the Holy Spirit and the principle of the cross bring death to our self-effort, we obtain God's grace and become obedient from the heart. Walking in the new covenant faith, we are now able to uphold the law, that is, in Christ by the Spirit of God.

Apart from Christ working in us, with the cross bringing to death our self-power and inward self-righteousness, we cannot please God, let alone keep the law. In fact, the more we try in this manner, the more sin becomes sinful, and eventually sin goes beyond any kind of control or measure.

"For sin, finding opportunity in the commandment, deceived me and by it killed me. So the law is holy, and the commandment is holy and just and good. Did that which is good, then, bring death to me? By no means! It was sin, working death in me through what is good, in order that sin might be shown to be sin, and through the commandment might become sinful beyond measure. We know that the law is spiritual; but I am carnal, sold under sin. I do not understand my own actions. For I do not do what I want, but I do the very thing I hate. Now if I do what I do not want, I agree that the law is good. So then it is no longer I that do it, but sin which dwells within me" (Romans 7:11-17).

The old covenant cannot bring us to freedom. Therefore God allowed John the Baptist to die. Those who believed in the Christ were no longer vacillating as to whether they should follow John the Baptist or Christ.

Jesus explains that John's faith was a militant old covenant faith; *"From the days of John the Baptist until now the kingdom of heaven has suffered violence, and men of violence take it by force."* This militant faith accelerates the law of sin and death for those who begin to have faith in Christ. This was an aspect of John's ministry, *"For this is he who was spoken of by the prophet Isaiah when he said, 'The voice of one crying in the wilderness: Prepare the way of the Lord, make his paths straight'"* (Matthew 3:3).

John's ministry is a transitional work igniting once again the futile fight against the sin nature, pointing to Christ and a new covenant where the believer in God receives power over the sin nature, ending the futile—never ending—fight against sin.

Now those who followed Christ were taught and shown that the law of God could not change the believer's nature, but Christ Himself who is the new covenant, would internalize and fulfill the law, cleansing and changing the believer's conscience and nature. Under the new covenant in Christ, those who believe and obey Christ now have power to become children of God, having power over their sin nature and capable of dying to the works of the flesh.

Unfortunately, many believers today struggle to understand that the Old Testament faith, with its arrangement of worship, adherence to regulations and the law of God, will not change the heart and nature. Try as they may, and often courageously and sometimes violently, they cannot enter into a peaceful rest with God.

There is a mixture of belief in Christ and adherence to the old covenant, which incites the suppression of the sin nature by fighting sin and temptation in a never-ending battle. There is no final victory and there can be no rest.

Again, this is a mix of the new covenant faith and old covenant faith and is often characterized by a militant and courageous faith, but this faith does not allow the true disciple of Christ to enter into the full rest of God. In fact, it is a form of disobedience nullifying the grace of God found in the new covenant.

Those Christians who fail to die to their self-powered efforts in suppressing sin will be considered least in the kingdom of heaven. Many Christians are taught to muster up this kind of *pull-yourself-up-by-the-bootstraps faith*, which works as long as the trials of faith are not too severe, or if the Christian is not double-minded.

A John-the-Baptist type of faith must die. It was the best type of faith the old covenant could facilitate. John the Baptist knew who the Christ was and worked as God's messenger to prepare the way for the Lord, but he also ended the old covenant faith found in the law and the prophets.

John, as all those before him, lived on the old covenant side of the cross, looking forward to the new dispensation of God's revealed plan of salvation, which has power to destroy our sin nature and facilitate eternal life in Christ.

Christians who try to live with Christ but walk in a militant old covenant faith (such as that in which John the Baptist walked, but portrayed that we are to leave when the new covenant came) will struggle and never find the promised life in Christ. These are stuck on John the Baptist's side of the cross.

What do I mean by being stuck on John the Baptist's side of the cross? Simply this; all the prophets, including John the Baptist, looked to the coming of the Savior and the power of the cross that brings to death the power of the sin nature and carnal works of the flesh. These precious saints of the Old Testament had the power of God upon them and they worked for God, yet they still constantly fought and struggled in suppressing and fighting the sin nature.

Christ and the work of the cross will bring to death this effort, and under this new covenant, God opens up the heart exposing its thoughts and intentions and dealing with them. The heart is purified and changed under the new covenant process called sanctification. The new covenant is the Gospel of Christ inclusive of all that He taught, which the Spirit of Christ and the Holy Spirit minister.

All that Jesus did on the cross and how we embrace our own cross, which is meant to bring to death our carnal personalities and motives, will result in the true rest of God where we have Christ working through us for God, not us working for God!

Concerning those of old, including John the Baptist, the following Scripture gives insight: *"These all died in faith, not having received what was promised, but having seen it and greeted it from afar, and having acknowledged that they were strangers and exiles on the earth... And all these, though well attested by their faith, did not receive what was promised, since God had foreseen something better for us, that apart from us they should not be made perfect"* (Hebrews 11:13; 39,40).

John the Baptist came near to Christ, but also was retired by God, not seeing the new covenant working in his own life. Of course, John, Elijah, Moses, Abraham and all the saints before, those whose faith attested to God's forthcoming plan, now see it all, from heaven's grandstands.

Those who teach and practice a mix of old and new covenant faith are actually in disobedience. We are expected to learn of the Old Covenant faith, the law and the prophets, which is part of the whole counsel of God, but we are expected to keep it in proper perspective, not mixing the two and attempting to apply the Old to our current faith walk. The New Testament authors wrote from deep understanding of God and His plan of salvation from the solid foundation of the old covenant as recorded in the Old Testament.

We all know John the Baptist was of God and did God's will. So were the prophets and true servants of the old covenant. Now the new has come. To practice the old way of approaching and working for God is to open up doorways for impure and self-powered faith in God. Taken to the extreme, we can see how Satan has opportunity to counterfeit this type of faith by empowering these carnal efforts with a counterfeit spirit.

Many hear the Gospel of Christ and a new covenant faith is ignited. It takes very little New Testament faith to move mountains: *"The apostles said to the Lord, "Increase our faith!" And the Lord said, "If you had faith as a grain of mustard seed, you could say to this sycamine tree, 'Be rooted up, and be planted in the sea,' and it would obey you"* (Luke 17:5,6). This is faith in Christ who gives us faith to do great things according to God's will.

This is the new covenant faith that comes from God through Christ. The problem is that many take the beginning of this faith and then add to it in their own strength, regressing back to an old covenant faith—trying to move mountains and uproot sycamine trees. This will eventually pervert true faith in Christ into presumptuous self-driven, self-powered faith, that is, faith in one's own faith and righteousness.

Satan attacks the new covenant faith in most believers, getting them to misunderstand John the Baptist's mission and message to activate a militant John-the-Baptist faith. John walked rightly under the old covenant, but his walk is not to be encouraged as an example to live by today.

Many teach that we are to take the kingdom of heaven by force. However, this approach will only lead to failure. God is not advocating a militant John the Baptist faith. It ended when John died. We must believe in Christ and not adhere to how John the Baptist walked in an old covenant faith.

Here is an important passage concerning John the Baptist and the end of the Old Covenant way of faith.

"John also was baptizing at Aenon near Salim, because there was much water there; and people came and were baptized. For John had not yet been put in prison. Now a discussion arose between John's disciples and a Jew over purifying. And they came to John, and said to him, 'Rabbi, he who was with you beyond the Jordan, to whom you bore witness, here he is, baptizing, and all are going to him.' John answered, 'No one can receive anything except what is given him from heaven. You yourselves bear me witness, that I said, I am not the Christ, but I have been sent before him. He who has the bride is the bridegroom; the friend of the bridegroom, who stands and hears him, rejoices greatly at the bridegroom's voice; therefore this joy of mine is now full. He must increase, but I must decrease' He who comes from above is above all; he who is of the earth belongs to the earth, and of the earth he speaks; he who comes from heaven is above all. He bears witness to what he has seen and heard, yet no one receives his testimony; he who receives his testimony sets his seal to this, that God is true. For he whom God has sent utters the words of God, for it is not by measure that he gives the Spirit; the Father loves the Son, and has given all things into his hand. He

who believes in the Son has eternal life; he who does not obey the Son shall not see life, but the wrath of God rests upon him'"* (John 3:23-36).

Christ authors and perfects our faith, bringing death to our sin nature and our attempts to be good in our self-strength. Remember our righteousness is as filthy rags. Our good efforts that the old covenant called upon must die! *"For no human being will be justified in his sight by works of the law, since through the law comes knowledge of sin. But now the righteousness of God has been manifested apart from law, although the law and the prophets bear witness to it, the righteousness of God through faith in Jesus Christ for all who believe. For there is no distinction; since all have sinned and fall short of the glory of God"* (Romans 3:20-23).

God allowed John the Baptist to be martyred. Herod had John beheaded. John the Baptist was not resurrected on the third day. John is among the saints of old in the presence of God!

Christ is the mediator of a new and much better covenant. To mix old covenant faith with the new will eventually corrupt the new faith and lead to disobedience. This is where Christian legalism is spawned and promotes hypocrisy.

Many who persist in the John the Baptist old covenant type of faith will eventually lose their composure in suppressing sins and have sin rise up, to their utter dismay.

Others will continue to struggle and fight the sin nature by the old covenant faith where the new covenant faith they once had will diminish more and more. They will become discouraged and fall into frustration where the "rest in the peace and presence" of God is never obtained. Many Christians will, allegorically speaking, lose their minds (their heads) in this futile attempt to overcome the sin nature trying to follow a John the Baptist walk with God.

A little leaven leavens the whole lump. Having the old covenant mixed with our relationship with Christ will allow Satan to inject carnal teachings to get our faith in Christ decreased and our faith in the old covenant increased. We must have our newly ignited New Testament faith purified through fiery trials that expose impure motives of heart and inner defilements of soul and spirit. This is one aspect of how the new covenant in Christ brings death to the sin nature. *"Count it all joy, my brethren, when you meet various trials, for you know that the testing of your faith produces steadfastness. And let steadfastness have its full effect, that you may be perfect and complete, lacking in nothing"* (James 1:2-4).

Many refuse to see their carnality of faith. Some are double-minded or 'twice-souled'. For these, a sifting by Satan will be required to expose and remove the carnality of their faith.

Peter had this same militant old covenant faith in Christ. But Jesus knew Peter had inner issues of character he refused to accept, and the only way for Peter to see these inner issues was through a severe trial of faith. So Jesus allowed the work of Satan to break Peter's stubborn resistance. Fortunately, Jesus, as the Good Shepherd, warned that Satan desired to sift Peter—all of Peter, and interceded for Peter's true faith.

Peter was in denial of his double-minded nature. Jesus said to Peter, "Simon, Simon, behold, Satan demanded to have *you*, that he might sift *you* like wheat." The use of the word *you* in Greek is plural—that is, *both of you*. In the next verse: "But I have prayed for *you* that your faith may not fail; and when *you* have turned again, strengthen your brethren;" the use of the word *you* in this portion is singular—that is, *one of you*. You see, Peter had an *unfaithful you* hidden and a *faithful you* outwardly leading the way. We know the actual sifting and trial Peter went through, which allowed him to finally see what he had refused to see. Peter still had an old covenant, I-can-do-it faith!

Now we have a little more insight to Peter's encouraging words, *"In this you rejoice, though now for a little while you may have to suffer various trials, so that the genuineness of your faith, more precious than gold which though perishable is tested by fire, may redound to praise and glory and honor at the revelation of Jesus Christ"* (1 Peter 1:6,7).

Many Christians are insecure and "two-souled," and compensate for this condition by mustering up a carnal militant, I-can-do-it faith, putting trust in a self-powered faith, as Peter did.

The shortcut teachings mentioned earlier trap the dear saint in a constant battle of suppressing the carnal nature and its desires, never allowing the work of the cross to bring to death these unseen carnal issues.

Most twice-souled Christians fall into the false teachings that resurrect an old covenant militant faith in which John the Baptist walked. Now we have potential for real trouble, not unlike the trouble Peter had to endure before he saw the hidden issues of his carnal personalities and sin nature.

Mixing the old and new covenant faith, and lacking understanding of how to cooperate with the Holy Spirit in dealing with a hidden carnal personality, gives Satan a right to attack.

Many of us are like Peter, where his "Simon" personality had to die and be changed to a Christ-like nature. When finally exposed, Peter wept bitterly and later went back to fishing. Christ was able to point out Peter's dividedness, how he really loved Christ far less than the things of this life. Peter's love for the world was meshed into the love of ministry, how it brought him recognition from others. This was a major reason Peter opposed Christ's death.

When struggling in this mixed faith, often a religious spirit, or counterfeit spirit impersonating the Lord's voice, will speak in these battles. The battle is against the hidden issues of the carnal, which is yet to be exposed and crucified. Satan does not want the saint to find full rest in the Lord, but rather stay carnal, vulnerable and weakened.

This voice, that counterfeits the Lord, will keep whispering in the saint's ear shortcut teachings, calling the saint to muster up more self-empowered faith. Scriptures taken out of context will be cited over and over by the devil. This will keep the saint in one battle after another, where the outcome is always a stalemate. Sooner or later inner self-power strength will break, creating disillusionment, causing many to fall away from God.

Many are caught up in a John-the-Baptist faith, misunderstanding the passage of Scripture where Jesus pointed out: *"From the days of John the Baptist until now the kingdom of heaven has suffered violence, and men of violence take it by force."* They use this verse as a license to stir up a militant faith.

Jesus was not at all advocating that the men and women drawing near to God should take the kingdom of God by force. That is why He said, "until now," referring to His work on the cross, His teachings, and the new covenant. This new covenant is in Christ where the work of the cross brings to death the militant self-powered faith of the Old Testament and is replaced by the faith that brings us to a rest in God, as the old nature is crucified and replaced by a Christ-like nature.

As Peter, when our practical theology does not allow us to see what we automatically do in the flesh, Jesus will allow Satan to sift. The Lord will do this for our own good, breaking our denial of being 'twice-souled'. The double-minded Christian must receive decisive and firm help in this hour. Like Peter, thousands upon thousands of Christians, including ministers and pastors, suffer this issue.

Unfortunately, many in leadership will feel threatened because this doctrine challenges their misunderstanding of Scripture, carnal faith or quick-fix doctrines. Many in ministry have painted themselves into a corner with doctrines that short-circuit the work of the cross and will cause severe sifting for the twice-souled. Correcting this, after years of preaching and teaching a mixed faith, is not easy to do. I see many denouncing this teaching that exposes the implementation of a John-the-Baptist type of faith. They will attack this sound doctrine for fear of losing their authority that keeps their ministry indispensable in the eyes of the struggling Christian.

Remember, John the Baptist lived under the old covenant and only saw the beginning of Christ's ministry and work. Christ's disciples saw John the Baptist's life, work and death. They finally realized why John the Baptist said, *"He must increase, but I must decrease"* (John 3:30).

Paul, the apostle wrote: *"For I through the law died to the law, that I might live to God. I have been crucified with Christ; it is no longer I who live, but Christ who lives in me; and the life I now live in the flesh I live by faith in the Son of God, who loved me and gave himself for me. I do not nullify the grace of God; for if justification were through the law, then Christ died to no purpose"* (Galatians 2:19-21).

John the Baptist fulfilled his call and purpose under the old covenant. His example of a perfect old covenant faith must end, and the Author and Finisher of our faith must become our Champion. It is faith in Him and His life in us, working His righteousness into us along with His wisdom, His faith, and His leadership, that brings us to the fullness of life with God!

"For the word of the cross is folly to those who are perishing, but to us who are being saved it is the power of God. For it is written, 'I will destroy the wisdom of the wise, and the cleverness of the clever I will thwart.' Where is the wise man? Where is the scribe? Where is the debater of this age? Has not God made foolish the wisdom of the world? For since, in the wisdom of God, the world did not know God through wisdom, it pleased God through the folly of what we preach to save those who believe. For Jews demand signs and Greeks seek wisdom, but we preach Christ crucified, a stumbling block to Jews and folly to Gentiles, but to those who are called, both Jews and Greeks, Christ the power of God and the wisdom of God. For the foolishness of God is wiser than men, and the weakness of God is stronger than men. For consider your call, brethren; not many of you were wise according to worldly standards, not many were powerful, not many were of noble birth; but God chose what is foolish in the world to shame the wise, God chose what is weak in the world to shame the strong, God chose what is low and despised in the world, even things that are not, to bring to nothing things that are, so that no human being might boast in the presence of God. He is the source of your life in Christ Jesus, whom God made our wisdom, our righteousness and sanctification and redemption; therefore, as it is written, 'Let him who boasts, boast of the Lord.'" (1 Corinthians 1:18-31).

To the Jew and now also to the Gentile, the promise of God's salvation from the sin nature, and His grace through a New Testament faith is given to us, leading unto eternal life. It is a gift for all who receive Christ, who is the New Covenant.

"To them God chose to make known how great among the Gentiles are the riches of the glory of this mystery, which is Christ in you, the hope of glory. Him we proclaim, warning every man and teaching every man in all wisdom, that we may present every man mature in Christ. For this I toil, striving with all the energy which he mightily inspires within me. For I want you to know how greatly I strive for you, and for those at Laodicéa, and for all who have not seen my face, that their hearts may be encouraged as they are knit together in love, to have all the riches of assured understanding and the

knowledge of God's mystery, of Christ, in whom are hid all the treasures of wisdom and knowledge" (Colossians 1:27 – 2:3).

Ministry case: The Inverted Camel-Haired Evangelist.

A traveling evangelist contacted our ministry; he wanted to share with us insights he had about ministry and find if we were like-minded in preaching the Gospel. We held conversations with each other a few times over the course of two months.

He had a prison ministry and would visit various fellowships in the area. We saw his sincerity and took him and his family under our wing, trying to give financial and fellowship support.

This couple had been in ministry for years, traveling and staying wherever they could. Often, he would pick up odd jobs to help meet ends financially. Their family consisted of four girls, one boy and one on the way.

We included him and his family on special events and even held a birthday party for two of his daughters. His family was short on just about everything, from clothes to basic furniture. They lived in a one-bedroom mother-in-law house adjoined to the home of a friend who also was trying to help them. The girls slept on the floor and their small son slept with the couple. Both were very grateful for our support and fellowship.

His message was basic, and he preached repentance. Then we began to see a harsh outer judgment come out in some of his preaching, as he looked for problems or issues in the lives of others. He then would exploit these uncovered issues in his exhortations. His messages to the inmates were laced with Scripture taken out of context such as *"there is nothing good in them"* and pound on them that we do not deserve salvation, trying to help them understand their wickedness of nature versus God's grace. I had to correct him on these misinterpretations, such as, *"For I know that nothing good dwells within me, that is, in my flesh. I can will what is right, but I cannot do it."* Explaining that Paul went on to say in Romans that, *"For I delight in the law of God, in my inmost self,"* in an attempt to help him out of this "beat up on sin and the body." We continued our effort to get him to see that this self-righteous rigorous devotion will not stop the indulgences of the flesh. I explained that this is an Old Testament faith and effort. It will put us back under the curse of the Law, trying to fulfill the laws of God in self-strength.

John the Baptist was the last prophet under the Old Testament call. He lived a very demanding and difficult life in the wilderness. He maintained a self-demeaning lifestyle, calling the people away from the comforts of their homes and cities, out into the wilderness as he preached repentance and baptizing for repentance of sins. His attack on immorality and wearing the vestments of the prophets of old, a camel hair coat and leather belt, led many to think of him as Elijah, who was to return and make way for the Messiah of Israel. Some legends say that John's camel hair mantle was worn inside out, purposely making the coarse hair of the camel prickly against his skin and helping subdue the deeds of the body.

Our evangelist brother seemed to live a very similar life. As we became more familiar with him, we saw a pattern where he would come by and fellowship, and somehow, he would leave with something: money, money for gas, extra food, toys for the kids. Our support was a real sacrifice on our ministry and fellowship since we were having our own financial challenges, as well. Nevertheless, we shared from our poverty and were very blessed.

He would often visit other fellowships or other friends, being gone an exorbitant amount of time from his family. We noticed that he did not pay appropriate attention to his children. Even at his daughter's birthday party, his attention had to be diverted to this activity—away from chatting with other adults about the Gospel and ministry.

Finally, he gave a message at our fellowship that was manipulative in nature, and upon seeing these issues, we confronted him and parted fellowship. We saw his self-demeaning lifestyle was part of his approach to ministry to get support as he dragged his wife and children through a difficult wilderness-type traveling ministry. This austere approach to the work of the Gospel was poverty by choice to manipulate others for support.

We had grown fond of the children and his wife. It was difficult not to be involved with them any longer. Holding him accountable and avoiding his abuses might wake him up. Knowing this was the Lord's will, even then we wondered if we had done the right thing.

About two weeks after we broke off fellowship, I had a peculiar dream that I knew was from the Lord. Often the Lord gives us dreams that confirm direction that the Holy Spirit is leading in or warns about people or situations.

In the dream, this evangelist was going around to different men in ministry and pinching them on the arm. The men in the dream did not flinch or take notice, but I saw that this was wrong, so in this dream I confronted his behavior and chased him away from these men.

I woke up and could not figure out exactly what this dream meant, especially the pinching. I knew he would often visit other ministries and churches in our area. I had discerned that he had a spirit of witchcraft that emanated to others with thoughts of giving him money or filling his car up with gas and so forth.

Later, I was explaining this person's issue to one of our members, and saying, "He had a pattern of going around and putting the pinch on people for money."

This was an old saying that my parents had when relatives came around unannounced, asking to borrow money. Often it was just $10 or maybe $50, something to help get them by with buying milk or gas. My parents could never say no but would often complain later about the pressure.

Then the meaning of the dream hit me. God indeed has a sense of humor. This evangelist was going around "putting the pinch on people." He wasn't there for fellowship, in love of God; he was there for money, subtly laying a guilt trip on his *"marks"* to pinch a few bucks for gas or basics for his family. Yes, he marked out people who had a soft heart and made his rounds to raise support, without coming right out and asking.

He followed the teachings of former minister Milt Green, who is now deceased. Green's ministry was a John-the-Baptist-type ministry. Green mixed the old covenant and the new covenant faith, leading to a carnal fight against sin, pounding on sins and casting out demons, but never really preaching the work of the cross that deals with the source of sins, that is, crucifying the works of the flesh and destroying the power of the sin nature.

This John-the-Baptist-faith does not bring a Christian to the fullness of God's grace and into the rest. I see many hardworking, Pentecostal ministries preaching holiness and commending themselves in order to gain support. Like this evangelist, they are working hard, but hardly working in the power and grace of God. This evangelist, like so many, are working hard for God but getting nowhere.

Those who practice this John-the-Baptist-faith will experience increasing struggles with their own sin nature. Satan will demand to sift many, like Peter. Others will lose their mental faculties, as they wear themselves out suppressing the old nature in self-powered faith. Still others will fight a militant moral war against an increasingly Sodom-like society. Many of these misguided Christians will be attacked and some will die prematurely.

Some will just burn out, quit, and fall away. Others will live out their self-imposed wilderness lifestyle and find themselves as least in the kingdom to come. *"Truly, I say to you, among those born of women there has risen no one greater than John the Baptist; yet he who is least in the kingdom of heaven is greater than he"* (Matthew 11:11).

WHEN IN DOUBT—MAGIC OUT
Christian superstitious acts

"And he took a cup, and when he had given thanks he gave it to them, saying, "Drink of it, all of you; for this is my blood of the covenant, which is poured out for many for the forgiveness of sins" (Matthew 26:27,28).

"Is any among you sick? Let him call for the elders of the church, and let them pray over him, anointing him with oil in the name of the Lord; and the prayer of faith will save the sick man, and the Lord will raise him up; and if he has committed sins, he will be forgiven" (James 5:14,15).

"Put on the whole armor of God, that you may be able to stand against the wiles of the devil" (Ephesians 6:11).

The misinterpreted shortcut: *"If I am overwhelmed, attacked by demons, or in some tremendous need, I must remember to pray a special prayer and 'Plead the blood of Christ for protection', or 'Ask that the armor of God be put on me now!' If there is opportunity, I will anoint the house, my car, my family, myself or even my property with oil while I plead the blood of Christ."*

When I was in the Marine Corps electronic repair schools, our tests came from a computer bank of tests. The questions had four possible answers, answer A, B, C or D.

There was a myth among the students. We all knew this myth, as each class passed it on to the next. The myth was to help us during tests, when a question on the test had no choice of A, B, C or D that stood out as the best answer. The myth was, *when in doubt, Charlie out!*

In the military, we used the NATO phonetic alphabet. For the letter A, the phonic was Alpha, B was Bravo, C was Charlie, and D was Delta. Our little myth was easy to remember. The basis for the myth was that the computer arrangement of the correct answer had a tendency to predominately use answer C. Of course, this was not true, but the myth was often used.

This allegory helps show how superstitious many Christians have become in their tests in life. Many operate in the Christian myth of *"when in doubt—magic out."* God's people want to believe in an instant method to remove pain, invoke protection of angels and walk within an invisible force field that keeps the *boogeyman* at bay. Yes, many immature Christians live in fear of the devil. They have all manner of defilements from the past.

Part of the discipline that comes at the hand of God is learning to stand against evil and resist the devil. Through trials and battles with the demonic, we grow in the faith of Christ, having His nature become ours.

Praying magic incantations is not a substitute for the discipline of the Lord. Christ's shed blood is not some magic potion delivered by God for Christians to throw all over spiritually, like a water sprinkling system.

The blood of Christ was given for the forgiveness of sins, not to be applied mysteriously over stressful situations, demonic attacks, and material property. This superstitious act is like the Roman Catholic act of the Eucharist, where the priest, through ceremony and special prayer, invokes the transubstantiation of the blood and body of Christ into wine and wafers. This is a foul doctrine inspired by demons, as is with this false doctrine of pleading of the blood of Christ.

The prayer that magically puts on the full armor of God is another superstitious myth and incantation that does nothing. Oh, Satan loves to play possum and pretend these myths and incantations work. Later he will come and destroy; uprooting these deceived Christians who will be blown away like tumbleweeds in a storm.

We are to *put* on the armor of God, not *pray* it on. Putting on the armor of God is done through the discipline of the Lord. For example, the breastplate of righteousness is part of the armor of God mentioned in Scripture and it means putting on true righteousness from the heart. This requires unbelief, impurity and defilements within the heart come to the light (our awareness) to be dealt with.

Anointing everything with oil for protection is another error. In the Old Testament certain people were anointed with oil symbolizing being set apart for God's purposes. New Testament accounts direct the use of oil to be used to anoint the sick for healing. There is the anointing of the Holy Spirit upon all true believers for understanding, wisdom, and the love of God. Many people think that walking in the gifts of the Holy Spirit makes them special, as someone anointed of God. Remember, God is no respecter of persons. Do not fall for this false doctrine either.

Another ministry case will give more insight to what Satan wants to hide by getting Christians sucked into these magic incantations.

Ministry case: Devils from Outer Space or—Get me the hell out of here!

"A spirit glided past my face; the hair of my flesh stood up. It stood still, but I could not discern its appearance. A form was before my eyes; there was silence, then I heard a voice" (Job 4:15,16).

"For God speaks in one way, and in two, though man does not perceive it. In a dream, in a vision of the night, when deep sleep falls upon men, while they slumber on their beds, then he opens the ears of men, and terrifies them with warnings, that he may turn man aside from his deed, and cut off pride from man; he keeps back his soul from the Pit, his life from perishing by the sword. 'Man is also chastened with pain upon his bed, and with continual strife in his bones; so that his life loathes bread, and his appetite dainty food. His flesh is so wasted away that it cannot be seen; and his bones which were not seen stick out. His soul draws near the Pit, and his life to those who bring death'" (Job 33:14-22).

In 1989, shortly after the beginning of our counseling ministry we moved into a bi-level three-bedroom rental. We used the large den and family room for counseling. When we first moved in we went through the house praying and anointing certain parts of the house with oil. We still had not seen the full error of these activities. Indeed, it was lack of faith. As we have learned and grown in faith, a simple prayer of faith with discernment will chase out any demonic activity.

There was a small storage area under the stairs that gave us the chills. We took special concern in prayer binding any demonic haunts left over from previous renters. We have found that bathrooms, special closets and storage spaces became places of abuse and molestation. Demons will often hide in a vacant house waiting to see what new wickedness they might inspire with the new occupants. Familiar spirits can transfer and stick around for a while looking for rest in another human being or setting up shop with another dysfunctional abusive family.

The chills seemed to leave with prayer, and we began to enjoy our new home. About six months passed when a peculiar spiritual attack came upon me. This caused restless sleep and for a couple of nights I stayed up praying in the family room. We had a couch there so when I was tired, I just slept there. This was adjacent to that creepy storage space.

This first night I prayed and fought spiritually, as I sought the Lord for answers to find out the root or source of this oppression. Finally, tired, I laid down on the couch ready to go to sleep. Just then I sensed an evil presence in the room, standing right by my head. I saw a vision of a midget-like being in metal pants. I was indeed fearful but prayed; commanding whatever it was to leave. Eventually it left and I fell asleep. Then a dream came where some kind of evil presence was in the corner of the room. In the dream, I got up, fearful but advancing toward this entity, commanding it to go in the name of Jesus, which I repeated over and over. I knew it was demonic. Finally, I woke up in a fearful cold sweat.

All through the day I contemplated these spiritual encounters. I knew the Lord was trying to give me clues concerning an issue I had that gave this *evil spirit of the night* a right to attack. The fear was not like me, so I knew there was something fearful within my spirit that Satan was attacking. God was allowing this to expose defilements of spirit and soul not yet cleansed.

The next evening, I knew there would be more work in prayer and seeking the Lord for answers. Again, I was restless and finally after much prayer fell asleep. Another vivid dream came.

This time, in the dream I was outside lying on a lawn chair in the patio area. I was reclining on my side looking at the tree line afar off. In the dream it was daylight. Suddenly I saw a small glowing white ball floating above the tree line in the distance. My heart began to race as I watched it grow bigger and suddenly appeared right in front of me, hovering in the air. At this point in the dream, I was again terrified and began commanding this object to leave in Christ's name. I finally woke up but this time I was more encouraged, knowing this was allowed by God to give me more information with which to work.

I began to think about the two dreams and then it hit me. These dreams reminded me of UFO encounters. As a child and through my teen years, my parents exposed me to many sci-fi movies. Some of these movies were very terrifying. An additional aspect in the second dream was that the floating ball was similar to the good witch appearing to Dorothy in the movie, *The Wizard of Oz*. This movie was a family tradition to watch each year on TV, when growing up in the early and mid-sixties.

Now it was obvious. There were defilements lodged in my spirit with the inner belief that extraterrestrial beings (ET) and witches were more powerful than God. I had to repent of this belief, and through the course of repentance some memories laced with fear came up. One was a terrifying movie where two teens were out in a car and they hit an ET. One of its hands was cut off and crawled into the back seat of the car, after the teenage boy had gotten out seeing what they had hit. It crawled up on the back of the front seat and was going to attack the girl. As it was approaching the girl, long needles came out of its fingertips dripping with liquid, ready to stab.

Growing up old sci-fi movies were a big hit during family TV time. This was the source of the chilly creepy feelings I had concerning the storage area under the stairs when we first moved into this house.

There was much relief and increased trust in God after repentance and cleansing. I had to repent of the belief that extraterrestrials and witches are more powerful than God is. Of course, I knew in my conscious mind God is greater, but in my twice-souled condition, my divided spirit believed otherwise.

Years later I shared this account with my mother. She apologized and recalled something very interesting. My mother and father had taken me to see that very movie about seven years before my first recollection, at the age of five. It was showing at an indoor theatre, and my parents took me to see this classic sci-fi film. She recounted that, at that very scene, I stood up and yelled, "Get me the hell out of here", and I started to leave on my own. They of course had to leave with me.

Pleading the blood of Christ over this defilement would never cleanse me of this fearful demonic stronghold in my life. Magically putting on the armor of God to keep the *boogeyman* away would not have worked either. And of course, our anointing the house, especially the storage area under the stairs did nothing to keep the demons from coming back to harass me.

God's faithfulness and His discipline in making me fight and see my issues of heart that Satan helped create in childhood was the only way to grow in faith. This is part of, *"and having done all, to stand. Stand therefore ..."* (See Ephesians 6:11-20).

Many Christians believe that life on other planets exists and that there are other beings from space that can visit the earth.

This is a lie of Satan and may well be what the Antichrist will claim concerning his source of power. Satan can appear as an "angel of light" and may use these lies so that he and demons can physically manifest in the last days, claiming to be extraterrestrial life, thus putting earthlings at ease when exposed to such grotesque beings.

INNER HEALING: NEW AGE OCCULT OR REVIVAL AND SANCTIFICATION?

Another movement that has gained much attention and confusion is the doctrine of inner healing, often called inner transformation, healing of memories, or healing of damaged emotions. Other variations are multiple personalities healing (MPD recovery) or dissociative identity disorder healing (DID recovery).

Again, inner cleansing, which is part of the process of being sanctified by God, will bring inner healing to defiling wounds still residing in the personal spirit. We are to learn how to work with the TRUE Holy Spirit allowing Him to expose, comfort and heal. This indeed is a teaching in the New Testament. *"Since we have these promises, beloved, let us cleanse ourselves from every defilement of body and spirit, and make holiness perfect in the fear of God"* (2 Corinthians 7:1).

Of late, many have taught on inner healing. Some of it is very sound. Some of it is carnal and even New Age in its application.

Division has sprung up over this issue within the body of Christ. The blame for division and controversy can be put on those who advocate the doctrine of inner cleansing/healing and those who reject it.

Again, the truth is the doctrine of inner cleansing and healing of the personal spirit has always been taught in Scripture, in both the Old Testament and New Testament. Unfortunately, few on both sides of this issue have truly sought the Word of God in order to see clearly what the Scripture teaches on inner cleansing and how to cooperate with God in His discipline that draws out hidden, forgotten memories, wounds and dividedness of soul and spirit.

Most who oppose or reject altogether the sound doctrine and teachings found in the Word of God on this aspect of sanctification are ignorant, fearful and in some cases blinded by the god of this world due to their self-righteousness and Gospel-hardened hearts.

On the other hand, rejection is partly due to the carnal and even New Age approach many use in promoting inner sanctification or inner cleansing/healing.

Those who teach against inner cleansing/healing are in error as are those who teach that the gifts of the Holy Spirit have stopped. The belief that the office of apostle and prophet has ceased is wrong.

I do understand that the irrational behavior and examples by most Christians involved in the Latter-Rain, Toronto Blessing type movements gives good reason to reject the biblical principle of the gifts of the Holy Spirit, office of apostle and prophet and inner sanctification (inner cleansing/healing). Nevertheless, those who reject truth in the Word of God have no excuse when Christ will judge their error, as well as judge the carnal or counterfeiting of these truths.

I believe the harder judgment will fall upon those who received insight and then allowed these works of the Holy Spirit to become impure and hijacked by the counterfeiting of Satan. Many ministries have taken these truths found in the Word and tampered with them for ill-gain and for a carnal self-kingdom building agenda. Self-promoting ministers of the Gospel have been a plague upon the church for centuries.

You may ask, who am I to be in a position of authority, and speak and write on such controversial issues within the body of Christ? According to men or the institutionalized church standards—I have no recognized authority, none whatsoever, nor do I care to get this type of approval.

But, as to my own inner sanctification and recovery, my relationship with the living true Christ, my study and knowledge of the Word of God, and fruit that bears witness—I have the authority of God's Word and the promises of God in Christ Jesus and the true Holy Spirit as my witness.

I know what I was like before and I know what I am like now. I know the confusing struggle I had due to the hypocrisy perpetrated by the Pentecostal, evangelical and charismatic Christians who either rejected these sound biblical teachings or misused and abused them.

Some inner healing ministries have built a vast network of counselors in an effort to help struggling Christians. Most have not given the wounded, double-minded Christian the full counsel of God. Unfortunately, like the shepherding movement, counselees can let the counselor do their work for them. Many Christian counselors' baby the double-minded or twice-souled, making them dependent on the counselor, not teaching the counselee how to carry their own load, learning to work out their OWN salvation in fear and trembling.

The emphasis should be to teach struggling Christians on how to work with the true Holy Spirit as THE Counselor and Spirit of Truth Who, in His time, will reveal hidden issues and secrets of the heart. Parachurch ministries should focus on teaching the body of Christ how to provide biblical support and accountability for true restoration and growth in Christ.

If you don't agree—then I trust God to show you what you need to do in order to become saved in soul and spirit, and how to help others become whole in Christ, for the great and terrible day of the Lord is coming soon.

Christian theologians and Christians who reject truth often do so because they want to believe they are okay on the inside when they are not! This is how the carnal religious and self-righteous people fight off the conviction of the Holy Spirit. For those who embrace the carnal or counterfeiting of these teachings, likewise, you had better take a good look at how the work of the cross for the believer has been avoided in these inner healing/latter rain movements, causing truth that starts out in the Spirit to end in the flesh with demons running the show.

Satan will soon be allowed to sift many dear saints who have played the fool, jumped on the shortcuts and refused to allow the living Word of God to become active in the division of soul and spirit. Many wounded and double-minded Christians refuse to allow God to expose, change or heal their inner thoughts and intentions of the heart. Many who oppose any challenge to false movements or teachings often, indeed, suffer these very issues.

Many on both sides of this division have become a stumbling block. Our double-minded brothers and sisters who desperately need to have these teachings put before them rightly, flounder in living hell. Their blood will be on the hands of those who tampered with, ignored and even opposed these biblical truths; these will find themselves enemies of the cross of Christ, opposing what God is about to do.

An important foundational Scripture concerning inner cleansing and inner sanctification is: *"For the word of God is living and active, sharper than any two-edged sword, piercing to the division of soul and spirit, of joints and marrow, and discerning the thoughts and intentions of the heart. And before him no creature is hidden, but all are open and laid bare to the eyes of him with whom we have to do"* (Hebrews 4:12,13).

Here the word of God specifically calls for the Christian to be obedient and enter into the rest of God. This simply means that we follow the Holy Spirit's leading in all of life and we work with the written word of God, which is made alive by the Holy Spirit. We learn to deal with our inner hidden issues, having our spirit and soul distinguished or separated. We then know where the source of spiritual strength, insight and direction comes from. Until then our personal spirit is impure and tied to our own soul, which can be influenced by the demonic—especially if we are two-souled. We do not discern what is of God and what might be our own inner motives and thoughts laced with a selfish agenda.

The next work we will publish will have a thorough explanation grounded in Scripture with characteristics of doublemindedness, and how to cooperate with the true Holy Spirit in the process of inner cleansing and sanctification, as well as ministry case examples.

The spirit and soul of a person can be crushed, bruised, defiled, broken, embittered, severely damaged, and divided. Many suffer from brokenness of heart (the heart is the seat of our emotions—thus we can suffer from broken or damaged emotions). The New Testament refers to Christians suffering from damaged emotions and a crushed or shattered spirit as being double-minded (twice-a-soul). As mentioned earlier, Peter was divided; Jesus affirmed this when he told Peter, *Satan desires to have you*, again. The word "you" here is plural, both of you or—two of you.

<u>We can have unbelief and a broken spirit from abuse:</u>
"Moses spoke thus to the people of Israel; but they did not listen to Moses, because of their broken spirit and their cruel bondage" (Exodus 6:9).
"A gentle tongue is a tree of life, but perverseness in it breaks the spirit" (Proverbs 15:4).
<u>Sorrow of heart and continued broken promises can break the spirit:</u>
"A glad heart makes a cheerful countenance, but by sorrow of heart the spirit is broken" (Proverbs 15:13).
<u>A downcast spirit affects the immune system causing sickness and illness:</u>
"A cheerful heart is a good medicine, but a downcast spirit dries up the bones" (Proverbs 17:22).
"A man's spirit will endure sickness; but a broken spirit who can bear?" (Proverbs 18:14).
<u>Caretaking in leadership can cause burnout and inner bitterness:</u>

"They angered him at the waters of Meribah, and it went ill with Moses on their account; for they made his spirit bitter, and he spoke words that were rash" (Psalm 106:32,33).

"Every one utters lies to his neighbor; with flattering lips and a double heart they speak" (Psalm 12:2).

<u>We can suffer from damaged emotions:</u>

"I have passed out of mind like one who is dead; I have become like a broken vessel" (Psalm 31:12).

"For that person must not suppose that a double-minded man, unstable in all his ways, will receive anything from the Lord" (James 1:7). The Greek word for double-minded literally means 'twice souled' where the soul includes mind, spirit of the mind, heart and the personal spirit.

My soul melts away for sorrow; strengthen me according to thy word!" (Psalm 119:28).

"Oil and perfume make the heart glad, but the soul is torn by trouble" (Proverbs 27:9).

The following verses give direction on dealing with inner issues, damaged emotions, broken spirit or double mindedness.

<u>God desires that we walk in truth within the inward being and with wisdom in the secret heart:</u>

"Behold, thou desirest truth in the inward being; therefore teach me wisdom in my secret heart" (Psalm 51:6).

"Who can search out our crimes? We have thought out a cunningly conceived plot. For the inward mind and heart of a man are deep!" (Psalm 64:6).

"The purpose in a man's mind is like deep water, but a man of understanding will draw it out" (Proverbs 20:5).

"The heart is deceitful above all things, and desperately corrupt; who can understand it? 'I the LORD search the mind and try the heart, to give to every man according to his ways, according to the fruit of his doings" (Jeremiah 17:9,10).

"And Simeon blessed them and said to Mary his mother, "Behold, this child is set for the fall and rising of many in Israel, and for a sign that is spoken against (and a sword will pierce through your own soul also), that thoughts out of many hearts may be revealed" (Luke 2:35,25).

"All the ways of a man are pure in his own eyes, but the LORD weighs the spirit" (Proverbs 16:2).

<u>We must allow God to cleanse and purify our hearts, sometimes through chastisement and fiery trials:</u>

"Create in me a clean heart, O God, and put a new and right spirit within me. Cast me not away from thy presence, and take not thy Holy Spirit from me. Restore to me the joy of thy salvation, and uphold me with a willing spirit" (Psalm 51:10-12).

"Since we have these promises, beloved, let us cleanse ourselves from every defilement of body and spirit, and make holiness perfect in the fear of God" (2 Corinthians 7:1).

"Submit yourselves therefore to God. Resist the devil and he will flee from you. Draw near to God and he will draw near to you. Cleanse your hands, you sinners, and purify your hearts, you men of double mind. Be wretched and mourn and weep. Let your laughter be turned to mourning and your joy to dejection. Humble yourselves before the Lord and he will exalt you" (James 4:7-8). The Greek word for double-minded literally means 'two souled', or 'twice a soul' where the soul includes mind, spirit of the mind, heart and the personal spirit.

"Beloved, do not be surprised at the fiery ordeal which comes upon you to prove you, as though something strange were happening to you" (1 Peter 4:12).

"Why are you cast down, O my soul, and why are you disquieted within me? Hope in God; for I shall again praise him, my help and my God" (Psalm 42:11).

"When my soul was embittered, when I was pricked in heart" (Psalm 73:21).

"Blows that wound cleanse away evil; strokes make clean the innermost parts" (Proverbs 20:30).

"See to it that no one fail to obtain the grace of God; that no "root of bitterness" spring up and cause trouble, and by it the many become defiled; that no one be immoral or irreligious like Esau, who sold his birthright for a single meal" (Hebrews 12:15,16).

"The sacrifice acceptable to God is a broken spirit; a broken and contrite heart, O God, thou wilt not despise" (Psalm 51:17).

"Take care, brethren, lest there be in any of you an evil, unbelieving heart, leading you to fall away from the living God. But exhort one another every day, as long as it is called "today," that none of you may be hardened by the deceitfulness of sin" (Hebrews 3:12,13).

<u>We must be transformed by the renewing of the mind and the spirit of the mind (unconscious mind):</u>

"Do not be conformed to this world but be transformed by the renewal of your mind, that you may prove what is the will of God, what is good and acceptable and perfect" (Romans 12:2).

"Put off your old nature which belongs to your former manner of life and is corrupt through deceitful lusts, and be renewed in the spirit of your minds, and put on the new nature, created after the likeness of God in true righteousness and holiness" (Ephesians 4:22-24).

<u>We must search our spirit and past memories during times of trouble, oppression and trial, looking for defilements and inner issues to find wrong motives of the heart:</u>

"For the word of God is living and active, sharper than any two-edged sword, piercing to the division of soul and spirit, of joints and marrow, and discerning the thoughts and intentions of the heart. And before him no creature is hidden, but all are open and laid bare to the eyes of him with whom we have to do" (Hebrews 4:12,13).

"But if all prophesy, and an unbeliever or outsider enters, he is convicted by all, he is called to account by all, the secrets of his heart are disclosed; and so, falling on his face, he will worship God and declare that God is really among you" (1 Corinthians 14:24,25).

"To the choirmaster: according to Jeduthun. A Psalm of Asaph. I cry aloud to God, aloud to God, that he may hear me. In the day of my trouble I seek the Lord; in the night my hand is stretched out without wearying; my soul refuses to be comforted. I think of God, and I moan; I meditate, and my spirit faints. Selah Thou dost hold my eyelids from closing; I am so troubled that I cannot speak. I consider the days of old, I remember the years long ago. I commune with my heart in the night; I meditate and search my spirit" (Psalm 77:1-6).

"The spirit of man is the lamp of the LORD, searching all his innermost parts" (Proverbs 20:27).

"For what person knows a man's thoughts except the spirit of the man which is in him? So also no one comprehends the thoughts of God except the Spirit of God" (1 Corinthians 2:11).

<u>God heals and binds the brokenhearted, crushed in spirit and double-minded (twice-a-soul):</u>

"The LORD is near to the brokenhearted, and saves the crushed in spirit" (Psalm 34:18).

"For thus says the high and lofty One who inhabits eternity, whose name is Holy: "I dwell in the high and holy place, and also with him who is of a contrite and humble spirit, to revive the spirit of the humble, and to revive the heart of the contrite" (Isaiah 57:15).

"The Spirit of the Lord GOD is upon me, because the LORD has anointed me to bring good tidings to the afflicted; he has sent me to bind up the brokenhearted, to proclaim liberty to the captives, and the opening of the prison to those who are bound; to proclaim the year of the Lord's favor, and the day of vengeance of our God; to comfort all who mourn; to grant to those who mourn in Zion—to give them a garland instead of ashes, the oil of gladness instead of mourning, the mantle of praise instead of a faint spirit; that they may be called oaks of righteousness, the planting of the LORD, that he may be glorified" (Isaiah 61:1-3).

"That according to the riches of his glory he may grant you to be strengthened with might through his Spirit in the inner man" (Ephesians 3:16).

"May the God of peace himself sanctify you wholly; and may your spirit and soul and body be kept sound and blameless at the coming of our Lord Jesus Christ" (1 Thessalonians 5:23).

"[H]e restores my soul. He leads me in paths of righteousness for his name's sake" (Psalm 23:3).

"For I will satisfy the weary soul, and every languishing soul I will replenish" (Jeremiah 31:25).

"So we do not lose heart. Though our outer nature is wasting away, our inner nature is being renewed every day" (2 Corinthians 4:16).

True leadership in the body of Christ must equip themselves with knowledge on how to minister in the whole counsel of God and learn how to lead, train and facilitate inner cleansing as part of true sanctification for those under their tutelage or leadership.

CHRISTIAN COUNSELING, DISCIPLESHIP OR PSYCHOANALYSIS-ISM

"If there be for him an angel, a mediator, one of the thousand, to declare to man what is right for him; and he is gracious to him, and says, 'Deliver him from going down into the Pit, I have found a ransom; let his flesh become fresh with youth; let him return to the days of his youthful vigor'; then man prays to God, and he accepts him, he comes into his presence with joy. He recounts to men his salvation, and he sings before men, and says: 'I sinned and perverted what was right, and it was not requited to me. He has redeemed my soul from going down into the Pit, and my life shall see the light.' 'Behold, God does all these things, twice, three times, with a man, to bring back his soul from the Pit, that he may see the light of life. Give heed, O Job, listen to me; be silent, and I will speak. If you have anything to say, answer me; speak, for I desire to justify you. If not, listen to me; be silent, and I will teach you wisdom'" (Job 33:23-33).

Psychoanalysis and psychotherapy have become integrated into the American culture. Trying to help the emotionally and mentally disturbed has created a multi-billion-dollar industry. Christians throng to counselors, psychiatrists and therapists paying top dollar to have someone give them inner peace and joy. Most medical insurance policies and government medical assistance have mental health options where some, if not all, diagnosed mental-emotional disorder treatments are covered.

People are going to therapists for any kind of stress. There are psychoanalysts specializing in treating unique anxieties, even to help Democrats deal with Kerry's loss in the 2004 Presidential election.

The number of Christian counselors and Christian psychiatrists has grown dramatically as well. An inordinate number of the so-called born-again, spirit-filled and tongue-speaking Christians seek help for all kinds of instability and anxieties.

As the counseling pastor of a Foursquare church with over 400 members, my work load was exhausting. Christians complained of all manner of temptations, sins and problems. They suffered from many severe dysfunctional and disabling issues where, indeed, James's divinely inspired statement still holds true: *"If any of you lacks wisdom, let him ask God, who gives to all men generously and without reproaching, and it will be given him. But let him ask in faith, with no doubting, for he who doubts is like a wave of the sea that is driven and tossed by the wind. For that person must not suppose that a double-minded man, unstable in all his ways, will receive anything from the Lord"* (James 1:5-8).

Somehow, Christians in our society have believed the lie that Christ cannot heal their emotional and psychological instabilities. Instead, they run to the world looking for help. Unfortunately, they run to and fro because leadership is not much better off, as most in the pulpit hypocritically preach soothing words that bring false peace to the troubled Christian mind.

There are over 250 psychotherapy models with a myriad of psychotherapeutic counseling methods. The number of secular, New Age and Christian counseling organizations continues to increase at a phenomenal rate.

Hundreds of psychology self-help books, both Christian and secular, have been published on inner healing, counseling, and trauma recovery. Terms such as: Multiple Personality Disorder, Dissociation Identity Disorder, Posttraumatic Syndrome—Stress Disorder, bi-polar, schizophrenia, and many more have become common terms in society.

There are over 180 mental health medications such as Prozac, Zoloft, Valium, Thorazine, Paxil, and Haldol.

I toured the Glore Psychiatric Museum in St. Joseph Missouri to see replicas, models and explanations of mental health treatment changes over the last 400 years. One display showed a giant hamster-type exercise wheel where mental patients were locked in to help tire themselves out from hysterical fits (many expired in this contraption). There were weird diabolic restraint methods, lobotomy instruments, and ice bath water treatments. Macabre and torturous would best describe most of the treatments and medical procedures practiced on the so-called mentally ill.

For years those considered mentally ill or emotionally unstable were diagnosed as having a mental disease. Now most instability is seen as disorders stemming from past abuse that caused trauma to the psychological formation of the victim. The abuse could have been physical, sexual, emotional and psychological wounding the spirit and dividing the soul. In the book of James, the writer states that evil and perverse words can set on fire, the cycle of nature or wheel of birth within the soul, and that newly created nature set on fire by hell. (See James 3:6)

Current treatments focus on psychotherapy and the use of medication to help stabilize and manage symptoms. Unfortunately, many of the prescribed medications produce psychotic episodes, suicidal tendencies, and other harmful side effects. Millions, including a multitude of Christians, are medicated for emotional and mental symptoms.

Christian counseling ministries and pastoral counseling are in high demand as struggling Christians seek help in overcoming mental and emotional maladies. Again, many Christians are prescribed anti-depressants and anti-psychotic drugs to help maintain stability.

My caseload became almost overwhelming. Through word-of-mouth my schedule was booked out three months in advance. It appeared that hurting and unstable Christians came out of the woodwork, as seemingly stable Christians came to their appointments describing secret obsessions, strained marriages, nightmares, abuse, hysterical episodes, uncontrollable lust and shameful sins. Their backgrounds and denominational affiliations varied. Even those in ministry heard about this work, came seeking help, plagued with anger, and sexual temptations that often led to secret sin. Some were already under the care of a mental health practitioner and on various medications yet seeking help from the Gospel of Christ.

During these seventeen years of counseling, I saw confusion and grief plaguing many of these Christians seeking help, as one book after another, pro and con, hit Christian bookstores. Inner healing, counseling and Christian psychology became a battleground for Christian authors stating their point of view. These writings and views went from one extreme to the other where inner healing was declared a cure-all move of God, or New Age and occult practice.

Many with whom we worked would hear another point of view and drop out. Some went to Christian clinics for in-patient stays, only to come out more confused. Others were told all is past, there are no hidden issues—it's just lack of faith in chasing off the devil. All this seemed so maddening and futile.

Most look for a shortcut, a painless cure or someone to do the hard work for them. When we shared about the work of the cross, requiring one to work out their own salvation, digging deep and getting at the bitter roots, many quit. They rejected the sound teachings of Christ, Peter, James, and Paul concerning inner sanctification and true discipleship. The discipline of the Lord scares them and these doubt-ridden Christians run to the pillow prophet or a soft gospel peddler that will help them to pretend away their hurt.

As one pastor acquaintance put it, they "shrink wrap" their problems and expect God to magically make their troubles go away. Therefore Prozac and other psychological pain numbing drugs are so popular with Christians.

Exposing hidden issues, roots of bitterness, unforgiveness and double-mindedness or two-souled issues is hard work; and the Holy Spirit, along with the word of God, is the Gospel of Christ's prescription to receive wholeness. This is the true Gospel work of inner sanctification that leads to stability, peace and joy in the Lord. Most who are willing to embrace God's recovery program just need solid teaching, true fellowship and support from sold-out disciples who walk in the true gifts of the Holy Spirit.

We warned those coming for help who were strung out on medications, that the required eventual weaning of medication (under care of their physician) would be necessary. They would need to feel the inner pain that the medication was suppressing. These medications mask the root issues and minimize the symptoms, almost never allowing Christ to bring to the surface that which must be cleansed and healed. Emotional, spiritual, and psychological pains are indicators and clues pointing to the root causes, wounds and other issues. Many took the warnings to heart and chose to not allow Christ to bring to the light the true source or root issues of the heart and spirit, opting to stay medicated and keep the symptomatic pain sedated.

Others chose to courageously but slowly lessen the medications (again, under the care and supervision of a licensed health professional) and get in touch with hidden issues, bitterness and doubled mindedness.

As we work out our own issues and embrace the discipline of the Lord, the work of the cross becomes the instrument of our own death and resurrection concerning the hidden carnal character structures. True cleansing, healing and transformation takes place for those who embrace God's recovery and inner cleansing program.

Our goal in counseling was true discipleship, sharing sound teachings and doctrine that gave each counselee understanding, and allowing them to work with the Holy Spirit on their own. We worked our way out of counseling, handing over the counselee to the Counselor and Spirit of Truth. We would meet with counselees once a week for one-hour sessions and then reinforce Christ's teachings with weekly meetings and fellowship services.

Finally, these twice-souled brothers and sisters began to work with the Holy Spirit as their Counselor and found His comfort and truth was there 24 hours a day—7 days a week.

Every true fellowship should walk in this type of ministry, allowing the true gifts of the Holy Spirit to expose, heal, comfort and regenerate the wounded and divided Christian.

You have read a few of our ministry case examples but there are so many more. I have chosen several to help you grasp how important it is for the sound doctrines of true inner cleansing and inner transformation to be restored to the body of Christ. This has always been in the word of God. Indeed, this is part of discipleship for the sincere Christian worker and minister of the Gospel. This work is not to be hijacked for exclusive use by special elitist Christians who create parachurch ministries, charging exorbitant fees and practicing quick-fix doses of counterfeit spirit touches. Nor should this all-important work of the Holy Spirit be given into the hands of secular psychiatrists who scientifically experiment with the soul and spirit of God's creation—arbitrarily using a psychoanalysis-ism theory and drugs and leaving God completely out of the healing process.

Ministry case: You'll Get Custody.

"The word of the LORD came to me: 'Son of man, prophesy against the prophets of Israel, prophesy and say to those who prophesy out of their own minds: 'Hear the word of the LORD!' Thus says the Lord GOD, Woe to the foolish prophets who follow their own spirit, and have seen nothing! Your prophets have been like foxes among ruins, O Israel. You have not gone up into the breaches, or built up a wall for the house of Israel, that it might stand in battle in the day of the LORD. They have spoken falsehood and divined a lie; they say, 'Says the LORD,' when the LORD has not sent them, and yet they expect him to fulfill their word. Have you not seen a delusive vision, and uttered a lying divination, whenever you have said, 'Says the LORD,' although I have not spoken? Therefore thus says the Lord God: 'Because you have uttered delusions and seen lies, therefore behold, I am against you,' says the Lord GOD" (Ezekiel 13:1-8).

Often, we held services for prayer and ministry in our support group work. Dozens of people would come primarily to receive a word of wisdom, knowledge, discernment, or prophecy, but few would apply the work of the cross during the week to bring death to their carnal issues. A pattern began to develop, like the pattern we see common within the body of Christ. They came to receive these encouraging manifestations of the Spirit, but continued in their self-indulging lifestyles.

Many received prophecies that immediately came to pass, while others took longer. One distraught woman, abused by her former husband and tricked into giving up custody of her children, came for ministry. The Lord told me to tell her: "You'll get custody!" And this happened quickly.

Most of these ministry meetings would last way into the night. The struggling Christians who participated in our support work also received the message of the cross and counseling.

Then the Holy Spirit increasingly prompted tough-love words and these people slowly drifted away. One Christian man who was trying to push himself into ministry would come. He refused to receive sound counsel and work on his carnal issues. He was unemployed and requested prayer for a job. He had an application at Boeing and expected I would prophesy that job into reality. I prayed and received: "A job here, a job there—don't worry about it." He said, "I can't receive that, pray again." I told him I would not; that was what the Lord told me to tell him. As it turned out, this person did have temporary jobs here and there.

Later, he came to me privately and asked me to hear from the Lord for him about going into full-time ministry. The Lord told me that he was going to go through a real fiery trial. He did not want to hear that.

His wife exposed his abuse to her and her children and asked him to leave. Their divorce caused bankruptcy. A few years later, we ran into him; he was living in his car, acting as if nothing was wrong. This man refused to hear the harder corrective messages and the whole counsel of God. He only wanted things prophesied to him that were pleasant.

Many of these people came for personal ministry to receive a prophetic message that suited them. Much of the body of Christ struggles in this condition, and they stay in this weak narcissistic state because there are plenty of ministries, pastors and false prophets hearing from their own spirit and prophesying out of their own minds. The coming trouble is going to shut down these lying ministries and false prophets.

Ministry case: Secrets of the Heart Revealed.

"Behold, thou desirest truth in the inward being; therefore teach me wisdom in my secret heart" (Psalm 51:6).

"But if all prophesy, and an unbeliever or outsider enters, he is convicted by all, he is called to account by all, the secrets of his heart are disclosed; and so, falling on his face, he will worship God and declare that God is really among you" (1 Corinthians 14:24,25).

Many Christians suffer issues of heart they keep secret; some are completely forgotten. The gift of prophecy, when functioning properly, exposes these hidden or suppressed secret problems of the heart. Having God expose these things should be normal ministry in all fellowships. Unfortunately, few understand this, or the gift is practiced improperly with impurity.

Often, in counsel or group ministry, hidden issues of heart would surface related to unresolved anger and fear, usually stemming from childhood abuse from parents. The most destructive are those hidden and forgotten secret heart issues of abandonment or rejection from their father.

Due to these hidden secret issues of heart, these Christians struggle with angry-bitter expectations misdirected toward their Heavenly Father. Once exposed and emotionally resolved, they begin to keenly sense closeness in the heart toward God and readily feel the love of God.

There are many accounts to choose from, but the one that might affect the reader the most is my own account in dealing with a secret issue of heart. This occurred in 1987, a year before the Lord released me back into ministry.

I started counseling with a pastor who worked in a faith ministry. It was a 100-mile round trip and those he counseled gave what they could in the form of an honorarium. One day I came to my session frustrated with God. In fact, I hit the pastor's desk and asked, "Where is God? It's like five steps forward, ten back."

Carl was the pastor's name, a big burly man, and full of the love of God. He motioned that he understood and started thumbing through his notes. About a minute later, with a puzzled look on his face, he said, "Chuck, I'm depending on the Holy Spirit here." And then he asked, "Did your father ever tell you he wanted to kill you?"

He searched his notes and could not find inference to this kind of abuse in any previous sessions.

I had never shared that with him or any other. This was something hidden deep in my heart. I said, "Yes, many times he would get me and my brother into a corner, from five years old and up, shake his fist and threaten to kill us, right then and there!"

Carl looked at me intently and said, "Our relationship with our Heavenly Father is initially founded in our relationship with our earthly father. You have taken that fear and rejection from these death threats in early childhood and transferred them to your relationship with your Heavenly Father. You think in your heart that God wants to kill you, too!"

It was as if a light turned on. It made sense. I know now it was the Holy Spirit bearing witness to what the Lord was having Carl prophesy. The Holy Spirit drew out of my heart a forgotten wound and brought it to my conscious awareness.

He followed up by saying, "That is not true of God. You have unbelief in your heart, which is sin." He continued, "You need to repent."

I could feel pressure in my heart. He led me in a simple prayer of repentance. When I finished praying, I wept and wept. It was like a ton of bricks had been lifted off my heart and spirit.

Carl stood by me as I continued to weep. I felt like jelly inside and became physically weak. Carl gave me a bear hug to give comfort, which also helped stabilize me. We finished that session and I continued to weep on and off during the drive home.

There have been about thirty different issues of heart and spirit that I have since dealt with that produced weeping that helped resolve unforgiveness, anger, fear and feelings of abandonment.

The true gift of prophecy, when in operation, will expose hidden issues of the heart. Most are wounds that carry damaged emotions that need resolution, forgiveness and cleansing—where the Holy Spirit brings the healing, cleansing power of Christ's blood to bear.

We fashioned our counseling ministry after this model. Many of the same powerful Holy Spirit manifestations exposed deep wounds and secrets that became a break-through for struggling Christians. I counseled with another person present at all times. We only asked that an honorarium be given. Sometimes it came in the form of food—one time a fresh salmon.

This kind of Holy Spirit counsel should be available in every fellowship.

> **Ministry case:** Revealing Wounds and Dividedness of the spirit by the Holy Spirit.
>
> *"The spirit of man is the lamp of the LORD, searching all his innermost parts"* (Proverbs 20:27).
>
> *"Put off your old nature which belongs to your former manner of life and is corrupt through deceitful lusts, and be renewed in the spirit of your minds, and put on the new nature, created after the likeness of God in true righteousness and holiness"* (Ephesians 4:22-24).
>
> Our heart can be broken, our spirit crushed or divided. The Bible speaks of another condition of heart—a double heart. A double-hearted person has similar symptoms to someone suffering from schizophrenia. The double-minded Christian referenced in James has the same symptoms of those suffering from D.I.D. (Dissociative Identity Disorder) or what used to be termed M.P.D. (Multiple Personality Disorder).
>
> Often, we suffer from wounds that crush our personal spirit into pieces. These pieces can carry or hold onto trauma and defilements for years. The born-again experience deals partially with these conditions. Until the Holy Spirit exposes these issues, with our understanding and cooperation, we cannot receive full cleansing, healing and wholeness.
>
> Helping wounded Christians understand this process and learn to cooperate is crucial to recovery and walking in the fullness of Christ. Counseling is a solid approach to assist Christians in grasping the doctrine of sanctification. The faster Christians understand and embrace these biblical principles of recovery, the faster each Christian can cooperate with the Holy Spirit as counselor.
>
> When wounded Christians gain understanding of the sanctification process, the Holy Spirit will accelerate cleansing and healing, since the Christian has learned to submit to His counsel. Eventually, we as counselors will walk away, no longer needed.
>
> Often, wounds to the personal spirit are deep and reside within for a long time. The following ministry case is a good example.

During a counseling session with a young Christian woman, the Holy Spirit prompted me to inform her of a wound that occurred to her spirit, before she was born, that is, while she was still in her mother's womb.

After prayer, she closed her eyes and began to describe a vision recounting an incident. The gift of knowledge was in operation. The Holy Spirit revealed to her that her father had punched her mother while pregnant with her. *"The spirit of man is the lamp of the LORD, searching all his innermost parts"* (Proverbs 20:27). Her spirit was wounded and the Holy Spirit gave light for her personal spirit to reveal this event.

We prayed over this revelation and for a healing for this trauma to her spirit. The healing would take some time, since there can be fragmented parts of her spirit contaminated by such perverse abuse.

I suggested that she also talk to her mother about this for confirmation. Indeed, at the next session this woman described a past incident that totally confirmed what the Holy Spirit was trying to heal within her spirit.

Her mother said, "When I was nine months along with you, your father and I were playing cards and I was winning. He became enraged and punched me in the stomach."

The Holy Spirit revealed many other defiling and cruel abuses. Each required cleansing and emotional resolution. This wounded Christian was getting at the truth concerning why she also abused and neglected her own children.

The body of Christ has perhaps millions of wounded Christians struggling in life and told by their pastors and other ministries to *just "mimic Christ and eventually you will make it."*

Yes, those who came for counsel were troubled, unstable and experienced demonic oppression and devilish attacks on a regular basis. Many expressed despair much like Job's description concerning his terrible time.

We eventually saw that the counseling ministry we worked in was similar to the ministry God gave Elihu, the one man who correctly counseled Job. Job had three other counselors who tried to help him see the reasons why suffering came upon this righteous man. Few theologians understand Job's true problem and label Elihu's ministry given to Job as better than Job's first three counselors, but still done in error. This is not true.

This ancient but very contemporary story about suffering at the hand of Satan needs to be understood and the principles applied, allowing the true disciple to effectively counsel others in trouble. Elihu confronted Job with his dependence on his own righteousness to protect him from Satan. He had a fear of God, but also a presumptive expectation that God had to protect and bless, because of righteous living. This he believed was his right.

Many Christians are vexed and troubled. They are attacked by Satan but do not see that God allowed these trials to warn and humble, causing them to seek out help from a true servant of God.

As Elihu said, *"For God speaks in one way, and in two, though man does not perceive it. In a dream, in a vision of the night, when deep sleep falls upon men, while they slumber on their beds, then he opens the ears of men, and terrifies them with warnings, that he may turn man aside from his deed, and cut off pride from man;.... If there be for him an angel, a mediator, one of the thousand, to declare to man what is right for him; and he is gracious to him, and says, 'Deliver him from going down into the Pit, I have found a ransom; let his flesh become fresh with youth; let him return to the days of his youthful vigor'; then man prays to God, and he accepts him, he comes into his presence with joy. He recounts to men his salvation, and he sings before men, and says: 'I sinned and perverted what was right, and it was not requited to me. He has redeemed my soul from going down into the Pit, and my life shall see the light.' 'Behold, God does all these things, twice, three times, with a man, to bring back his soul from the Pit, that he may see the light of life.'"* (Job 33:14-17, 23-30).

James spoke into the lives of the twice-souled Christians in his day, and this New Testament book is God's recovery program for the last-day divided Christian. James did not prescribe drugs or medicine to avoid dealing with the issues of heart Satan was attacking. The word sorcery in the Greek is *pharmakia*, translated in English, *pharmacy*. Sorcery is mentioned in the works of the flesh found in Galatians 5 and signified the use of medicine, drugs and spells. *"In sorcery, the use of drugs, whether simple or potent, was generally accompanied by incantations and appeals to occult powers, with the provision of various charms, amulets, etc., professedly designed to keep the applicant or patient from the attention and power of demons, but actually to impress the applicant with the mysterious resources and powers of the sorcerer"* (Vine's Expository Dictionary of Biblical Words, Thomas Nelson Publishers, NY, 1985, p. 587).

Many psychiatrists employ New Age occult methods and make use of the many drugs manufactured by the multi-billion-dollar pharmaceutical industry. Many Christian ministries funnel unstable Christians to so-called Christian psychiatrists where root issues are glossed over, and drugs are prescribed. One popular family ministry had a guest on their radio talk show discussing the topic of post-partum blues. The woman interviewed praised the drug Prozac for saving her from potential severe depression and perhaps harmful behavior.

Most women who suffer this malady do so because they carry a twice-souled agenda for having children. When a wounded and insecure woman becomes pregnant, there is often an inner motive for attention gathering during her pregnancy. Then when her child is born attention diverts to the baby. This can incite unconscious jealousy and even hatred toward the new baby. These and most other syndromes come from our sin nature and carnal personalities that produce sinful and evil desires within Christians. Left hidden, simple challenges in life become insurmountable mountains leaving hopelessness and bitter jealousy to take their destructive course.

When a sincere but divided Christian understands these principles, the Holy Spirit can work with that twice-souled child of God and get to the root of the problem. Masking the symptomatic pain with drugs, carnal activities and counterfeit sensuous spiritual touches may work for a while, but sooner or later Satan will gain the upper hand.

True Elihu type ministries and Christian workers, when raised up and trained, will be able to assist the double-minded Christian, work with the Holy Spirit and get God's recovery program started. Sooner rather than later, these hurting Christians will learn to work out their own salvation with fear and trembling, leaning on the true Holy Spirit as counselor and comforter.

GROWING UP INTO THE UNITY OF TRUE FAITH

"And his gifts were that some should be apostles, some prophets, some evangelists, some pastors and teachers, to equip the saints for the work of ministry, for building up the body of Christ, until we all attain to the unity of the faith and of the knowledge of the Son of God, to mature manhood, to the measure of the stature of the fullness of Christ; so that we may no longer be children, tossed to and fro and carried about with every wind of doctrine, by the cunning of men, by their craftiness in deceitful wiles" (Ephesians 4:11-14).

Such division and confusion within the body of Christ! Such weak, ignorant and lazy saints—gullible to accept almost any ear-tickling lie!

Such weak and selfish leadership; setting wrong examples, leading eagerly for the appearance of success, ignoring Christ's teachings on making true disciples. As shepherds, how will you and I be received when the Chief Shepherd appears?

Jesus said, *"Nevertheless, when the Son of man comes, will he find faith on earth?"* (Luke 18:8). That is the question!

Jesus calls men and women into leadership, expecting these newly called disciples to be taught by the existing true leadership. Unfortunately, very few in leadership today teach and lead by example, as Christ would have them.

Today, church leaders rubberstamp new leaders by brainwashing them, training them to follow denominational ideology, methods and carnal doctrines and not follow after Christ. Few are made into true disciples of Christ.

Leadership's great commission is, *"Go therefore and make disciples of all nations, baptizing them in the name of the Father and of the Son and of the Holy Spirit, teaching them to observe all that I have commanded you; and lo, I am with you always, to the close of the age"* (Matthew 28:19,20).

This commission and plan lasted for about 300 years, until Constantine turned Christianity into the state religion of the Roman Empire. Through slow apostasy and political alliances with most Western European states and the Holy Roman Emperors of Germany, all of European Christendom fell under control of the Roman Catholic Church for about a 1,000-year period, which is known as the medieval Dark Ages. Not until the end of this period did some of the Roman Catholic heresies come under strong attack, led by John Wycliffe, who, among other issues, repudiated the occult practice of the Eucharist and the false doctrine of transubstantiation. This started the reformation movement, leading to the Protestant revolt against Papal supremacy and doctrinal error.

Since the Reformation there have been strides made in restoring sound doctrine and inspired teachings concerning faith and sound doctrine, incorporating all that Jesus taught. True Christianity is still in process of reformation and restoration, getting back to biblical New Testament Christianity, without the control and influence of carnal or corrupt leadership and their foul teachings. The model Christ gave, and the teachings of the original apostles did not manipulate, use underhanded methods or promote pet doctrines that created factions and divisions. In fact, the apostles, in their writings addressed these issues that were already starting to corrupt Christianity.

The end of this age is approaching quickly. All the biblical prophecies of terrible things to come are beginning to unfold; there will be restoration of true leadership that will focus on shepherding the flock and making disciples—to follow Christ, and not themselves.

There is coming a clear distinction between the true and the false, where those who love truth will separate from the phony and apostate church. However, this coming out will not be a new denomination or another strange movement, rather a searching out and bonding in likeminded fellowship among the true saints. These are Christians eager to attain unity of the true faith in Christ and be changed into the fullness of His character, in the true love of God.

These saints will meet with each other and demand leadership by example from sold-out shepherds, regardless of denominational background. The leadership litmus test will be *example living* and teaching all that Jesus taught. This cannot be faked; therefore, leadership must first become a true disciple of Christ, and then follow the call of God to fulfill duties as an apostle, prophet, evangelist, pastor or teacher. These true leaders, whom God is about to make visible, will not stand on a title or crave recognition but be known as true sold-out servants of Jesus. They will require those under their tutelage to grow up into Christ, standing on their own two feet of faith, no longer troubled by the cunning of men and Satan's wicked schemes.

God's true leaders will not allow the followers of Christ who are in their care to make them into idols, or special *"Holy Ghost Bartenders!"* That is right; one of the current leaders in the Toronto Blessing movement refers to himself as a special envoy for the Holy Spirit who dispenses feel-good spiritual touches.

The coming persecution and increasing tribulation will shake up Christians everywhere. Leadership will wake up, preach and teach truth by example, or fall away, joining the deceived Christians aligning with the false church, empowered by the ever-increasing antichrist spirit.

The bride of Christ will be made pure, without spot or wrinkle for the whole world to see. This is the promise Christ will fulfill, and He will showcase His bride to a lost and dying world, terrified by the dark and terrible days coming upon all of mankind.

Unity of the true faith in Christ will be accomplished. You can count on it.

BY WHAT AUTHORITY–GOD'S OR MAN'S?

"And they came again to Jerusalem. And as he was walking in the temple, the chief priests and the scribes and the elders came to him, and they said to him, 'By what authority are you doing these things, or who gave you this authority to do them?' Jesus said to them, 'I will ask you a question; answer me, and I will tell you by what authority I do these things. Was the baptism of John from heaven or from men? Answer me.' And they argued with one another, 'If we say, 'From heaven,' he will say, 'Why then did you not believe him?' But shall we say, 'From men'?'—they were afraid of the people, for all held that John was a real prophet. So they answered Jesus, 'We do not know.' And Jesus said to them, 'Neither will I tell you by what authority I do these things'" (Mark 11:27-33).

Imagine how confused God's people became as Christ taught. He attacked the teachings of those in authority and upset a system of worship *gone bad*. Christ did not attack God's word, rather He showed in the Word of God how corrupt and wayward God's people had become, especially leadership.

Jesus walked in an authority none had seen before, *"And when Jesus finished these sayings, the crowds were astonished at his teaching, for he taught them as one who had authority, and not as their scribes"* (Matthew 7:28,29).

This authority came from a true relationship with the living God. The Pharisees were constantly nipping at His heels, trying to undermine God's message and Christ's ministry. They were the established leaders of God and claimed authority from history, the law, the Temple, and their man-made system of worship. Through the years, wayward leadership developed a slick system for worship by adding manmade rules and precepts to the word of God that made the worshippers feel religious and good about themselves. Money was key to this perverse system. When the people came to sacrifice, the Temple inspectors constantly rejected the people's lambs, doves, and other sacrifices. Those worshippers had to buy a sacrifice from the Temple vendors—often at exorbitant prices. Nevertheless, many followed the teaching of the scribes, Sadducees, and Pharisees in blind obedience.

Jesus wasn't after their pocketbook. He gave the Good News of the kingdom of God and also offended the selfish, the game player, the phony and the evil people dressed as sheep. He preached about a death to their soulish-carnal life by using a metaphor, the Roman's cruel death penalty—the cross. He spoke of receiving a higher life in God that required a death to the self-centered life on earth. He healed the sick and cast out demons setting many free—at no charge. When He healed them in the power of God, He told those restored to tell no one. He did not promote the work God gave Him to do at the expense of the lame, crippled and diseased.

When the crowds formed, He did not raise money to build a giant amphitheater and a network of disciples to herd in the people like cattle. He had compassion on them and trained the disciples to be true shepherds who served God above all else, choosing men who would be obedient in feeding and caring for God's flock.

The people responded, began to follow Christ, and listened to His teachings and instruction by His disciples. The Temple rulers and Pharisees became indignant and jealous, and soon plotted to kill Jesus. You see, Jesus came from outside the religious structure of His day. John the Baptist did not rise from within Israel's temple-synagogue system. Jesus called His disciples, ordinary common men—apart from the religious system.

Christ's authority was Truth and a true relationship with God. This kind of authority always offends the carnal and self-promoting hypocrites who come into power over God's people, exercising a manipulative and controlling authority, building up themselves at the expense of others.

He taught His disciples not to lord it over each other, not to seek recognition or to exercise authority over each other.

Christ's teachings turned the sincere lover of God, to God, to depend on a living relationship with God. He taught with an authority that broke the spell of the religious system and exposed the hypocrisy-soaked men who ran it. These men were envious of Christ and the apostles. Out of their intense jealousy, they sought to destroy the work of God through Jesus and His disciples. Even Pilate, an ungodly ruler, perceived that the high priest delivered Christ up out of envy.

After Christ's resurrection and the ensuing outpouring of the Holy Spirit, the disciples caused a big stir within Jerusalem as they taught with an authority from God, backed by signs and wonders. Soon the religious leaders tried to stop the disciples and put down a true Holy Spirit-led move of God.

"Now when they saw the boldness of Peter and John, and perceived that they were uneducated, common men, they wondered; and they recognized that they had been with Jesus. But seeing the man that had been healed standing beside them, they had nothing to say in opposition. But when they had commanded them to go aside out of the council, they conferred with one another, saying, 'What shall we do with these men? For that a notable sign has been performed through them is manifest to all the inhabitants of Jerusalem, and we cannot deny it. But in order that it may spread no further among the people, let us warn them to speak no more to any one in this name.' So they called them and charged them not to speak or teach at all in the name of Jesus. But Peter and John answered them, 'Whether it is right in the sight of God to listen to you rather than to God, you must judge; for we cannot but speak of what we have seen and heard.' And when they had further threatened them, they let them go, finding no way to punish them, because of the people; for all men praised God for what had happened" (Acts 4:13-21).

There was much persecution against the apostles and one man named Saul wreaked havoc on the church, throwing many into prison. Saul was a staunch Pharisee who believed this new sect, called The Way, was heretical and must be stamped out. Jesus intervened from heaven and confronted Saul as he was traveling to Damascus to gain more authority from the synagogues to arrest more followers of The Way—that is, Christians and Christ's disciples.

Jesus stopped Saul, soon to be called Paul, and commissioned him, saying *"... he is a chosen instrument of mine to carry my name before the Gentiles and kings and the sons of Israel; for I will show him how much he must suffer for the sake of my name"* (Acts 9:15,16).

Not too many Christians saw Saul after this, as Paul himself wrote, *"And I was still not known by sight to the churches of Christ in Judea; they only heard it said, "He who once persecuted us is now preaching the faith he once tried to destroy"* (Galatians 1:22,23).

As Christians grew in numbers, many of the Pharisees believed in Christ and some formed their own group promoting circumcision. Corrupt and jealous priests were indignant toward the new church and the apostles, though there was some peaceful coexistence for a time.

God's new church started to become tainted with rules, regulations and rites of passage that allowed the believer to boast before God. Even Peter struggled with God's commission for the church to reach the Gentiles with the message of salvation and vacillated about whether these new Gentile converts should become circumcised.

Saul, now a true believer in Christ, went into seclusion for 14 years in Arabia. (Read Galatians 1:1-2:14). Here Paul is raised up by God to ensure the true Gospel of Christ stays on track. Christ taught the apostle Paul by the Holy Spirit apart from the original disciples. *"For I would have you know, brethren, that the gospel which was preached by me is not man's gospel. For I did not receive it from man, nor was I taught it, but it came through a revelation of Jesus Christ"* (Galatians 1:11,12).

Paul walked in an authority worked into him by Christ, though Paul conferred with the original disciples. *"Then after fourteen years I went up again to Jerusalem with Barnabas, taking Titus along with me. I went up by revelation; and I laid before them (but privately before those who were of repute) the gospel which I preach among the Gentiles, lest somehow I should be running or had run in vain.... And from those who were reputed to be something (what they were makes no difference to me; God shows no partiality)— those, I say, who were of repute added nothing to me"* (Galatians 2:1,2,6).

And so it is throughout the history of Christianity. Christ has found ordinary untainted men and women, who were not taught man's gospel. These men and women are often called of God apart from the institutionalized church and taught the true Gospel through His discipline and the Word of God, then He raises them up to confront waywardness that often creeps back into Christianity.

True leadership walks in an authority that does not need the approval of others. Many in leadership water down the Gospel for fear of rejection. These are men-pleasers who desire to have a following. A shepherd after God's heart will lead by example and minister the Word of God to encourage and promote faith in the hearer, resulting in maturity. A sincere saint submitting to a true leader will know that he or she cannot make that leader responsible for their maturity, but rather desire to stand on their own two feet of faith.

Jesus came in this kind of authority. People who heard and saw Christ preach and minister knew they could not manipulate the Lord. He told them truth and if they did not receive it, that was the hearer's problem, not His. His disciples walked in that same authority.

Jesus warned of much end-time counterfeit activity: false ministers, false prophets, false signs and wonders, false brethren and false teachings that would, if possible, deceive those truly born of God.

The true disciple has an authority bestowed upon them by God apart from the institutionalized church, pastor, prophet, apostle, and bishop—any so-called pillar or leader in the church. This authority is not to be insubordinate, rebellious or undermining leadership, but rather an authority to make sure that any leader or doctrine is authentic—of God and biblical. There are many biblical teachings where Scripture text is taken out of context, making the teaching a damning heresy, a teaching of men.

Many will be deceived at the end of the age. These Christians will have no excuse. They cannot blame the destructive results on anybody but themselves. Most Christians blindly follow a leader who claims to have authority. These Christians listen to anybody but they themselves never arrive at the truth. They do not dig deep into the Word of God; seek the real Christ and desire to be taught of God. It is hard work, and we are held accountable to hear from the Holy Spirit and the written Word of God for ourselves on matters pertinent to doctrine, fellowship and personal discipleship.

It is much easier to let someone tell us what we should believe. Jesus said, *"No one can come to me unless the Father who sent me draws him; and I will raise him up at the last day. It is written in the prophets, 'And they shall all be taught by God.' Everyone who has heard and learned from the Father comes to me"* (John 6:44,45).

In Catholicism, the rank and file Catholic follows the Pope rather than Christ. Protestants have their own brand of leadership idolatry as well.

Christ is the mediator and facilitator of a new and better covenant with God. You and I, as ordinary everyday believers, and lovers of God, can now come to God individually and know God—personally. The old covenant set up a system of mediators and all were taught to know about the Lord. Now, through the person of Christ, we can know the true God on a personal basis.

"This is the covenant that I will make with the house of Israel after those days, says the Lord: I will put my laws into their minds, and write them on their hearts, and I will be their God, and they shall be my people. And they shall not teach every one his fellow or every one his brother, saying, 'Know the Lord,' for all shall know me, from the least of them to the greatest" (Hebrews 8:10,11).

Do you know Christ, or know about Him through your pastor, denomination or favorite *international superstar* leader? If you are deceived, it will be your own fault, for Jesus said, *"My sheep hear my voice, and I know them, and they follow me"* (John 10:27).

You have authority and power to become a true son or daughter of the Living God. It is your responsibility to make sure you have a right relationship with the true Jesus. Then it is your responsibility to fellowship with other likeminded sincere Christians. So, to what authority will you submit—God's or man's?

CHAPTER 5

The Self-Righteous Are Fighting A Losing Battle

THE RISE OF THE SELF-RIGHTEOUS ARMY

Over the last 30 years, Christians have gained strong political influence. This powerful voting block focuses on national immorality, fighting abortion, fighting for religious freedom, and restoring our Christian heritage.

The "moral majority" was based on the evangelical Christian rally call that lost steam with so many church scandals. Now a new rally cry has risen, creating a focus on revival and evangelizing the lost before the rapture of the born-again Christian occurs. A self-righteous arrogant doctrine espousing that born-again Christians are exempt from enduring the Great Tribulation spearheads this new rally cry.

Other Christians, as mentioned previously, are driven to establish the kingdom of God by restructuring society, praying, and hoping for a massive revival that will usher in an era of dominant Christian ideology throughout the world.

These lying doctrines, along with the so-called prosperity teachings embraced by many Christians, present an "in-your-face" message that alienates most lost sinners. Those who do come to Christ receive a maze of carnal religious doctrines that make them feel superior. Millions of lukewarm Christians are blind to their precarious relationship with Christ as they arrogantly prance around showing off a self-righteous lifestyle. Soon this pitiful condition will be challenged by a world fed up with Christian hypocrisy.

God is about to judge the self-righteousness running amuck in His church. Like Job, millions of self-righteous Christians will be thrown into deep trouble that will boggle the mind. Christians will be forced to become humble and take to heart Christ's words, *"It is the Spirit that gives life, the flesh is of no avail"* (John 6:63, Zechariah 4:6,7).

THE POWER OF THE WICKED WILL INCREASE

The wicked are learning to gain more demonic spiritual power than ever. They will receive satanic protection as they become bolder and arrogant. Demonic forces will enlist and empower the wicked to facilitate Satan's work, assaulting Christians and imposing a one-world order political agenda.

This nation and the church have gradually taken themselves further away from the protection of God's grace and mercy. We have pushed God out of our schools, government, businesses, and far too many of our church sanctuaries. God has chastened America and the church of America repeatedly with natural disasters, calamities, scandals and Wall Street scares. September 11 was the first severe attack with more to come. This was a direct satanic attack allowed by God as judgment.

Miraculously, through the prayers of a small number of devout and repentant Christians, judgment seems to be suspended. This was another of God's merciful warnings to America to repent!

We as Christians must take this reprieve to get ready! We can count on this momentary blessing to end quickly if the elected leadership of this nation turns more immoral and embraces Satan's end-of-the-world plans. Only if the church truly repents and enters into a "knee-bending and weeping" revival can there be a continuation of godly moral leadership in parts of the government and in the White House!

Judgment is coming, regardless of who is President. God is looking for His people to truly repent of their own wickedness, and only then will they be able to be a true witness to the lost and dying.

We as a nation and most of God's people have not heeded these disciplines and warnings from the Lord. Now the abandonment has truly begun. God's restraint against the spiritual forces of evil is lifting. We have spurned the Son of God, profaned Christ's sacrifice and outraged the Spirit of grace. (Heb. 10:29-31). We are sinning deliberately and flaunting our evil in God's face. Moreover, God's people smugly point the finger at these national abominations but do not give up their own secret sins and idolatrous lifestyles.

We have given God no other alternative than to turn us over to the power of the wicked to get our attention. Satan has demanded to sift this nation and this generation of American Christians, who are about to get a dose of demonic power directed at them that will be so humbling and terrifying that many will lose faith. Panic will sweep over many Christians and they will retreat into hiding like the disciples, running to their homes and hiding from the perpetrators of Christ's crucifixion.

The wicked will receive protection and increased demonic power as this society becomes even more soaked in films and TV shows depicting sorcery and other occult activity. Now children and teens are learning how to practice witchcraft on the Disney channel. The *Harry Potter* series of children's books is sweeping across this nation, as millions of children now learn to become wizards and sorcerers. *Harry Potter* movies teach millions of children across our nation and all around the world how to appreciate sorcery. Amazingly, many Christian leaders and so-called Christian psychologists label critics of these things as alarmists, as they give the green light to Christian parents. The Roman Catholic

Church recently announced that *Harry Potter* and their so-called Christian teachings are not in conflict. Millions of Christian families are now letting their children watch these foul and demonic images and learn about the occult. I know of many adults who innocently got into witchcraft as children by watching the "Wizard of Oz" as a child. Think of what the children are being exposed to today and inviting into their spirits!

Revulsion is coming upon this nation concerning any Christian who arrogantly displays Christian jewelry, posters, T-shirts, bumper stickers and the like. Attacks against arrogant Christians will increase. A spiritual landslide of oppression will overwhelm millions of unprepared Christians causing many to fall away, sin, and develop a cold heart toward God. Mockery, maligning and verbal stoning will be directed at Christians, especially those who continue in the public war against our national moral decay. This generation of Christians will know what it means to suffer for the name of Christ. In almost every level of government, from social services to the court room, anyone who proclaims Christ will be looked upon as evil and the truly evil will start to win many battles and appear to be protected and blessed.

Evil people will have more rights than the righteous person. Godly men and women opposing the wicked will suffer loss after loss in standing up against these evils. Recall the former Hewlett Packard employee fired recently for displaying "hate scripture" over the company's diversity policy and awareness campaign. He challenged his dismissal and the higher court ruling sided with HP.

The spiritual "witchcraft" power amongst the wicked will increase. Evil spirits will direct the wicked to curse, proclaim hexes and cast spells against Christians and prominent Christian leaders. Satan and his demons will start "hate and destroy" campaigns in the spiritual realm. True, as God's Word declares, *"Like a sparrow in its flitting, like a swallow in its flying, a curse that is causeless does not alight"* (Proverbs 26:2). Unfortunately, most Christians do not walk in purity of heart, and so give cause for these curses to take effect. Soon, the far left will begin to secretly organize attacks against Christians and Christian moral crusaders.

Only the truly righteous who are grounded in the Lord will be able to ward off these attacks. They will walk in wisdom, humbly keeping their heads down during this horrific spiritual attack on God's people. They will only contend with darkness when God directs.

Revelation 13:1-10 speaks of a Beast that will arise, saying and performing great and wicked things against God and the saints. We have seen many beasts come and go throughout history. This new onslaught is leading up to the final Beast that will deceive the whole world.

Soon, much lawlessness and evil will be legal in this nation. During this time, Christians must endure and trust their souls to a faithful Creator. (See 1 Peter 4:19).

The Mayor of San Francisco openly defied state laws by granting thousands of homosexual and lesbian marriages, performing ceremonies at city hall in celebrating Saint Valentine's Day, 2004. The State of Massachusetts is also grappling with this Sodomite issue. Yes, we will see more and more vile practices become legal. More Janet Jackson-type shocking exposures will become the norm, as if it were a contest for entertainers to push the moral limits.

Until now, society and Christians had the choice whether or not to carry on a sinful lifestyle and expose one's self to immorality. We can go to an adult bookstore secretly; we can access pornography on the Internet or watch X-rated videos in the privacy of our home. Christians can participate in all of this secretly and still act like a saint on Sunday and Wednesday. The temptations have always been there, but soon we will not have a choice. Filth and perversion will knock at our doors, demanding participation, just as it was in the days of Lot!

The civil government of Sodom and Gomorrah sanctioned the attempted assault of the two men (angels) sent by the Lord to warn Lot. Evil men knocked on Lot's door, demanding that Lot's guests come out to them so they could sexually assault them. The laws of the city did not protect Lot or his guests. Lot could not call on the city for any legal or police protection. The wicked were within their rights! The only way Lot and his family received protection and deliverance was by direct intervention from God. *"...[T]hen the Lord knows how to rescue the godly from trial, and to keep the unrighteous under punishment until the day of judgment, and especially those who indulge in the lust of defiling passions and despise authority"* (2 Peter 2:9-10). Today, evil men and women are bold and willful, having no fear to revile and assault others. Society is regressing to animalistic behavior and reveling in it in broad daylight.

Increasingly, new laws make way for lewd and obscene public behavior. This activity is looked upon as a Constitutional freedom, freedom of speech and expression, which will open doors to market perverse lifestyles and enlist new recruits. Soon public nudity will gain legality in certain places in our nation, as different levels of government increasingly license lewd conduct in the name of freedom of speech and freedom of expression.

Christians everywhere are hoping and praying for the restoration of morality, but the church must turn to God and clean house if any true change in society is to take place.

The doctrines of demons that many Christians have embraced concerning spiritual warfare and protection under God's grace will be like cardboard walls against a hurricane! The Satanic power that evil people will obtain can only be withstood by the pure saint who truly has Christ formed within them.

I have outlined a few doctrines that Satan has gotten many Christians to practice. If you believe these lies, it is time for you to renounce these superstitious faithless teachings for what they are and have the *real* armor of God put on you.

Evil will demonstrate its power arrogantly and the weak, selfish, undisciplined Christian will not have any strength or protection against this onslaught. Many of these deceived Christians will wonder what happened and try to find answers. They will question their phony and weak minister or pastor and the old pat answers will be seen for what they are: whitewashed lies. In dismay, many of these spiritually wounded Christians will find help from the righteous remnant that God has trained to minister during this coming dark hour. They will have the answers and the anointing of the true Christ to help others begin the cleansing work of the Holy Spirit and stand victoriously.

As for the rest, they will wander in a spiritual wasteland, groping in darkness, looking for an easy way out. Satan will deceive them even more. Christians who hate reproof and correction will find false safety and false peace. These false Christians will become part of the false church. They are the foolish maidens about whom Jesus prophesied concerning the end of the age.

Many of these Christians were deceived by the false doctrines propagated through the *Left Behind* series. This line of theology puts Christians at ease, thinking the Rapture will include the carnal, lukewarm, sin-ridden Christian. When the trouble comes, those who embrace this false hope will not have the discipline and spiritual authority to fight or follow the Holy Spirit's protective guidance during the Great Tribulation and the final fight for lost souls.

After the flood of evil runs its course and the days of abandonment to prosperity cease, great trouble will hit everywhere. The financial markets will collapse, food shortages will be common in America and the bankruptcy courts will be overwhelmed. Already the bankruptcy courts' caseloads are behind because of the 2002-2003 economic downturn. Panic will hit the impure and unprepared Christian, driving them like sheep to the slaughter. They will put their faith in government bailouts and different frantic plans to straighten out the mess. Millions of Christians will buy the lie and take the mark of the beast in their hearts long before the actual mark of the beast becomes the law, imposed on the masses. They will have made a complete shipwreck of their faith.

Christians who rejected sanctification and the discipline of the Lord *will be left behind*, while the righteous Christian will be raptured to safety. This will happen near the end of the days of trouble of which Jesus spoke, not before the start of the Great Tribulation. (See Matthew chapters 24 and 25).

Soon many outspoken Christians, who confront the wicked without God's mandate can expect to be the target of hate crimes and practitioners of witchcraft. Many in society have become quite familiar with occult practices.

During these last 20 years of increased immorality, many Christians have stayed very religious (legalistically) and attacked the sinner to counterbalance their own inner uncleanness. They do this to keep up self-deceit, just as the Pharisees did in the Gospel accounts.

It is similar to the popular evangelist in the late 1980s that attacked prostitution from the pulpit, when all along he suffered torment from past defilements from his youth. Finally, he succumbed to the very behavior he condemned. None of this minister's condemnation helped him, nor did the self-righteous pretentious teachings ward off his inner desires. I hope by the grace of God that this brother has been restored. Another brother, Jim Bakker, has come a long way in restoration and seems to be warning, with sound doctrine, the error of the prosperity message and other false teachings that led him astray.

Increasingly, Christian hypocrites will fall, losing power to ward off inner lusts and wickedness. Already there is a high rate of addiction to pornography for those in ministry. This is just the beginning!

Jesus is coming to His temple (the body of Christ) with a whip, exposing actors and charlatans for all to see. He will allow the demonic to make hypocrisy visible and to make the consequence fearfully understood. This will not be a light housecleaning, but a thorough purging.

LOSS OF CREDIBILITY

These things have already started! The former Clinton administration passed dozens of executive orders and pushed through legislation that undermined our moral freedoms and expanded the freedoms of immorality and governmental control over private and religious rights. The Bush administration will continue to try to change some, but many will stay on the books as this administration concentrates on fighting terrorism and a faltering economy.

Why is this happening? Why are the wicked gaining power and becoming so cynical toward Christians?

Americans see no difference between the ungodly and the supposed godly Christian. Most see through the self-righteous hypocrites and have developed distain for so-called leadership accountability. The church should have done its own housecleaning; instead, the legal system had to step in.

God has called Christians to be a peculiar and special people. As it reads in 1 Peter 2:9-12, *"But you are a chosen race, a royal priesthood, a holy nation, God's own people, that you may declare the wonderful deeds of him who called you out of darkness into his marvelous light. Once you were no people but now you are God's people; once you had not received mercy but now you have received mercy. Beloved, I beseech you as aliens and exiles to abstain from the passions of the flesh that wage war against your soul. Maintain good conduct among the Gentiles, so that in case they speak against you as wrongdoers, they may see your good deeds and glorify God on the day of visitation."*

Hypocrisy is the example that God's people are giving the world today. There are few safe fellowships to which a tired lost sinner can run. Instead, the church, for the most part, has become a "brood of vipers." In the eyes of the world, there is no distinction between the frauds of the world and the televangelist; between the Christian abortion protestors and terrorists; nor between the moral majority advocates and the self-righteous stoners described in John 8:1-11; between greedy corporations and megachurch growth programs; between Christian higher education and secular universities; between madness seen in worship services and *voodoo rituals*; nor distinguish between the prosperity hyper-faith Christian ministries and secular get-rich-quick infomercials.

The world does not see the light of the church any longer and revulsion toward the Christian is about to break out in every corner of society. Peter prophesied that this would happen. *"But false prophets also arose among the people, just as there will be false teachers among you, who will secretly bring in destructive heresies, even denying the Master who bought them, bringing upon themselves swift destruction. And many will follow their licentiousness, and because of them the way of truth will be reviled. And in their greed they will exploit you with false words; from of old their condemnation has not been idle, and their destruction has not been asleep"* (2 Peter 2:1-3).

SECRET SIN IN THE CAMP

Godly men and women have been crying out against the flood of filth and immoral decay in America. There have been some victories, but more and more battles are being lost. Again, why are we losing ground? Why is God not backing these moral crusaders? Is God not witnessing against the immoral evil that is flooding our country?

It is because these godly men and women did not see to it that supporters and congregations in their charge and influence embrace purity, godliness, and humility and practice what they preach. They did not teach them how to clean house! Instead, most are taught to gloss over their inner rotten attitudes, to tolerate sin and deceit in the camp, and to ignore backbiting, jealousy and accept reprobates into fellowship! There was no warning of the consequences for allowing these kinds of evils to flourish in the congregation. Shortcuts and quick fixes replaced sound doctrine and the preaching of sanctification and fear of the

Lord. The goal is to look good on the outer appearances and pretend the inner sickness will magically take care of itself.

Let's face the truth. The work of the cross within the believer's life is not easy. We are to humble ourselves under the mighty hand of God and do the painful work concerning our inner wrong motives. Therefore, the easy way is *avoidance*. It is no wonder many refer to the church in America as the church of Laodicéa— *lukewarm, wretched, pitiable, poor, blind, and naked.* (See Revelation 3:14-22).

In 1998 a prominent national ministry began to intensify its opposition to the homosexual and gay rights movement. Secret sin was "in the camp" of this ministry, as it is in many other *ministry camps*. Those ministries that attack the wicked and point the finger will begin to take severe beatings. This prominent national ministry did take a beating two years later in 2000. Two scandals rocked this national ministry, one right after the other. News of this hit the media, a sad and unfortunate situation concerning this prominent national ministry. Let us hope this message strikes home that good works continue within this ministry. We will see more and more of these kinds of disappointments as long as the church refuses to uncover and deal with secret sin in individual ministry camps.

Read what happened to Israel when they crossed over into the Promised Land. The Lord gave the city of Jericho into the hands of the Israelites, with clear orders not to take any of the city's devoted idols. Some broke faith with the Lord and smuggled out a few forbidden items.

"But the people of Israel broke faith in regard to the devoted things; for Achan the son of Carmi, son of Zabdi, son of Zerah, of the tribe of Judah, took some of the devoted things; and the anger of the LORD burned against the people of Israel. Joshua sent men from Jericho to Ai, which is near Bethaven, east of Bethel, and said to them, 'Go up and spy out the land.' And the men went up and spied out Ai. And they returned to Joshua, and said to him, 'Let not all the people go up, but let about two or three thousand men go up and attack Ai; do not make the whole people toil up there, for they are but few.' So about three thousand went up there from the people; and they fled before the men of Ai, and the men of Ai killed about thirty-six men of them, and chased them before the gate as far as Shebarim, and slew them at the descent. And the hearts of the people melted, and became as water. Then Joshua rent his clothes, and fell to the earth upon his face before the ark of the LORD until the evening, he and the elders of Israel; and they put dust upon their heads. And Joshua said, 'Alas, O Lord GOD, why hast thou brought this people over the Jordan at all, to give us into the hands of the Amorites, to destroy us? Would that we had been content to dwell beyond the Jordan! O Lord, what can I say, when Israel has turned their backs before their enemies! For the Canaanites and all the inhabitants of the land will hear of it, and will surround us, and cut off our name from the earth; and what wilt thou do for thy great name?' The LORD said to Joshua, 'Arise, why have you

thus fallen upon your face? Israel has sinned; they have transgressed my covenant which I commanded them; they have taken some of the devoted things; they have stolen, and lied, and put them among their own stuff. Therefore the people of Israel cannot stand before their enemies; they turn their backs before their enemies, because they have become a thing for destruction. I will be with you no more, unless you destroy the devoted things from among you. Up, sanctify the people, and say, 'Sanctify yourselves for tomorrow;' for thus says the LORD, God of Israel, 'There are devoted things in the midst of you, O Israel; you cannot stand before your enemies, until you take away the devoted things from among you'" (Joshua 7:1-13). Israel was defeated and God said that they would be "a thing for destruction" if they did not sanctify themselves immediately and get rid of the secret sin in the camp.

Christians must repent and embrace sanctification by embracing the work of the cross. Most Christians avoid the painful process that destroys the passions of the flesh. There is little true humility in repentance! If secret sin and the works of the flesh are not crucified, it may be too late, and millions of Christians in America may be spewed from the mouth of Christ. As Christ warned the church of Laodicéa, so, too, we must receive this same warning now, before it is too late.

GOD IS WARNING BUT NOT MANY LISTEN AND TAKE HEED

Killer hurricanes one after another, forest fires, floods, earthquakes, deadly tsunamis, droughts, all point to nature seeming to be out of control. There are wars, rumors of war, perplexities among nations, and diseases that once were under control are now a threat. There are flu and virus epidemics, mad cow disease, shortages of vaccines, and famine in various places and ancient religious wars threatening world peace. Terrorists seek weapons of mass destruction. They kidnap, behead and attack to sway international opinion and control national elections around the world.

Jesus described this trouble as birth pangs leading up to the Great Tribulation, the coming of the lawless one by activity of Satan, the Rapture and the coming wrath of God.

My eldest son lived through the third hurricane in Florida of 2004. He reported how damaging it was in certain areas. One interesting thing he noted was that many churches were damaged, but property next to the churches were not harmed. One church had its steeple lifted up, turned upside down and slammed right through the roof into a pew. He reported another peculiar observation that came from a radio commentator describing damage. Billboard after billboard along a stretch of freeway had been knocked down by the hurricane, except for one. It had about five layers of old signage lifted and torn off, yet the billboard itself was still standing. The layer of signage that was left plainly read: *"We need to talk! God."*

Those familiar with Christ's warnings should recognize where we are in God's sovereign plan of Christ's return. God is warning but few are listening and many who do hear do not take it to heart. We hear of Christians having nightmares where they are running from nuclear mushroom clouds, dreams where an unknown enemy attacks this nation, and others having dreams and visions of earthquakes and volcano eruptions bringing devastating destruction. Few ministers warn from the pulpit about the coming trouble and judgment that Jesus clearly warned would come. What is most disturbing is that the majority of pastors and teachers soothe disturbed and shaken Christians by saying the Rapture will occur before any really bad trouble comes to America.

Since few shepherds warn of the coming trouble, God is speaking and shaking everything that can be shaken, in hopes of waking in time, as many as possible. If this shaking by God stirs up fear within you, then good! You may have time to get ready. You still might have time to allow Christ to build within you an unshakeable faith that will get you through the coming terror-filled days.

"See that you do not refuse him who is speaking. For if they did not escape when they refused him who warned them on earth, much less shall we escape if we reject him who warns from heaven. His voice then shook the earth; but now he has promised, 'Yet once more I will shake not only the earth but also the heaven' This phrase, 'Yet once more,' indicates the removal of what is shaken, as of what has been made, in order that what cannot be shaken may remain. Therefore let us be grateful for receiving a kingdom that cannot be shaken, and thus let us offer to God acceptable worship, with reverence and awe; for our God is a consuming fire" (Hebrews 12:25-29).

DISNEYLAND CHRISTIANS
LIVING IN THE MAGIC KINGDOM INSTEAD OF THE KINGDOM OF GOD

Many Christians were outraged over Disney and many other companies in the entertainment business abandoning the so-called family-oriented products, shifting to the bizarre, perverse, more explicit, and violent types of programming. This generated Christian protests and boycotts, as most of Hollywood and the entertainment media began to give themselves over to a satanic worldview.

Boycotting much of Disney's products should have happened years ago by Christians, without being a suggestion by any church denomination or national Christian leader. Christians have exposed themselves to *Snow White, Fantasia, The Black Hole, Escape from Witch Mountain, Return to Witch Mountain, The Gnome Mobile, The Lion King,* and many other titles that are loaded with occult messages.

The world is going to get more satanic in nature and God is allowing this to slap the body of Christ to wake up a sleeping Church. God's people are more concerned about preserving a "Magic Kingdom" of entertainment than walking in the kingdom of God having their minds set on things that are above. (See Colossians 3:1-4).

Christians are more knowledgeable of philosophies, fantasies, romance novels and movies than the deep things of God. Christians and their children are easily influenced by myths and stories that are full of empty deceit. Gradually, more and more Christians are embracing perverted translations of the Bible containing radical interpretations. The more accurate translations—the King James Version and Revised Standard Version—are being replaced by errant translations.

A few years ago, a Christian couple I know raved about the movie, *Field of Dreams*. This is a story full of spiritualism and necromancy! Thousands of Christians sat and idolized the *Star Wars* trilogy. Christians are blindly watching movies loaded with sorcery, demonic figures, and perverse behavior. TV commercials have increasingly become explicit, filling the TV family hour with filth and perversion. "*I will not set before my eyes anything that is base*" (Psalm 101:3).

These families will reap the whirlwind unless the spirit and soul of each family member become cleansed from these defilements. One local pastor who was popular enough to have a 15-minute Christian radio spot said to his listeners that he loved to watch horror movies; in fact, he said the more "horror" the better. One of Satan's best ploys in grooming and programming a society, including Christians, is to get them to accept evil by gradually presenting evil in mild, bite-sized pieces dressed up in comedy.

A little leaven leavens the whole lump. Inch by inch, worldly and satanic forces slowly seeped into this nation's inner psyche. Many godly men and women have warned and warned over the years—some warned in a wrong manner, but regardless, when the true prophets warned, they were ignored. David Wilkerson (*The Vision, Racing Towards Judgment, Set the Trumpet to Thy Mouth*) and Phillip Keller (*Predators in our Pulpits*) as well as others spoke out only to be received with a deaf ear by most Christians. Let the scoffers pick up these same books now. They will see that the majority of these warnings have come to pass. The accuracy of these warnings should drive them to their knees in true repentance. Frankly, very few of those scoffers will come out of the darkness. Even if they did read these warnings again, God has given many of them over to their own self-deceit and darkness, for many are like Esau, who sold his own birthright! (See Hebrews 12:15-17).

SORCERY EMBEDDED IN SOCIETY THAT BLINDS CHRISTIANS

Gradualism has been Satan's tool for centuries. He is patient to sow evil into the mindset of God's people. Blinded by the god of this world, thousands of Christians embraced worldliness and wickedness in mild forms. There was no discernment, no ferreting out the deceit; then they turned around and boycotted! How hypocritical!

The TV shows *Bewitched, I Dream of Jeannie, The Adams Family, The Munsters, Scooby Doo, Casper the Friendly Ghost, The Smurfs, Superman,* were demonic in nature, but were presented as innocent fun and escapism. Many Christians still consider this as just fun and fantasy. One of the most occult movies of all, *The Wizard of Oz*, left an indelible defiling impression on the spirits of millions across this nation. (It is sad, but interesting to note that many of the actors and actresses portraying these evils have died early in life, become crippled, or failed as functional people).

I Dream of Jeannie and *Bewitched* were a gradual exposure to sorcery that led to *Carrie, Sabrina the Teenage Witch, Hocus Pocus* and, now any type of horror and witchcraft movie that is imaginable. All this demonic activity develops a mindset to accept the next level of evil. The American culture and far too many Christians accepted this gradualism. Evil has seeped into society until what was considered quite evil just a few years ago is considered really funny and no big deal for today. Thus, *Harry Potter* became so widely accepted, read, and viewed!

Almost every heartthrob on the wide screen takes their turn acting in a wicked vampire movie. Satan is being glorified, and evil drips off billboards, oozes out of movie screens and flows into homes across this nation during the "TV family hour." There is not one medium left untouched by Satan.

Sorcery is subtly taught to our children repeatedly within this culture, and most Christians endorse it or are blind to its power. In the last days, powerful demonic spirits will influence and attack others through the practice of sorcery. This evil is starting to dramatically increase already!

Violence has become commonplace and Hollywood keeps giving the public what they demand. Could class action suits succeed against Hollywood, blaming tinsel town for all the teen deaths caused by handguns and other violent crimes?

The church has tried to stop all this immorality, but the efforts have been too little too late. Dare Christians correct the world of evil, yet embrace milder forms of wickedness? We are getting what we asked for. Moreover, God's people always pay the price when they make concessions with evil and bring base and unclean things into their home. We play church, seek the worldly American Dream, and give our children over to the entertainment industry as baby-sitter while we try to obtain the material world. Satan has come to the last-day Christian and is demanding his pay. Many souls will come to ruin and their faith will be shipwrecked because of the love of money and the use of sorcery to advance in this world. (See 1 Timothy 6:3-10). Revelation forewarns that many will not repent, even after severe judgment.

"The rest of mankind, who were not killed by these plagues, did not repent of the works of their hands nor give up worshiping demons and idols of gold and silver and bronze and stone and wood, which cannot either see or hear or walk; nor did they repent of their murders or their sorceries or their immorality or their thefts" (Revelation 9:20, 21).

STOPPING THE IMMORAL FLOOD IN THE STRONG ARM OF THE FLESH

The self-righteous still pound the pulpits, becoming more politically outspoken, and campaigning against public immorality. Christians gather in front of abortion clinics, protesting the murder of the unborn, while they practice all manner of wickedness in secret; some even justifying murdering abortionists. Leadership has ignored the sick condition of the church and turned outward, hurling followers and themselves into society's morality conflict. Yes, we Christians should speak out, but by the power of God and in true righteousness. God will no longer honor these efforts, and some will lose personal battles with devastating losses. Secret sin will overtake many Christians; hypocrisy will be exposed at all levels.

One reason failure is coming to the Christian moral protestor is because this battle has become a personal battle for many. Jesus warned *the flesh is of no avail*. (See also Jeremiah 17:5-8) Those who continue to fight evil without a mandate from God will be putting themselves and others in harm's way.

Much of this work became a tool to raise money in the guise of doing something to stop the immoral flood. The church is throwing stones while living in glass houses. They continue to ignore Scriptures about self-righteous finger pointing and attacking the lost and the sinner.

Leadership continues to keep silent concerning these evils that persist within the body of Christ. They avoid preaching the cross and crucifixion of the flesh. They refuse to challenge the church to become the salt of the earth. They soften the message, tickle ears, stand on their moral soapbox and then hinder true servants of the Lord who protest this hypocrisy.

MORAL CRUSADERS WILL START TO LOSE MORE BATTLES
AND SOME WILL DIE UNEXPECTEDLY

This is a prophetic warning, and you can count on it coming to pass! I wrote an open letter to several of our morality fighters several years ago. I warned those who are in this public battle against the evils of this nation that God is not standing behind these valiant efforts any longer. Leave them alone! Let's turn to getting the body of Christ ready to endure the Great Tribulation. Warn God's people to repent of their sins. God will judge the lost sinner, the ungodly, and the wicked.

Unless these carnal moral crusades stop, some wonderful men and women of God will unexpectedly take ill or die. The demonic spiritual attacks will strike—in some cases instantly! I am grieved to have to warn in this manner. I personally believe witchcraft and hate prayers spewing from the homosexuals and liberals brought on physical setbacks, heart attacks and strokes to prominent Christian moral crusaders. They have a right to beat up on our moral crusaders because of hidden idols and secret sins within their ministries and the general lukewarm condition prevalent throughout the body of Christ.

WANTING TO CONVERT AMERICA FOR THE WRONG REASONS

Deep down inside, most American Christians do not really want Christ to return! We are living in the lap of luxury—fat and sassy, even though we know that His coming will be terrible and very soon. We are trying to convert America so God will not have to come and judge America with the rest of the world. We do not want to end up losing our "treasures here on earth." Many would like to believe otherwise, but the fact is this: Jesus warned that it would be terrible and that we as Christians must endure this terrible time all the way to the end.

The world and all that is in it will be burned! Yes, we will escape wrath, provided we deal with our attachments to this world, become able to leave this all behind, and not look back! I think many Christians subconsciously expect the Rapture to include homes, cars, TVs, lost loved ones, boats, vacations, money, clothes, jewelry and the like.

I am not against possessing appropriate material and temporal things to properly function and live contented. As it says, *"There is great gain in godliness with contentment; for we brought nothing into the world, and we cannot take anything out of the world; but if we have food and clothing, with these we shall be content. But those who desire to be rich fall into temptation, into a snare, into many senseless and hurtful desires that plunge men into ruin and destruction. For the love of money is the root of all evils; it is through this craving that some have wandered away from the faith and pierced their hearts with many pangs"* (1 Timothy 6:6-10).

DRAGGING REPROBATES INTO THE CHURCH

Many in leadership, as well as Christian workers, have become very gullible and naïve. We listen to any kind of sob story, practice Christian hospitality, and with this mindset many become deceived and end up attempting to convert reprobates. A reprobate is someone who has become unredeemable. Few are knowledgeable in proper discernment of this type of person.

Many molesters of children have crossed the line, becoming reprobate in nature. They come to church and hide. They lurk in the darkness of lies and self-deception. They defile and practice their evil under the noses of the elders, pastors and Christian workers. Few teachings are available or taught on the subject of "evil people" and how to confront, expose and/or avoid them.

Psalms and Proverbs discuss this subject thoroughly, as well as the New Testament Scriptures. Jesus warned His disciples and trained them in discerning evil amongst the brethren. One reason the Lord allowed Judas to stay with the original disciples to the very end was to teach how evil "sons and daughters of the devil" sneak into the midst undetected. In 2 Peter 2 you will find a good account of their method of operation.

CULT FAMILY SYSTEMS ENDORSED BY THE CHURCH

The preservation of the family is one of the foundational messages of the church, and rightly so. Unfortunately, in an attempt to stem the tide of divorce and the breakup of the family, evil adults in abusive family systems are not properly dealt with. Many churches pity abusers and blame victims, letting the cycle of abuse and violence stay hidden. The church, for the most part, harbors these abusers—especially men. Christians who are victims of family abuse and violence get more support and help from the world than from their own church fellowships. Some denominations and individual fellowships are correcting this injustice, but far too many deny the problem.

Many of the families considered foundational members of thousands of churches across this nation are self-righteous and legalistic hypocrites trying to control and manipulate the pastor. They attempt to influence the congregation by way of seniority, money, the appearance of righteousness and good works. These people, when allowed to do so, will destroy revival after revival. When the Holy Spirit moves upon a fellowship to bring repentance, true confession of sin, forgiveness and a sincere love of the brethren, these people will douse the movement with religiosity and dampen the young convert's zeal. Their hidden bitter jealousy and selfish ambition will channel demonic attacks to shut down true movements of God.

On the other hand, if they can get into the limelight, they will help foster false revival through fleshly church growth programs. These are the "good-evil" type of families hidden in many fellowships, appearing to be good as they tithe faithfully, thus they get away with murder. That is right, murder! These are false brethren, born of the flesh, not by the Spirit of God, and they persecute those who have true faith, trying to destroy their divinely inspired life and liveliness. *"But as at that time he who was born according to the flesh persecuted him who was born according to the Spirit, so it is now"* (Galatians 4:29). (Also, read Matthew Chapter 23).

Christian Relationship Idolatry
Enthrallment that blinds one to evil, hinders true faith and stifles life.

Relationship idolatry: searching, dreaming, and lusting after the perfect mate, raising "super" children, obtaining the American Dream while maintaining non-stop romantic sensuous experiences—this is the worldview of relationships, and millions of Christians embrace this mindset. Christian romance novels and Christian fantasy fiction are in high demand. Christian marriages are troubled with divorce, abuse, and child neglect; all of these are on the rise. Most of these troubling relationship issues in the body of Christ hide from the light of the Gospel, but each day more and more secrets are exposed. The cares of this world are taking their toll on the Christian and Christian family.

Paul wrote, *"...I mean, brethren, the appointed time has grown very short; from now on, let those who have wives live as though they had none, and those who mourn as though they were not mourning, and those who rejoice as though they were not rejoicing, and those who buy as though they had no goods, and those who deal with the world as though they had no dealings with it. For the form of this world is passing away"* (1 Corinthians 7:29-31). The form of this world is passing away; but as the end of the age draws near, Christians are growing more and more obsessed with marriage, the perfect mate, material possessions, entertainment and financial freedom.

Inner craving for a sense of stability, self-worth and security have not driven Christians to God, who will demand that these carnal desires come to death on the cross, making Christ their all and in all. To the contrary, Christian fad teachings and false movements harness these fleshly passions to make Christians lust after the perfect marriage to the perfect Christian spouse, find and attend the perfect church, as well as follow the perfect ministry and idolize the perfect "anointed" teacher. They wrongly teach that in finding perfection in the right relationships, the right church, and the right dynamic leader, one's heart will find fulfillment. Unfortunately, these are temporal fulfillments offered by the world, and those preaching and teaching these fad doctrines make Christians dependent on their ministries, rather than trusting God in true faith and storing their treasures in heaven as Christ commanded.

Christians demand that relationships and material possessions continually feed these inner narcissistic needs and most of these false Christian teachings cater to these cravings. These boastful teachings produce naïve, self-centered and lust-driven Christians who will believe anyone who makes temporal "abundant life" promises and instant freedom. *"For, uttering loud boasts of folly, they entice with licentious passions of the flesh men who have barely escaped from those who live in error. They promise them freedom, but they themselves are slaves of corruption; for whatever overcomes a man, to that he is enslaved. For if, after they have escaped the defilements of the world through the knowledge of our Lord and Savior Jesus Christ, they are again entangled in them and overpowered, the last state has become worse for them than the first. For it would have been better for them never to have known the way of righteousness than after knowing it to turn back from the holy commandment delivered to them. It has happened to them according to the true proverb, The dog turns back to his own vomit, and the sow is washed only to wallow in the mire"* (2 Peter 2:18-22).

These Christians are never content with the person they are with, their family or their material status; rather, they yearn for worldly perfection in all these things. Single Christian men and women fall for mates whose hearts are far from God. Christians are bilked daily by charlatan evangelists and false prophets or the unscrupulous businessman marketing bogus or illegal get-rich-quick schemes.

The defilements of their former life in the world blind a multitude of Christians to evil, cloaked in a veneer of decency and religious hype. Far too many Christians are loaded down with the cares of this world and lusting for sensuous freedom in spousal intimacy, finances, romance, recognition, and success.

Even devout married Christians become ensnared within their relationships due to lack of discernment and misleading doctrine. They struggle with anxiety in their relationships, allowing the cares of this world and for each other to divide their devotion to Christ. I have counseled many troubled Christian couples confused by these false teachings that spawn relationship idolatry. Paul saw this forming within the church at Corinth as he expounded further about trusting God for all things and for each other, rising above the legitimate needs and cares in this life.

"I want you to be free from anxieties. The unmarried man is anxious about the affairs of the Lord, how to please the Lord; but the married man is anxious about worldly affairs, how to please his wife, and his interests are divided. And the unmarried woman or girl is anxious about the affairs of the Lord, how to be holy in body and spirit; but the married woman is anxious about worldly affairs, how to please her husband. I say this for your own benefit, not to lay any restraint upon you, but to promote good order and to secure your undivided devotion to the Lord" (1 Corinthians 7:32-35).

Some single women (and men) come to church looking for a mate. Their relationship to Christ is nominal at best, with their hearts bent on finding the perfect mate. Again, Paul warned in 1 Timothy 5 that the sincere single woman or widow should put their hope in God and the mature should be enrolled in fellowship and ministry work. Others who came were self-indulgent, being already dead while living. There is a flood of young men and women coming to the church looking for a mate, who are narcissistic, full of deception, lusting after the opposite sex. They are Christian in name only, going to church to cover up their selfish agenda.

Paul continues with his letter to Timothy stating, *"... for when they grow wanton against Christ they desire to marry, and so they incur condemnation for having violated their first pledge"* (1 Timothy 5:11). In this exhortation he points out that some have already strayed after Satan.

Children are pushed into sports, vocations, professions, and marriage in order to fulfill their parents' lost dreams or to make a showing to others that their son or daughter has arrived. From generation to generation, the cycle of relationship idolatry grows. Having children became a means for attention; eventually it all becomes a burden, not a blessing, and subtle abandonment and rejection seep in. This lust for the world and relationship idolatry creates Christian children with no sense of belonging.

We have extreme hero worship and personality enthrallment as sports figures, entertainers, flamboyant preachers, and Hollywood heroes become gods in the daily lives of the American Christian. Christian parents are creating spiritually dead and dysfunctional children, living for attention and acceptance from anyone who will look their way. Many of these adult children of dysfunctional Christian families enter church work or the ministry for all the wrong reasons—to gain glory and attention.

This nation's love of sports heroes has degenerated into worshipping the human physical body. Like many children of dysfunctional families, a sport becomes an escape with fantasies of heroic accolades and attention.

As a youngster, I idolized sports—especially football—and had my own unfulfilled dreams. This was a subtle pressure on my children. Years ago, when the Lord began to challenge this carnal issue, I was led to pray for a release from this invisible, yet powerful spiritual impingement. Within two days of this prayer, my oldest son decided not to play football during his senior year in high school. I had some difficulties accepting his decision; he certainly had the build and the attitude to compete at college level: 6' 3", aggressive, and tough as nails. He told me he loved to compete on the high school swim team and chose to make that his main sport to help him develop physically. For a while I thought God answered that "Abraham-Isaac" sacrificial prayer a little too quickly. I finally submitted to the will of God, and in my heart let my son live his own life.

After he graduated from high school, he joined the Coast Guard. His first duty was aboard the USCGC Vigilant; Cape Canaveral, Florida was homeport. He volunteered and trained to be the ship's rescue swimmer and was involved in the Haitian trouble in the early nineties.

On one of his first rescue missions, the Vigilant was dispatched to help search for a father and son overdue from a scuba diving excursion just off the Florida shores. The search had been frustrating, since there were no flags, boat, or specific location information—just a general vicinity of where they might be.

The cutter was making its planned search pattern as the crew had *eyes on the water*, looking for the lost scuba divers. My son manned the "big eyes," which is a permanently mounted high-powered binocular set on the cutter's flying bridge. Finding two divers bobbing on the ocean waves was an almost impossible chore, and dread soon set in.

My son began to think of what he would do if he were in their place. The thought came quickly: swim to the nearest buoy. He began to scan for the closest buoy and saw two figures clinging for life onto a buoy about a mile from the cutter and quite a distance from the shore. These two men were exhausted, and very thankful when brought aboard.

Tears swelled up as my son told me this account. It was very inspirational, his being so new to the demands of such service for our country; I was very proud. Then the Holy Spirit started to remind me of the prayer and sacrifice of heart to which the Lord had led me, just a couple of years prior. Christian parents must die to living out their lives through their children. Relationship idolatry and enthrallment destroys people, drains life from others, and often subverts God's plans.

THE ZEALOT APPROACH WILL NO LONGER BE BACKED BY GOD

In our zeal to stem the tide of immorality and wickedness in which this nation wallows, many Christians have become very vocal, and, in some cases, militant.

This militant approach is like the zealots who believed in the Law of Moses, as did the Pharisees. The zealots were distinguished from the Pharisees because they thought it was treachery against God to pay tribute to the Roman emperor. They became increasingly fanatical, willing to fight unto death for Jewish independence. Eventually, the zealot sect worsened in their opposition to Roman rule and became a group of assassins, or "dagger men." Their fanaticism increased to the point of being a major factor that helped incite the Roman-Jewish war. These fanatics took control of Jerusalem in AD 66, which led the Romans to lay siege to the city. Jerusalem fell in AD 70 and the temple was destroyed, as Jesus had predicted. The last stronghold of the zealots was the fortress of Masada, which fell to the Romans in AD 73.

The "foot in mouth" mistake made recently by one of the moral *religious right* leaders makes this point clear. This moral zealot had to retract his statements concerning the causes of the September 11 attack. In an interview on the 700

Club, this Christian leader accused the wicked, lesbians, homosexuals, occultists, civil liberty unionists, and such for the cause of the 9/11 attack on America!

You see God did not back him up whatsoever. In fact, Pat Robertson, the founder of the 700 Club and host of this interview, listened in agreement, but later backed away by saying that he himself was shocked and confused at these condemning words.

Expect in the very near future severe attacks on moral protesters and any public displays against sin, homosexuality, and abortion. There will be severe abuse given to any Christian and group of Christians who stand out and express disapproval of these blatant sins, especially homosexual public rallies and parades. God is saying: *Leave them alone*! Lot was nearly assaulted when he confronted the roving band of homosexual rapists in Sodom.

There comes a time when we must let God judge the wicked. We Christians must bow out of the protest arena and fall on our faces before God. This persecution and trouble will produce true intercession, repentance and cleansing, something we refused to do when all was well!

MORAL PROTESTS WILL BE CONSIDERED INFLAMMATORY AND WILL BE ATTACKED

The courts will start increasing the protection of the homosexuals and abortionists. They have already begun to use anti-racketeering laws against abortion protests. The hate crime law is just the beginning. Though this current White House administration may overturn some of these laws, you can expect a flood of laws to come later in support of the wicked.

There is such a fear sweeping the courts, local governments, and police units concerning homosexual reprisal and protest that they will sell out, and in some cases even back these evil agendas. They will consider moral protesting of any immoral event, gathering, or abortion clinic demonstration as inflammatory and see the participants as riot inciters. Christians who continue confrontational witnessing can expect attacks. People will start rejoicing as news accounts report these violent acts against moral protesters and militant Christians.

The pharisaical leaders who persist in fighting immorality in the flesh will fuel the war between the religious right and the liberals. This war will escalate with the self-righteous Christians throwing larger and larger stones. Already we see people like Dr. Laura Schlesinger backing down, with protesters demanding retractions. Again, consider the 700 Club comment previously mentioned. Those comments drew scathing attacks from the press and others.

There will be more sudden turns of events such as the mistake mentioned here that will cause many of these leaders to be crushed, like Rome crushing

Jerusalem and destroying the temple. All of this will incite more and more persecution to come upon the Christian. Those who desire to do God's will in these last days and be used of God mightily must refrain from this battle and deal with the evil hidden secret sins in the Church's midst and in their own lives. (See 1 Corinthians 5:9-13).

PERSECUTION MADNESS AND THE GREAT FALLING AWAY

Jesus prophesied a coming time where great persecution toward Christians would consume the world. He warned in Matthew 24 of a false spiritual awakening with many who would come in His name proclaiming lies and leading many astray. With this spiritual awakening, there would be wars and rumors of war, where nation would rise against nation. Alliances of nations would battle each other with famines and earthquakes in various places. This, He said, would be the beginning of the birth pangs just prior to the end of this age. What Christ said to the disciples next is what most Christians are not prepared for. All these signs are building up to the great persecution that Jesus spoke of in Matthew 24:9-13. *"Then they will deliver you up to tribulation, and put you to death; and you will be hated by all nations for my name's sake. And then many will fall away, and betray one another, and hate one another. And many false prophets will arise and lead many astray. And because wickedness is multiplied, most men's love will grow cold. But he who endures to the end will be saved."*

Satan is about to unleash a spirit of persecution upon the church, and we can expect it to be near the level of persecution that the early church suffered in ancient Rome. It will be illegal to murder, but if a Christian is murdered many will say that the death was a service to mankind.

The liberal Christian church will have to go all the way with the immoral agenda to avoid persecution. Many will succumb to this pressure and go all out with ordaining homosexual ministers. Even nudity as a form of worship will be made legitimate in some of these liberal churches. The liberal and lukewarm church will socially embrace government programs that supposedly help the poor, the homeless, and the welfare recipient. They will speak out for more social reform programs, appear socially righteous in helping the poor and downtrodden, but will only succeed in selling their souls to Satan.

I am reminded of the famous evangelists Dr. Robert Schuller who praised Bill Clinton during his first inauguration party, declaring this man a "repairer of the breach"—what a terrible judgment of character. This Christian leader—as so many others—is daubing the wall with whitewash by not speaking the truth!

The true church will have a hard time regrouping. The confusing doctrines and the independent spirit within each local fellowship must end. Persecution will burn it out! There is coming a time when the truly righteous will hide in their homes until the storm of evil passes over.

True ministries will keep their mouths shut, help those whom God calls out of darkness, do good to the household of faith, and wait upon the Lord humbly and in a true state of repentance. Judgment is coming and must come to the household of God first, in the form of great persecution, because we, His people, are so wayward. Jesus warned that Christians would be turned over to trouble and persecution. The hate would be worldwide. Why is God allowing this to happen?

Most Christians, through hypocrisy and secret wickedness have put themselves in danger. Since God's people refuse to do any sort of housecleaning, God will allow the wicked to "beat up" Christians for a season. This will bring true cleansing and strengthening, but Jesus also warned that many would fall away and betray one another. Soon we will see who are genuine and those who are a phony Christian playing church.

CHRISTIAN-BASHING WILL BE THE "IN THING TO DO"

This will shut down the boisterous Christians for fear of their lives. Christian symbols and "in-your-face" slogans on bumper stickers will meet with harassment and hate. People who wear Christ hypocritically around the neck and wrist will be targets for thugs, gang members and outraged homosexuals who will "bash" Christians for the fun of it.

God will allow this to happen to see who is genuine and who is phony. He already knows, but the problem is that we do not. There will be a separation of the wheat and tares that will allow the righteous to be clearly seen on that day when God finally acts.

God will act with great fierceness and wrath against all the ungodly sinners and wicked people who opposed Him and His true servants. First, He must cleanse and purify His people and chase out the wicked. A day of vengeance is coming, and in that day, God will have a glorious church that will shine in the darkness as millions of sinners flee to this beacon as the end of the Great Tribulation nears.

An army of true servants of Christ will walk in spiritual authority and power that in some cases will cause outright the death of some who practice evil openly. Just as Ananias and Sapphira fell dead at Peter's feet, many false Christians and wicked people will be made examples of God's terrible power.

"It was of these also that Enoch in the seventh generation from Adam prophesied, saying, "Behold, the Lord came with his holy myriads, to execute judgment on all, and to convict all the ungodly of all their deeds of ungodliness which they have committed in

such an ungodly way, and of all the harsh things which ungodly sinners have spoken against him" (Jude 14,15).

THE CRY OF JOB WILL BE HEARD THROUGHOUT THE CHURCH

Here is an ancient story found in the Old Testament that has stumped many theologians. Few Christians understand the message of Job.

Job was a man of faith who lived an exemplary life following the law of God faithfully. In fact, as the story of Job unfolds, God mentions to Satan Job's uprightness, a man who turns from evil and fears God. In reading this account, it would seem that God was bragging about Job to the devil.

Out of a vindictive nature Satan challenges God's assessment of Job by stating, *"Does Job fear God for nought? Hast thou not put a hedge about him and his house and all that he has, on every side? Thou hast blessed the work of his hands, and his possessions have increased in the land. But put forth thy hand now, and touch all that he has, and he will curse thee to thy face"* (Job 1:9-11).

Astoundingly, God allows Satan to attack Job. As you read the account of Job's suffering it becomes clear that God is not protecting Job whatsoever. He lost everything, including his children. The only thing that Satan was not allowed to bring upon Job was his physical death. Finally, Satan afflicted Job with terrible sores all over his body. This physical disease was so bad that Job ended up sitting on hill of ashes, scraping his sores. Even his wife turned against him and said, *"Do you still hold fast your integrity? Curse God, and die"* (Job 2:9).

In all of these terrible afflictions, tribulation and evil at the hand of Satan, Job did not sin by cursing God with his mouth, nor turn from God in his heart.

Let us consider the issue of the ages, the suffering of the righteous. Does God allow the righteous to suffer arbitrarily?

Job had three friends who came to console him. These three friends tried to convince Job that somehow, he had a secret sin that caused God to allow such terrible affliction to overtake him. Job contested their advice and counsel holding to his innocence and stated, *"Teach me, and I will be silent; make me understand how I have erred. How forceful are honest words! But what does reproof from you reprove?"* (Job 6:24,25).

However, there was a problem with Job's relationship with God. There was no secret sin, no bad attitude, but Job does direct his complaint against God, unable to see that Satan was the perpetrator of the evil that befell him. Job says of God, *""How then can I answer him, choosing my words with him? Though I am innocent, I cannot answer him; I must appeal for mercy to my accuser. If I summoned him and he answered me, I would not believe that he was listening to my voice. For he crushes me with a tempest, and multiplies my wounds without cause; he will not let me get my breath, but fills me with bitterness. If it is a contest of strength, behold him! If it is a matter of justice, who can summon him? Though*

I am innocent, my own mouth would condemn me; though I am blameless, he would prove me perverse. I am blameless; I regard not myself; I loathe my life. It is all one; therefore I say, he destroys both the blameless and the wicked. When disaster brings sudden death, he mocks at the calamity of the innocent. The earth is given into the hand of the wicked; he covers the faces of its judges—if it is not he, who then is it? 'My days are swifter than a runner; they flee away, they see no good. They go by like skiffs of reed, like an eagle swooping on the prey. If I say, 'I will forget my complaint, I will put off my sad countenance, and be of good cheer,' I become afraid of all my suffering, for I know thou wilt not hold me innocent. I shall be condemned; why then do I labor in vain? If I wash myself with snow, and cleanse my hands with lye, yet thou wilt plunge me into a pit, and my own clothes will abhor me. For he is not a man, as I am, that I might answer him, that we should come to trial together. There is no umpire between us, who might lay his hand upon us both. Let him take his rod away from me, and let not dread of him terrify me. Then I would speak without fear of him, for I am not so in myself. 'I loathe my life; I will give free utterance to my complaint; I will speak in the bitterness of my soul. I will say to God, Do not condemn me; let me know why thou dost contend against me. Does it seem good to thee to oppress, to despise the work of thy hands and favor the designs of the wicked?'" (Job 9:14–10:3).

Throughout the first half of the book, Job and his three friends argue with each other concerning the reason for Job's suffering. In chapter 32:1 it states, *"So these three men ceased to answer Job, because he was righteous in his own eyes."*

There was another man there, Elihu, who was younger than Job and the other three. Due to his youth, Elihu refrained from any comments or counsel. When the argument stopped, Elihu confronted all four in their error. Elihu saw that Job's three friends had declared Job was in error but could not find the true reason. Elihu also saw that Job had justified himself rather than God. Elihu points out to Job the real problem—which was counting on his own righteous living as reason why God should always protect and bless him.

The reason for Job's suffering was simple; this righteous man had faith in God, but also had faith in his own righteousness. To keep Job from going down to the pit in his self-righteous condition, God allowed Satan to sift and attack Job to a point. God used Satan to break Job of his inner self-righteous stance. Satan has learned to keep most Christians blind to this condition, for the devil knows in the end how damning self-righteousness will be for the deceived Christian.

This is a terrible lie that many Christians live by today: a lie promoted by leadership throughout the body of Christ, which concerns faith in faith and trust in one's own righteousness rather than trusting in God's grace and mercy. This stance will give Satan a free rein to test Christians with affliction, trouble and calamity.

Job blamed God for his sorrow. In fact, though he did not curse and sin against God, he did ascribe to God being ambivalent and arbitrary by allowing trouble to come to the righteous as well as the wicked. Job says, *"He destroys both the blameless and the wicked."* (Job 9:22).

The complaint and cry that came from Job during his sufferings will come from many Christians in the coming days, as they suffer calamity like Job's. You see, much of the church is in the same spiritual condition that Job was in, that is, before he was humbled.

These Christians love God but believe the lie that prosperity and temporal blessings are a right, based on their righteousness. Many will say in the near future, *"I am innocent, and God has taken away my right; in spite of my right I am counted a liar; my wound is incurable, though I am without transgression.... It profits a man nothing that he should take delight in God"* (See Job 34:5-12).

This was Job's stance, but Elihu saw Job's real issue and confronted it head on. When Elihu ceased his words to Job, Job was silent. Remember Job himself said, *"Teach me, and I will be silent."*

It is interesting to note that when Elihu finished, Job kept his silence, but also God spoke directly to Job and confirmed that which Elihu had spoken. Finally, when God finished, Job broke his silence and admitted, *"I had heard of thee by the hearing of the ear, but now my eye sees thee; therefore I despise myself, and repent in dust and ashes"* (Job 42:5,6).

Many Christians do not see their true ugliness. Paul came to this conclusion as well. He was a New Testament Job. Paul wrote, *"For we are the true circumcision, who worship God in spirit, and glory in Christ Jesus, and put no confidence in the flesh. Though I myself have reason for confidence in the flesh also. If any other man thinks he has reason for confidence in the flesh, I have more: circumcised on the eighth day, of the people of Israel, of the tribe of Benjamin, a Hebrew born of Hebrews; as to the law a Pharisee, as to zeal a persecutor of the church, as to righteousness under the law blameless. But whatever gain I had, I counted as loss for the sake of Christ. Indeed I count everything as loss because of the surpassing worth of knowing Christ Jesus my Lord. For his sake I have suffered the loss of all things, and count them as refuse, in order that I may gain Christ and be found in him, not having a righteousness of my own, based on law, but that which is through faith in Christ, the righteousness from God that depends on faith; that I may know him and the power of his resurrection, and may share his sufferings, becoming like him in his death, that if possible I may attain the resurrection from the dead"* (Philippians 3:3-11).

After Paul's conversion to Christ, he found how truly wicked the sin nature is. He discovered a great revelation; that he was a "wretched man" who desperately needed a Savior to change him. He discovered this after he became a Christian!

God desires to show the self-righteous Christian the truth about their inner self, its ugly wretchedness that can be just as vile through self-righteousness as that of a terrible sinner through their unrighteousness.

Today, Christians are counting on an inner self-righteous stance with God to be exempt from suffering, trials and not have to depend on God for everything. Far too many saints are righteous in their own eyes, have not been humbled and cleansed of their inner self-righteousness, which is as murderous and hateful as the vilest sinner.

Soon many shallow Christians will ascribe to God what Job ascribed to God during his suffering, *"For Job said, 'I am innocent, and God has taken away my right; in spite of my right I am counted a liar; my wound is incurable, though I am without transgression.' What man is like Job, who drinks up scoffing like water, who goes in company with evildoers and walks with wicked men? For he has said, 'It profits a man nothing that he should take delight in God.' Therefore, hear me, you men of understanding, far be it from God that he should do wickedness, and from the Almighty that he should do wrong. For according to the work of a man he will requite him, and according to his ways he will make it befall him. Of a truth, God will not do wickedly, and the Almighty will not pervert justice."* (Job 34:5-12).

Mark it down; many will fall from their shallow walk into a mournful condition. God sent Elihu to Job to break the denial of self-righteousness. Elihu was a *"nobody"* in Job's circle of fellowship. Remember what Paul wrote concerning the nobodies whom God will use.

"For consider your call, brethren; not many of you were wise according to worldly standards, not many were powerful, not many were of noble birth; but God chose what is foolish in the world to shame the wise, God chose what is weak in the world to shame the strong, God chose what is low and despised in the world, even things that are not, to bring to nothing things that are, so that no human being might boast in the presence of God. He is the source of your life in Christ Jesus, whom God made our wisdom, our righteousness and sanctification and redemption; therefore, as it is written, "Let him who boasts, boast of the Lord" (1 Corinthians 1:26-31).

There is no condemnation from God when the saint comes to the true assessment of his or her own self. That is the vital understanding that the true saint must receive in order to overcome the sin nature and the works of the flesh.

"For by grace you have been saved through faith; and this is not your own doing, it is the gift of God—not because of works, lest any man should boast" (Ephesians 2:8,9). Unfortunately, many start out having faith in the grace of God, but fall back into religious self-righteousness, never having Christ formed within them. (See Galatians 3:22-4:10).

Now is the time to get ready, God's way. Allow the Holy Spirit to show you your dependence on religion that stems from an inner self-righteous stance.

GOOD-HEARTED PEOPLE, TURNED OFF TO THE GOSPEL

Christians often are more treacherous than the good-hearted lost sinner. I am afraid that much of Christianity has progressively become hardened and hypocritical, just as Christ observed of the religious leaders, priests, and the so-called righteous of his generation.

There are millions of good-hearted people in this nation who are turned off to the Gospel. The Gospel, preached and presented, does not match up with a Christ-like example in day-to-day life, not to mention the sickening criminal and financial scandals or the madness demonstrated in some of the rallies and revival meetings. Indeed, if the true Holy Spirit of God were to move upon the masses, there would be only a few solid congregations and ministries that would teach sound doctrine and make true disciples. To solve this problem, God is about to allow suffering to come and then do a new thing.

PROPHETIC TURF WARS WITH NO WINNERS

In attempting to recognize the office of apostle and prophet within the church, many have embraced the counterfeit and the carnal. A movement called the Five-Fold ministry has sprung up over the last twenty or so years that emphasizes the restoration of the function of apostle and prophet within the local church and in the body of Christ.

Just as there are evangelists, teachers and pastors, this teaching, taken from the Ephesians 4:11-16 and 1 Corinthians 12:27-31, affirms that apostle and prophet are also part of Christ's gift to the church to equip the saints for the work of the ministry, until there is true unity of faith.

Many in this movement esteem an apostle and prophet more important than a pastor, evangelist, and teacher. A leadership hierarchy is established.

Of course, we see this in many other denominations as evangelists and certain teachers and pastors become nationally and internationally recognized and highly esteemed. Recognized leaders such as Hank Hanegraaff, Billy Graham, Dr. R. C. Sproul, Dr. Charles Stanley and many more command a high place of honor with many Christians today. Some deserve to be recognized for their contribution, but many are put on a pedestal.

Yes, we need leaders appointed, prepared, and disciplined by Christ today, more than ever. The mission for all godly leadership is to equip God's people to stand on their own two feet of faith, obtaining the full knowledge of Christ, no longer being deceived by false teachers, evil men and women disguised as sheep.

Again, true leaders who are personally trained by Christ are, *"to equip the saints for the work of ministry, for building up the body of Christ, until we all attain to the unity of the faith and of the knowledge of the Son of God, to mature manhood, to the measure of the stature of the fulness of Christ; so that we may no longer be children, tossed to and fro and carried about with every wind of doctrine, by the cunning of men, by their craftiness in deceitful wiles. Rather, speaking the truth in love, we are to grow up in every way into him who is the head, into Christ, from whom the whole body, joined and knit together by every joint with which it is supplied, when each part is working properly, makes bodily growth and upbuilds itself in love"* (Ephesians 4:12-16).

This movement has produced apostles and prophets who allow themselves to be elevated. These self-elevated leaders gain authority through deceived Christians, who believe these leaders have an anointing that the poor weak saint needs in order to be set free.

There is now a war of prophetic ministries and prophetic messages inundating the body of Christ through this movement. Again, they take the passage from Malachi that states, *"Behold, I will send you Elijah the prophet before the great and terrible day of the LORD comes. And he will turn the hearts of fathers to their children and the hearts of children to their fathers, lest I come and smite the land with a curse"* (Malachi 4:5,6).

Jesus said of Elijah's returning, *"Elijah does come, and he is to restore all things; but I tell you that Elijah has already come, and they did not know him, but did to him whatever they pleased. So also the Son of man will suffer at their hands"* (Matthew 17:11,12). Jesus was speaking of John the Baptist.

Jesus spoke of many false prophets arising as the end of this age draws near. These prophets are dispensing one prophetic word after another. A pattern has emerged where these "superlative" apostles (superlative was Paul's description for the false apostle) and highly touted prophets compete for recognition. These preach deceitful messages that minimize Christ's warnings and teachings on the end of the age, the treachery of the Antichrist and the trouble Christians must endure.

More and more ear-tickling prophecies spew out of their mouths to those who idolize their anointing. Yet, they dispense stern warnings for those who don't jump on their bandwagon.

These promote an exclusive club of elite apostles and prophets to whom the deceived must submit. These teachings speak of the Lord's return as a process dictated by the purification of the church and restoration of the earth. There is a subtle mix of premillennial and postmillennial teachings and—*who knows if there will be a Rapture of the saints.* They do not see the Rapture occurring at the end of the Great Tribulation.

I quote John Sandford from his book, *Elijah Among Us*, where he prophesies of a coming wave or move of God, *"The second wave will be marked by healing of the earth. His messengers, in this coming wave, will lead into the healing of the nations and the healing of the earth.... How much shall be accomplished by, or during, this coming wave, I cannot say. I know all will be done, but perhaps much awaits another great wave—or wait our Lord's return, to be accomplished only after His Parousia. I want to celebrate the Father's purposes and His eminence, as He acts among us and in the earth. I call the Church to look up, to expect and receive the maturation of His prophets and apostles, and to respond in obedience"* (Page 239).

This movement is counterfeit for the most part. Some in this movement started out with insight concerning inner sanctification, but hijacked it, mixing New Age and pop psychology, producing a carnal ministry to build a reconstructionist approach in getting the church ready for Christ's return. This allows an elitist approach to ministry, making a living on helping cure the double-minded or 'twice souled' Christian.

This is ministry-kingdom building through making themselves indispensable to the body of Christ. *"We hear from God, you don't. We have the anointing, you don't."*

They are ignoring Christ's commission to make disciples, teaching them to observe all that Jesus commanded and taught. True leadership is commissioned to teach God's people to be taught and led by the Holy Spirit. Again, Jesus said, *"My sheep hear my voice."*

But instead, these false or at best carnal prophets and apostles parade as though they have it together, hear from God, and have the answers for inner healing and transformation. They believe that when the next wave or move of God comes they will be the foundation or glue that holds it all together. There will be a purging of the filth, as Sandford puts it, through a baptism of fire.

Again, quoting from Sandford's same book, *"In this work of purging by fire and judgment, God's Nathanic prophets who understand and decipher the deceptions of the human heart will become crucial. Purging and fire only become blessing and joy where ministry turns them into mercy and kindness. Where Christians do not avail themselves of such ministry, or cannot find it, the Lord will accomplish the same purging and sanctification the hard way, by pain and suffering"* (Page 236).

The fire Sanford speaks of is an increased outpouring of God's presence where those in this movement will be ushered into the presence of God and somehow whisk through any trouble because they embraced their brand of inner healing and inner transformation. They are ignorant of James' teachings concerning the twice-souled Christian who, if told how to cooperate with the

Holy Spirit as counselor in the discipline of the Lord, can become pure, without their super-sensational host of counselors, prophets and apostles.

No evangelist, pastor, teacher, apostle, or prophet should try to elevate himself or herself to a position of being indispensable. Counseling is good, but we should have true discipleship at the local church where the gift of prophecy and the sound counsel of God are available without fees. One of these prophets, John Paul Jackson, has distinguished himself from the other ministries by specializing in dream interpretation. Others specialize in counseling, prophecy and/or other special teachings.

You must understand, the counterfeit can look like the true item, but upon examination and with discernment, the carnal, and in some cases, New Age or Native American spiritualism, becomes apparent.

The terrible thing about the false or carnal that engages in this prophetic turf war is that in the end, there are no winners. They do not walk in the true prophetic where the secrets of the heart are disclosed; rather they see some issues but keep the anointing for themselves, lest they work themselves out of a job. These false and carnal teachers have hijacked the restoration of the office of apostle and prophet, counseling, and the prophetic gifting, along with their carnal brand of revival—building for themselves a business out of ministry.

They miss the mark! Case in point, in Sandford's book he praises Paul Cain stating, "In 1988, the Holy Spirit showcased the prophets in what was then a large Vineyard church in Denver. Paul Cain, perhaps the foremost and most well-known of the early modern prophets, was there. After his teaching, he called people to receive personal words."

All these years Paul Cain sat right under the *discerning* noses of John Sandford, Mike Bickle, Rick Joyner, Bob Jones, Jack Deere, Cindy Jacobs, John Arnott and a host of others. Cain ministered within this movement heavily, prophesying and laying hands on others. The truth finally came out about this showcased prophet of this wayward movement. Rick Joyner, Jack Deere and Mike Bickle went public with their attempt to help Paul Cain get out of alcohol and stop engaging in homosexuality.

Joyner, Bickle and Deere tried to restore Cain with confrontational counseling, but as these three men put it, *"Paul has resisted this process and has continued in his sin."*

The apostle Paul taught, *"I wrote to you in my letter not to associate with immoral men; not at all meaning the immoral of this world, or the greedy and robbers, or idolaters, since then you would need to go out of the world. But rather I wrote to you not to associate with anyone who bears the name of brother if he is guilty of immorality or greed, or is an idolater, reviler, drunkard, or robber–not even to eat with such a one. For what have I to do with judging outsiders? Is it not those inside the church whom you are to judge? God judges those outside. 'Drive out the wicked person from among you'"* (1 Corinthians 5:9-13).

These men are to be commended for confronting and exposing this kind of immorality. There needs to be a thorough housecleaning within this movement, starting with the false doctrines. The root problem of this tragedy is the false doctrine that elevates a self-proclaimed apostle-prophet into leadership. How much more is hidden within the dark recesses of this and other movements that practice leadership idolatry?

In 1992, I had an opportunity to listen to Cain in person and was warned by the Holy Spirit to avoid his ministry. The leadership idolatry was subtle but noticeable then and has become obvious as the meetings demonstrate more and more spiritual sensuousness.

Having wicked people in leadership is not unique to this movement. Recently, I discussed this problem with a friend and senior leader in a noted evangelical denomination. He shared about a young woman coming to him in private during a recent denominational conference, asking for counsel. This woman reported that one of the high leaders in this conference was a pedophile and had molested her during her teen years. My friend listened and then offered to go to leadership and confront this predator, but she begged him not to for fear of hurting this wicked servant's family. My friend felt he could do nothing to expose this evil. So, this high-ranking leader is free to molest others.

Our ministry was led to pray that this man be exposed and brought down, even if the denomination gets a black mark. Enough is enough—we are to drive out the wicked from amongst the brethren!

As I mentioned earlier, evangelical, Pentecostal and charismatic denominations and other Christian groups look to promote flamboyant leaders who have the *"anointing."* The thinking is to present the best to build the church, denomination, or movement, giving these spotlight-seeking apostles the high seat of honor. A true apostle or prophet is not interested in self-promotion or carving out his or her own turf.

God uses those who are not so elegant in speaking, but whose hearts loves Christ above all else and truly avoid sharing His glory. These true servants do not lust after power, but rather have been disciplined to empty themselves, taking on true servanthood, having Christ formed within. These run the race without taking shortcuts. *"Therefore, since we are surrounded by so great a cloud of witnesses, let us also lay aside every weight, and sin which clings so closely, and let us run with perseverance the race that is set before us, looking to Jesus the pioneer and perfecter of our faith, who for the joy that was set before him endured the cross, despising the shame, and is seated at the right hand of the throne of God"* (Hebrews 12:1-2).

Lust for prophetic power and anointing has truly dampened discernment, entrapping this movement in a no-win situation. The only possible way to salvage true faith for those involved is to have a movement-wide renouncement of the false doctrine of postmillennialism that incorporates New Age and Native American spiritualism, renounce leadership idolatry and stop the counterfeit manifestations. In a clean sweep, the movement must preach sound doctrine that teaches on true discipleship that will build a foundation for true revival, a true end-of-the-age revival that God will facilitate during the Great Tribulation period.

The foundation of this Five-Fold ministry movement is faulty, its key doctrines do not embrace all that Jesus taught and commanded. The love they preach is a love for ministry, the world, the earth and recognition, showcasing each other's accomplishments. Those who truly love Christ will follow all His commandments, including the troubling death-to-self teachings and the end-of-the age terror that will come. Unfortunately, the false doctrines found in this movement will not allow the sincere saint to win the full prize, having Christ becoming all and in all. Some will not win the race at all being deceived and taking ease concerning the end-of-the-age trouble, persecution, and fiery trials that will face the church.

"And this is love, that we follow his commandments; this is the commandment, as you have heard from the beginning, that you follow love. For many deceivers have gone out into the world, men who will not acknowledge the coming of Jesus Christ in the flesh; such a one is the deceiver and the antichrist. Look to yourselves, that you may not lose what you have worked for, but may win a full reward. Anyone who goes ahead and does not abide in the doctrine of Christ does not have God; he who abides in the doctrine has both the Father and the Son. If any one comes to you and does not bring this doctrine, do not receive him into the house or give him any greeting; for he who greets him shares his wicked work" (2 John 1:7-11).

No one will win this prophetic turf war and those who follow and support this deceitful work will partake in its judgment. Leadership in this movement will encounter more trouble as God brings judgment and discipline to its lascivious practices of false prophecy, empty manifestations, and greed for recognition. This is a false movement that counterfeits what the Lord will soon do. This movement would like to manage and control the maturing of the church through a hierarchy of apostles and prophets that they appoint and recognize. They like to believe that God would use this movement to restore all things so Christ can return.

No, Christ will prepare His Church Himself through the coming persecution and fiery trials. *"That he might sanctify her, having cleansed her by the washing of water with the word, that he might present the church to himself in splendor, without spot or wrinkle or any such thing, that she might be holy and without blemish"* (Ephesians 5:26,27).

A remnant will arise, unorganized by any man-made movement, yet walk in unison as the true Holy Spirit directs true ministry through true disciples. This end-of-the-age revival will have Christian workers and pure saints supported and served by true apostles, prophets, evangelists, pastors, and teachers who will not rob Christ of His preeminence within the Church.

Those in leadership who do not become humble, repent, and build disciples, teaching them to be taught by the Holy Spirit will be exposed, driven out, shut down, ignored and in some cases taken home prematurely.

OLD WINE SKINS DISCARDED
MAKING WAY FOR THE LAST-GENERATION WARRIOR CHRISTIANS

Indeed, a true New Testament body of believers will arise as trouble and personal trials shape each new enlistee of this last generation of Christian disciples. Jesus gave a parable concerning old and new wine skins.

"And the Pharisees and their scribes murmured against his disciples, saying, 'Why do you eat and drink with tax collectors and sinners?' And Jesus answered them, 'Those who are well have no need of a physician, but those who are sick; I have not come to call the righteous, but sinners to repentance.' And they said to him, 'The disciples of John fast often and offer prayers, and so do the disciples of the Pharisees, but yours eat and drink.' And Jesus said to them, 'Can you make wedding guests fast while the bridegroom is with them? The days will come, when the bridegroom is taken away from them, and then they will fast in those days.' He told them a parable also: 'No one tears a piece from a new garment and puts it upon an old garment; if he does, he will tear the new, and the piece from the new will not match the old. And no one puts new wine into old wineskins; if he does, the new wine will burst the skins and it will be spilled, and the skins will be destroyed. But new wine must be put into fresh wineskins. And no one after drinking old wine desires new; for he says, 'The old is good'" (Luke 5:30-39).

These last few generations of Christians have labored long and hard to bring the Gospel to the lost. From the reformation in the 1500s to the sweeping crusades of Billy Graham, vast amounts of books, literature and teachings have been produced to touch the lost and encourage the saint. Most efforts were commendable works, but with this heritage came stagnation and religiosity to the body of Christ. Denominational pride, evangelical self-righteousness,

Pentecostal fanaticism, and charismatic spiritualism have overtaken much of the body of Christ throughout North America.

God's people are set in their ways, clinging to half-truths and doctrines that emanate prideful distinction. I am not referring to the liberal denominations, false Christian cults, or New Age spiritualism. No, just as Jesus confronted God's people during His ministry, so today the Lord must confront God's people who have received the blessings of all these last generations of sold-out saints who have fought for reformation and the restoration of truth found in the written Word of God. In these many battles for the Gospel over the last 40 years, most have run their course and become proudly set in their portion of truth. They are completely convinced that they hold the proper worship and walk before God. In the strength of prideful religiosity, they have made themselves feeble for the last-day battle. Some will adjust to what God is about to do, but unfortunately, many will stand in the way, as did the Pharisees of Christ's day when they opposed the first-generation disciples and apostles.

These old warriors cannot embrace the work of the cross that lays bare religious self-righteousness and denominational pride. Some will give up these issues that hinder, but not many, especially those in power and control.

Can you imagine veterans of the two World Wars, Korean or Viet Nam fighting in today's military services? They would be of very little use, set in their old training ways and unable to adapt quickly to make use of the power available in equipment and communications. They would be unable to mobilize promptly in today's high-tech *command and control* environment. The new wine of technology for America's fighting forces, with its intensive training demands and its constant fluid changes in strategy and tactics, makes the old soldier obsolete in effective deployment for battle. This does not mean the old soldier was not heroic, courageous, and obedient to duty and service of country.

Likewise, many faithful Christians throughout these last 40 to 50 years of service will not be able to give up old habits of carnal religious duty. They will not be able to endure the spiritual warfare that works through the satanic implants or adapt to confronting evil in the power of God that may require instant death to the wicked, as the case of Ananias and Sapphira. (See Acts 5). These old saints will struggle with the restoration of the foundational message of the New Testament—salvation by God's call, sanctification through fiery trials and the work of the cross for the believer—that destroys confidence in self and in religious methods.

What is the main message that the old wineskins cannot bear to hear and embrace? It is the true work of the cross for the believer.

I recall, as a young assistant pastor in an evangelical denomination, a doctrine that was very enslaving: holding Sunday as the Sabbath in which no one was to work, or even dine out or go grocery shopping. These precious saints reverted to a legalistic gospel that Paul fought in his writings to the body of believers at Galatia. Other epistles confront these same disqualifying observances, which, on the surface appear to be wise in promoting devotion and self-abasement. Nevertheless, these doctrines, as well as other errant teachings, have no value in stopping the works of the flesh. (See Galatians 3:1-5, 6:11-16 and Colossians 2:8-23).

The many self-enforced holiness doctrines—baptism preferences, required spiritual gift experiences as evidence of the baptism in Holy Spirit, and other special teachings—all add up to fleshly methods. These promote distinction in order to present a good showing, but they do not bring the saint to the rest of the Lord or into the fullness of His presence.

The last generation "true saint" and "true disciple" will be the new wineskins that will hold the last day outpouring of God's presence and demonstrated power. Remember that Jesus prophesied about this added work force that would intimidate the old saint who had worked all day long, leading up to the final harvest. (See Matthew 20:1-16).

In the last decades a prayer movement called *concerts of prayer* sprang up. I had opportunity to share in a few of these gatherings. Usually there were four or five topics given by as many speakers, and my topic was *brokenness*. I would expound on the work of the cross in the believer's life that produced death to self, death to the flesh, and death to religious self-righteousness. I was usually one of the last to speak. The first part of this message received a warm embrace. When the end of the message came, not many stayed receptive.

At the end, I challenged them with a call to a sacrificial life in Christ; astonishingly, faces on most turned ashen and many that I made eye contact with portrayed a terrible anguish and fear.

Here is what I said: *"If you desire to come into the fullness of life in Christ, becoming a true disciple, then you must make an unreserved covenant with God by giving Him permission to do whatever it takes to change you and destroy every ounce of carnal nature within. This means you must also give God permission not to stop any trial or fiery ordeal that would cause you to want to break the covenant as a living sacrifice–no matter how much you would kick, yell or falter."*

This final call would send terror through the old saint. They knew intuitively that their scope of control and power through religious doctrine would be one of the first things *axed* by God. Many saw the loss of financial status, knowing deep inside that they were trying to serve two masters: God and mammon. Some feared the loss of loved ones as they sensed the Holy Spirit's conviction concerning relationship idolatry and their unwillingness to let their children go, as God required Abraham to do concerning the promise of God through Isaac.

My dear brothers and sisters, this is what I present to you now! You may have part of your heart fastened to a special hobby, an idolatrous love of a new home or car, ministry success, money, power, control or a relationship. You must count the cost and let it go! This is the demand of Christ for all true disciples, or else you cannot be His disciple.

Part two of this message will help you cooperate with God in this process and learn to give up these idols of heart. You must make the above covenant and you must consider this: you had better sit down and count the cost, because anything and everything will be subject to the work of the cross, where death to the love of the world, the pride of life and the lust of the eye will be destroyed!

Here is some Scripture to help you accept this exhortation.

"I appeal to you therefore, brethren, by the mercies of God, to present your bodies as a living sacrifice, holy and acceptable to God, which is your spiritual worship. Do not be conformed to this world but be transformed by the renewal of your mind, that you may prove what is the will of God, what is good and acceptable and perfect" (Romans 12:1-2).

As you consider these warnings and the harder teachings of Christ, you must look at the whole purpose of God and set your hope and desire on His coming and the kingdom of God. The end of the age is upon us and the return of Christ is soon.

"But do not ignore this one fact, beloved, that with the Lord one day is as a thousand years, and a thousand years as one day. The Lord is not slow about his promise as some count slowness, but is forbearing toward you, not wishing that any should perish, but that all should reach repentance. But the day of the Lord will come like a thief, and then the heavens will pass away with a loud noise, and the elements will be dissolved with fire, and the earth and the works that are upon it will be burned up. Since all these things are thus to be dissolved, what sort of persons ought you to be in lives of holiness and godliness, waiting for and hastening the coming of the day of God, because of which the heavens will be kindled and dissolved, and the elements will melt with fire! But according to his promise we wait for new heavens and a new earth in which righteousness dwells. Therefore, beloved, since you wait for these, be zealous to be found by him without spot or blemish, and at peace (2 Peter 3:8-14).

If you choose to be zealous, part two of this message will help you work out your salvation and be ready for our Lord's appearance!

"He who testifies to these things says, 'Surely I am coming soon' Amen. Come, Lord Jesus!" (Revelation 21:20).

PART TWO

HOW TO STAND AND ENDURE TO THE END

PRELUDE

...The Great and Terrible Day of the Lord Approaches, but Who Can Endure It?

"BLOW the trumpet in Zion; sound the alarm on my holy mountain! Let all the inhabitants of the land tremble, for the day of the LORD is coming, it is near, a day of darkness and gloom, a day of clouds and thick darkness! Like blackness there is spread upon the mountains a great and powerful people; their like has never been from of old, nor will be again after them through the years of all generations. Fire devours before them, and behind them a flame burns. The land is like the garden of Eden before them, but after them a desolate wilderness, and nothing escapes them. Their appearance is like the appearance of horses, and like war horses they run. As with the rumbling of chariots, they leap on the tops of the mountains, like the crackling of a flame of fire devouring the stubble, like a powerful army drawn up for battle. Before them peoples are in anguish, all faces grow pale. Like warriors they charge, like soldiers they scale the wall. They march each on his way, they do not swerve from their paths. They do not jostle one another, each marches in his path; they burst through the weapons and are not halted. They leap upon the city, they run upon the walls; they climb up into the houses, they enter through the windows like a thief. The earth quakes before them, the heavens tremble. The sun and the moon are darkened, and the stars withdraw their shining. The LORD utters his voice before his army, for his host is exceedingly great; he that executes his word is powerful. For the day of the LORD is great and very terrible; who can endure it? (Joel 2:1-11).

CHAPTER 6

Refiner's Fire and Fullers' Soap

SIT DOWN AND COUNT THE COST

Jesus warned His followers to sit down and count the cost of becoming a true disciple. Many Christians have never heard this admonishment. Christ desires to deal with you and me thoroughly. This means everything that interferes with the lordship of Christ in our life, those things that we love more than Christ, must come under His discipline. We must submit to His discipline and we cannot control or speed up this process, but we can abort or slow it down if we do not learn how to cooperate. We must consider the demands of His discipline, for many underestimate the difficulties and trials God ordains and become discouraged and quit.

We must learn how to present our lives to this all-demanding work of Christ. We must be willing to renounce all that we control and expect fiery trials and pressuring circumstances to purify our hearts. We must brace for the worst, hope for the best, and expect Christ to complete that which He started. We must let go and trust God with our lives and for those we love. *"So therefore, whoever of you does not renounce all that he has cannot be my disciple"* (See Luke 14:25-35).

UNQUENCHABLE FIRE

John the Baptist said Christ would come and baptize with the Holy Spirit and baptize with unquenchable fire. *"Even now the axe is laid to the root of the trees; every tree therefore that does not bear good fruit is cut down and thrown into the fire. I baptize you with water for repentance, but he who is coming after me is mightier than I, whose sandals I am not worthy to carry; he will baptize you with the Holy Spirit and with fire. His winnowing fork is in his hand, and he will clear his threshing floor and gather his wheat into the granary, but the chaff he will burn with unquenchable fire"* (Matthew 3:10,12).

Christian writers have written volumes concerning the many workings of the Holy Spirit, yet most Christians have little understanding concerning Christ's work and the baptism of the Holy Spirit in conjunction with the baptism of fire. Many equate the baptism of fire aspect of Christ's work with some special ecstatic spiritual and emotional experience.

The Holy Spirit has many ministrations or works. He will give counsel, comfort, and spiritual gifts; reveal truth, bring to remembrance truth, illuminate or give understanding to the written Word of God, convict of sin, judgment, and righteousness, bear witness to the Person and personal work of Jesus Christ and bear fruit within the character of a true Christian. Many Christians misunderstand that the Spirit of Christ ministers in conjunction with and directs the work of the Holy Spirit as God wills. Remember, the spiritual Person of Christ is distinct from the work of the Holy Spirit, who is God and abides in us, the Father and the Son.

Christ desires to have the Holy Spirit dwell fully within the true Christian. Christ begins the process of discipline and cleansing to change our character, so the Holy Spirit's fullness is unhampered. To accomplish this Christ will baptize with fire.

When we receive the Holy Spirit, peace, assurance, and the building up of the believer's faith will begin. New Christians need steady nurturing and encouragement by mature disciples. This prepares the new Christian to grow and receive the deeper things of God. When the new believer is ready, Christ will arrange stringent discipline, which will include trials and challenges that purify our faith. Some trials will be fiery and continue with no end in sight until the issues God wants us to see are exposed and properly dealt with.

This process is the baptism of fire and is required of every true disciple of Christ. Today, most Christians are basic followers of Christ. They lack sound doctrine and proper support to submit to the discipline of the Lord and become disciples.

Christians suffer from shallowness, weak character, immaturity and an insecure relationship with God. Paul addressed this concern in his letters to the Christians at Corinth and elsewhere in his epistles.

"But I, brethren, could not address you as spiritual men, but as men of the flesh, as babes in Christ. I fed you with milk, not solid food; for you were not ready for it; and even yet you are not ready, for you are still of the flesh. For while there is jealousy and strife among you, are you not of the flesh, and behaving like ordinary men? For when one says, 'I belong to Paul,' and another, 'I belong to Apollos,' are you not merely men?" (1 Corinthians 3:1-4).

Unfortunately, most Christians stay in the basics and never receive solid teaching that allows Christ to burn up the chaff and crucify the works of the flesh. *"For though by this time you ought to be teachers, you need someone to teach you again the first principles of God's word. You need milk, not solid food; for every one who lives on milk is unskilled in the word of righteousness, for he is a child. But solid food is for the mature, for those who have their faculties trained by practice to distinguish good from evil. Therefore let us leave the elementary doctrine of Christ and go on to maturity, not laying again a foundation of repentance from dead works and of faith toward God, with instruction about ablutions, the laying on of hands, the resurrection of the dead, and eternal judgment"* (Hebrews 5:12- 6:2).

Christians must learn how to embrace the discipline of the Lord. This requires that sound doctrine be distributed and made readily available to exhort the Christian in these important issues that lead to maturity. Pastors, teachers, TV evangelists, seminar professors, and adult Sunday school teachers must present the meat of the word as well as the milk of the word. Then Christ can discipline in everyday circumstances of life.

"And have you forgotten the exhortation which addresses you as sons? 'My son, do not regard lightly the discipline of the Lord, nor lose courage when you are punished by him. For the Lord disciplines him whom he loves, and chastises every son whom he receives.' It is for discipline that you have to endure. God is treating you as sons; for what son is there whom his father does not discipline? If you are left without discipline, in which all have participated, then you are illegitimate children and not sons" (Hebrews 12:5-8).

Indeed, today many Christians go through life avoiding the discipline from the Lord and are at risk of rejection as illegitimate children. Hebrews continues by informing us that God, *"...disciplines us for our good, that we may share in his holiness. For the moment all discipline seems painful rather than pleasant; later it yields the peaceful fruit of righteousness to those who have been trained by it"* (Hebrews 12:10-11).

It is the training and discipline of the Lord that destroys and burns the chaff in our lives. What is chaff? Chaff is the outer protective layer of carnal (selfish and sin centered) attitudes, character, unbelief, and bitterness that most Christians have. Christ desires to baptize us in fire so the chaff completely burns away. Indeed, this baptism is an unquenchable fire that relentlessly brings pressure to expose and transform the old nature into the new. After the work of sanctification, then one can expect the baptism of power, by the Holy Spirit, for the purpose of ministry and witness.

Far too many Christians believe that receiving Christ and receiving the Holy Spirit automatically destroys the old nature within the new believer. This is an error and is one major reason why so many Christians fall away when trouble and trials come. The Holy Spirit is more interested in cleansing and purifying our heart and spirit and destroying the old carnal sin nature within new believers than in releasing them into the ministry or giving an outer spiritual gift. Unfortunately, most new Christians are released into ministry and told to seek the gifts of the Holy Spirit long before they are ready.

Due to the confusion from so many false teachings concerning the baptism of the Holy Spirit, many older Christians in the body of Christ should be mature by now, but are no better off. The results are catastrophic, giving license to immature Christians who rush prematurely into a ministry. These carnal Christians, laying hands on others, enter into others' sins as they defile others with their own sins. (See 1 Timothy 5:22). In many cases, the blind are leading the blind, causing little advancement for the kingdom of God!

Once a true born-again Christian's faith becomes strong enough and there is wise support available from mature Christians, Christ will begin to allow fiery trials to purge, cleanse and heal their heart, mind and spirit. *"...He will baptize you with the Holy Spirit and with fire. His winnowing fork is in his hand, and he will clear his threshing floor and gather his wheat into the granary, but the chaff he will burn with unquenchable fire."* (Matthew 3:11,12).

Not too many Christians understand this process, nor are there many who want to enter the sanctification process. Soon the body of Christ is in for a purifying ordeal that will not stop until the last-day church is spotless. For, *"...Christ loved the church and gave himself up for her, that he might sanctify her, having cleansed her by the washing of water with the word, that he might present the church to himself in splendor, without spot or wrinkle or any such thing, that she might be holy and without blemish"* (Ephesians 5:25-27).

Most Christians are not ready for Christ's return. *"But who can endure the day of his coming, and who can stand when he appears?"* (Malachi 3:2). Cleansed and disciplined Christian leaders and workers will stand and be weapons in God's hand on the day that God acts. The Lord Jesus is preparing His disciples. *"For he is like a refiner's fire and like fullers' soap; he will sit as a refiner and purifier of silver, and he will purify the son's of Levi and refine them like gold and silver, till they present right offerings to the Lord"* (Malachi 3:2-3).

The purification process is difficult and trying. Some have paid the price by enduring this process and many others have already begun this work and are near the end. If you have not started this process, now is the time to begin. Simply make a personal covenant (contract) with God. Make an agreement with God that gives Him permission to do whatever it takes to bring you to purity, obedience, and the fullness of His grace. God is faithful and submitting to this process governed by His hand will never fail.

Present your life as a living sacrifice that is acceptable and pleasing to God. Prepare by bracing for fiery trials and circumstances that will sift and test you to the very core of your being. Through this process He will bring to your awareness every ill feeling, selfish motive, weak character structure, defilement, and filthy attitude and thought. He will show you things that you had completely forgotten about. He will expose hidden judgments, forgotten unconfessed sins, bitter jealousies, insecurities, inner fears, unbelief, bitter expectations, self-deception, and false doctrine.

It may take months, and even years of dealing with dividedness of heart, mind, and spirit. You must be ready to weep and mourn; you must be willing to humble yourself—so God will not have to.

Partner with like-minded brothers and sisters who have made the same commitment. Count the cost of the potential loss of friends, idols of heart, family members turning against you, persecutions, calamities, and the like. Be willing to renounce in your heart all that you own. Be willing to sacrifice everything that is dear to you. In this, you must trust your soul and all that you are responsible for to a faithful Creator who will see you through to the finish.

"And Peter said, *'Lo, we have left our homes and followed you.'* And he said to them, *'Truly, I say to you, there is no man who has left house or wife or brothers or parents or children, for the sake of the kingdom of God, who will not receive manifold more in this time, and in the age to come eternal life'"* (Luke 18:28-30).

Does this mean we are to abandon our spouse and children and run here and there? No, rather it is giving up controlling ownership in these relationships and no longer being controlled by others but led by the Spirit of God. Following Christ is a radical change in all of life, and many relatives and family members may oppose such a move. Often a disciple may find, like Peter, that they love work, people and family more than they love Christ.

When these issues are cleared up in the heart of the disciple, Christ will personally restore *in manifold measure* homes and significant relationships, unless a particular person in a relationship continues to reject the Gospel, which in that case the person may be evil and must be avoided. The alternative is, if we do not leave the emotional, and sometimes, physical hold others have on us, we may run the risk of falling away from Christ and losing eternal life.

When you have gone through this sanctification process (where you put to death the deeds of the body by the Holy Spirit), the abundant joyful life in Christ is yours, a life in which you are safe, where Satan can't blackmail or tempt you beyond your strength, since the passions of the flesh are now crucified. This is the life of a true disciple, which always carries in the body the death of Christ so the life of Christ is manifest in and through the true disciple. This is a life where rivers of pure living water (the Holy Spirit) flow through you and out to others.

This life will have wisdom, boldness, surety, confidence (in God, not the flesh), discernment to judge evil from good, and faith to move mountains while not glorifying self in the process.

Your life will be a life of prayer and humility. You will not care about the appearances of righteousness, but you will live in righteousness from the heart. You will not put on a pretense of righteousness to make sinners feel lost. You will share your faith graciously, without manipulation, pressure or haughtiness. You will not waste time on liars, game players and hypocrites. You will pray things through and then watch God's will be done, since that is what God asked you to pray. You will live daily to do God's will above all else. You will not have an attitude of working for God, but rather a rest in God, where His Spirit works through you to get His agenda done—*not yours or man's*.

This new life is the life of grace that comes only by the work of the cross and the baptism of fire. The cross brings to death our mixed motives—those hidden motives that drive us to serve God for our own exaltation and glory. The desires of the flesh are in check, now that your personal spirit is no longer tied to the old nature. You will be able to put off the old nature, which was like your former manner of life, because your inner mind, heart and spirit have been renewed and healed.

Your heart and mind will be set on heaven and fighting for God's will to be done on earth, above all else! You will know the will of God and fight for it. You will suffer the sufferings of Christ as you stand in the gap for those people in your life that God desires to be set free. Your body will take beating after beating, spiritually and physically, as you stand in the gap, warding off Satan's attacks against those he holds captive, while all through the battle you will be sustained and strengthened by Christ until victory is achieved.

Your life will not be fanatical and religious. The lost and weak Christian will feel safe to confess sins and ask for prayer and counsel. You will be stable, strong, caring, frank, loving, firm, courageous, meaningful, non-threatening, encouraging, sober yet fun loving, childlike but mature, slow to speak but having words full of wisdom and grace, intolerant toward evil and evil people but patient with sinners, the brethren and those who are weak. Say! Isn't this how Jesus walked?

You will not be afraid to confront evil and stand up for righteousness, even in the face of persecution. You will be proactive in your continued sanctification, ever pressing on to the high call of God in Christ Jesus. You will rejoice and not panic when trouble sweeps the land, even when afflictions strike home. You will be a pillar for loved ones to gather to for support and strength.

You will know how and when to say no to those who flatter and use you, as you avoid doing for others what they need to do for themselves. You will wean the game players after a season of support, knowing that Christ, not you, must now become all and in all to them. You will learn to catch flattery and not let it deceive you. You will learn to die to the work God gives you so you can hand it to your replacement when God calls you to higher things or take a break before starting something new.

People will see your strength, seek your help, and ask you to pray for them. You will learn to graciously, but firmly, tell those who seek your counsel what they need to hear, not what they would like to hear in the flesh. You will stick to your word, even if it personally turns out for the worst.

Satan will know that he cannot buy you, blackmail you, pressure you or intimidate you. Demons will know of you as a true enemy. They will harass you and attack you so your victories and accomplishments in Christ will not puff you up. You will know you are a soldier for Christ whose heart and treasure are in heaven, and fight in the "war of the universe" that never ends until the Great Day. You will understand the cost and be willing to give it for the glory of your King. In all of this, you will become a true disciple of Christ and walk as He walked. You will overcome, endure to the end, and be saved!

All that I have written here is in Scripture. It is obtainable! The old nature *can and must be dealt* with, through Christ, in His discipline and His leadership. Grace will abound and sin will no longer have dominion over you. You will succeed in crucifying the deeds of the old self, maintaining power over the old nature, and being at rest, ready to meet the Lord in physical death or at His appearance.

When God's leaders and workers, those whom He sets aside as a remnant, have been thoroughly cleansed, then He will start to do some mighty and terrible things.

What will the Lord do when this purification is complete? *"Then I will draw near to you for judgment; I will be a swift witness against the sorcerers, against the adulterers, against those who swear falsely, against those who oppress the hireling in his wages, the widow and the orphan, against those who thrust aside the sojourner, and do not fear me, says the Lord of hosts"* (Malachi 3:5). Also *"Since we have these promises, beloved, let us cleanse ourselves from every defilement of body and spirit, and make holiness perfect in the fear of God"* (2 Corinthians 7:1).

The Lord will have at His disposal a mighty army who will demonstrate the true power of God as they gather souls in the final great harvest!

This is the time to get ready, dig deep, get right with God, and allow Him to crucify the works of the flesh within you. Let Him lay bare your motives, thoughts, and intentions of the heart. Embrace His discipline now, so you may stand at His coming.

WORD OF THE CROSS: THE TRUE SOURCE OF POWER FROM GOD

The cross is all that the pure in God desire to glory in. Yes, we rejoice in what the Lord did at Calvary, but that work was three-fold: to pay the debt that we could not pay; to disarm Satan and the ruling principalities of their right and power over sin-enslaved mankind; and to set the example for every genuine disciple to follow, that is, to pick up his or her own cross and enter into a death like Christ's—then be raised with Him in newness of life!

God backed up the whole work of Christ by raising Him from the dead. This is the Father's stamp of approval and our hope: the resurrection from the dead. However, herein lies trouble for most Christians: they think in terms of eternal life only. They focus on the Lamb of God as the procurer of our salvation, given freely by faith to those who call on Christ's name. However, the more important aspect of Christ's work, missed by most, is *that His death has purchased our freedom to enter into a death like His. This is the believer's work, allowing the work of the cross to bring death to the old carnal nature.*

Most of Christianity rejoices and jumps for joy concerning the victories obtained when Christ died for our sins to set us free. Nevertheless, the last and most important aspect of Christ's work on the cross is this: we can now die to our old sin nature, transforming our character permanently on the inside. This is where many have missed the whole point of God's redemptive work. The born-again experience is just the beginning, which leads to death of the old carnal nature and fullness of life in Christ, continually filled with the Holy Spirit, ever abiding in Christ and His words.

Christ is the firstborn of many, leading us to our own cross that we might gain full entrance back to a personal daily fellowship and communion with God the Father. Christ's work in the flesh was to purchase all mankind by grace. When we believe on the Lord Jesus, we come under an *"umbrella of grace"* in order to work out our salvation through a process of trials, disciplines and revelation of God concerning His ways. In this process, He will write His laws upon our hearts and give us His life in fellowship with Him!

This is done by God, directing circumstances that force us to die to our old inner nature that unconsciously and automatically reacts to life our way—not God's way. The new Christian is put under this umbrella of grace to learn to cooperate with God as He lays bare the inner thoughts and intentions of the heart that are not Christ-like in nature. When Asaph the psalmist was in trial and distress, he humbled and examined himself.

"To the choirmaster: according to Jeduthun. A Psalm of Asaph. I cry aloud to God, aloud to God, that he may hear me. In the day of my trouble I seek the Lord; in the night my hand is stretched out without wearying; my soul refuses to be comforted. I think of God, and I moan; I meditate, and my spirit faints. Selah Thou dost hold my eyelids from closing; I am so troubled that I cannot speak. I consider the days of old, I remember the years long ago. I commune with my heart in the night; I meditate and search my spirit" (Psalms 77:1-6).

Slowly, in a process of discipline and challenges, there is a breaking down of the denial and blindness concerning the old self with its motives, thoughts, and intentions of the heart. These motives and thoughts come from our old carnal life or the flesh. The old carnal life or the flesh is still within Christians and has a life of its own. This carnal life wars against the new life given by the Holy Spirit, which is received at the new-birth experience. Now if a new believer understands this process and humbles himself to accept the hand of God in these pressuring trials, then grace and spiritual help will be given to the willing new believer for miraculous inner changes.

The hidden old motives and desires die and give way to Christ-like beliefs and inner character. Transformation takes place from one degree of revealed glory of God to the next, until most of our inner self is in Christ's likeness. Finally, there is the culminating point of the death and resurrection process whereby we obtain the grace of God, and obedience becomes indelibly written on the heart, forever to stay! Until we obtain the grace of God, the believer is at risk. Inner wounds, bitterness and self-righteousness within the heart can allow the heart to become evil and unbelieving, or self-dependent and prideful, causing a believer to fall away. The deceitfulness of sin can blind the heart, inspiring sin to become deliberate and more flagrant than ever.

"Take care, brethren, lest there be in any of you an evil, unbelieving heart, leading you to fall away from the living God. But exhort one another every day, as long as it is called 'today,' that none of you may be hardened by the deceitfulness of sin. For we share in Christ, if only we hold our first confidence firm to the end, while it is said, 'Today, when you hear his voice, do not harden your hearts as in the rebellion'" (Hebrews 2:12-15).

The believer can suffer from a divided heart, mind and spirit. This condition allows Satan and demons to torment and maintain oppression. In some cases, demons can be lodged in a divided heart or wounded parts of a split or divided personal spirit. They can stay there because the divided parts missed being regenerated. The work of the cross is God's plan to grow up Christians into salvation, making the believer whole by His sanctifying processes.

Paul wrote, *"For the word of the cross is folly to those who are perishing, but to us who are being saved it is the power of God"* (1 Corinthians 1:18).

So many Christians are looking for the power of God to be manifest in their lives. Thousands throng to meetings and seminars, listening to various teachers, collecting literature, tapes and notes as they try to obtain the power of God. Many attend revival meetings, looking for a powerful touch from an "anointed" speaker that will send them into the fullness of God with power and glory.

For Christians today the directive from most pulpits and most national teachers is: *grasp the power of God*! They want power from on high. They want to move mountains. They want to raise the dead. They want to perform miracles. They want to walk in the gifts. They want recognition and glory as a believer who has the power of God. Why is this lust for power so strong? Simply put, Christians mistakenly believe the outer manifest power of God will give them power over their carnal nature, inner wounds, and unbelief.

Few Christians understand Christ's example. An extreme lack of sound doctrine exists concerning the true power of God and what God requires of the true believer in order to walk in His strength. Many believe that the inner strength of God in the disciple's life comes from the outer demonstration of God's power. Let us look at this passage.

"For he was crucified in weakness, but lives by the power of God. For we are weak in him, but in dealing with you we shall live with him by the power of God. Examine yourselves, to see whether you are holding to your faith. Test yourselves. Do you not realize that Jesus Christ is in you? Unless indeed you fail to meet the test!" (2 Corinthians 13:4,5).

Most refuse to examine themselves as they attempt to grasp the power of God. Indeed, they miss Christ's example.

"Have this mind among yourselves, which is yours in Christ Jesus, who, though he was in the form of God, did not count equality with God a thing to be grasped, but emptied himself, taking the form of a servant, being born in the likeness of men. And being found in human form he humbled himself and became obedient unto death, even death on a cross" (Philippians 2:5-8).

Most treat the power of God as an object to manipulate and grasp. They treat Christ as a means to an end. These wayward and misled children follow any teacher or so-called prophet or super apostle, seeking a supposed *nirvana* of Christianity. These deceived Christians hunger for the perfect teaching or the right "Christian religious formula" or spiritual experience to grasp that perfect and sublime state of being.

The intrinsic power of the sin nature will never come to submission by the outer demonstrating power of the Holy Spirit. Read this passage, dealing with the power of God that brings grace.

"And to keep me from being too elated by the abundance of revelations, a thorn was given me in the flesh, a messenger of Satan, to harass me, to keep me from being too elated. Three times I besought the Lord about this, that it should leave me; but he said to me, 'My grace is sufficient for you, for my power is made perfect in weakness.' I will all the more gladly boast of my weaknesses, that the power of Christ may rest upon me. For the sake of Christ, then, I am content with weaknesses, insults, hardships, persecutions, and calamities; for when I am weak, then I am strong" (2 Corinthians 12:7-10).

Does the external, demonstrated power of God deal with the sin nature? No! It is the narrow path and difficult road, often in anonymity, that leads to a break with the sin nature. Then, when the process is complete, there will be rest, peace and a full connection with God. The hand of God will form a splendid and divine relationship through the work of the cross. The true disciple will seek His abiding presence in humility—not to gain His power, but to bless the Lord and be His pleasure and delight.

The true strength of God comes into the sincere believer as grace when the cross has finished its work. This is a process that takes time, long enough to work

Christ's true nature deep within, as the power of the old nature comes to a complete death.

The outwardly demonstrated power of the Holy Spirit comes to those who have been disciplined, cleansed and trained. The disciple will not misuse His power or seek self-glorification in ministry. This discipline, facilitated by Christ and the Holy Spirit, is what John the Baptist meant by the baptism of fire. Indeed, fiery trials will be required. No genuine believer in this training will want out of this process prematurely, nor will God allow the process to be terminated or minimized. It is unquenchable! The only way out is to fall away and turn your back on God. You may plead and try to get out of this discipline or minimize the baptism of fire, but God will continue to work until it is done. He knows how much we can stand. We must learn to trust our souls to a faithful Creator. (See 1 Peter 4:12-19).

Unfortunately, because few understand this process, many sincere Christians circumvent God's sanctification process and abort the complete work of the cross. God will come back later and start it up again, and often a more troubling trial is required.

Indeed, restoring the work of the cross in the believer's life is paramount. Purity and strength will come to the body of Christ by the work of the cross!

EMBRACING THE DISCIPLINE OF THE LORD

Christ works this death into the truly committed Christian. He uses circumstances, trials, blessings, and healing or whatever He sees fit. Death of the old carnal nature allows regeneration within our nature to be made Christ-like, where new *attitudes of heart, of a divine origin become ours.*

"His divine power has granted to us all things that pertain to life and godliness, through the knowledge of him who called us to his own glory and excellence, by which he has granted to us his precious and very great promises, that through these you may escape from the corruption that is in the world because of passion, and become partakers of the divine nature. For this very reason make every effort to supplement your faith with virtue, and virtue with knowledge, and knowledge with self-control, and self-control with steadfastness, and steadfastness with godliness, and godliness with brotherly affection, and brotherly affection with love. For if these things are yours and abound, they keep you from being ineffective or unfruitful in the knowledge of our Lord Jesus Christ. For whoever lacks these things is blind and shortsighted and has forgotten that he was cleansed from his old sins. Therefore, brethren, be the more zealous to confirm your call and election, for if you do this you will never fall; so there will be richly provided for you an entrance into the eternal kingdom of our Lord and Savior Jesus Christ" (2 Peter 1:3-11).

We can receive this new, Christ-like nature, provided we cooperate with the Lord and His discipline. This is where many fail. The trials seem too difficult, and many quit.

"It is for discipline that you have to endure. God is treating you as sons; for what son is there whom his father does not discipline? If you are left without discipline, in which all have participated, then you are illegitimate children and not sons. Besides this, we have had earthly fathers to discipline us and we respected them. Shall we not much more be subject to the Father of spirits and live? For they disciplined us for a short time at their pleasure, but he disciplines us for our good, that we may share his holiness. For the moment all discipline seems painful rather than pleasant; later it yields the peaceful fruit of righteousness to those who have been trained by it. Therefore lift your drooping hands and strengthen your weak knees, and make straight paths for your feet, so that what is lame may not be put out of joint but rather be healed. Strive for peace with all men, and for the holiness without which no one will see the Lord" (Hebrews 12:7-14).

If we endure to the end, we will receive what God promises! Far too many Christians take the easy road and avoid the discipline. They avoid the pain as they hang onto their worldly life. They learn to pretend to walk in holiness and develop religious pride. These, who avoid the discipline, will not be able to stand before the Lord on the day that He appears, but rather will flee in shame. We must take courage and embrace the work of the cross daily!

OBTAINING THE PURE GRACE OF GOD

Most in society become exposed to defilements that infect soul and spirit. The human spirit soaks up these things like a sponge. Contrary to popular opinion, America and most Christians are sick and filthy on the inside. Yes, the initial rebirth implants a new nature within the new Christian. The old nature, with defilements from the past, will coexist with our new nature born of God. We reckon or consider the old nature dead to us so we can destroy the power that the old nature retains. This is where the grace of God succeeds and where the law of God fails. (See Romans 7:21-8:17).

Christ's sacrifice and God's *grace* allow us to look at who we truly are on the inside without condemnation. Now we can deal with issues of bitterness, selfishness, and hidden wounds by grace and forgiveness, with accountability. Grace does not condone sin, for when we sin deliberately, we receive retribution.

The law of God says we must not sin. When we apply the law, we find that sin gets worse, so we try harder, and sin gets worse yet, until finally sin gets out of hand. When we understand salvation, faith, Christ and grace, we can deal with sin by way of the cross and grace. Our inherent sin nature needs changing, and the law of God enforced by self cannot accomplish that.

Though many Christians experience the forgiveness of sins when they first come to Christ, defilements, sinful nature and inner attitude of heart still have power. The new nature in Christ has temporal power by grace to hold off the sin nature for a season. The new Christian now needs instruction to gain understanding concerning how to crucify the old sinful nature and embrace sanctification. Unfortunately, proper teachings on how to cooperate with God in the sanctification process are difficult to find.

Consider all the self-help psychology lecturers, authors and professionals. People are clamoring for help to overcome their inner problems. They will buy any book that promises "instant inner peace."

Humans have a sin nature problem to begin with. Further, we know that living in a corrupt and godless society can magnify that problem. Family systems tend to hand down secret sins and abuse of children from generation to generation. All this piles up—layer after layer of defilements compounded by emotional and spiritual wounds. The soul and spirit of men and women can truly become destitute and perverse, and yet appear good on the outside.

I have counseled hundreds of Christians who shared shame and hurt from a destructive childhood. Most of them were genuine Jesus-loving believers who, try as they may to live for Christ, never do so in peace and joy. They were continually frustrated as they covered up their unstable lives. They came to church and requested counseling, trying to obtain the grace of God. Their inner lives were in turmoil as they confessed that none of the "quick fix and cheap grace" gospel messages were succeeding in helping them receive the true, restful grace of God.

Even more discouraging, once told of the true cleansing process, many shudder and quit. Many say they would rather not deal with the hidden pain. In spite of encouragement and informing them what Christ warned—to count the cost of following Him all the way—most backslide. They are hardened with unbelief because of the abundance of false teachings and the *abridged gospel of instant life in Christ* spewing from most pulpits.

They fall back into the status quo of being a *quietly frustrated* Christian, settling for a false peace by "playing church." Many go from church to church, looking for a magic formula or combination of church work, fellowship and a "baby me" pastor who will cater to their selfish pride and attention-seeking antics. These pastors are false shepherds who oppose Christ's recovery program by telling these wounded sheep what they want to hear. This helps their congregation grow in numbers and maintain financial support.

There are true ministers out there who fight the good fight and support true discipleship and healing for God's wounded. They refuse to play the games. They present the whole Gospel of Christ, which includes those painful and terse teachings of Christ that most Christians avoid. This handful of Christian ministries and congregations are producing disciples that obtain the pure and true grace of God. These believers have cleansed their heart, mind and spirit and walk in humble holiness. They are earthen vessels of honor emanating the pure grace of God, giving light to those around them. They serve Christ from pure motives, not from bitter jealousy and selfish ambition. They have emptied themselves and found a precious jewel, the pure grace of God!

The pure grace of God, when obtained, brings eternal security, fullness of life and mountain-moving faith. Therefore, obtain the true grace of God! *"See to it that no one fail to obtain the grace of God; that no "root of bitterness" spring up and cause trouble, and by it the many become defiled; that no one be immoral or irreligious like Esau, who sold his birthright for a single meal. For you know that afterward, when he desired to inherit the blessing, he was rejected, for he found no chance to repent, though he sought it with tears"* (Hebrews 12:15-17).

GRACE WITHIN — POWER UPON

"And the Word became flesh and dwelt among us, full of grace and truth; we have beheld his glory, glory as of the only Son from the Father. (John bore witness to him, and cried, 'This was he of whom I said, 'He who comes after me ranks before me, for he was before me.'") And from his fulness have we all received, grace upon grace. For the law was given through Moses; grace and truth came through Jesus Christ" (John 1:14-17).

Jesus called His disciples individually, a handpicked group of men He would teach and train personally. Some were told, *"Follow me, and I will make you fishers of men"* (Matthew 4:19). Others He just called, beckoning them to follow Him. Little did they know what kind of life they would lead, what kind of attitude changes were in store, what kind of controversy and shameful failure He would take His disciples through. Their worlds were turned upside down.

Walking with Jesus was demanding, rigorous, elevating and then crushing. They were awed, stumped, challenged, anointed to cast out demons and heal the sick; and they were constantly subjected to parables that sometimes seemed impossible to understand.

Then Jesus became very controversial. A war of words and slanderous attacks was directed at Christ and His disciples. The religious leaders of the day became jealously enraged, since so many people followed Christ and adhered to His teachings. The disciples were worried and even told Jesus, *"Do you know that the Pharisees were offended when they heard this saying?' He answered, 'Every plant which my heavenly Father has not planted will be rooted up. Let them alone; they are blind guides. And if a blind man leads a blind man, both will fall into a pit'"* (Matthew 15:12-15).

He taught them what it meant to be servants of each other, having no competition, not elbowing one another to gain elevated recognition. Mercy, grace, judgment, fear of God, obedience from the heart, honesty and courage, nothing was left undone.

The final lessons were betrayal, denial, fear and shame. Disciples saw their own true inner nature, as their lives spun out of control during Christ's passion. They were taught, and then they were trained in what they learned.

Jesus went to the cross and took the disciples through a death like His. They feared for their lives, as death on a cross became a real possibility for them. They had left their homes, jobs, and family—everything to follow Jesus. As the miracles and the fame grew, the disciples felt assured they made the right decision. What heady days, when Jesus gave them authority to heal the sick and cast out demons. Then it all ended abruptly! What embarrassment, shame and fear.

Then Christ is risen, appears to His disciples and it all makes sense. He walks and talks with them, opening their eyes to prophecy and the true meaning of all that had just happened.

Jesus imparts to them the Holy Spirit and finalizes their training. Through these rigorous three-and-one-half years, Christ's disciples were turned inside out and given an example of what divine nature looks, acts and lives like.

Christ's ministry of grace and truth replaced the law. His disciples had God's grace worked into their inner being, transforming their attitude of heart and spirit to be modeled after Christ, Who, as God in the flesh, was the true life-giving Spirit. Grace and truth were the new foundation from which the disciples' newly changed character would now continue to grow.

This is how Jesus called and made His disciples then, and this is still the way He teaches and trains a true disciple today.

The Father had Jesus call, lead, teach and train so that this handful of men could make disciples in a similar manner, working with the ascended Christ and the Spirit of God.

The day of Pentecost, where the power of the Holy Spirit came upon the disciples for witnessing, came after the disciples were transformed and the Holy Spirit was given to them. The trial they endured revealed to them their selfish sin nature and carnal personalities.

The work of the cross within the disciples accomplished a death to the old nature, allowing the new nature, rooted in grace and truth, to be a temple for the indwelling presence of God.

The power to witness and minister the Gospel came upon them on the day of Pentecost—this power did not come into their inner beings! New converts were baptized with the Holy Spirit as confirmation, and the disciples taught these new believers. Now, for each individual convert, the Holy Spirit began a similar process of discipleship.

Today Christians who desire to become a true disciple of Christ are told they need Pentecostal power to come upon them and within them, in order to allow them to be a witness for Christ and walk in newness of life. The process of discipleship that Christ expects to be taught to new disciples, so the Holy Spirit can orchestrate true training in life, is virtually ignored.

Instead, these new Christians are taught that grace will come when one is baptized with a sensuous power from God. The special power from God will magically subdue the old nature, keeping it suppressed. If you have problems, depression or sinful desires return, then you have leaked this special power and you must get a new infilling. Often larger doses of this supposed Holy Spirit power filling the believer with ecstasy are required. The issues of heart and the demonic oppression develops immunity to the previous level, so more power is needed to help keep the old nature, with its sinful desires, held down. This is an addictive process keeping wounded Christians dependent on these false and empty manifestations.

This is a terrible lie that short circuits Christ's discipleship training, where trials and the discipline of suffering and affliction exposes, cleanses and purifies unbelief, carnal desires, and bitter roots.

Most Christians who are deceived by this doctrine get power upon them all right, but that power is not God's power, but a counterfeit power with counterfeit feelings. Lust for this power is often driven by bitter jealousy and selfish ambition.

The true discipleship plan of Christ is to teach new converts how Christ will discipline and allow Satan to buffet, to expose and bring to death ill motives of the heart. Then, when this work is done, however long it may take, that true disciple is ready to have Pentecostal power come upon them. This power is meant to draw attention to Christ and his nature within. Those who embrace the discipline of Christ will live by example and emanate God's grace, not a fanatical hype that draws attention to self.

In the coming days, Christ will make known His true disciples, many of whom have been hidden while in training. We know of many great men and women of God throughout the history of the church. God has always hidden a remnant that has stayed the course. Many pastors and leaders today, men and women never heard of, will be released in a mighty way to lead by example in the coming true move of God.

Over these last 30 years the world and the lost have had to look hard to find a true servant of God. There is much confusion as many proclaim to have the power of God, but, walk in the counterfeit. Soon the world will be able to identify a true disciple of Christ once more, one who has the grace of God worked within, and the true power of God upon them, as a testimony to the true Christ.

Right Offerings Presented To The Lord

These pure ministries, fellowships and Christian workers produce like kind. They fulfill the Great Commission of our Lord, *"Go therefore and make disciples of all nations, baptizing them in the name of the Father and of the Son and of the Holy Spirit, teaching them to observe all that I have commanded you; and lo, I am with you always, to the close of the age"* (Matthew 28:19,20).

Lukewarm congregations avoid the preaching of the cross and the discipline of the Lord. The message of the cross that includes how to embrace Christ's discipline exposes the believer's carnal nature and hypocrisy. Today this message is not popular with the sheep, so the pulpit becomes silent on the most powerful life-changing principles of the Gospel!

Every fellowship should become a spiritual and social community hospital, ministering in the power of God, with a confrontational tough love, yet full of grace, understanding, support, and compassion. There must be freedom for the ministry of the Holy Spirit to comfort, demonstrate the true gifts, encourage, and also confront sin, especially secret sin. Those who embrace the discipline of the Lord will be transformed in nature and emanate Christ-like character. These are true Christians, and it is these whom God will use to facilitate congregational holiness and bring true revival.

Today, sound Christian character is rare. In its place is a "Christian welfare mentality" that caters to the wounded, giving out large doses of feel good prophecies that perpetuate self-pity and narcissism. Most churches offer God "lukewarm believers," who fall at the first sign of difficulty. The hard battles, that require longsuffering and fighting for God's perfect will to be accomplished in fellowship, family, neighbors, community, and country, are left to a tired and overworked handful.

This will change, for He will come to His temple and chase out the wicked. *"...he will sit as a refiner and purifier of silver, and he will purify the sons of Levi and refine them like gold and silver, till they present right offerings to the LORD"* (Malachi 3:3).

The Righteous Will Be Spared

There is severe judgment coming to America. This will prepare a holy remnant that will endure to the end and be a powerful witness all through the Great Tribulation! (Again, see Revelation 7:13-17).

Dear friend, we must be prepared to walk in righteousness and holiness, doing God's perfect will. We must overcome the world, the flesh, and the pride of life.

"But the day of the Lord will come like a thief, and then the heavens will pass away with a loud noise, and the elements will be dissolved with fire, and the earth and the works that are upon it will be burned up. Since all these things are thus to be dissolved, what sort of persons

ought you to be in lives of holiness and godliness, waiting for and hastening the coming of the day of God, because of which the heavens will be kindled and dissolved, and the elements will melt with fire! But according to his promise we wait for new heavens and a new earth in which righteousness dwells. Therefore, beloved, since you wait for these, be zealous to be found by him without spot or blemish, and at peace" (1 Peter 3:10-14).

God will spare His own people! All historical accounts of Christian martyrs—those great men and women of God—are given to us for encouragement that we might stand against evil and not give in to temptation. God will spare the righteous, even as the fires roar all around them!

We can be ready if we embrace the discipline of the Lord and the fiery trials that God may ordain for His beloved. While prosperity abounds for the wicked and the lukewarm Christian, those who truly love Christ will leave these pleasures behind and allow His discipline to run its course. Many times, we have seen the wicked and the phony Christian prosper in their ways while we struggle to make ends meet with very few supporting this work. Occasionally we complain, but the Lord confronts our murmuring, reminding us of what we will escape in the coming days. He will set our feet upon the Rock; and no tribulation, persecution, or even death will shake us. Beloved friends, God will appoint an hour of testing to prepare you for the coming horror that will fall on all Christians. Those who took the wide gate and easy road will fall to the coming destruction. Those who allowed Christ to bring His discipline and became prepared will walk in true power of God. Christ will save those who belong to Him.

"Beloved, do not be surprised at the fiery ordeal which comes upon you to prove you, as though something strange were happening to you. But rejoice in so far as you share Christ's sufferings, that you may also rejoice and be glad when his glory is revealed. If you are reproached for the name of Christ, you are blessed, because the spirit of glory and of God rests upon you. But let none of you suffer as a murderer, or a thief, or a wrongdoer, or a mischief-maker; yet if one suffers as a Christian, let him not be ashamed, but under that name let him glorify God. For the time has come for judgment to begin with the household of God; and if it begins with us, what will be the end of those who do not obey the gospel of God? And "If the righteous man is scarcely saved, where will the impious and sinner appear?" (1 Peter 4:12-18).

When they bound Shadrach, Meshach, and Abednego with their own clothes and threw them into the fiery furnace, Christ was there in the fire with them. The only thing that the fire touched was the strip of cloth binding their hands. They experienced a wonderful closeness with the living God—yes, in the furnace!

When thrown into the furnace of affliction, it is to purify you, to destroy hindrances that prevent you from having a pure and close fellowship with Christ. It is this kind of relationship that will spare you when the fires of the

Great Tribulation roar all about. He will make a way for His beloved and spare them in the coming hour of fire and trouble. We must be prepared God's way in order to endure until the moment of Rapture at the end of the great harvest, during the Great Tribulation.

THE TRULY RIGHTEOUS SERVANT WILL FINALLY BE SEEN

The church has lost its vision of greatness that upholds justice (fighting for what is right), truth and righteousness. True leadership for this country and in Christianity is rare.

That is not to say that true godly leadership no longer exists. On the contrary, the hand of God throughout the land is forging true leaders. Soon you will see more of these sold-out Christians released for ministry—locally, nationally and internationally.

The people of America are demanding leaders who cater and pander to them. We see this in the election of government leaders, as well as the ministers appointed (elected) by the congregation. This approach to leadership appointment is like king Saul in the Old Testament. The people wanted a king just as the surrounding nations, so God appointed Saul as king over Israel. The people preferred an egotistical, weak leader whom they could manipulate. God granted Israel their desire. God turned them over to their greed and special interests. Soon the nation of Israel fell into trouble and all the while God had His leader under His wing.

David was set aside and put in God's leadership training processes, under the disciplining hand of God through affliction and trouble. God honed a man of God. God told Samuel, His prophet, to choose a replacement for the corrupt king Saul and directed Samuel to the house of Jesse.

The new leader of Israel was to come from one of the sons of Jesse. Jesse introduced Samuel to each son, one by one. As the first son stood in front of the prophet of God, Samuel said to the Lord, *"Surely the LORD'S anointed is before him. But the LORD said to Samuel, 'Do not look on his appearance or on the height of his stature, because I have rejected him; for the LORD sees not as man sees; man looks on the outward appearance, but the LORD looks on the heart'"* (1 Samuel 16:6,7).

Samuel examined each, looking at their stature and thinking that surely this must be the man of God's choosing. None passed the Lord's interview. One son was not present. That was David, Jesse's youngest son, who had a healthy vibrant complexion and brilliant eyes. But as Scripture points out, David's brothers were constantly putting him down. Nevertheless, this was the man God would choose!

There are servants of the Lord throughout this country, hidden and under the training and discipline of the Lord. Many struggle as their Christian brothers and sisters ignore them, brush them aside and consider them weak and imperfect. When trouble comes and God's people, as well as millions of lost souls, are at their wit's end, full of panic, then God will make visible His true servants. They will give sound counsel with wisdom and teachings that will help many overcome and be ready to meet Christ.

"Then those who feared the LORD spoke with one another; the LORD heeded and heard them, and a book of remembrance was written before him of those who feared the LORD and thought on his name. 'They shall be mine,' says the LORD of hosts, 'my special possession on the day when I act, and I will spare them as a man spares his son who serves him. Then once more you shall distinguish between the righteous and the wicked, between one who serves God and one who does not serve him. For behold, the day comes, burning like an oven, when all the arrogant and all evildoers will be stubble; the day that comes shall burn them up,' says the LORD of hosts, 'so that it will leave them neither root nor branch. But for you who fear my name the sun of righteousness shall rise, with healing in its wings. You shall go forth leaping like calves from the stall. And you shall tread down the wicked, for they will be ashes under the soles of your feet, on the day when I act,' says the LORD of hosts" (Malachi 3:16–4:3).

CHAPTER 7

Purity That Shines in the Darkness

THE BEATITUDES WILL BE INNER CHARACTER OF THE TRUE BELIEVER

Christ laid out a simple standard for believers to walk in. Christians are to be the light of the world, giving direction and vision for the lost sinner in each level of society. Today America is stumbling. Citizens, politicians, teachers, corporate executives and even Christians grope for direction. Most are blind, unable to recognize the warning signs, let alone interpret them rightly. September 11th should have awakened millions to true repentance. Instead, "God Bless America" is sung repeatedly and prayers for protection are uttered, but there is no repentance from our national sins or our false Christian ways.

The warning voice of the church has been asleep, lulled to believe that a great revival or move of God is coming and will deter any terrible judgments. Most leaders, from national evangelist to the local pulpit, give soothing messages and orchestrate ear-tickling prophecies. These errant ministers of the Gospel jockey for recognition, building for themselves a kingdom on earth. They are unwilling to hear the truth from God and in turn warn God's people. These false prophets will have the blood of many on their hands. They oppress any true voice of warning, controlling what is presented to the body of Christ. This, along with a lukewarm condition, has numbed God's people to His warnings. Christ's predictions concerning the last days of this age are ignored, as most Christians busy themselves sanctimoniously playing church, in love with this world and its pleasures. That will soon change!

Jesus warned the church of Laodicéa that He would spew them out of His mouth. They were not on fire for Christ but had all the outer trappings of Christianity. This weakened condition is prevalent everywhere across America! Christians who live in the most prosperous nation in the world are at grave risk of eternal damnation.

What is the standard attitude of heart that the sincere believer must maintain? Here it is, in Christ's words ringing forth from the Sermon on the Mount!

"And he opened his mouth and taught them, saying: 'Blessed are the poor in spirit, for theirs is the kingdom of heaven. Blessed are those who mourn, for they shall be comforted. Blessed are the meek, for they shall inherit the earth. Blessed are those who hunger and thirst for righteousness, for they shall be satisfied. Blessed are the merciful, for they shall obtain mercy. Blessed are the pure in heart, for they shall see God. Blessed are the peacemakers, for they shall be called sons of God. Blessed are those who are

persecuted for righteousness' sake, for theirs is the kingdom of heaven. Blessed are you when men revile you and persecute you and utter all kinds of evil against you falsely on my account'" (Matthew 5:2-11).

Christians cannot mimic these Christ-like character attributes. Church attendance, Bible study, Bible College, seminary or any earthly discipleship program or hyper-faith ministry cannot instill or create this kind of purity. Nor can this character be prophesied into existence or transferred by the laying on of hands by any *superlative apostle* or *great prophet*.

Christ is working with individual people, a handful of Christians here and there who have given the Lord permission to make them into Christ-like believers, who walk the walk and refrain from bragging about their achieved purity and their relationship with God.

They will bring Light to the lost. They will not seek their own recognition or glory in what they do. They will be courageous and do the hard thing. They will work behind the scenes, making disciples—one life at a time. Some will become visible on local, national and international levels as they minister powerfully, but they will not make themselves kings over God's people. They will serve His purposes, not a fleshly agenda.

Many true prophets will predict destruction and confront national evil publicly. These will be forerunners to the last-day prophets spoken of in the book of Revelation. This nation and the world will see the last-day true church in all her splendor and power!

FOXHOLE FELLOWSHIP AMONGST THE RIGHTEOUS

As more and more trouble and persecution come upon Christians, sincere believers will begin to put away foolish and selfish agendas and learn to walk with each other in true and meaningful fellowship.

Jesus led the disciples through one challenge after another, preparing them for proper fellowship with one another. At the end of the Lord's training, He told his disciples, *"A new commandment I give to you, that you love one another; even as I have loved you, that you also love one another. By this all men will know that you are my disciples, if you have love for one another"* (John 13:34,35).

There is an unbelievable amount of infighting, betrayal, backbiting, bickering, selfishness, and jealousy prevailing within most ministries and fellowships. Large ministries attempt to control, organize, and influence the body of Christ for their own greedy agendas. This carnal silliness is about to end!

The trouble coming to the church and America will cause Christians to grow up in a hurry. Christian wolves will be exposed and driven out of fellowship. The holy presence of God will be so powerful; game players will stop their hypocrisy or flee fellowship out of holy terror. Pet denominational doctrines, preferential forms of carnal worship, and non-essential doctrine will no longer hamper genuine fellowship between believers across the nation.

A loving bond will grow out of suffering. Those who continue to embrace false doctrines will not find acceptance, but in love, they will receive correction. Those who hang onto heretical issues or continue in sin will receive sharp rebuke that demands correction and restoration; if not, they will have to leave the fellowship.

Suffering and persecution will form this New Testament bond in fellowship. Just as He trained His disciples in person, He will also train His last-day disciples in pure love, reigning as Lord of all.

The institutionalized Christian churches will have a fight on their hands as they try to control local fellowships which refuse to tolerate false doctrines promoted for the sake of growth and false ecumenical unity. The sick abominable practices that are causing pastors to leave the Episcopal Church with its newly elected homosexual bishop will spread to evangelical, Pentecostal and charismatic congregations. The sincere pastor will realize the manmade doctrines in their conservative denominations are just as deceiving and destructive, with false teachings keeping Christians lukewarm.

The Holy Spirit has inspired men and women in the past to try to bring reform to the institutionalized church, only to be kicked out, burned at the stake, or branded "heretics," as they narrowly escape with their lives. Throughout the history of Christianity, God's true people have had to "come out from amongst the false church" in order to maintain integrity and the truth of the Gospel.

Now, more than ever, there is an increased effort for unity between the Protestants and the Catholics. This is flowing over to the charismatic, evangelical and Pentecostal groups. Christians and ministries who stand against these false unity movements that contradict Christ's teachings will suffer persecution. Yes, persecution will come to the true believer from false backslidden denominations and false Christians.

The current Second or Third-Wave, Toronto Blessing and Latter-Rain movements that try to control fellowships and other ministries will soon be seen as false, just as Christ prophesied.

Members of the true body of Christ will have a sincere love one for another that comes from intense battle. They will develop a "foxhole camaraderie" bond of love, even laying down their lives for one another—in some cases literally!

NO MORE EGO MONUMENTS

"Then said Jesus to the crowds and to his disciples, 'The scribes and the Pharisees sit on Moses' seat; so practice and observe whatever they tell you, but not what they do; for they

preach, but do not practice. They bind heavy burdens, hard to bear, and lay them on men's shoulders; but they themselves will not move them with their finger. They do all their deeds to be seen by men; for they make their phylacteries broad and their fringes long, and they love the place of honor at feasts and the best seats in the synagogues, and salutations in the market places, and being called rabbi by men. But you are not to be called rabbi, for you have one teacher, and you are all brethren. And call no man your father on earth, for you have one Father, who is in heaven. Neither be called masters, for you have one master, the Christ. He who is greatest among you shall be your servant; whoever exalts himself will be humbled, and whoever humbles himself will be exalted'" (Matthew 23:1-12).

These last 30 years, Christianity has experienced a large influx in leadership that practices exactly what Jesus taught not to do! They build ego monuments of massive building programs, giant crusades, spawn quick-fix teachings, all sold for ill gain, as they demand to sit in the seat of honor and recognition.

Christians embrace teachings that appoint leadership based on outer appearances, rather than by content of heart and sound character. Christ has ordained leadership for the body of Christ, and He appoints after He destroys their need to build up their ego. Unfortunately, God's people appoint by judging outwardly and those truly called of God have a fight to keep going, for the false receive the bulk of prayer, ministerial recognition and financial support.

These people exalt themselves, often in a subtle manner, purporting to have the answers for successful living. They market their carnal teachings like TV infomercials where participants become millionaires overnight. These false prophets and wolves in sheep's clothing pander to millions of Christians who refuse to deal with their selfish agendas for success.

Christians defrauded by these false teachers and prophets become victims, due to their own dark sin nature. Greed, covetousness, jealousy and selfish ambition drive struggling carnal Christians to these flamboyant charlatans. Peter wrote concerning this type of leader, *"These are waterless springs and mists driven by a storm; for them the nether gloom of darkness has been reserved. For, uttering loud boasts of folly, they entice with licentious passions of the flesh men who have barely escaped from those who live in error. They promise them freedom, but they themselves are slaves of corruption; for whatever overcomes a man, to that he is enslaved"* (2 Peter 2:17-19).

These false teachers with their destructive lies are about to be exposed, and God's people will finally see the falseness and reject the *super apostles, great teachers, flamboyant evangelists, and special prophets* who teach a watered-down gospel that tickles the ear.

True servants, recognized as leaders, will walk in authority that truly comes from God, not from a demonic spirit that produces empty signs and wonders! Christians will see the difference and false teachers will have their evil reign end;

God's people will stop supporting the false, for they will see them for who they really are! As Paul warned about this very issue, *"...so these men also oppose the truth, men of corrupt mind and counterfeit faith; but they will not get very far, for their folly will be plain to all"* (2 Timothy 3:9).

NEW LEADERS THAT ARE BOLD, COURAGEOUS AND HUMBLE

The Lord makes leadership by His call and purposes. One does not enter into the ministry as an occupation, or with motives of self-glory and fame. Jesus will refine and discipline those whom He calls. This training is hard—a grueling ordeal that takes a long time. Far too many believe that higher Christian education for the ministry qualifies someone for leadership.

Bible colleges and seminaries can help leadership with an intellectual understanding of ministry and leadership responsibility, but unfortunately, most do not teach and train on dealing with individual people and their problems as Christ would. Ask most pastors who have served in the trenches; they will tell you how unprepared they were for ministry. They had to learn to minister effectively only by Christ's discipline and Holy Spirit-inspired illumination of the Word of God. The most effective are men and women who have dealt with their own issues, wounds, and finally learned to daily die to self and live in the fullness of life—abiding in Christ.

Most leaders are afraid to tell the congregation what they need to hear. A board of elders or some other committee has hired them, and that pastor or minister works for a salary. Unfortunately, money has far too much influence in the church.

God is preparing pastors, ministers, apostles, prophets, teachers and evangelists, workers and disciples who will minister above reproach. Congregations will begin to demand truth and tough love from the pulpit. These true servants will be spiritual eunuchs for the sake of the kingdom of heaven, shepherding Christ's bride, honoring Christ as the one and only bridegroom. These sold-out servants will hold true to the teachings of Christ, assisting the bride of Christ to come to her fullness of splendor and glory.

The brash leader who brags of easy power formulas and conceals a self-recognition agenda can expect exposure, judgment, and rejection. The humble servant leader who is bold and courageous with the truth will finally be in demand. These people will not work in "pretense" and "appearances," but rather will minister from *built-in* true Christ-like character.

THE MONEYCHANGERS WILL BE CUT OFF AND CHASED OUT

Today, in all sectors of Christianity you see ministries selling their wares. They offer quick-fix gimmicks, prosperity formulas, and trinket sales for large donations. Recently Trinity Broadcasting Network advertised a TBN doorknocker to place on the front door of your home as a tool to witness by. Of course, this requires a donation.

Gimmicks like this are common on the national ministry level as well as in local churches. The messages are "give to get" and "speak it into existence," as well as many other success formulas that all involve giving money to receive this mountain-moving power. God's people allow leadership to sell them this bill of goods because they are spiritually lazy, pampered and babied.

Do not mistake this message as a callous, cruel or hardhearted belittlement of God's people. True ministries and servant leaders will indeed walk in compassion, love and understanding, just as Jesus walked. Remember, Jesus also confronted, rebuked, and taught the disciples to do the same. God demonstrated from the beginning His disdain for liars and hypocrites by instantly ending the life of Ananias and Sapphira. This put the fear of God in the new church and respect for true leadership. The phonies stayed clear!

Paul prophesied this: *"For the time is coming when people will not endure sound teaching, but having itching ears they will accumulate for themselves teachers to suit their own likings, and will turn away from listening to the truth and wander into myths"* (2 Timothy 4:3).

This passage has the excellent word, *myths* to describe these false teachings discussed in this volume. Yes, many are superstitious mythical doctrines, which the naïve and foolish Christian learns to love, choosing lies over truth. As I said earlier, Satan has been playing possum concerning these myths. Many of these teachings encourage and facilitate Christian witchcraft (prayers in the flesh) and are becoming more popular than ever.

Soon Satan will turn on them and come to collect souls. Millions of panic-stricken Christians, who are spiritually doped-up from embracing these myths, will be caught off guard and buy into the new world order. As Jesus said of this coming delusion, *"If possible deceive even the elect!"*

Jesus is coming to the temple of God, that is, the body of Christ, with a whip. He will have a pure bride on the day He appears.

"In the temple he found those who were selling oxen and sheep and pigeons, and the money-changers at their business. And making a whip of cords, he drove them all, with the sheep and oxen, out of the temple; and he poured out the coins of the money-changers and overturned their tables. And he told those who sold the pigeons, "Take these things away; you shall not make my Father's house a house of trade" His disciples remembered that it was written, "Zeal for thy house will consume me" (John 2:14-17).

A MOVE OF GOD THAT CANNOT BE HIJACKED

Many Christians expect a powerful move of God to come soon. False and carnal teachers are also expecting this move of God. These false teachers, prophets and self-proclaimed apostles, prophesy and tout this coming move of God as something to which only they are privy.

These prophecies of a coming move of God are partially true, for there will be a powerful move of God. These apostles and prophets speak by a spirit of divination, as did the slave girl who followed Paul; here is a partial account: *"As we were going to the place of prayer, we were met by a slave girl who had a spirit of divination and brought her owners much gain by soothsaying. She followed Paul and us, crying, 'These men are servants of the Most High God, who proclaim to you the way of salvation.' And this she did for many days. But Paul was annoyed, and turned and said to the spirit, "I charge you in the name of Jesus Christ to come out of her" And it came out that very hour"* (Acts 16:16-18).

Yes, a spirit of divination and a counterfeit anointing is stirring the Latter-Rain and Kingdom Now movements, as its leaders continue in their attempt to hijack the coming true move of God. Another great awakening is hoped for, which falls into the errant ministries' game plan for building a kingdom on earth that they become prominent in, not the true kingdom of God. They will try to showcase their ministry, talent, gifts and work—where they become the center of attention making Christians dependent on their gifting and anointing.

The majority of leaders expecting a coming new wave of God's power will add to the current so-called revival they facilitate. In their doctrine, this added power will be God's progressive work in using the church to reconstruct society, restore all things and establish the kingdom of God on earth—reclaiming the world for Christ, so He can now return.

Of course, this is not what Jesus taught concerning His return. A terrible persecution will come, a great falling away and a separation between false Christians and true Christians will occur. This will be the foundation for the coming true move of God, a terrifying, but glorious move of God, which will bring the true Gospel of Christ to the forefront of humanity as a testimony to all the nations. (See Matthew 24:14)

Many Christians will believe the Antichrist's lies, backed by the false church and false prophets who say Christ will come back through the reconstruction and restoration work of the church. These lies will cause a multitude of deceived Christians to be in the *valley of decision* soon, as the testimony and message from a true, pure and separate people warn with truth concerning Christ's return.

The Great Tribulation will produce a final harvest of souls and a revival that will jolt many sincere but asleep Christians, such as the awakening of the wise maidens in Matthew 25:1-13.

Judgment, trouble, and persecution will accompany the coming true move of God. This move of God cannot be bought, canned, video produced, sold or manufactured. This move of God will have leaders who have paid the price, like the first disciples, confronting false brethren, liars, cowards and evil people trying to infiltrate the true church. These leaders will guard the sheep and speak forth God's terrible power. They will continue to expose the false, chase out the wolves and undermine the false apostles and deceitful workmen whom Satan has been setting up.

There is a showdown coming between true leadership and the false. Paul prophesied in 2 Timothy 3:1-9 about these last day false leaders opposing the coming true move of God. *"As Jannes and Jambres opposed Moses, so these men also oppose the truth, men of corrupt mind and counterfeit faith; but they will not get very far, for their folly will be plain to all, as was that of those two men"* (2 Timothy 3:8,9).

WORSHIP THAT IS IN SPIRIT AND IN TRUTH
"God is spirit, and those who worship him must worship in spirit and truth." (John 4:24).

Worship services in most churches in America are hymns sung by rote, or entertaining songs sung in the spirit of the flesh. Back in the late eighties as counseling pastor, I witnessed worship in our Foursquare church evolve from genuine praise unto the Lord, to carnal manipulation of the human spirit.

Truth left this fellowship as the senior pastor became charmed with false revival and false worship, lusting after church growth. The following is an account of a discerning sister who finally saw worship degenerate to a narcissistic form of entertainment.

> "One thing I always loved in the church was the music. I loved to sing praises to the Lord and enter into full-hearted worship. God was beginning to reveal to me the things that were ungodly in the church I attended. One morning, in church, the praise and worship began. With eyes closed, I could always shut everything else out and sing directly to the Lord. This particular morning, I found I could not enter in at all. No matter how much I closed my eyes or prayed to the Lord, I could not enter into worship. The Lord was opening my eyes for the first time. I heard the music differently. It sounded harsh and deliberately contrived. I looked around at the people. Everyone seemed to be acting, trying to conjure up a devout attitude of worship. At first, I thought it

was me, so I tried harder to enter in. I could not—it was phony. It was so upsetting to me, that in my spirit, I was weeping. Weeping for the people and yes, for myself not being able to enter in.

At last, I asked God to let me enter in. He did! Immediately, all that I was discerning lifted. I could praise and worship along with everyone else. However, I knew it was wrong! I had asked God for something to make me feel better, not what was on His heart. Immediately, I repented and asked God to forgive me for being selfish and wanting a *buzz* from the worship service. I said, 'God, your will, not mine.' I had prayed for discernment many times and now God was granting that request. In my selfishness to **feel good** I did not realize the gift of discernment comes with a high cost to the self-life. God in his grace and mercy answered my prayer, took away the false worship, and allowed me to see spiritually what He saw in this congregation concerning praise and worship."

We must worship our Father in spirit and in truth. Many come to fellowship having painful issues of heart to bring before the Lord. The Holy Spirit should always lead worship service where truth about ourselves can be expressed in worship. It may be that several in the congregation need a song unto the Lord that deals with the forgiveness of sin or draws out hidden bitterness. Yes, joy should be expressed to the Lord as well.

The belief that all things are new in Christ and any oppression or depression is of the devil is a terrible error. This lie will influence worship to become conjured or pumped up to move any who might be feeling low into a *feel-good* state, a form of spiritual mesmerization.

Spiritually sensuous expressions of worship become a lie covering up the true condition of the heart. In reality, worshippers come to get spiritually pumped up, not come before God in His Spirit and in truth.

In the coming days, persecution and trouble will restore genuine Holy Spirit led worship for many fellowships. The glitter and entertainment so prevalent in church will lose its deceptive hold.

WOE TO THE PHONY AND WEAK SHEPHERDS

Jesus said of the leadership of His day, *"The scribes and the Pharisees sit on Moses' seat; so practice and observe whatever they tell you, but not what they do; for they preach, but do not practice. They bind heavy burdens, hard to bear, and lay them on men's shoulders; but they themselves will not move them with their finger. They do all their deeds to be seen by men; for they make their phylacteries broad and their fringes long, and they love the place of honor at feasts and the best seats in the synagogues, and salutations in the market places, and being called rabbi by men. But you are not to be called rabbi, for you have one teacher, and you are all brethren. And call no man your father on earth, for you have one Father, who is in heaven. Neither be called masters, for you have one master, the Christ. He who is greatest among you shall be your servant; whoever exalts himself will be humbled, and whoever humbles himself will be exalted"* (Matthew 23:2-12).

He went on, as recorded in Matthew 23 and elsewhere; that these leaders over God's people were in deep trouble. He said: *Woe to you*; meaning trouble or grief to you. Here is a summary of Christ's charges concerning their evil works.

- They preached God's word but did not practice what they preached.
- They laid heavy burdens on the people that were hard to bear, but made life easy for themselves.
- These false and weak leaders made a show of themselves in front of others, seeking recognition.
- They loved the place of honor and sought the accolades of men.
- They sought out salutations and special titles.
- They worked hard to control and lord it over others under their influence.
- They opposed genuine believers from entering into the fullness of life in God, for they themselves could never enter the true kingdom of God.
- They competed with each other to draw men after themselves, making converts who became more evil than they themselves had become.
- They made up rules, sayings and teachings holding money, gifts and religious artifacts more sacred than having a right relationship with God.
- Christ called them blind guides, children of hell and hypocrites.
- They worried about religious appearances but neglected justice, mercy and faith.
- Christ exposed their perverse priorities saying; *"You blind guides, straining out a gnat and swallowing a camel."* (Camels were considered an unclean animal).
- These made their lives look good on the outside, but their hearts were full of extortion and greed.

Christ referred to these leaders as people who appeared beautiful or outwardly righteous to men, but were full of hypocrisy and iniquity, like a whitewashed tomb full of dead men bones and all uncleanness.

Jesus pointed out that their hypocrisy was a witness against themselves, equating them to be like the rebellious leaders in Israel's past, who murdered the prophets and true servants of God.

Christ called these phony and weak leaders serpents, a brood of vipers and murderers, saying they were of the same nature as their father, Satan. Jesus said these things to their faces in public for all to hear.

Jesus, Peter, Jude, Paul, and others warned of a coming day when there would be an abundance of phony, corrupt and weak shepherds deceiving many of God's sheep. Today we see one rotten, foul exposure after another.

Woe to the last day shepherds who feed themselves and not the sheep. Woe to the phony minister, pastor, self-proclaimed apostle, and prophet who domineeringly care for God's people, who take money to heal, only to heal the wounds of God's people lightly, saying peace, peace when there is no peace.

Retribution is coming. Judgment is coming to the false leader; trouble and vexation of soul are coming to the wolves in sheep's clothing.

True leadership will shine and walk in the true power of God. These phony leaders and shepherds will either repent in true humility, learning to take the narrow gate and hard path, and submitting to the example of true leadership, or they will end in shame, see their followers leave, or die prematurely at the hand of God.

The true leaders of God's choosing will not exercise church or denominational control or facilitate any disciplinary action, but rather confront the false, head-on, in the true power of God, as Moses did when he was opposed by Jannes and Jambres. The true power of God will be obvious and terrifying. In many cases, these false leaders simply will not have a great following any longer, as the sincere and hungry Christian flees and drops their support.

The coming revelations of sexual perversion, greed and corruption will make the Christian's head swim. Even while I am writing this update, headlines in ChristianityToday.Com announced allegations of a gay relationship between Paul Crouch, founder and president of Trinity Broadcasting Network and a former employee, resulting in bribery, payoff, and extortion. On the heels of that public revelation, another tragedy is starting to surface concerning a famous so-called prophet, Paul Cain, allegedly a confirmed alcoholic and practicing homosexual, who resists correction and restoration, yet proceeds with ministry. The news of Cain was published directly on the website of Morningstar Ministries, founded by prophet Rick Joyner.

As Peter prophesied, *"But false prophets also arose among the people, just as there will be false teachers among you, who will secretly bring in destructive heresies, even denying the Master who bought them, bringing upon themselves swift destruction. And many will follow their licentiousness, and because of them the way of truth will be reviled. And in their greed they will exploit you with false words; from of old their condemnation has not been idle, and their destruction has not been asleep"* (2 Peter 2:1-2).

The wicked and the lost sinner revile the Gospel more than ever. Many follow the false and weak shepherd.

Mark it down, trouble and pain are coming to the false and weak shepherd, for their destruction has not been asleep, but is to be revealed—soon. God is about to fire many in leadership and replace them with genuine sold-out shepherds who serve the Lord Jesus Christ and not money, fame and fortune. (See Ezekiel 34)

FOOLISH CHRISTIANS LEFT BEHIND

Jesus foretold that the lies coming from false Christian leaders would blind many Christians of the last day.

"Then the kingdom of heaven shall be compared to ten maidens who took their lamps and went to meet the bridegroom. Five of them were foolish, and five were wise. For when the foolish took their lamps, they took no oil with them; but the wise took flasks of oil with their lamps. As the bridegroom was delayed, they all slumbered and slept. But at midnight there was a cry, 'Behold, the bridegroom! Come out to meet him.' Then all those maidens rose and trimmed their lamps. And the foolish said to the wise, 'Give us some of your oil, for our lamps are going out.' But the wise replied, 'Perhaps there will not be enough for us and for you; go rather to the dealers and buy for yourselves.' And while they went to buy, the bridegroom came, and those who were ready went in with him to the marriage feast; and the door was shut. Afterward the other maidens came also, saying, 'Lord, lord, open to us.' But he replied, 'Truly, I say to you, I do not know you.' Watch therefore, for you know neither the day nor the hour" (Matthew 25:1-13).

The five foolish maidens represent many Christians who succumb to deception by the lies of the world as the Antichrist comes into power. The Great Tribulation will plunge the world into great darkness and distress. These Christians will not be able to see what is happening nor know what to do. They will turn to those who built their lives on the Rock, seeking help, only to be told, "No!" Terrified, these foolish Christians will run back and forth in frantic desperation begging, buying and grappling for sustenance and help.

What these five foolish maidens are asking for is something no other Christian can give them. It is a true relationship with Christ, forged in truth and the discipline of the Lord. The wise Christian knows that trying to do for someone else what he or she must do for themselves will bring trouble. Many sincere Christians suffer burnout helping false brethren. If not stopped in time, this care taking of the false Christian can actually destroy one's own faith.

"Now the Spirit expressly says that in later times some will depart from the faith by giving heed to deceitful spirits and doctrines of demons, through the pretensions of liars whose consciences are seared, who forbid marriage and enjoin abstinence from foods which God created to be received with thanksgiving by those who believe and know the truth.... Have nothing to do with godless and silly myths. Train yourself in godliness;

for while bodily training is of some value, godliness is of value in every way, as it holds promise for the present life and also for the life to come" (1 Timothy 4:1-8).

I encourage readers to examine yourselves and determine if you are building up a true and sincere faith in the living Christ. Again, *"Examine yourselves, to see whether you are holding to your faith. Test yourselves. Do you not realize that Jesus Christ is in you? Unless indeed you fail to meet the test!"* (2 Corinthians 13:5).

CHAPTER 8

Spiritual Warfare That Is Effective

RESPECT FOR THE ENEMY'S POWER

Christians take on spiritual warfare, not having a clue as to what they are really facing. True spiritual warfare will be the most difficult thing you will ever attempt.

Yes, a new Christian has authority to stand against Satan, as Christ said, *"All authority in heaven and on earth has been given to me"* (Matthew 28:18).

Believers receive delegated authority over Satan and the demonic, provided they abide in Christ. We are to obey Christ, walk in purity and follow the Holy Spirit's guidance in all matters, especially in spiritual warfare. There is a fundamental error with most teachings concerning spiritual warfare and fighting Satan. Read the following passage carefully.

"Humble yourselves therefore under the mighty hand of God, that in due time he may exalt you. Cast all your anxieties on him for he cares about you. Be sober, be watchful. Your adversary the devil prowls around like a roaring lion, seeking someone to devour. Resist him, firm in your faith, knowing that the same experience of suffering is required of your brotherhood throughout the world. And after you have suffered a little while, the God of all grace, who has called you to his eternal glory in Christ, will himself restore, establish and strengthen you. To him be the dominion for ever and ever. Amen" (1 Peter 5:6-11).

The fear of God is desperately lacking throughout the body of Christ. Christians do not understand that Satan can have permission to buffet, attack and challenge Christians for the sake of discipline. Many times, Christians take on a satanic issue or demonic strongholds without regard to God's timing or even knowing God's will in the matter. The results are far-reaching and can be very serious, even resulting in premature loss of life.

Do not be misled into thinking that spiritual warfare is easy and that any Christian will be able to put Satan and demons to flight just by uttering "in the name of Jesus." Remember what happened to the sons of Sceva who invoked the name of the Lord, but who did not personally know Jesus. (See Acts 19:11-17).

On the other hand, Satan sometimes plays possum to allow naïve or arrogant Christians to believe they have great spiritual power and authority over the devil, when actually they have very little—if any.

Here are a few principles to consider:

- Be humble. Satan devours Christians who think they know it all and walk in spiritual pride and arrogance. Remember what happened to Job and Peter.

- God will raise you up in true authority and power over the works of Satan when you are ready. You must deal with any hidden issues of heart and walk in obedience. You need to have proper understanding with wisdom. Most of all learn to be patient!
- Satan may sift you, test you, and attack all that is dear to you. Peter refused to believe he had issues that Satan could attack. Jesus did not stop Satan from sifting Peter. Idols of the heart will be challenged: relationships, money, education, reputation etc. God will allow these challenges until all idols of the heart are hammered out of you. The fear of men and the fear of death will be exposed as well.
- When you set out to be obedient, Satan will challenge you every step of the way. Hidden areas of self-confidence are big on Satan's list. Pressing and anxious circumstances will be directed your way that will force you to cast all your cares on God and mean it!
- God requires that the Christian endure a season of suffering where Satan will be allowed to challenge and sometimes attack. This is to discipline, train, and strengthen your faith. A deeper purpose is to facilitate cleansing of any hidden defilements and bring to death sin-centered inner personalities. This is training in true spiritual warfare; be attentive, sober-minded and watchful. Satan will attack and counterattack when and where you least expect it, *especially when you have had a recent victory*.
- Be encouraged that you are experiencing these challenging trials and battles. The discipline you are receiving is confirmation of acceptance as a son or daughter by your Heavenly Father. You are being trained as a true worker and warrior that Satan and demons will respect and fear *in Christ*.
- In this process, Christ's character will be established within you. As you grow in grace and in His righteousness, His power will flow with minimal hindrance (coming from you) and God (in His peace) will crush Satan under you. (See Romans 16:17-20).
- There will be a time when your fight is directed at evil people being used by Satan. Many will be false Christians, some even extended family members. You will learn that spiritual warfare may include prophetic declarations of destruction and premature death to evil people who no longer have faith, who have a seared conscience and have crossed the line concerning God's saving grace. (See Acts 5:1-11, Acts 8:14-24, Acts 13:4-12, 1 Corinthians 5:1-13, 2 Corinthians 11:12-15, Ephesians 5:1-20, 2 Thessalonians 3:1-5, 1 Timothy 1:18-20, 5:17-22, Titus 1:10-16, 1 John 5:16,17 and Revelation 2:21-29).

Paul ran into powerful resistance in his missions to Asia. Satan was behind these attacks and was used as a tool to bring Paul to the following understanding and discipline.

"For we do not want you to be ignorant, brethren, of the affliction we experienced in Asia; for we were so utterly, unbearably crushed that we despaired of life itself. Why, we felt that we had received the sentence of death; but that was to make us rely not on ourselves but on God who raises the dead; he delivered us from so deadly a peril, and he will deliver us; on him we have set our hope that he will deliver us again. You also must help us by prayer, so that many will give thanks on our behalf for the blessing granted us in answer to many prayers" (2 Corinthians 1:8-11).

So expect weaknesses, insults, hardships, persecutions and calamities. In all these things, you will be more than a conqueror and God will deliver you each step of the way. This He will do if you are humble, sober-minded, alert, and depending on Him. You must maintain a willingness to continue with the cleansing of all defilements, doublemindedness and hardness of heart.

The body of Christ must have a healthy fear of God restored, which will put an end to so much boastful arrogance and presumption upon God. Be forewarned. There is coming a time in the very near future when Satan will be allowed to sift arrogant Christians.

THE SWORD OF THE SPIRIT: HOLY SPIRIT-LED ENGAGEMENT

Christians who decide to wrestle against evil must understand the difference between applying memorized verses of Scripture in spiritual battle and the Word of God, quickened by the Holy Spirit.

Paul wrote that we are to take up *"...the sword of the Spirit, which is the **Word of God"*** (Ephesians 6:17, ***emphasis is mine***), as we stand against the evil dark forces in heavenly places.

I have highlighted "word" in this passage to point out a difference. In this case, the Greek for "word" is *rhema*, which is different from other usages of "word." This implies a direct command by the Holy Spirit as He quickens to memory the appropriate written Word of God to apply in each situation.

"The significance of rhema (as distinct from Logos) is exemplified in the injunction to "take the sword of the Spirit which is the word of God," in Eph. 6:17. Here the reference is not to the whole Bible as such, but to the individual Scripture which the Spirit brings to our remembrance for use in time of need, a prerequisite being the regular storing of the mind with Scripture" (*Vine's Expository Dictionary of Biblical Words*, Thomas Nelson Publishers NY 1985. page 683).

When Christians lack sound doctrine to aid in rightly dividing the written Word of God, then the memorization of the Scriptures will be out of context. This will hinder the Holy Spirit's efforts to bring to remembrance appropriate Scripture that would reflect God's will on a particular situation.

Many Christians apply Scripture out of context when they do spiritual warfare. They fall out of God's timing and purpose, and in some cases actually oppose the will of God.

Some pray for God's protection for people, when in fact God has turned them over to judgment and in like manner the reverse often occurs as well, where Christians turn people over to judgment in prayer, when they were to stand in the gap for that person.

Christ will discipline us to rightly divide God's word and hear from the Holy Spirit correctly. Discerning the true voice of the Holy Spirit is paramount to the success in *taking up the sword of the Spirit.*

UNDERSTANDING THE ENEMY

Satan is devious and smart. He loves to puff up Christians, convincing them they are standing, when in fact they are one blow away from destruction. Many ministries avoid teaching the schemes and deceit of Satan. Their thought is that this would glorify Satan, so just concentrate on worshiping Christ and adhering to pet doctrines and formulas that maintain prosperity.

Paul wrote, *"I appeal to you, brethren, to take note of those who create dissensions and difficulties, in opposition to the doctrine which you have been taught; avoid them. For such persons do not serve our Lord Christ, but their own appetites, and by fair and flattering words they deceive the hearts of the simple-minded. For while your obedience is known to all, so that I rejoice over you, I would have you wise as to what is good and guileless as to what is evil; then the God of peace will soon crush Satan under your feet. The grace of our Lord Jesus Christ be with you"* (Romans 16:17-20).

We are to take note of people and so-called Christians who create trouble. They do not serve Christ, but their own hidden agendas, and manipulate and deceive naïve Christians with flattery. Though we may be obedient, we can still be ignorant concerning what is truly good and deceived as to what is evil.

Once we understand that evil often appears good and uses a cloak of decency to cover wickedness, and then God will have an overcoming Christian to destroy the work of Satan. Knowing the difference will make us a weapon in God's hand. We also must know the devil's devices and understand how he employs these insidious schemes.

Often Christians unknowingly give opportunity to Satan. If we harbor resentment, lack forgiveness, hang onto unresolved anger, maintain sinful alliances, or have secret sins, then Satan has a right to come to tempt and destroy. In addition, if you have impure motives in life or disregard sound doctrine pertaining to healthy fellowship and matters of proper relationships, you can expect trouble.

Satan loves to use unclean and defiling people who worm their way into relationships with naïve and carnal Christians.

EXPOSING HIDDEN DARKNESS

When we are willing to do battle for God, we can expect the Lord to lead us into exposing hidden evil around us.

CAUTION: This activity can be a shock. There were cases when we exposed evil, where relatives, close friends and other Christians became directly affected; and occasionally they themselves were the instruments of evil.

Evil is real and evil people exist. Evil likes to hide and burrow deep into family systems, perpetuated by generational sins. God wants these things exposed.

"Therefore be imitators of God, as beloved children. And walk in love, as Christ loved us and gave himself up for us, a fragrant offering and sacrifice to God. But fornication and all impurity or covetousness must not even be named among you, as is fitting among saints. Let there be no filthiness, nor silly talk, nor levity, which are not fitting; but instead let there be thanksgiving. Be sure of this, that no fornicator or impure man, or one who is covetous (that is, an idolater), has any inheritance in the kingdom of Christ and of God. Let no one deceive you with empty words, for it is because of these things that the wrath of God comes upon the sons of disobedience. Therefore do not associate with them, for once you were darkness, but now you are light in the Lord; walk as children of light (for the fruit of light is found in all that is good and right and true), and try to learn what is pleasing to the Lord. Take no part in the unfruitful works of darkness, but instead expose them. For it is a shame even to speak of the things that they do in secret; but when anything is exposed by the light it becomes visible, for anything that becomes visible is light. Therefore it is said, 'Awake, O sleeper, and arise from the dead, and Christ shall give you light.' Look carefully then how you walk, not as unwise men but as wise, making the most of the time, because the days are evil. Therefore do not be foolish, but understand what the will of the Lord is" (Ephesians 5:1-17).

Yes, the days are evil, and evil people do evil things in secret! Be careful and be diligent in learning discernment from the Lord. Jesus warned about judging wrongly. The following principle will help you understand and seek proper discernment of evil.

> Many sinners do evil but have faith and a good heart that will respond to the Gospel when prayer is offered on their behalf. At times, an intercessor must stand in the gap for them. These will respond to effective witnessing, truly renounce their evil practices and grow in the grace of the Lord. The Holy Spirit

> must lead with keen discernment when working with such people, because …
>
> Evil people look like any sinner, but do evil from the heart and have a seared conscience. Many in this condition will never be granted repentance by the Lord. They may respond to testimony, come to church, and attempt to be religious, only to be false through and through. Some look very righteous and even do-good deeds. The self-righteous evil builds up themselves at the expense of others and in the process destroy life. This is true evil; it is to be exposed, confronted, avoided if there is no fruit of repentance, and driven out of fellowship!

Many pastors cry out for revival and "lo and behold" trouble comes to the congregation. Adultery is exposed, fights break out, schisms develop, roots of bitterness spring up, and a host of other sin and carnal problems crop up. One major issue is domestic violence and marriage troubles that have finally come to the surface. Sadly, in some cases family pedophilia is exposed.

This indicates that prayer for revival is working. The wicked, corrupt, and wayward, which are needful of correction, are coming to the light as the Holy Spirit begins cleaning house in preparation for revival and adding souls to the fellowship.

Many congregations are perfect hideouts for child molesters. Abuse toward children—physically, emotionally, and sexually—is at an epidemic level within Christian homes just as it is in our society as a whole.

Many Christians and pastors tend to let sleeping dogs lie and avoid exposing any evil that is lurking within the flock. They do not want scandal, trouble, gossip and irate relatives howling when the church holds an abusive husband or wife, father or mother, grandfather or grandmother accountable. Most churches are under the influence of the uncrucified sin nature and learn to prefer hypocrisy and leave evil hidden. They want to present to the community a wonderful rosy picture of congregational unity and harmony, a Shangri-la portrait!

Sound preaching and teaching of the entire Gospel and embracing the work of the cross will create a supportive atmosphere within the congregation. This facilitates true Christian healing and restoration. The congregation will rise above the worry of what others think, and as did Christ, "despise the shame" when working in messy situations and receiving flack for doing the perfect will of God as darkness and evil are exposed.

In some cases, the exposed evil can bring repercussions to the whole community, as well as the local church. Nevertheless, the command is *expose it* and drive that which is wicked from our midst as well as to see evil exposed in our community and society.

FIGHTING THE EVIL HUMAN SPIRIT

This battle is the most difficult to explain, and perhaps the most potent in Satan's arsenal. Most Christians are completely unaware of this spiritual threat. The potential power of the "unregenerate" personal spirit of a human being can be lethal. A great misunderstanding exists within the body of Christ concerning the nature of our personal spirit.

We, as humans, have a personal spirit. It is that part of us that is alive and invisible yet held in place within the human physical body. If the human spirit departs from the body, the body dies.

Some might be aware of the New Age books written by Shirley MacLaine and other writers. Simply put, these deceived people stumbled onto (by satanic influence) the power of the human spirit. They developed demonic-inspired methods to help induce astral projection of their own spirit. That is, they develop the ability to send their inner person (or spirit) out of the body to travel to other places. Demonic spirits intertwined with their human spirit provide the spiritual power. These deceived people crave power, and these lies open their spirit to a "power demon" that helps their personal spirit leave their body.

Similar teachings have even infiltrated parts of the charismatic movement as these wayward teachers cite Paul's statement in 1 Corinthians 5:3-5, *"For though absent in body I am present in spirit, and as if present, I have already pronounced judgment in the name of the Lord Jesus on the man who has done such a thing. When you are assembled, and my spirit is present, with the power of our Lord Jesus, you are to deliver this man to Satan for the destruction of the flesh, that his spirit may be saved in the day of the Lord Jesus."*

If indeed, Paul's personal spirit was out of body, it was in the power of the Holy Spirit, not in his willful choice with demonic assistance.

The teaching of Catholicism calls this spiritual activity "bilocation" and it is defined as follows:

Bilocation. Multiple or simultaneous presence of the same substance of soul in two places distant from each other. Bilocations have been frequently reported in the lives of the saints. (Modern Catholic Dictionary, by John A. Hardon, S.J. Doubleday & Company, Inc., 1980. Page 67).

Occult practice makes astral projection a fundamental goal for beginners, a rudimentary aspect of witchcraft or sorcery. A particular aspect of the satanic spirit world activity allows a demonic force to enlist a human spirit to attack another person or another Christian. This is done with or without the knowledge of the person whose personal spirit is being enlisted to attack.

Satan and demons can enlist human spirits virtually at will, due to the many doorways that Christians and non-Christians have created and allowed to stay within their spirit.

Doorways are defilements to our spirit from exposure to occult practices and teachings. The following practices are what many fall into: necromancy, the Ouija board, psychic readings, palm readings, movies depicting sorcery (the TV series, *Bewitched*, was a powerful doorway exposing millions of adults and children to sorcery), self-hypnotism and childhood abuse to name a few. The *Harry Potter* books and movies have defiled and lured millions of children worldwide into occult practices, sorcery and spiritualism. Satan's plans have become bold, taking masses of children into darkness. Christ warned those who cause little ones to stumble that instant execution would be a light sentence. God will hold the author and others accountable who promote *Harry Potter*. (See Matthew 18:6-9).

Unresolved anger and lack of forgiveness embedded within the heart and spirit of a person is another tool that Satan can use to gain access to use a human spirit, especially when coupled with the aforementioned doorways. As it says in Scripture, these things give opportunity to Satan. (See Ephesians 4:25-31).

> **Note:** We have found that adults who suffered molestation in childhood can have multiple satanic doorways. The pain of the often-forgotten defilements forced victims to suppress, repress and many cases instantly dissociate from these abuses. Proper emotional response and cries for help were also buried in like manner. The sun went down many times on anger along with other damaged emotions. These indeed give Satan an opportunity to gain access to the abused child's spirit. As adult born-again Christians, many of these wounds, defilements and doorways are lodged deep within, waiting like time bombs to be satanically ignited. Very significant symptoms are dreams where one is flying in the air indicates a doorway to close. The Holy Spirit should be allowed the freedom in healthy fellowship to expose these hidden wounds. The local body of believers should be trained to help facilitate a support and recovery program that will effectively foster healing and wholeness.

When Christians battle evil, often Satan will attempt to enlist a human spirit in his scheme of attack and counterattacks. Many Christians have unhealthy relationships with people who have not cleansed themselves of such defilements. These defilements are what allow the intertwining of the demonic with the human spirit. Often Christians doing warfare are unaware of their own defilements that can make battles more intense and more dangerous than necessary. True Christians who find themselves in this type of warfare must look to their own issues that will magnify these curse-filled attacks. Many Christians give cause for these attacks to land due to their own defilements not yet exposed and cleansed. As quoted earlier, *"Like a sparrow in its flitting, like a swallow in its flying, a curse that is causeless does not alight"* (Proverbs 26:2).

Jesus warned us concerning hidden or harbored issues of heart such as unforgiveness and revenge. Millions of Christians have hearts loaded down with issues of jealousy, hate, unforgiveness and sin. This condition allows Satan and demons to create a torrent of defiling curses and spiritual oppression that attack each other. Many fellowships struggle with all manner of disorder and vile practices. These double-minded carnal Christians spew poison when they open their mouths.

"But no human being can tame the tongue—a restless evil, full of deadly poison. With it we bless the Lord and Father, and with it we curse men, who are made in the likeness of God. From the same mouth come blessing and cursing. My brethren, this ought not to be so. Does a spring pour forth from the same opening fresh water and brackish? Can a fig tree, my brethren, yield olives, or a grapevine figs? No more can salt water yield fresh. Who is wise and understanding among you? By his good life let him show his works in the meekness of wisdom. But if you have bitter jealousy and selfish ambition in your hearts, do not boast and be false to the truth. This wisdom is not such as comes down from above, but is earthly, unspiritual, devilish. For where jealousy and selfish ambition exist, there will be disorder and every vile practice" (James 3:8-16).

Satan will drive this condition to its maximum effectiveness, using defiled human spirits against each other. Indeed, as James put it, out of the double-minded Christian flows blessing and curses, clean and foul water. This causes trouble, sickness, strange events and all manner of evil situations.

The unclean human spirit of the lost and the sinful double-minded Christian can incite common symptoms of severe headaches, nausea and extreme loss of energy. In more extreme cases, symptoms of such attacks may include severe physical pain, near fatal accidents and overwhelming oppression. Often sickness and severe illness manifest themselves by the continued spiritual attack upon the immune system. The following quote from *Soul and Spirit* by Jessie Penn-Lewis will point out some symptoms of this kind of spiritual attack. Penn-Lewis referred to this power as *soul or psychic power* as opposed to *spirit power*.

> "How this ignorant bringing into action of psychic force can affect spiritual believers has come to me in a recent letter. The writer says, 'I have just come through a terrible onslaught of the enemy. Hemorrhage, heart affection, panting and exhaustion. My whole body in a state of collapse. It suddenly burst upon me while at prayer to pray against all psychic power exercised upon me by (psychic) 'prayer'. By faith in the power of the Blood of Christ, I cut myself off from it, and the result was remarkable. Instantly my breathing became normal, the hemorrhage stopped, exhaustion vanished, all pain fled, and life came back to my body. I have been refreshed

and invigorated ever since. God let me know in confirmation of this deliverance, that my condition was the effect of a group of deceived souls who are in opposition to me 'praying' about me! God has used me to the deliverance of two of them, but the rest are in an awful pit.'" (Soul and Spirit, Jessie Penn-Lewis, Christian Literature Crusade, 1989 page 58).

A more modern description of this spiritual power is that Satan harnesses the unregenerate human spirit or the divided portion of the personal spirit of the double-minded Christian. The devil can capture and channel inroads through the human soul (mind and emotions) into the personal spirit by years of grooming and inciting forbidden practices. This condition can progress to demonic possession or demonic infestation. God's desire is to be in communion with true Christians through their regenerated spirit. God's plan is to regenerate the human spirit and separate the soulish and carnal influence, as well as the demonic influences, by way of rebirth, cleansing, and sanctification, in conjunction with the work of the cross.

I can attest to this type of demonic-human spirit power. When hit by this power, you will know firsthand its serious effect and murderous potential. Passivity or disassociation is symptomatic of possessed humans, as well as demon-infested or double-minded Christians. This passivity is a disconnection to the physical or life's realities and characterized by a lack of empathy and/or a seared conscience.

Yes, this is Satan's most insidious war plan: to enlist human spirits who have become zombie-like agents of satanic principalities and world rulers of this present darkness.

Paul wrote to Timothy; *"Do not be hasty in the laying on of hands, nor participate in another man's sins; keep yourself pure"* (1 Timothy 5:22).

There can be transference of familiar and defiling spirits, as well as hidden jealousy and hatreds directed by these types of people against Christians, and double-minded Christians against each other. You can be sure that Satan will drum up this type of person once a Christian makes a stand to do true spiritual warfare.

When fighting this, the disciple must understand that the human spirit, coupled with the demonic spirit, has additional power to inflict spiritual, emotional, physical, and even severe illness or death upon their targeted victims.

We must understand this aspect of Satan's work, but also Christians must be pure in heart and cleansed of all defilements of soul and spirit in order to gain victory in this type of spiritual warfare. Rebuking the demonic in the name of Jesus is part of the battle, but also, we must develop discernment that a human spirit might be an accomplice in the attack.

The human spirit has free will, therefore one must work with the Holy Spirit and reject a human spirit attack by invoking a prayer that states, "The Lord rebuke you!" Often the battle to ward off such attacks may take days where intermittent one- or two-hour etc. prayer sessions take place. Another important aspect in fighting an evil human spirit is to identify the human spirit involved. Here the gifts of the Holy Spirit are vital—especially prophecy, words of wisdom, words of discernment and words of knowledge concerning the invisible works of Satan against the saint.

Examining the ties between the person and persons with whom you are fighting will help bring insight and understanding. You may need to tactfully break off the relationship. Pray for the exposure of their hidden agenda, then confront them, and above all, hold no resentment or revenge against them. Forgiveness is an important key for victory in these cases. The reason Satan snares so many in this scheme stems from unresolved anger, unforgiveness and bitter jealousy. A reminder, *a curse without cause will not take hold*.

The best approach is to avoid such people. The Lord may require you to pray that the person involved has their eyes opened to the Gospel. In some cases, turning them over to judgment may be required. (See 1 Corinthians 5:1-5 and 1 Timothy 1:18-20).

There is one last, but very important concern to express on this subject. Satan uses many Christians in this manner because they never embraced the cross. They maintain a carnal state of *being* and often carry defilements of soul and spirit wherever they go. Their spirit and soul are intertwined, and this condition can cause demonic infestation if they are divided or double-minded.

Again, *double-minded* Christian is the term used concerning this critical area of spiritual warfare. These Christians can be very dangerous to work with, confront, and support. Studying the book of James will lay out the characteristics and symptoms of these unstable Christians whom Satan often enlists in his most brutal spiritual attacks.

The above was an overview concerning the spiritual power of the human spirit. A more in-depth discussion is in the appendix: *"The Human Psychic and Spirit Power Unleashed by Satan."*

IDENTIFYING THE PRINCIPALITIES OPPOSING THE CHURCH AND THE LOST

Over the years, I have seen movements come and go concerning spiritual warfare and prayer. I remember Larry Lea's program in the late eighties. This movement attempted to network parts of the body of Christ into a massive organized spiritual warfare system on a national level.

God did not back this effort. Satan delights in beating up on Christians who take him on in the flesh. (See Acts 19:11-17). This carnal attempt at spiritual warfare was stopped—*right in its tracks*! The last campaign that I remember was that of taking on the witches in the San Francisco area. The plan was to identify the different principalities that were gripping different communities, then launch an all-out assault, enlisting local congregations and Christians in the community to pray. Rallies were held and large amounts of donations were received to get this national movement off the ground. This effort to identify and fight the forces of darkness and principalities ended in failure and scandal.

The World Prayer Center in Colorado Springs, hosted by New Life Church, pushes spiritual mapping and facilitates a worldwide prayer network. Review of the different prayer groups, spiritual war campaigns and the humanistic atmosphere will send chills through the discerning saint. This is another carnal attempt to raise and enlist an army of carnal prayer warriors to take on Satan's strongholds. The momentum, dollars spent and massive numbers of deceived workers involved in this misguided effort will not withstand Satan's sifting in the coming days.

Any attempt to take on opposing principalities must be done by the direction of the Lord, by solid disciples who are ready to endure suffering, trouble, persecution, blackmail, harassment and frequent physical misery and mental anguish.

Paul wrote of his mission into Asia and the opposition that he encountered, *"For we do not want you to be ignorant, brethren, of the affliction we experienced in Asia; for we were so utterly, unbearably crushed that we despaired of life itself. Why, we felt that we had received the sentence of death; but that was to make us rely not on ourselves but on God who raises the dead; he delivered us from so deadly a peril, and he will deliver us; on him we have set our hope that he will deliver us again. You also must help us by prayer, so that many will give thanks on our behalf for the blessing granted us in answer to many prayers"* (2 Corinthians 1:8-11).

Many Scriptures back up the fact that fighting the demonic requires purity of heart and must be directed by God. In addition, it is to be carried out by those who have counted the cost. Intercessors and Christian workers are in high demand in this great fight. These people cannot be just anybody. The call of God is the prerequisite, and they must experience the refining fires of sanctification. (See Ephesians 4:25-30, Romans 16 verses 17-20, 2 Corinthians 2:9-11, 2 Corinthians 4:7-10, 1 Thessalonians 2:7-18, Revelation 2:10, and 1 Peter 5:6-11).

Many of the prosperity and hyper-faith leaders contend that the apostle Paul was ignorant of the power of God and that the personal suffering described by this true apostle was unnecessary. How arrogant and deceived are these modern day charlatans! To declare an author of the Scriptures in error and not fitting into their description and teachings concerning the deeper things of God and true spiritual warfare is indeed heresy!

We must learn what the Scriptures teach and understand the cost of doing God's will in spiritual warfare. Some of these errant teachings come up with the wildest descriptions of the demonic and of the spiritual powers controlling people, communities and nations.

The main names of the principalities are the names of the false gods and idols worshipped by the Gentiles in biblical times. Through the years and in different cultures, their names have changed. To give an example, Asherah worship—found in Canaan—is closely like Ishtar and Isis worship found in Babylon and Egypt respectively. Later, this female false god appeared in Greek and Roman mythology. In New Testament times, Asherah was "Diana of the Ephesians" and today in the Catholic Church is "Mary, mother of God—Queen of Heaven."

You can see this impact in our culture with the resurrection of these principalities in the TV characters of She-Rah, Isis, Wonder Woman and so forth. The male counterparts traced into our culture are Baal, Hercules, and Superman.

Certain principalities continue to spawn the Middle East crisis. These satanic powers are determined to destroy Israel. In the book of Daniel, it states that the prince of Persia (a demonic governing power over Persia) opposed the archangel Michael and delayed God's answer to Daniel's prayers concerning the release of Israel from their captivity.

Baal and Asherah worship are the biblical counterpart to relationship idolatry. The name Baal means husband, owner and Asherah means wife. This kind of idolatry swept into Israel. Soon this idolatry mingled into their worship of God. Here you see Satan's work continued from Adam and Eve: *you will be like God*. These relationship issues stem from making each other a god in all the issues of life. This results in each spouse requiring the other to be responsible for inner peace, joy and happiness, leading to weaknesses and dependencies. This carnal and selfish relationship dynamic becomes destructive, controlling, and manipulative where each learns how to dominate the other. The current legalistic submission teaching concerning husbands and wives within many denominations, demanding the wife be submissive and treated as a second-class creation, is the work of these principalities.

Moloch is another pagan cult god worshipped in biblical times. This pagan cult god was a more radical form of Baal and Asherah worship where children were made to walk into fire as a sacrifice. Today child abuse, child abductions, child rape and child pornography are widespread. There is an epidemic of child molestation in different Christian sects. The Roman Catholic heresy of celibacy and other sick doctrines facilitates a harbor of safety for the wicked and the pedophile. Of late, Mormonism is being exposed for its wayward doctrines that facilitate, yet conceal the practices of polygamy and sexual child abuse.

Paul made it clear that Satan was involved in deceiving Christians by sending evil human agents into the midst of God's people. The demonic powers behind this scheme can be called *angel of light* principalities. Satan attempted to destroy Christ; you and I know that failed. Then, in like manner he attempted to destroy the first century Christians by persecution and martyrdom. That did not work either. So, he began a campaign of infiltration and institutionalization of Christianity. Rome makes Christianity its state religion and we see Roman Catholicism take root and begin to suppress truth and bury the true Gospel in religion. This and other so-called orthodox Christian sects twisted the Gospel to the surrounding pagan culture, making Christianity attractive to pagans by using similar rituals and myths. These *angels of light principalities* inspired all manner of heresy, disguised with half-truths. Those in leadership took on these false teachings to compete for souls and keep converts from going back to the pagan cults.

Today, this practice is widespread. Even evangelical denominations allow worldly entertainment and false teachings with pretended signs and wonders to sway converts.

The message of instant change and gold dust falling from the air comes from an *angel of light* principality stemming from the ancient practices of alchemy. (See 1 Corinthians 11, Acts 20:29-32, 1 Timothy 4:1-10, 2 Timothy 3:1-9 & 4:1-5 and 2 Thessalonians 2:3-15).

Ask God to open your eyes to the powerful principalities that control relationships, marriages, church services and many other activities in the community and in fellowship. Demons run in the works of the flesh as listed in Galatians 5:19-21, blinding Christians to inner carnal passions and desires. For example, a familiar demonic spirit of strife can incite quarrels within relationships and whole family systems, feasting on hidden bitter jealousies.

Until the work of the cross gains access to the inner roots of bitterness, these familiar spirits within family systems will perpetuate secret sin, abuse, and carnality—perpetuating deep hidden ruts of defiling family of origin sins. These will be handed down from generation to generation until they are exposed, and secret sin is brought to the light.

Be forewarned, you must patiently endure a demanding personal learning curve. This will equip the sincere Christian for spiritual battle with the full armor of God as well as instill Christ-like character. Christian workers, intercessors and those in ministry who graduate from Christ's training course will enable Christ's authority to flow through the disciplined saint. The sold-out warrior of Christ will break the demonic strongholds in the lives of the people in community, families and in the congregation.

DEFENSIVE WARFARE

The concept of defensive warfare is simple. Like defensive driving, we must be always on the alert.

As Peter wrote, *"**Humble** yourselves therefore under the mighty hand of God, that in due time he may exalt you. **Cast** all your **anxieties** on him, for he cares about you. **Be sober, be watchful**. Your adversary the devil prowls around like a roaring lion, seeking someone to devour. Resist him, firm **in your faith, knowing** that the same experience of **suffering is required** of your brotherhood throughout the world. And after you have suffered a little while, the God of all grace, who has called you to his eternal glory in Christ, will himself **restore, establish, and strengthen** you. To him be the dominion for ever and ever. Amen"* (1 Peter 5:6-11).

The emphasized areas in the above text are my highlights and are the basic attitudes and actions required for day-to-day living as a Christian. I also emphasized the divine benefits. Faithful adherence is required. If you submit to the training and discipline of the Lord and consistently practice defensive warfare principles, you will be ready when evil comes near.

There are times when God will grant us "rest and recreation" and we can temporarily lower our defenses and relax. Unfortunately, we are a generation that loves leisure, entertainment, and rest. We become passive in our warfare, and we then wonder why we are surprised at the success of the enemy's attack.

Again, defensive warfare requires constant humility, soberness in all things, and keeping constant vigilance. When Satan attacks you, resist him in faith, the faith that relies on God and not on self or on religious prayers. God is not pleased with the hardhearted Christians who give lip service to Him. These people do spiritual warfare by rote. They babble faithless incantations, such as pleading the blood over themselves, or magically don the armor of God to fend off the demonic. This type of Christian refuses to admit that they may have carnal character structures and foul motives in serving God, allowing Satan the right to harass and torment.

Note: *The practice of saying a prayer that pleads the blood of Christ stems from the belief that Christ's blood, shed on the cross (once and for all) can be mystically directed to cover a person, situation or material element for protection. This is similar to the Roman Catholic practice where the priest speaks a mystical prayer (transubstantiation) where the bread and wine of the Eucharist are transformed into the body and blood of Jesus, although its appearances remain the same.*

You must remember that suffering will be involved. Sometimes it will be impossible to endure (humanly speaking), thus we grow to rely on His grace, and not our own carnal spiritual strength.

Yes, our success is by God's unmerited grace; however, we must work out our own salvation and become obedient in all things. We learn obedience from the heart through the discipline of the Lord and partaking in the sufferings for Christ. We become motivated to love God unconditionally, not to accumulate points that allow boasting in His presence. (See Hebrews 5:7-10).

OFFENSIVE WARFARE

There are times when God calls us to attack. We must allow God to crush the enemy's work through our prayers and wrestling, which may require that we turn someone over to Satan for discipline. This may end up causing premature death. We may be involved in confronting evil people, as did Peter when he dealt with Ananias and Sapphira. Training and discipline tempers our ability, boldness and spiritual skills to wrestle with the powers of darkness and destroy strongholds, expose evil and evil people and sometimes confront sin straight on. As we walk in a defensive posture, we must not shy away from attacking evil and the powers of darkness when instructed to do so by our Heavenly Father.

Those who proactively take on Satan must do so with a clear mandate from God. Foolish pride and presumptuous arrogance are traps for carnal Christians. Fellowships that attempt to take on Satan's territory apart from the Holy Spirit's leadership and guidance are subject to severe trouble that could result in destruction, even loss of life.

If there is secret sin in the camp, the congregation—and even leadership—can expect to get a real beating. When false brethren join in on the effort, for whatever reason, there will be unnecessary casualties. Never enlist immature Christians to do this kind of warfare. Do not; I say again, *do not* involve Christians who are not likeminded or have not submitted to the discipline of the Lord and the work of the cross.

Christians who take on the enemy knowingly must be seasoned prayer warriors and true disciples who maintain a stable walk with Christ. Even then, one can expect suffering and more discipline.

Remember, Jesus commanded His disciples to wait until power came upon them before they went out on the Great Commission. They had been prepared for this power, so we also must be prepared in the discipline of the Lord and the work of the cross so that our day of Pentecostal power might come, in the time of His choosing. This includes being commissioned with spiritual power in combating evil and the dark work of the prince of the air.

"He gives power to the faint, and to him who has no might he increases strength. Even youths shall faint and be weary, and young men shall fall exhausted; but they who wait for the LORD shall renew their strength, they shall mount up with wings like eagles, they shall run and not be weary, they shall walk and not faint" (Isaiah 40:29-31).

CHAPTER 9

Standing in the Gap

"And I sought for a man among them who should build up the wall and stand in the breach before me for the land, that I should not destroy it; but I found none. Therefore I have poured out my indignation upon them; I have consumed them with the fire of my wrath; their way have I requited upon their heads, says the Lord GOD" (Ezekiel 22:30,31).

God is asking His people to stand in the gap for this great nation and a lost generation. Will He find His people willing to pay the price? The church has her example of a Man who stood in the breach. Indeed, it was Christ; now it is our turn to follow His lead.

Many come to church wounded and struggling, trying to work out their salvation. The coming persecution and the preaching of the cross will flush out the phonies who control most congregations. This house cleaning will allow God to bring solid disciples into leadership who will fulfill the law of Christ, bearing the burdens of weaker, new Christians. (See Galatians 6:1-10).

TRUE MINISTRIES LIVING AND PREACHING THE CROSS WILL BE BEACONS OF LIGHT AND HELP

Christ's message to His followers was the cross. The theme of redemption is the cross! The road to the fullness of life in Christ is the cross! This message must be restored to the body of Christ! Most importantly, this is the only message that God will back up.

Jesus declares, *"If any man would come after me, let him deny himself and take up his cross daily and follow me. For whoever would save his life will lose it; and whoever loses his life for my sake, he will save it"* (Luke 9:23,24).

The great prosperity experienced in this nation has lulled God's people to follow a cross-less, painless gospel that accommodates selfishness and laziness within Christians. The inner motives, thoughts and intentions of the heart remain unchallenged. In fact, many churches cater to this root attribute of the carnal sin nature!

Christians are misled to jump into the resurrected life by a shortcut that bypasses the work of the cross in the believer's life. The teaching that Christ did it all, we don't have to suffer death to our carnal self is a deadly doctrine, leading millions of Christians down the easy path that results in destruction.

Christ promises abundant life, but He also said that one must have his or her life come to a death. This seems to be a contradiction. Not so, if you understand that there are two meanings for the Greek word life, one is *zōē*, the other is *psuchē*.

Looking at the word "life" in the Greek with relationship to the abundant life, this Greek word is *zōē*, meaning life as the Father has in Himself. It is God's life shared through Christ to the believer, imparted by the Holy Spirit.

The life that must die within the true disciple is different. The Greek word for "life" in this context is *psuchē* which means that natural life of the soul, mind and heart, or if you will, the seat of our carnal personality or flesh, which is still active in most believers. This soul life feeds on relationship idolatry, pride of life, lust of the eye and lust of the flesh.

Thousands of hurting sinners and unstable Christians flock to most churches only to receive a watered-down gospel that does not help the sincere Christian loose their *psuchē* carnal life as Christ commands. Messages on how to look like a Christian on the outside are preached, rather than the transforming power of the cross. The work of the cross in the believer's life is painful and it is not instant. So, death to this selfish *psuchē* life is avoided. Thus, the abundant *zōē* life in Christ can never fully come.

Most Christians are taught that the abundant life in Christ is the fullness of a *psuchē* life. This is a false life in Christ, which can only mimic the *zōē* life in God. What a travesty of deception, which sets up wrong expectations for the new Christian.

Jesus said that Satan was a thief and a murderer from the beginning. Thousands of Christians struggle and eventually fall prey to Satan, the murderer of the *zōē* life found in Christ. The perverted gospel coming from far too many pulpits produces Christians in name only, where few get a glimpse of Christ's mission, *"I came that they may have life, and have it abundantly"* (John 10:10).

In 1988, our counseling ministry began in a 400-member charismatic church. Our appointments were booked out three months in advance by word of mouth. The number of hurting Christians in this medium-sized church was overwhelming. Soon Christians from other churches heard about the help available, which put even greater demand on our ministry. These Christians carried misery and pain because they lacked understanding concerning God's healing and restoration processes. Most suffered from abuse as children and many in supposed Christian homes.

We relied on honorariums from counselees, and often my family received food from a food bank ministry. A few special offerings from the congregation that we served came at the nick of time. Unfortunately, the senior pastor asked for offerings for us reluctantly. Few messages from the pulpit addressed the work of the cross and sound doctrine on learning to cooperate with the Holy

Spirit as Counselor and Healer of past wounds. This same pastor brought one evangelist after another to the pulpit in an attempt to get the congregation hyped-up to bring in more converts. Each time the congregation was encouraged to give generously for these guest speakers. This describes a deplorable situation quite common throughout the body of Christ.

This trend is about to come to a halt. The economic trouble that will soon befall America will be devastating and demoralizing. Fear and panic will grip the hearts of once confident and arrogant Christians. Millions of unsaved people will look to the church for help and see quite clearly that the phony ministries and fellowship can't and won't offer hope during these hard times.

True Leadership That's Immune To The Moses Syndrome

Moses and Aaron experienced a terrible pressure to keep God's people in line, walking before the Lord in a faithful manner. Something finally snapped with Moses and Aaron. These two men of God fell into a leadership trap or syndrome.

When God sent Moses and Aaron to Egypt to start the exodus of Israel, leading them out from under their cruel bondage, they spoke as such to the Pharaoh, *'Thus says the LORD, the God of Israel, Let my people go, that they may hold a feast to me in the wilderness.' But Pharaoh said, 'Who is the LORD, that I should heed his voice and let Israel go? I do not know the LORD, and moreover I will not let Israel go'"* (Exodus 5:1,2).

The battle began between Moses and the Pharaoh over God's people. Finally, after ten powerful signs and destructive judgments against Egypt, the Pharaoh relented.

We remember how God showed one sign after another as Moses spoke and warned on behalf of God, as Israel struggled and rebelled in the wilderness on the way to the Promised Land.

God calls Moses to Mount Sinai, to receive God's commands and while Moses is delayed the people of Israel rebel. *"And the LORD said to Moses, 'Go down; for your people, whom you brought up out of the land of Egypt, have corrupted themselves; they have turned aside quickly out of the way which I commanded them; they have made for themselves a molten calf, and have worshiped it and sacrificed to it, and said, 'These are your gods, O Israel, who brought you up out of the land of Egypt!'"* (Exodus 32:7,8).

God says to Moses, *"Your people, whom you brought up out of the Land of Egypt, have corrupted themselves."*

Yes, God's people were no longer His; they were now Moses' people.

Moses fell into a deadly leadership trap, where false responsibility for God's people to succeed makes the unsuspecting leader become embittered in a no-win double-bind situation.

A double-bind situation for leadership is where the leader assumes responsibility for the success of those under their leadership, when in fact those being led are wholly responsible to apply true leadership example and succeed by the working out of their salvation in their own faith and obedience.

Jesus would not succumb to this pressure. Many pastors are bogged down with sorting out one mess after another within their congregation. *"One of the multitude said to him, 'Teacher, bid my brother divide the inheritance with me.' But he said to him, 'Man, who made me a judge or divider over you?' And he said to them, 'Take heed, and beware of all covetousness; for a man's life does not consist in the abundance of his possessions'"* (Luke 12:13-15).

Sound doctrine and the harder teachings of Christ chase out the game players and bring the sincere to a pure faith in Christ. The pastor who makes true disciples, living by example and preaching and teaching the cross, will find rest rather than burnout. Though at first many may depart, the result will be a solid core of true disciples working as elders and Christian workers doing the work of the ministry.

True leaders will be made immune to the Moses syndrome and avoid the pitfalls, burnout and destruction to which so many leaders succumb to. *"They angered him at the waters of Meribah, and it went ill with Moses on their account; for they made his spirit bitter, and he spoke words that were rash"* (Psalm 106:32,33).

HEALING FOR THE DOUBLE-MINDED CHRISTIAN

"Count it all joy, my brethren, when you meet various trials, for you know that the testing of your faith produces steadfastness. And let steadfastness have its full effect, that you may be perfect and complete, lacking in nothing. If any of you lacks wisdom, let him ask God, who gives to all men generously and without reproaching, and it will be given him. But let him ask in faith, with no doubting, for he who doubts is like a wave of the sea that is driven and tossed by the wind. For that person must not suppose that a double-minded man, unstable in all his ways, will receive anything from the Lord" (James 1:2-7).

Over the many years of pastoral counseling, I have learned that God's word is accurate in identifying the cause and describing the symptoms of millions of unstable Christians. I have counseled hundreds from most denominations and backgrounds. The resounding root of the problem was simple, scriptural and all encompassing; these people are double-minded! (That is, two-souled or twice a soul).

I investigated, studied and worked out my own issues based on this scriptural diagnosis and prognosis. This is important, so I have underlined the method and source of healing and recovery for "unstable Christians." It is the **Word of God!**

You see, I am not a psychiatrist, clinical therapist, or psychologist. My higher formal education is in biblical studies, computer science and technology, with my completed undergraduate studies in Business Administration. I do not hold a license to pronounce a mental or emotional diagnosis or give any kind of medical or pharmaceutical prescription to make someone better.

Here is what I do claim:

> That by having a proper relationship with Jesus Christ and sound knowledge of the Word of God, I was able to recover from an abusive childhood which was the cause of much difficulty and instability in my walk with Christ and in daily living.
>
> Further, because of the call of God to full-time ministry, and with the lessons I learned from my own recovery, searching and study as a layperson, I was able to help others to learn to work with God in their own healing.
>
> Indeed, the Word of God with the leadership, counsel and comfort of the Holy Spirit can heal the wounded and double-minded Christian, if that Christian is sincere and willing to learn how to cooperate with God and apply these biblical principles as well as find solid like-minded fellowship. Again, the New Testament term double-minded (two-souled or twice-a-soul) describes a condition Christians can suffer from, as being "divided in soul and spirit."
>
> Far too many double-minded Christians who suffer from wounds to their spirit go to secular healers at the direction of their pastor. Many psychiatrists and clinicians try earnestly to help, but cannot and do not apply God's healing grace nor help the wounded fully recover God's way.

In a future published work, *Can Christ Heal the Divided?* We will expound on the principles, symptoms and issues concerning recovery for the two-souled Christian.

For now, the following are some paraphrased biblical principles that will help set the right frame of mind to start cooperating with God in becoming sanctified:

- Embrace trials by humbly submitting to God and stop blaming Satan for everything. Understand that Satan has a right to tempt us when we have hidden desires.
- Be willing and obedient—that is, hearing the Word and doing it.
- Stop putting on a religious pretense to cover up an insecure relationship with God. Religiosity covers bitter jealousy and selfish ambition.

- Be quick to listen, slow to speak; that is, keep your mouth shut and examine what and why you want to say something before you blurt it out. Remember, out of the heart the mouth speaks.
- The tongue is a powerful tool and can cause the birthing of inner character structures, so watch what you say to others (especially children) for the tongue can be a deadly poison.
- Be sincere and give up the love of the world. Look for mixed motives in your prayers and petitions. It may be God's will to pray a certain way, but we may also have an additional motive of hatred or revenge based on lack of forgiveness and bitterness. When these mix within our motives, they can skew or even sabotage our prayers.
- Above all, humble yourself, for the true Christian must maintain humility. Submit to God. This means we must submit all of life into God's care, even when suffering and trouble comes, so trust in Him to work it out, for He will, if you cooperate.
- Stand firm in faith and resist Satan; if you mean business, he will flee. Draw near to God and He will draw near to you. Admit and confess your sins and make every effort to stop sinning. You may need support, so be with like-minded brothers and sisters who are sincere and are not phonies who condemn and put-on religious airs.
- If you sin deliberately, knowing it is wrong and do it anyway, it will come back on you. God judges His people when they sin deliberately, and the repercussions can be quite fearful. (See Hebrews 10:19-39).
- Examine the thoughts and intentions of your heart for purification, and deal with the double-minded condition. Many inner thoughts are contrary to what you know to be God's will for you. Thoughts that are impure and come from past defilements and wounds will need to be examined. Take them captive and submit them to the Scripture and all of Christ's teachings. Practice self-examination and capture your inner thoughts without self-condemnation but hold yourself accountable to change on the inside. Be renewed in the spirit of your mind. (See Ephesians 4:17-24).
- Turn from fleshly doctrines and going to meetings that promise "a quick-fix"; there are no shortcuts.
- There must be a deliberate and intense effort in working out the double-minded parts within the spirit of your mind, heart, and personal spirit. The sincere child of God can put off the old nature by renewing the spirit of the mind. God gives grace to the humble. Persevere to the end, until you know that Christ's character has become yours, no matter how long it takes. In due time the Lord will exalt you. (See 1 Peter 5:6-11).

- In this humbling process, God will grant you grace for cleansing and healing. He will exalt you after you humble yourself. Do not make God humble you first, but rather dig deep and build upon the Rock while there is still time.

Recovering from doublemindedness can be an intense process. Many Christian leaders believe dealing with inner issues stemming from past wounds and defilements is not of God. There are many passages of Scripture that teach the contrary. Here is what Jesus says concerning these lies, *"Woe to you, scribes and Pharisees, hypocrites! for you cleanse the outside of the cup and of the plate, but inside they are full of extortion and rapacity. You blind Pharisee! first cleanse the inside of the cup and of the plate, that the outside also may be clean"* (Matthew 23:25,26).

Another verse specific to inner cleansing after one becomes a Christian written by Paul states, *"Since we have these promises, beloved, let us cleanse ourselves from every defilement of body and spirit, and make holiness perfect in the fear of God"* (2 Corinthians 7:1).

Note: the word *body* in this verse in the original Greek is *sarx* and in this context means, human nature with its frailties and passions, or specifically a carnally minded person.

The false doctrines noted earlier in chapters three and four, which teach avoidance of inner cleansing, have left many Christians polluted with all manner of inner vileness covered by a self-created religious personality. Their relationship with Christ started out in the Holy Spirit but as they continued in false doctrine, Christ became a self-made false *Christ*, formed from these false doctrines. This is one major reason why Christ will say to many, *"I never knew you; depart from me, you evildoers."*

SIN NATURE: DIVIDED HEART AND MIND, WOUNDED SPIRIT— NOT A MENTAL DISEASE

The world has reaped many blessings from science, as it helped create many innovative products, medical cures, medical procedures and amazing technological tools. In our over zealousness and arrogance, science was given a blank check concerning research into almost all areas of life. Some of this was absolute folly. Society accepted the false assurances of science as we plunged into the nuclear age. Scientific research and reports assured the whole nation that there would be negligible effects from nuclear contamination. Our many nuclear experiments and public programs turned lethal as these reports and scientific research were found to be half-truths and, in some cases, a plain lie! We are now reaping trouble for buying into one of science's greatest mistakes.

Science in all areas became an idol and society's savior. Our educational system is giving our children false hope in what science can do and how science is usually correct.

One thing Christians have always rejected from science was Darwinism and evolution. It was clear that this was a flaw in science and now, even though it's too late to stop the lies, sound and credible information is being presented scientifically to refute this error of "science."

What is just as disturbing and should have been addressed immediately was the error in science concerning the human heart and mind; there is a real problem here!

Far too many Christian's buy, hook line and sinker, the notion that secular psychiatrists, counselors or psychologists empowered by scientific research can figure out what is wrong with people emotionally and mentally. This research ignores the fact that humans are spiritual beings who possess a personal spirit, which, when wounded, presents psychological, emotional and even physical symptoms.

"Ask, and it will be given you; seek, and you will find; knock, and it will be opened to you. For every one who asks receives, and he who seeks finds, and to him who knocks it will be opened. Or what man of you, if his son asks him for bread, will give him a stone? Or if he asks for a fish, will give him a serpent? If you then, who are evil, know how to give good gifts to your children, how much more will your Father who is in heaven give good things to those who ask him! (Matthew 7:7-11).

More than ever children are prescribed different chemicals in an effort to quell the symptoms of lazy, narcissistic parents who allow, among other societal evils, the defiling images of TV, a powerful programming tool of Satan to penetrate their children's psyche.

The truth is leaking out into society. We now see, more than ever, support groups, self-help tools and even Christian ministries springing up as the truth in God's Word comes clear.

God's Word became clear for me. Sinful behavior is hidden everywhere in society. Families and family systems look good on the outside, but under closer inspection, evil and abuse that create dysfunctional members of society are becoming evident. Children who suffer these symptoms are finally having their parents become suspect.

Throughout each generation, families will hand down their own brand of sin nature characteristics and wounds. Unless the Gospel of Christ changes these tendencies, each new family in succession will suffer. (See Exodus 34:6,7).

GOD'S PRINCIPLES FOR RECOVERY:
APPLYING LESSONS FROM THE BOOK OF JAMES

God is faithful and has provided an excellent *step recovery* book in the Bible. The book of James paints a clear picture of what the problem is, the consequences, and how to overcome double mindedness.

This divinely-inspired book contains a very practical and hard-hitting message that addresses real issues in the church—a true biblical step program that changes Christians on the inside. These principles will not allow Christians to religiously mask root problems and spiritually dope themselves up to ease symptomatic pain. God's recovery program will not allow a cover-up concerning the sin nature and wounds to the spirit.

I suggest doing an outline of James, taking an attitude that this book was specifically written to you. You will find sound principles that you can apply with the counsel and leadership of the Holy Spirit. The key is to study, seek, ask and knock on the closed doors of your heart, allowing God to expose what is hidden.

Keep your outline handy and use it as guidelines in your prayers, times of meditation and self-examination. Look for mixed or ill motives of heart in all that you do and speak.

PROPER APPLICATION OF THE WHOLE ARMOR OF GOD

"Finally, be strong in the Lord and in the strength of his might. Put on the whole armor of God, that you may be able to stand against the wiles of the devil. For we are not contending against flesh and blood, but against the principalities, against the powers, against the world rulers of this present darkness, against the spiritual hosts of wickedness in the heavenly places. Therefore take the whole armor of God, that you may be able to withstand in the evil day, and having done all, to stand. Stand therefore, having girded your loins with truth, and having put on the breastplate of righteousness, and having shod your feet with the equipment of the gospel of peace; besides all these, taking the shield of faith, with which you can quench all the flaming darts of the evil one. And take the helmet of salvation, and the sword of the Spirit, which is the word of God. Pray at all times in the Spirit, with all prayer and supplication. To that end keep alert with all perseverance, making supplication for all the saints, and also for me, that utterance may be given me in opening my mouth boldly to proclaim the mystery of the gospel, for which I am an ambassador in chains; that I may declare it boldly, as I ought to speak" (Ephesians 6:10-20).

Many Christians think that somehow by being born again, Spirit-filled or Spirit-baptized; they have a magical protection by God, which comes upon them by simply asking. Yes, God supplies abundant grace to new Christians, which includes a nominal amount of protection when they ask in simple prayers of faith. On the other hand, to think that only praying a special prayer will get the job done is presumptuous. For many Christians, "the putting on the whole armor of God" has become a superstitious incantation.

Strength comes from the Lord for those who love Him and have a real relationship with Him, not by what we know about Him.

Most Christians underestimate Satan. Few have really brushed up against true evil and been victorious. As one becomes purer in Christ, authority over Satan and the demonic becomes more powerful, swift and discerning.

People are instruments of Satan and his legions, but it is the spiritual power behind those people that must be conquered first, then evil people can be confronted more successfully. Even then, evil people will kick and fight right up until they are defeated, for their very character and heart has become evil.

The armor of God is "Christ-like character qualities," wrought within Christians through the discipline and training of the Lord.

Truth is to be worked into our nature. We must not be self-deceived. David wrote that God desires truth in the inward being. Most Christians avoid dealing with their true thoughts and intentions of the heart, which often contain impure or mixed motives.

There must be righteousness and holiness within the heart. Our private lives must be exemplary before God. That means the breastplate of righteousness and wisdom consists of what is in the heart. David wrote, *"Teach me wisdom in my secret heart."* There is no room for hypocrisy.

Many Christians venture into spiritual battle, spouting off memorized Scripture and think they are wielding the "Sword of the Spirit." This foolishness brings much trouble. They did not hear from the Holy Spirit, but rather presumptuously and arrogantly they attack evil and evil situations in "self-strength." Christ will say to many false and deceived Christians at the final judgment, *"Depart from me–I never knew you!"* In this passage of Scripture, the demons said to these itinerant exorcists, *"Jesus I know, and Paul I know; but who are you?"* Then the demons, working through the man whom they controlled, overtook all seven of these false exorcists, wounding them and forcing them to flee for their lives, beaten and naked. You see Jesus worked through Paul because He (Jesus) knew Paul, and that is the authority we have in Christ. So also, the demons know who has a true relationship with Christ and who does not.

When properly worked in, the full armor of God allows a true disciple to fight victoriously. Demons will know and fear that Christian who is truly in Christ and whom Christ works through, not what that Christian says or commands!

CHRIST-LIKE CHARACTER CREATED BY ENDURING FIERY TRIALS

I was sharing with a Christian whom I had just met. We discussed what the Lord was doing in our lives. I shared with him how our ministry concentrated on the work of the cross for the believer in everyday life. He listened as I explained that, so few Christians know how to cooperate with God as they enter the narrow gate and follow the hard path. Not too long into the discussion, I could tell that he was cringing on the inside. He carefully changed the subject and finished by saying that my work in this area was a "hard gig."

Unfortunately, most Christians do not want to participate in God's true discipleship-making program. They want to have God in their lives—but on their terms. For a Christian to give God permission to bring trials into their life in order to produce true Christ-like character, becomes too hard to accept and far too many believers *run from this kind of sacrificial life and covenant*.

Once I was associated with a pastor who had personal issues and difficulties and occasionally came to me for counsel and prayer support. Some of these issues were sexual in nature.

Finally, one day I encouraged him to give God permission to do whatever it took to change his inner nature by way of the work of the cross. His countenance turned pale, and I could tell deep fear arose within him.

After a moment of silence, he said to me, "I just can't; I am afraid God will take away one of my children!"

Through several situations and issues, this precious brother and I parted fellowship. About a year and a half later he fell into sin, committed adultery, and had to step down from ministry, at least for a while.

Jesus said, *"Enter by the narrow gate; for the gate is wide and the way is easy, that leads to destruction, and those who enter by it are many. For the gate is narrow and the way is hard, that leads to life, and those who find it are few"* (Matthew 7:13,14).

Like so many others, this Christian chose the easy way in attempting to get at the old sin nature and have it changed. The choice this man made ended in destruction.

Yes, the trials will be hard—but not too hard. This man's reason for not submitting to God's plan for inner character transformation was the fear that God would take away one of his children!

What great unbelief in God! This is what was indeed in his heart of hearts concerning his true attitude toward God. This man's faith and trust in our Lord was riddled with unbelief.

"Take care, brethren, lest there be in any of you an evil, unbelieving heart, leading you to fall away from the living God. But exhort one another every day, as long as it is called 'today,' that none of you may be hardened by the deceitfulness of sin. For we share in Christ, if only we hold our first confidence firm to the end, while it is said, 'Today, when you hear his voice, do not harden your hearts as in the rebellion'" (Hebrews 3:12-15).

Many Christians have unbelieving hearts. It is written, *"And they took offense at him. But Jesus said to them, 'A prophet is not without honor except in his own country and in his own house.' And he did not do many mighty works there, because of their unbelief"* (Matthew 13:57,58).

Jesus comes to believers and challenges them with the cross and true discipleship, but far too many today will not give up their own lives so Christ will have preeminence in all things. They hang onto life vicariously, clinging to others and making idols out of children, a spouse, ministry, work, material goods and reputation. They refuse to surrender to the "all-owning demands" of Jesus. They mistrust him! Jesus insists that we love Him above all else. Christ demands to transform our nature so that it becomes like His.

"Many of his disciples, when they heard it, said, 'This is a hard saying; who can listen to it?' But Jesus, knowing in himself that his disciples murmured at it, said to them, 'Do you take offense at this? Then what if you were to see the Son of man ascending where he was before? It is the spirit that gives life, the flesh is of no avail; the words that I have spoken to you are spirit and life. But there are some of you that do not believe.' For Jesus knew from the first who those were that did not believe, and who it was that would betray him. And he said, 'This is why I told you that no one can come to me unless it is granted him by the Father.' After this many of his disciples drew back and no longer went about with him" (John 6:60-66).

NO LONGER NAÏVE ABOUT GOOD AND EVIL

Paul wrote to the Christians in Rome, addressing the very same issue. *"I appeal to you, brethren, to take note of those who create dissensions and difficulties, in opposition to the doctrine which you have been taught; avoid them. For such persons do not serve our Lord Christ, but their own appetites, and by fair and flattering words they deceive the hearts of the simple-minded. For while your obedience is known to all, so that I rejoice over you, I would have you wise as to what is good and guileless as to what is evil; then the God of peace will soon crush Satan under your feet. The grace of our Lord Jesus Christ be with you"* (Romans 16:17-20).

God is building leaders who will teach all that Jesus taught. Evil people are sent by Satan to cause trouble and constantly lead Christians astray, but the sound teachings of Christ help Christians detect and avoid such people. Unfortunately, few read and embrace all that Jesus taught.

Remember Jesus warned, *"I came to cast fire upon the earth; and would that it were already kindled! I have a baptism to be baptized with; and how I am constrained until it is accomplished! Do you think that I have come to give peace on earth? No, I tell you, but rather division; for henceforth in one house there will be five divided, three against two and two against three; they will be divided, father against son and son against father, mother against daughter and daughter against her mother, mother-in-law against her daughter-in-law and daughter-in-law against her mother-in-law"* (Luke 12:49-53).

Jesus knew this would be one of the hardest lessons for the disciples. He was constantly warning His followers about wolves in sheep's clothing and false prophets. He had to correct His disciples repeatedly about the leaven of the Pharisees, which is the deceptive power of hypocrisy. Teaching them was one thing, training them in real life situations was even more difficult, but this is the only way to break denial that evil people exist and are more numerous than you would think. If not stopped, evil people will destroy others who get in their way.

One reason Jesus called Judas and allowed him to stay all through those years of fellowship with the other disciples was to train the remaining eleven in discernment. What a shock for the other 11. Judas betrayed Christ. How could that be?

When evil becomes visible, indeed, it seems surreal, baffling, and unbelievable. Nevertheless, evil people do evil and they live right under the noses of the naïve saint.

This is Satan's most effective way of hindering the work of the Gospel and causing dissensions and difficulties; just send in a Judas. Satan will never give up the "Judas Plan," at least until the end. We must always be alert and discerning.

Paraphrasing what Paul wrote: *until God's people are no longer deceived and have had enough trouble from these imposters, only then they will begin to avoid these people. Until then, Satan will run roughshod through the camp. Peace will be difficult to maintain.*

When the true body of Christ grows up and no longer is naïve concerning evil people, then God will have a people that He can use to crush the work of Satan.

BEING SEPARATE AND SALT OF THE EARTH

God's people are to stand in the gap and fill the breach that often breaks open in their nation. As the salt of the earth, we are to preserve the land so that corruption and evil do not overtake society, thus inciting extreme judgment and the wrath of God.

Jesus said we are to be light and salt. We are to be examples who testify in word and deed as to Who Christ is, and indeed that Christ lives in us, and to be a powerful spiritual influence in the world. Fulfilling the call of being light and salt will give direction in times of darkness and preserve and influence life all around us. Many Christians believe the hired minister or pastor is the one to do all those difficult things, while they sit in the pews demanding blessings and entertainment. On the contrary every Christian is in ministry to be salt and light, which is the normal work of a true disciple of Christ!

This goes hand in hand with the Great Commission to make disciples of all peoples (nations). Sad to say, the result of not doing this is as follows:

"You are the salt of the earth; but if salt has lost its taste, how shall its saltness be restored? It is no longer good for anything except to be thrown out and trodden under foot by men. You are the light of the world. A city set on a hill cannot be hid. Nor do men light a lamp and put it under a bushel, but on a stand, and it gives light to all in the

house. Let your light so shine before men, that they may see your good works and give glory to your Father who is in heaven" (Matthew 5: 13-16).

That is exactly what is about to happen. Christians in this nation will soon know what persecution feels like. The trampling of Christians by ridicule, harassment, and in some cases hate-crimes and murder are coming soon. This revulsion towards Christians has already begun, and soon it will be widespread and secretly approved by many in the government.

Only those sold out to Christ will be victorious. As this becomes prevalent, the church will start losing imposters as the hypocrites renounce their shallow beliefs.

Trouble is coming to the church in America and most are not ready to endure this persecution.

Those who endure and become pure and consecrated will be true servants of the Lord. Their lives will become living letters from God to a dying generation. They will be full of effectual prayer and boldness as they confront evil in the power of God, not in the flesh! They will suffer persecution, but this will only make them stronger and full of the Holy Spirit and the grace of our Lord Jesus Christ.

"You yourselves are our letter of recommendation, written on your hearts, to be known and read by all men; and you show that you are a letter from Christ delivered by us, written not with ink but with the Spirit of the living God, not on tablets of stone but on tablets of human hearts. Such is the confidence that we have through Christ toward God. Not that we are competent of ourselves to claim anything as coming from us; our competence is from God, who has made us competent to be ministers of a new covenant, not in a written code but in the Spirit; for the written code kills, but the Spirit gives life" (2 Corinthians 3:2-6).

CHAPTER 10

Winning the War

GOOD WORKS THAT ARE ORDAINED BY GOD

"FOR we are his workmanship, created in Christ Jesus for good works, which God prepared beforehand, that we should walk in them" (Ephesians 2:10).

Recently, two Christian women came knocking at the door. They introduced themselves as representatives from a local evangelical church. One was involved in the church's Christian education ministry; the other was the wife of the assistant pastor.

They were out talking to people about attending their church and explaining the many programs that were available. I shared with them about our fellowship and our work, explaining how we work with deeply wounded Christians and how I was pleased to hear about their work in the community.

The wife of the assistant pastor ignored what I was saying and kept pushing their programs, as if our work was in competition with theirs. I shared with them about the difficulty of our work and I could tell the other woman was excited to hear about what the Lord was doing in our ministry. The Holy Spirit brought out a kindred unity between her and me, as we glorified Jesus in our conversation and shared eagerly about the Lord's work being raised up, noting that not too many ministries are accomplishing this today.

Finally, the assistant pastor's wife interrupted once more and started extolling their church programs. After listening to me about our work, she still was trying to get my family and me to attend their fellowship. I could tell the other woman sensed that this was completely out of place. I closed the conversation, wished them well, and said we would pray for their "good efforts" in touching the community for Christ. I also asked for prayer for the work the Lord had chosen for us. The assistant pastor's wife became cold and left with a disappointed countenance. As they walked away, I remembered the account in Luke 17:35 where Jesus said, *"One will be taken, one will be left."*

So many works are just getting people to attend their church. This example is not an exception.

The Lord is about to release disciplined Christians who will walk in the good works that God ordains. Congregations and fellowships across this nation want credit and recognition for their programs and ministries. Many do very little to encourage and support the rest of the body of Christ's efforts. Local fellowships that humble themselves will start to work together and support solid, God-ordained works where Christ will get full credit. Partisan self-glorifying congregations within the body of Christ will experience death in the coming days.

Pastors must be alert and not unite with the false or carnal denominations or fellowships. A false unity and prayer movement is setting many up to commit an ecumenical suicide. Watch out, beware, and seek like-minded leaders and pastors who embrace the cross and know that judgment begins with God's people. Revival and true unity begin in the sanctuary, wrought by an ongoing baptism of fire and the work of the cross. Anything short of this is counterfeit.

True revival, a true turning to God in deep repentance starts with a preparation that closes down the false works, chases out the wolves and leaves a cleansed and purified band of disciples, who follow the Holy Spirit's leadership.

AN ARMY LED BY THE LORD JESUS

Jesus will take the reins back from the false shepherds and replace them with true shepherds who get their marching orders from Christ, not the church growth marketing programs, megachurch conferences, superlative false apostles or errant, marauding tickle-the-ear prophets.

These shepherds will help Christian workers minister the Gospel as sound doctrine and *all the teachings* of Christ become restored. These sold-out leaders will start to do their job: equipping the saints for the ministry. *"And his gifts were that some should be apostles, some prophets, some evangelists, some pastors and teachers, to equip the saints for the work of ministry, for building up the body of Christ, until we all attain to the unity of the faith and of the knowledge of the Son of God, to mature manhood, to the measure of the stature of the fullness of Christ; so that we may no longer be children, tossed to and fro and carried about with every wind of doctrine, by the cunning of men, by their craftiness in deceitful wiles. Rather, speaking the truth in love, we are to grow up in every way into him who is the head, into Christ, from whom the whole body, joined and knit together by every joint with which it is supplied, when each part is working properly, makes bodily growth and upbuilds itself in love"* (Ephesians 4:11-16).

A true revival will come during this time of great trouble. Persecution tends to purge out the false while disciplining and training the true. Then demonstrations of the true power of God will manifest in the form of miracles and in terrible acts of God, like the account of Ananias and Sapphira. These things will begin to restore the fear of God Almighty in the body of Christ and across this nation.

GOD WILL BE A WITNESS AGAINST THE WICKED

"Then I will draw near to you for judgment; I will be a swift witness against the sorcerers, against the adulterers, against those who swear falsely, against those who

oppress the hireling in his wages, the widow and the orphan, against those who thrust aside the sojourner, and do not fear me, says the LORD of hosts" (Malachi 3:5).

Many Christian leaders have spoken out against the tide of wickedness that is overflowing into society. We see more and more battles lost, as if God has not backed these efforts. Indeed, for the most part He has not!

True disciples will be raised up and will pronounce individual judgments against the wicked. First, this type of housecleaning will start within churches.

As with Ananias and Sapphira, so will hundreds of evil people hiding in the body of Christ begin to take ill, die, and many will die outright where they stand as true prophets of the Lord confront their wickedness. A holy terror will fall on Christians first; then, as word gets out about this, the wicked will lose their boldness and arrogance as they retreat underground in fear of their own lives. (See Acts 5:11).

Those who oppose God's work will be dealt with harshly on the day that God acts. This will be a sovereign work of God to restore healthy fear of God and respect for the true servant of the Lord. For a new believer or those ignorant of these accounts in the Scripture, this may seem radical and scary, but this kind of power is not at the discretion of the servant of the Lord, but rather a directive of the Holy Spirit. As you read you will see that the Holy Spirit directs these acts and we must trust God in His sovereignty and wisdom. (See Appendix for further discussion).

"When they had gone through the whole island as far as Paphos, they came upon a certain magician, a Jewish false prophet, named Bar-Jesus. He was with the proconsul, Sergius Paulus, a man of intelligence, who summoned Barnabas and Saul and sought to hear the word of God. But Elymas the magician (for that is the meaning of his name) withstood them, seeking to turn away the proconsul from the faith. But Saul, who is also called Paul, filled with the Holy Spirit, looked intently at him and said, 'You son of the devil, you enemy of all righteousness, full of all deceit and villainy, will you not stop making crooked the straight paths of the Lord? And now, behold, the hand of the Lord is upon you, and you shall be blind and unable to see the sun for a time.' Immediately mist and darkness fell upon him and he went about seeking people to lead him by the hand. Then the proconsul believed, when he saw what had occurred, for he was astonished at the teaching of the Lord" (Acts 13:6-12).

A few years ago, there was an account of a young prophet and his family addressing a congregation about this coming time of judgment to the household of God. The pastor allowed this young man to stand up and proclaim this warning for all to hear.

An elder took offense, came up to the pulpit, denounced this message, and bad-mouthed the prophet. The pastor of this church tried to get this elder to stop and sit down, but he would not, and continued his rebuke. Finally, the young prophet stood and said to this elder; "Get your house in order. The Lord is taking you home!"

The elder became even more indignant and forced the pastor to escort him from the pulpit. Two weeks later, this elder died instantly of a heart attack!

There have been times when we have had to speak forth a destructive judgment on an individual. The training that God put us through eventually brought us to a conviction that this was God's last resort in stopping an evil person and putting an end to their evil influence. When we saw enough suffering caused by the evil and learned from the word of God that in some cases there was no alternative, we then learned to deliver God's occasional prophetic messages of discipline and destruction.

Ministry case: Chasing out the wolves.

> "But Saul, who is also called Paul, filled with the Holy Spirit, looked intently at him and said, 'You son of the devil, you enemy of all righteousness, full of all deceit and villainy, will you not stop making crooked the straight paths of the Lord? And now, behold, the hand of the Lord is upon you, and you shall be blind and unable to see the sun for a time.' Immediately mist and darkness fell upon him and he went about seeking people to lead him by the hand. Then the proconsul believed, when he saw what had occurred, for he was astonished at the teaching of the Lord" (Acts 13:9-12).

Every Thursday night from 7 to 9, the ministry's support group worked with Christians who struggled with various issues. Addictions, abuse and destructive relationships were the primary issues addressed. On occasion, we would find a person attending to be *insincere*. We would confront them appropriately and if they did not repent and stop, they could not attend. One man was coming to hit on women. We went through the confrontational process, but he continued his sexual advances, so we barred him from the group and fellowship.

He continued to call one woman in the group. At our counsel, she had a restraining order served. He was not to call her, or me, as her pastor, or use anyone as a go-between to contact her. In spite of the legal restraint, he attempted to get me to pass on a message. He telephoned my residence and posed the request and I said, "No." He would not listen to reason and he started railing at me. Filled with righteous indignation, the Holy Spirit prompted me to tell him, *"You son of the devil, the next time I see you, I'll see you in handcuffs."* He finally hung up. I reported this to the police, and they served him a court appearance. About two months later, the prosecuting attorney requested that I testify at this appearance.

All the parties concerned had arrived, except the accused. He was late. Finally, we all heard his voice booming in the hallway. He was telling his attorney that this crazy minister was to blame for his court appearance. He continued his loud assessment of me as they walked into the courtroom.

He came in *handcuffed* to another person. Evidently his imprisonment was for some past felony. It never dawned on him that the prophetic word the Lord spoke through me two months prior had come to pass. The Lord knew he had warrants for his arrest and had a servant of the Lord speak forth his incarceration. Like Elymas the Magician, this man did not repent, even though the Lord executed his judgments.

Few see the slow judgments of the Lord over the years concerning the wicked, those who deceive and mislead many, even some who exalt themselves to be gods.

Recall Elizabeth Montgomery who played the lead role in the TV sitcom "Bewitched". She died before her time, so did Agnes Moorehead, as well as Dick York and Dick Sergeant. In 1966, Beatle John Lennon said, "we're more popular than Jesus now; I don't know which will go first—rock-n-roll or Christianity."

It was said of the Titanic before her maiden voyage, *God could not sink her.* Mama Cass was proclaimed omnipotent in her vocal range. Superman actors and the child actress in the movie *Poltergeist* all died untimely deaths. These are just a few examples.

"Now Herod was angry with the people of Tyre and Sidon; and they came to him in a body, and having persuaded Blastus, the king's chamberlain, they asked for peace, because their country depended on the king's country for food. On an appointed day Herod put on his royal robes, took his seat upon the throne, and made an oration to them. And the people shouted, 'The voice of a god, and not of man!' Immediately an angel of the Lord smote him, because he did not give God the glory; and he was eaten by worms and died. But the word of God grew and multiplied" (Acts 12:2-24).

Why do some live on in their arrogance and idolatry, while others who are wicked die soon, even instantly? We have many accounts in Scripture concerning this type of judgment at the hand of the Lord. Again, see Appendix for further discussion.

THE GREAT TRIBULATION WILL AWAKEN A MULTITUDE OF LOST SOULS AND MANY FOOLISH CHRISTIANS

A great harvest is coming, and millions will awaken to the call of God for salvation and sanctification. A holy fear will sweep over these precious lost children of God.

Many who read this may become disturbed as I challenge their Rapture theories. Sorry to burst bubbles, but Christ will not Rapture His dear saints to safety until the great harvest is complete, during the Great Tribulation! The church may endure ten months, two years, five years, or the entire tribulation period. No one will know the day or hour, but we must be ready, and we must be able to endure until that great moment and be called up at the sound of the last trumpet.

The Lord expects His people to shine as a witness for millions who are lost. There is coming a great harvest, and God is calling for His workers to be ready. He desires to purify and establish a people to stand as beacons of hope with the pure message of Christ's Gospel. (Read Revelations 7:9-17).

True Conversions By The Holy Spirit
True End-of-the-Age Harvest is Coming. You Can Count On It!

Over the last 30 years, we have seen a tremendous spiritual hunger manifest across this nation and in the world. Satan has taken advantage of this as we have seen the New Age movements and cults spring up.

Simply put, the "gospel" these people hear is not the true Gospel of Christ; it is a different gospel, and it is not found in the New Testament. Paul warned the Christians at Corinth about this. *"I feel a divine jealousy for you, for I betrothed you to Christ to present you as a pure bride to her one husband. But I am afraid that as the serpent deceived Eve by his cunning, your thoughts will be led astray from a sincere and pure devotion to Christ. For if someone comes and preaches another Jesus than the one we preached, or if you receive a different spirit from the one you received, or if you accept a different gospel from the one you accepted, you submit to it readily enough"* (2 Corinthians 11:2-4).

New converts must, in no uncertain terms, be set straight concerning the demands Christ has on their lives.

Many of these people coming to church are seeking a spiritual program that is rooted in *"What can God do for me to make my life better?"*

Many pastors and teachers take advantage of this and tell these seekers about a *magic Santa Claus Christ* who will cater to all their whims and wants. The stark reality of Christ's warnings is minimized and even left out of the message altogether. The messages in this false gospel boil down to selling "fire insurance" and "spiritual investment programs" that supposedly give instant returns. The cares of this world drive many to God, but God never called them. He knew their hearts!

Jesus sent the rich young ruler away by confronting him with his wrong motives for seeking God. I wonder how many ministers of the Gospel would chase off the rich by confronting their true motives.

In the coming days, true leadership and Christian workers will challenge the motives of these insincere Christians. But those who are called of God and come to Christ will understand exactly what the great price is and be willing to pay as they choose to follow Christ, the coming King of kings and Lord of lords!

True Fellowship Revival Will Not Be Short Circuited

Recently an associate in ministry informed me that her church is pushing the Toronto Blessing revival, trying to inspire this false revival to get started within their local fellowship.

Impressed with growth and outer manifestations that supposedly bring Christians closer to God to feel divine ecstasy, a key leader started speaking about how the Wales revival started this movement in 1904.

This teacher made a wild statement, saying that Jessie Penn-Lewis was responsible for stopping the Wales revival from spreading to the whole world. This misinformed teacher asserted that Penn-Lewis pulled Roberts aside and convinced him to back away from promoting this movement. As I have shared earlier, Jessie Penn-Lewis and Evan Roberts worked together in denouncing the counterfeit that overtook a true move of God and attempting to correct and teach why and how the demonic counterfeited the real. There will be more and more extraordinary assertions and lies spread about anyone who denounces this counterfeit activity.

Judgment is coming to the liars. God will start to severely discipline the counterfeit servants and false teachers who practice carnal methods in getting God's people stirred up.

True shepherds must learn how to avoid the pitfalls that befell the Wales revival and other true movements of God. Pastors and elders will have to give an account as to the care they exercised over God's vineyard.

Penn-Lewis and Roberts began to preach and teach against these errors. They saw the root problem being the lack of true disciples available to bring converts into the training and discipline of the Lord, embracing the work of the cross.

Penn-Lewis wrote, *"Now as to the perils of Revival: These again primarily may be briefly defined as, (1) the danger of acting or living by 'feeling', or the sensuous life, instead of the spirit-life; and (2) the peril arising from the spirits of evil counterfeiting the workings of the Holy Spirit. Alongside of the danger of becoming dominated by 'feelings' and emotions, the perils of Revival come mainly from the invisible world of spirits. The Counterfeiter is watching to counterfeit, and to insert his workings in the place of God's workings.... main peril.... A very small inserted 'stream', or 'tincture' from the enemy, causes mixture which may not be discerned at first, but which sooner or later produces fruit in confusion and trouble"* (Transcript from the message, *The Cross and Revival* by Jessie Penn-Lewis).

Jesus prepared the church for the day of Pentecost by making true disciples—first. These men were not obsessed with signs and wonders.

The true minister and shepherd who cry to God for revival must understand how God prepares for revival. A true move of God upon the lost, the backslidden and lukewarm Christian can only come when proper discipleship is established and maintained.

Jesus called twelve disciples, and He trained them intimately, losing only one—the son of perdition, Judas. He taught them lessons and exposed hidden issues within them that assured these men would not waver in the building of the first century Christian church.

This is the key for true revival to come within any local fellowship or congregation. The problem is learning to understand what true discipleship is.

During the late sixties and seventies, a discipleship movement began in the church here in the US. It was referred to as the shepherding movement. This movement had good intentions with the goal to build disciples of sincere believers.

Many Christians involved, who submitted to this discipleship program, were unstable and wayward (twice souled). To compensate for this, strict controls were put in place. A hierarchy of shepherds was established from national leaders down to local shepherds in charge of small groups. Unfortunately, leadership within this movement became overbearing and controlling.

Again, we have an example of failure due to a carnal effort in attempting to fulfill Christ's commission.

Let's read Christ's commission: "Go *therefore and make disciples of all nations, baptizing them in the name of the Father and of the Son and of the Holy Spirit, teaching them to observe all that I have commanded you; and lo, I am with you always, to the close of the age*" (Matthew 28:19,20).

The key is that in the beginning Christ built a foundation for the church, making true disciples. These men had Christ's nature burned within, thus they taught and led by example.

Jesus told the disciples to teach new disciples to observe all that He commanded. Few today teach others all that Jesus taught. The basic cause for this is many in leadership have never allowed Jesus to discipline them intimately in all that He commands.

In reality, true revival is founded on true discipleship teachings, where the training is done by the discipline of the Lord, with like-minded disciples supporting each other in what Jesus called, *"Entering the narrow gate and walking the hard path that leads to life."*

Part of the solution will come from God's people who no longer tolerate the false. When trouble comes, the false looses its power to decieve. And the sincere Christian, when burnt enough, will be outspoken and not tolerate the lies. Right now far too many of God's sheep choose to stay stupid, going along with anyone who promises a good time in the Lord. This is about to end and true revival in the local fellowship will stay the course as God's people start to wake up and reject the false.

MASSES WILL FOLLOW JESUS AND TRUE LEADERSHIP NOT SUPER HEROES

When the Great Tribulation revival begins, the masses will gather to hear sound doctrine by ministers of the Gospel who will not steal the glory from Christ, nor foster empty manifestations by a false spirit to hijack what God is doing.

Christ calls and disciplines true servants to lead, and not draw the sheep after themselves. Some are to be apostles, prophets, evangelists, pastors and teachers. A true servant will not elevate him or herself by way of title or push self-prominence. Yes, there are still apostles and prophets besides evangelists, pastors and teachers. If you will, Martin Luther was an apostle used by God to restore the true doctrine of justification by faith, not by works. The word 'apostle' means "one sent forth, or a messenger." The title "prophet" means "a seer," or one who has immediate intercourse with God, also translated, "one in whom the message from God springs forth" or "one to whom anything is secretly communicated." "Pastor" means "shepherd or guide, an overseer of God's flock." "Evangelist" means "a messenger of good news or a preacher of the Gospel." "Teacher" means "to carry on instruction, to teach what is good by word and example." Each office, by definition, has a specific function to build and equip Christians for successful living and effective ministry.

We are to respect, appreciate and support true leaders called of God. Unfortunately, few Christians discern between hirelings and those who have paid the price of true discipleship. Indeed, false apostles, false prophets, false teachers, false pastors and false evangelists prosper because God's people follow those who preach the easy way and avoid preaching and teaching what needs to be heard. Jesus warned not to elevate anyone in leadership to an exalted position. (See Matthew 23:1-39).

Many in leadership today use underhanded ways to preach the Gospel. Paul wrote, *"Therefore, having this ministry by the mercy of God, we do not lose heart. We have renounced disgraceful, underhanded ways; we refuse to practice cunning or to tamper with God's word, but by the open statement of the truth we would commend ourselves to every man's conscience in the sight of God. And even if our gospel is veiled, it is veiled only to those who are perishing. In their case the god of this world has blinded the minds of the unbelievers, to keep them from seeing the light of the gospel of the glory of Christ, who is the likeness of God. For what we preach is not ourselves, but Jesus Christ as Lord, with ourselves as your servants for Jesus' sake"* (2 Corinthians 4:1-5).

THE TRUE GIFTS OF THE HOLY SPIRIT MANIFESTED

Many of the manifestations of the so-called gifts of the Holy Spirit in these false revivals are bizarre and self-edifying. Many are false, cover up the secrets of the heart, and short-circuit the work of the cross.

When the true gifts of the Holy Spirit are in operation, secret sin comes to the light and wounds receive healing. Painful, unresolved issues of heart are confessed and wounds to the spirit receive healing and cleansing. True gifts that edify will manifest in a meaningful manner, bringing understanding to the hearers. Order and decency, with respect to newcomers and outsiders, will prevail.

Seeking power, for the sake of power, will stop. The cross is the life-changing power of God for the believer. The outwardly expressed power of God given for witness, ministry and preaching is manifested to draw attention to the Gospel and to the person of Christ. Christians lack the grace of God that maintains inner peace and security, because they avoid discipline that builds Christ-like character. These empty manifestations give outsiders and new believers the wrong message. As Paul wrote, *"will they not say that you are mad?"* (1 Corinthians 14:23).

Paul had to correct the power-hungry Christians at Corinth and stated specifically, *"For Christ did not send me to baptize but to preach the gospel, and not with eloquent wisdom, lest the cross of Christ be emptied of its power. For the word of the cross is folly to those who are perishing, but to us who are being saved it is the power of God. For it is written, 'I will destroy the wisdom of the wise, and the cleverness of the clever I will thwart'"* (1 Corinthians 1:17-19).

When the true power of God becomes manifest, there is a deep sense of holiness and reverence. There are times to rejoice and make a wonderful noise unto the Lord, but much of what is termed "the power of God" and "manifestations of the gifts of the Holy Spirit" are empty. They are counterfeit and distract from the true work of the Holy Spirit and sanctification.

When the true power of God is manifest, you will know the difference. To walk in the true power of God demands a price; that price is our life, given upon the believer's cross.

"For what we preach is not ourselves, but Jesus Christ as Lord, with ourselves as your servants for Jesus' sake. For it is the God who said, 'Let light shine out of darkness,' who has shone in our hearts to give the light of the knowledge of the glory of God in the face of Christ. But we have this treasure in earthen vessels, to show that the transcendent power belongs to God and not to us. We are afflicted in every way, but not crushed; perplexed, but not driven to despair; persecuted, but not forsaken; struck down, but not destroyed; always carrying in the body the death of Jesus, so that the life of Jesus may also be manifested in our bodies. For while we live we are always being given up to death for Jesus' sake, so that the life of Jesus may be manifested in our mortal flesh. So death is at work in us, but life in you" (2 Corinthians 4:5-12).

JESUS SAID, "REMEMBER LOT'S WIFE"

"Likewise as it was in the days of Lot—they ate, they drank, they bought, they sold, they planted, they built, but on the day when Lot went out from Sodom fire and sulphur rained from heaven and destroyed them all—so will it be on the day when the Son of man

is revealed. On that day, let him who is on the housetop, with his goods in the house, not come down to take them away; and likewise let him who is in the field not turn back. Remember Lot's wife. Whoever seeks to gain his life will lose it, but whoever loses his life will preserve it. I tell you, in that night there will be two in one bed; one will be taken and the other left. There will be two women grinding together; one will be taken and the other left. Two men will be in the field, one will be taken and the other left" (Luke 17:28-36).

Christ saw the last days as terrible, yet normal. He saw Christians taking their ease, living happily in the world with God's blessings. Our Lord warned to beware of this condition of heart throughout His prophecies and parables concerning the last day Christian. Even though trouble increases—most of the world will live a normal life, building, marrying, selling, planting and carrying on *as usual!*

The free world's prosperity and temporal blessings, especially in America and Canada, have a death grip upon the spirits and souls of most Christians! Jesus foresaw this and warned!

Good-hearted Christians are clinging to this world, many putting their eternal salvation at risk or at least storing up for themselves and their family unnecessary trouble. Their hearts are weighed down with the cares of this life and risk missing the rapture. Few read and take to heart these particular warnings of Christ. Many gloss over these warnings because they have been told not to worry about the end of the age—Christ has everything under control and you'll be raptured to safety before trouble comes your way.

The goodness of the world has a spellbinding power upon the normal Christian who desires to serve Christ and get along in this world. Many a Christian's heart is not prepared for Christ's return, and all the trouble leading up to His appearing.

Far too many Christians love the goodness of the world more than they love God. That is why Christ warned concerning *Lot's wife.*

Lot's wife was told in no uncertain terms—"Don't look back!" So, why is Christ using Lot's wife as a warning for the last day Christian, to not look back? The answer is in why Lot's wife looked back.

What made Lot's wife look back? Lot's wife did not look back at Sodom because of its evil or because she missed evil. She looked back because of her sentimentality toward the good that she had experienced as she and her family lived amongst that generation of evil people in Sodom.

All of us have been blessed by others who are nice and do *good*, or appear to be good in the world, but many of these so-called good people have no interest in God or the things of God. These are the *good-looking evil people* in the world who tolerate and even condone evil in others, though they themselves might not practice evil. An evil generation will proclaim God and look very good on the outside, serving God in talk, not indeed. There is a difference between the truly righteous and those who appear to be righteous.

We see many *good people* protest against certain evils such as war, abortion, and other disturbing or bad things such as capital punishment.

Most who are squeamish have chosen a "live and let live" philosophy for life, learning to tolerate and give concession to evil. King Saul had this attitude of heart, leading him to disobey God's orders. We see this same concession enveloping many nations, families and far too often many within congregations everywhere. Many pastors and ministers are afraid to call evil, evil and chase out the wolves. So concessions are made, evil is tolerated and often ignored. Peter confronted Ananias and Sapphira concerning their satanic evil devices and as a result they died instantly. Ask yourself this, how many in Christian leadership would confront evil as Peter did? How many *good* people would protest the death of Ananias and Sapphira?

So here is the issue with Lot's wife, she had made concessions within her heart concerning the *good* people of Sodom. She had fond memories of her relationships with the *good-looking evil people* in Sodom. Today, as well, most Christians have fond memories and nice feelings from worldly relationships, living, working, playing, as friendships are developed.

All these things have a spellbinding power upon the heart of a Christian as the end of the age draws near. Lot's wife was warned, and she began her journey to safety only to disobey and become frozen in her tracks, turning to salt. Most likely, in her heart she could not believe God would destroy *the good* with the *bad*. You see, self-righteous people who practice good can be as wicked as those we consider bad that practice evil.

Remember the parable that Christ told concerning the tax collector and the righteous man on the way to the temple? (See Luke 18:9-14).

Why does God want separation from the world and death to the love of the world?

Simply—the world is fashioned after Satan's nature—lust of the eye, pride of life, lust of the flesh, tolerance of sin and evil, manipulation, competition, jealousy, selfish ambition, control and deceit.

This is where many Christians are as the end of the age unfolds. When Christ calls, many will be unable to go—as their hearts resist separating from *the good* in a lost, dying and rebelling world. Few are ready in their innermost heart to let go now. How many Christians will be ready when the time comes?

Jesus tells us not to be alarmed at what takes place leading up to the beginning of the events that start the end of the age. We are now in wars and rumors of wars as well as natural upheavals, these are the birth pangs, but He does warn of the coming persecution, a great falling away, putting Christians to death and the growth of terrible wickedness.

Christ is warning Christians that at a certain time a massive persecution will come as the world turns against true Christians. Persecution will grow throughout the nations of the world and anti-Christian sentiment will increase within world governments. False and liberal Christians will hate the true Christian who cries out, warns, and defies the coming New World Order. Of course, Muslims, and other world religions will become even more hateful toward Christians. The current Iraqi war is galvanizing deep hatred throughout the world toward Jews and Christians. The Muslim world perceives that America and Israel are Christian and Jewish countries conspiring to rule their world. The reelection of President Bush and his conservative agenda are adding fuel to the fires of persecutions. Even now, many liberals are calling the red states, (those who voted for Bush) *Jesus land*.

The world as a whole is moving increasingly toward socialism where individual rights and freedoms are relinquished to government dominance, both in the private lives of their citizens and in business. Free enterprise and free trade will begin to disappear. Government will control more and more of our everyday life. All this is leading to the New World Order and the rise of the antichrist.

There is an awful time coming for Christians! Most will not stand during this time unless they get ready.

God's people of America and Canada are held spellbound by the "goodness" and "prosperity" we so cherish. It is hard for the sincere Christian to grasp the fact that evil is very pervasive and insidious, ready to be released in every level of society and across all nations. Much *good* is used to cover-up an evil heart. We find it hard to believe that God expects Christians to separate themselves from such before judgment. In fact, many find it incomprehensible that God will judge the so-called *good* in the world. Jesus said, *"He who is not with me is against me, and he who does not gather with me scatters"* (Matthew 12:30).

As I share the many accounts concerning our confrontations with evil most Christians are surprised, perplexed and frankly doubt the validity of our battles. Remember, evil sometimes comes in a cloak of decency!

We have found it necessary to completely let go of our false perception of the world as being *good* in order to recognize and fight hidden evil. Yes, we are to look for the good, but not to be deceived by the false good and the deception of the world. *"Look carefully then how you walk, not as unwise men but as wise, making the most of the time, because the days are evil"* (Ephesians 5:15,16).

God will break the spell over His people concerning the goodness of the world. God is trying to awaken the foolish and unprepared Christian to these issues and forebodings of trouble. Countless exposés of vile evil have surfaced throughout society and throughout Christian churches. These things will continue along with increased societal immorality. These birth pangs, the coming persecution, and the Great Tribulation are God's way of awakening His people to get ready. He will shake everything that can be shaken. (See Hebrews 12:26-29).

Not too many Christians agree that Catholicism is the worst of all cults. Even as this corrupt false church is being exposed, this cult is still sanctioned throughout evangelical, charismatic, and even many Pentecostal denominations and individual fellowships as a valid Christian denomination. This is the result of Satan's plan. The end of the age harlot church, consisting of unified Protestants and Catholics, will draw millions of wayward and unsuspecting Christians into the devil's grip.

The world says, "All roads to God are valid" and those who say otherwise are now suspect and will soon be considered opponents of the coming New World Order. Many Christians will be in the valley of decision long before the mark of the beast comes. Regrettably, many will choose a *New World false Christian and religious order* that fosters unity at the expense of embracing and teaching the true gospel of Christ.

More personal trouble, persecution, a Sodomite society and demonic oppression will awaken those who have faith but are spellbound. The false Christians who have shipwrecked their faith will take the full plunge and sell their birthrights to get along with a persecuting, hate-filled world.

Right now, the mission of many misguided Christians is sanitizing the world. If the world is somewhat moral, then it is easy to justify having an inordinate love of the world, with its deceitful trappings of goodness. This is rooted in the pursuit of worldly success, pleasure and prosperity. Indeed, this is an aspect of caring for the world in a way that weighs down the heart.

The prosperity message is in conflict with God's Spirit and soon this contradiction will either sear the conscience completely or free the Christian from trying to purify Disneyland and the *magic kingdom*, instead of themselves and *get ready* for the coming kingdom of God.

We are to be salt of the earth—not purifiers of the world, trying to make the world a sinless, sanitized place where the whole world is converted to Christianity. This ideology comes from embracing false doctrine that contradicts Christ's warnings concerning the end of the age.

"But the day of the Lord will come like a thief, and then the heavens will pass away with a loud noise, and the elements will be dissolved with fire, and the earth and the works that are upon it will be burned up. Since all these things are thus to be dissolved, what sort of persons ought you to be in lives of holiness and godliness, waiting for and

hastening the coming of the day of God, because of which the heavens will be kindled and dissolved, and the elements will melt with fire!" (2 Peter 3:10-12).

Great persecution for Christians in the so-called "free world" is about to be unleashed. What many of our brethren have experienced in the communist countries and third-world Islamic nations will soon come to us! Believe me—this is right around the corner.

This trend is already beginning and will certainly adjust the lukewarm Christian's priorities and attitude. A sifting is coming through persecution that will separate the weeds or tares from the wheat.

Persecution, along with other catastrophic problems that are coming, will break the budget of thousands of churches and fellowships across North America. Phony TV ministries will run short of money as the true body of Christ shapes up and pays attention to the leaner true ministries that are providing sound doctrine and honest leadership.

Home churches will start springing up everywhere. Hunger to meet with like-minded Christians will destroy the desire to be entertained with false worship and ear-tickling messages that miss the mark. True Christians will become nauseated with the lukewarm hypocrite as they spew out poison every time they open their mouth. A desire to discern and separate oneself from the phony and the world has already begun and will continue to grow, leading to a pure and powerful church—the bride of Christ.

Yes, true discipleship training and teachings will be the priority of those coming out from the false system of worship across North America—called "Churchianity."

A Christian exodus is about to begin as millions of Christians turn from the false to the true—and conversely, millions of phony Christians will seek out the harlot false denominations that still hold the form of godliness but deny the true power of God.

Many places of worship will wake up, set priorities straight and begin to make disciples of Christ rather than followers of denominations, leaders, and exotic movements. Many will realize that these man-made sectarian doctrines, flamboyant leaders, and exotic movements did nothing to help prepare them for the trouble they will be forced to endure.

Yes, trouble is coming, and we must be prepared to endure to the end and be saved: to be saved from unnecessary trouble, to be saved from being left behind, to be saved from an unclean heart that would look back when the final trumpet is blown.

Like Lot's wife, many are looking back. Lot's wife left with her husband and family, but her heart clung to Sodom. Again, it was the *good* things to which her *heartstrings* were tied. Like Lot's wife, many Christians have their hearts connected to this world for a variety of reasons, which may all seem legitimate. These Christians, perhaps even some of you who are reading this message, are unconsciously connected to this world.

Christ's simple statement, *"Remember Lot's wife,"* is a clear message for Christians who have the same condition of heart that caused this woman to look back. Like Lot's wife, these Christians are coming out and being identified with Christ and His teachings. They seem stable, walking away from sin and unhealthy relationships, nevertheless these Christians whom Christ warns of are in danger of being left behind.

Are you looking back in your heart of hearts? Perhaps you are spellbound with carnal relationships and how life used to be. Sentimentality is one of Satan's strongholds, concerning Christ's warning not to look back. We all have fond memories of the good times, pleasant memories of childhood, filled with picnics, outings and so on. Many reminisce with deep sentiment over how it used to be growing up. Nostalgia of the good times is ever growing as more and more stress, vile entertainment and supposed pleasurable events become shallow and unfulfilling. Many others have sentimental sorrow over past mistakes such as divorce, a lost childhood due to abuse, missed opportunities and mistakes. Give it all up! Look to the coming age and Christ's soon return. *Get ready*!

Don't pretend these issues are not there, but resolve the pain, sentiment and cares of the heart. You may need to weep and mourn over these unresolved wounds, emotional ties and lusts. Pretending away or shrink-wrapping these issues will cause you to be caught off-guard. These things are what Lot's wife was consumed with and caused her to look back.

You may be looking forward to Christ's soon return but are looking back in sentimentality and nostalgia, clinging to the good things in the world and to the way it used to be, or the way you would like it to be. This is a doomed world, and we must walk as foreigners who long for heaven and Christ's return. We must enjoy in appropriate portion God's blessings but simultaneously and continually break from the bonds of this world's lie.

Lot's wife was not sinning or wanting to live in sin. That is how many Christians live, avoiding sin but loving the world. But, just as Lot's wife had a weight within her heart that caused her demise, so too, many Christians are weighted down.

How many Christians will look up, begin to rise with the last trumpet sound and maybe go a few hundred feet through the air in the rapture, then look back, fall to earth and be left behind — dead!

Let us set aside every weight that so easily besets us and press on in the discipline of the Lord and not wallow in our sentiment and unhealthy worldly affections. Hebrews chapter 12 gives great insight concerning worldly affections and the discipline of the lord.

GIVE UP THE WORLD AND DON'T LOOK BACK

Lot's wife could not give up friendship with those in Sodom. Many Christians have become friends to this world.

James warns Christians in this condition by stating, *"Unfaithful creatures! Do you not know that friendship with the world is enmity with God? Therefore whoever wishes to be a friend of the world makes himself an enemy of God"* (James 4:4).

To be able to stand in these coming days, the true disciple must deal with the things of the world that remain in the heart. The Christian must dissolve his or her love and friendship with this world.

Christians were told that they need to be "born again," and rightly so, but that rebirth must be of God and one must then grow up into salvation. Many felt a spiritual experience, however their hunger for God and obtaining His righteousness ended there. They never grew up into salvation, having dealt with the world, the flesh and the pride of life. They think they have a "ticket to ride" when the rapture occurs, but they cannot be further from the truth. These words from the apostle John hold true for the last hour Christians:

"Do not love the world or the things in the world. If anyone loves the world, love for the Father is not in him. For all that is in the world, the lust of the flesh and the lust of the eyes and the pride of life, is not of the Father but is of the world. And the world passes away, and the lust of it; but he who does the will of God abides forever. Children, it is the last hour; and as you have heard that antichrist is coming, so now many antichrists have come; therefore we know that it is the last hour" (1 John 2:15-18).

How many Christians think they are following Christ and doing God's will, yet are letting the cares of life direct them? Many follow Christ for the blessings and never give up the world.

"As they were going along the road, a man said to him, 'I will follow you wherever you go.' And Jesus said to him, 'Foxes have holes, and birds of the air have nests; but the Son of man has nowhere to lay his head.' To another he said, 'Follow me.' But he said, 'Lord, let me first go and bury my father.' But he said to him, 'Leave the dead to bury their own dead; but as for you, go and proclaim the kingdom of God.' Another said, 'I will follow you, Lord; but let me first say farewell to those at my home.' Jesus said to him, 'No one who puts his hand to the plow and looks back is fit for the kingdom of God'" (Luke 9:57-62).

If you're worried about your retirement, stocks, homes, cars and your family, you must deal with these things in your heart now! They will crowd out Christ and you will find yourself unprepared spiritually to navigate in the coming tribulation. Deal with it now and do not look back, for Jesus said, *"As it was in the days of Noah, so will it be in the days of the Son of man. They ate, they drank, they* married, they were given in marriage, until the day when Noah entered the ark, and the flood came and destroyed them all. Likewise as it was in the days of Lot—they ate, they drank, they bought, they sold, they planted, they built, but on the day when Lot went out from Sodom fire and sulphur rained from heaven and destroyed them all—so will it be on the day when the Son of man is revealed. On that day, let him who is on the housetop, with his goods in the house, not come down to take them away; and likewise let him who is in the field not turn back. Remember Lot's wife"* (Luke 17:26-32).

Another Scripture underscoring this truth reads, *"And he told them a parable: 'Look at the fig tree, and all the trees; as soon as they come out in leaf, you see for yourselves and know that the summer is already near. So also, when you see these things taking place, you know that the kingdom of God is near. Truly, I say to you, this generation will not pass away till all has taken place. Heaven and earth will pass away, but my words will not pass away. But take heed to yourselves lest your hearts be weighed down with dissipation and drunkenness and cares of this life, and that day come upon you suddenly like a snare; for it will come upon all who dwell upon the face of the whole earth. But watch at all times, praying that you [may have strength] to escape all these things that will take place, and to stand before the Son of man'"* (Luke 21:29-36).

BIRTH-PANGS OF THE COMING KINGDOM

"And you will hear of wars and rumors of wars; see that you are not alarmed; for this must take place, but the end is not yet. For nation will rise against nation, and kingdom against kingdom, and there will be famines and earthquakes in various places: all this is but the beginning of the birth-pangs. Then they will deliver you up to tribulation, and put you to death; and you will be hated by all nations for my name's sake. And then many will fall away, and betray one another, and hate one another. And many false prophets will arise and lead many astray. And because wickedness is multiplied, most men's love will grow cold. But he who endures to the end will be saved" (Matthew 24:6-13).

Already we see terrible times. Jesus warned that as the end of this age nears there would be an increase in wars, natural disasters, calamities, *".... and upon the earth distress of nations in perplexity at the roaring of the sea and the waves, men fainting with fear and with foreboding of what is coming on the world..."* (Luke 21:25-26).

I have shared this message with many dear saints and far too many become panic stricken. Jesus consoled the true saint saying, *"See that you are not alarmed; for this must take place, but the end is not yet."*

Dear reader, we are well into the birth pangs of the coming kingdom of God. During these birth pangs of trials and trouble, God expects the true saint to wake up and become prepared spiritually and physically. If you have fear, then you are not right with God. He expects the true saint to stand and minister through these pre-tribulation distresses.

Many who read the first edition skimmed through the pages looking to the warnings concerning the wicked and the lukewarm church. These readers did not apply the message of sanctification to their own lives. These dear readers are saying to themselves, *"This message applies to others, I am okay!"*

Taking this approach is foolish. If you let this opportunity to get ready spiritually and physically pass you by, then you may be named among the "foolish maidens" Jesus warned of in Matthew 25:1-13.

This book has sound doctrine that when applied will help you cooperate with Christ's baptism of fire that will purge, cleanse, strengthen and heal you. In this process, you will learn to hear from the true Holy Spirit. Indeed, you must hear God perfectly in this hour. He is faithful and He will lead you and your family to safety.

Make sure you work with like-minded Christians. Do not divulge what God instructs you to do with anyone other than those whom God allows. There will be false and insincere Christians betraying one another is the days to come. Marshal law, UN occupation troops and refugee camps are just part of the coming trouble. Displaced masses will be herded into makeshift camps for safety, food and water.

Regardless of what God instructs you to do, whether to stay, move to a safer region or leave the county, be wise in taking precautions in preparing to leave your homes if necessary. When trouble hits the cities, there will be looting, murders, rape and pillaging by roving gangs and enraged-frantic citizens. This will even spread to many rural regions of the United States. Law and order will give way to anarchy in many places.

If you are prepared and hear from God correctly, you and your family will have opportunity to get to safer ground. Do not be lazy and presume upon God. Study the Word of God, research and learn how you can take common sense steps in order to be prepared. Do not wait to the last minute and expect miracles.

ENDURING TO THE END

"And to the angel of the church in Philadelphia write: 'The words of the holy one, the true one, who has the key of David, who opens and no one shall shut, who shuts and no one opens. I know your works. Behold, I have set before you an open door, which no one is able to shut; I know that you have but little power, and yet you have kept my word and have not denied my name. Behold, I will make those of the synagogue of Satan who say that they are Jews and are not, but lie—behold, I will make them come and bow down before your feet, and learn that I have loved you. Because you have kept my word of patient endurance, I will keep you from the hour of trial, which is coming on the whole world, to try those who dwell upon the earth. I am coming soon; hold fast what you have, so that no one may seize your crown. He who conquers, I will make him a pillar in the temple of my God; never shall he go out of it, and I will write on him the name of my

God, and the name of the city of my God, the new Jerusalem which comes down from my God out of heaven, and my own new name. He who has an ear, let him hear what the Spirit says to the churches'" (Revelation 3:7-13).

Again, in the coming days the true Christian will be challenged on all sides. Every believer who commits to an all-out relationship with Jesus will come under spiritual oppression, various afflictions, and persecution. In fact, at moments, the intensity will be so great it will seem God himself has come against us.

We struggle in our trials because suffering and discipline is foreign to us, but as we endure each trial we can see how meaningful and sovereign the discipline of the Lord truly is.

It will be hard to deny the temptation to quit or compromise. Many will find friends and family members become spiteful, callous, and even treacherous. At times the pressure in relationships, finances, ministry and trying circumstances will seem unbearable.

In Acts it describes part of Barnabas and Paul's ministry as, *"strengthening the souls of the disciples, exhorting them to continue in the faith, and saying that through many tribulations we must enter the kingdom of God"* (Acts 14:22).

Christian, we are at war. Scripture states that Satan has come down to make war upon the saints; and we must accept reality that in this war, to be a soldier of Christ, there is suffering. *"Share in suffering as a good soldier of Christ Jesus. No soldier on service gets entangled in civilian pursuits, since his aim is to satisfy the one who enlisted him"* (2 Timothy 2:3,4).

Suffering is part of fighting and learning to endure with patience. This is how we develop Christ-like character. It is this character that helps us overcome. *"More than that, we rejoice in our sufferings, knowing that suffering produces endurance, and endurance produces character, and character produces hope, and hope does not disappoint us, because God's love has been poured into our hearts through the Holy Spirit which has been given to us"* (Romans 5:3-6).

When we learn to patiently endure suffering we become steadfast in all of life. *"Count it all joy, my brethren, when you meet various trials, for you know that the testing of your faith produces steadfastness. And let steadfastness have its full effect, that you may be perfect and complete, lacking in nothing"* (James 1:2-4).

Even as we work out our salvation, dealing with our carnal issues, we are admonished to keep our confidence to the end that we might receive what is promised. *"For we share in Christ, if only we hold our first confidence firm to the end"* (Hebrews 3:14).

In our suffering and discipline, God is treating us as a true son or daughter, *"For the Lord disciplines him whom he loves, and chastises every son whom he receives. It is for discipline that you have to endure. God is treating you as sons; for what son is* there whom his father does not discipline? If you are left without discipline, in which all have participated, then you are illegitimate children and not sons" (Hebrews 12:7,8).

Do not be discouraged when you witness other Christians prospering in false doctrine and indulging in the pleasures of life. They are told to take their ease and be blessed with material wealth and prosperity. The terrible truth is; if they do not awaken in time, His day will come upon them like a snare. *"But take heed to yourselves lest your hearts be weighed down with dissipation and drunkenness and cares of this life, and that day come upon you suddenly like a snare; for it will come upon all who dwell upon the face of the whole earth. But watch at all times, praying that you [may have strength] to escape all these things that will take place, and to stand before the Son of man."* (Luke 21:34-36).

So, as you and I struggle in learning to endure suffering and embrace His discipline, we will receive strength to escape that coming day.

"Therefore we ourselves boast of you in the churches of God for your steadfastness and faith in all your persecutions and in the afflictions which you are enduring. This is evidence of the righteous judgment of God, that you may be made worthy of the kingdom of God, for which you are suffering—since indeed God deems it just to repay with affliction those who afflict you, and to grant rest with us to you who are afflicted, when the Lord Jesus is revealed from heaven with his mighty angels in flaming fire inflicting vengeance upon those who do not know God and upon those who do not obey the gospel of our Lord Jesus. They shall suffer the punishment of eternal destruction and exclusion from the presence of the Lord and from the glory of his might, when he comes on that day to be glorified in his saints, and to be marveled at in all who have believed, because our testimony to you was believed. To this end we always pray for you, that our God may make you worthy of his call, and may fulfil every good resolve and work of faith by his power, so that the name of our Lord Jesus may be glorified in you, and you in him, according to the grace of our God and the Lord Jesus Christ" (2 Thessalonians 1:4-12).

Indeed, we suffer for the kingdom of God, being made worthy of His call, and to walk in true faith by His power!

Satan will use our own unresolved issues, especially self-pity and hidden unbelief. Thoughts like, *"this is too hard... it's not fair, this is too much... God has forsaken me,"* are tip of the iceberg indicators. Do not ignore these thoughts, but press to the root of each as they come to your awareness.

Evil people cloaked in decency and unrepentant lukewarm Christians become strong weapons used by the enemy. Avoid involvement with such. They will attack your faith, drain you of the *zōē* life in Christ and distract you from doing God's perfect will.

Have consistent fellowship with like-minded Christians. Hold each other accountable and watch each other's back. Always be alert.

Christ is the pioneer and perfecter of our faith, He will not fail us. *"And I am sure that he who began a good work in you will bring it to completion at the day of Jesus Christ"* (Philippians 1:6).

"Who shall separate us from the love of Christ? Shall tribulation, or distress, or persecution, or famine, or nakedness, or peril, or sword? As it is written, 'For thy sake we are being killed all the day long; we are regarded as sheep to be slaughtered.' No, in all these things we are more than conquerors through him who loved us. For I am sure that neither death, nor life, nor angels, nor principalities, nor things present, nor things to come, nor powers, nor height, nor depth, nor anything else in all creation, will be able to separate us from the love of God in Christ Jesus our Lord" (Romans 8:35-39).

THE RIGHTEOUS ARE NOT DESTINED FOR WRATH

This message may seem difficult to bear for some of you. I will not apologize. The sound teachings of Christ and the rest of the Word of God support everything I have written here. If it has distressed you, then praise God! There is not that much time left. Playing church is not going to prepare you for the coming hard times.

This is a warning to all of us who are hearing the footsteps of Christ's soon return. Let us not be foolish and be barred from entering into the great celebration on the day that He appears.

The Great Tribulation will force many Christians to buy into Satan's scheme. If we are prepared in our hearts to hear from God rightly and have become true disciples, then we will be able to endure to the end, resist Satan's schemes, and succeed!

Some of us may lose our lives as a witness for Christ. So what? If we have allowed Christ to work true salvation into us, then there will be no sting (pain) in death. (Remember Stephen in Acts 6:8- 7:60) God expects His church to endure through much of the Great Tribulation and testify as to Christ, His great love and His redemptive plan. When the last great harvest of souls is complete, as His full fury comes against the world, then you can expect His appearance to quickly call us up, for we are not destined for wrath or to be condemned to judgment with the world.

"For the Lord himself will descend from heaven with a cry of command, with the archangel's call, and with the sound of the trumpet of God. And the dead in Christ will rise first; then we who are alive, who are left, shall be caught up together with them in the clouds to meet the Lord in the air; and so we shall always be with the Lord. Therefore comfort one another with these words. But as to the times and the seasons, brethren, you have no need to have anything written to you. For you yourselves know well that the day of the Lord will come like a thief in the night. When people say, 'There is peace and security,' then sudden destruction will come upon them as travail comes upon a woman with child, and there will be no escape. But you are not in darkness, brethren, for that

day to surprise you like a thief. For you are all sons of light and sons of the day; we are not of the night or of darkness. So then let us not sleep, as others do, but let us keep awake and be sober. For those who sleep sleep at night, and those who get drunk are drunk at night. But, since we belong to the day, let us be sober, and put on the breastplate of faith and love, and for a helmet the hope of salvation. For God has not destined us for wrath, but to obtain salvation through our Lord Jesus Christ, who died for us so that whether we wake or sleep we might live with him. Therefore encourage one another and build one another up, just as you are doing" (1 Thessalonians 4:16- 5:11).

The great day of Christ's wrath is coming. We are not destined for His wrath. The Great Tribulation is nothing, compared to the wrath of God.

"When he opened the sixth seal, I looked, and behold, there was a great earthquake; and the sun became black as sackcloth, the full moon became like blood, and the stars of the sky fell to the earth as the fig tree sheds its winter fruit when shaken by a gale; the sky vanished like a scroll that is rolled up, and every mountain and island was removed from its place. Then the kings of the earth and the great men and the generals and the rich and the strong, and every one, slave and free, hid in the caves and among the rocks of the mountains, calling to the mountains and rocks, 'Fall on us and hide us from the face of him who is seated on the throne, and from the wrath of the Lamb; for the great day of their wrath has come, and who can stand before it?'" (Revelation 6:12-17).

Indeed, we hear the thunder of the horsemen of the Apocalypse. September 11 was a major milestone for the end-of-the-age sequencing ordained by God! *REVELATION SIX* horrors are approaching fast. Let us be sober and get ready so that we will not be ashamed at His coming and left behind to suffer God's wrath! AMEN and AMEN!

Answering the question—
"What should I do?"

Many readers have asked, "What should I do?" or "What are you going to do, Pastor Pretlow?" or "Are you leaving the country?" Some have asked to pool resources hoping to live near our ministry in anticipation of terrible times coming (looking for a safe place to weather out the storm).

Please read carefully the following answer concerning these types of questions.

First, God is faithful, and Jesus Christ will protect that which is His. Each person must come to an absolute peace in the true Christ, trusting Him to lead and protect. If Christians do not repent, many will lose their life and much will be destroyed in the coming judgment. Nevertheless, Christ will protect that which is His. You must make Christ your all and in all!

If you are anxious, fearful and feel panicky, then I encourage you to search your heart and obey the admonition in Scripture to fast and pray in this hour and draw close to the Lord. You must become prepared spiritually in CHRIST above all else and learn to discern and obey His voice. There is no guide coming, which includes me or anyone else who is warning in this hour. You simply cannot follow another man; you must learn to follow the Lord.

Suggestions as to what you can do and how to prepare for you and your family, here is a web sites that may help. This list is not exhaustive, and you must determine for yourself if these suggestions are suitable and what steps you should take to be ready in the event of a catastrophe. www.ready.gov/index.html

To be very candid, I cannot and will not advise you. Nor will I disclose what the Lord is calling me to do. Nor do I recommend moving near our ministry to pool resources.

If you believe God wants you to stay where you are, then you must confirm that with prayer and fasting, making sure this is God's will for you and your family. If God directs you to move to a rural or mountainous place, then you must obey. If God instructs you to leave the country, then you should leave.

When you have confirmed God's will, He will make a way for you. He will provide all the necessities and resources in getting you and your family to a safer place, if you are led to move.

Some have reacted to the warning of the impending judgment of the Lord with anger and even with malicious behavior. This has always been the case. Search the scriptures and you will find every time the Lord gave warning to the people, there were those who refused to receive the word, and turned and hated and attacked the messenger. This hour is no different. (See Numbers 16:1-50 and

Jude 8-19.) The Lord instructed me to warn the people, but at no time did He ever tell me to convince the people. If you are unable to receive the warning, and then do what you believe the Lord is calling you to do.

We are convinced that God's judgment and wrath are about to be poured out upon America. As for the lukewarm, hypocritical and apostate Church, they can expect to be spewed out of Christ's mouth. For the deceived and carnal saint, the coming trouble will purify and make clean a multitude that Scripture says, *"These are they who have come out of the great tribulation; they have washed their robes and made them white in the blood of the Lamb. Therefore are they before the throne of God, and serve him day and night within his temple; and he who sits upon the throne will shelter them with his presence. They shall hunger no more, neither thirst anymore; the sun shall not strike them, nor any scorching heat. For the Lamb in the midst of the throne will be their shepherd, and he will guide them to springs of living water; and God will wipe away every tear from their eyes"* (Revelation 7:14-17).

For the true saint, this is the hour Jesus warned of, so be encouraged, for He said, *"Now when these things begin to take place, look up and raise your heads, because your redemption is drawing near"* (Luke 21:28).

Appendix A

Judgment, Premature Death, Wrath of God and the Prophetic

A Brief Look at God's Tough Love

"There were some present at that very time who told him of the Galileans whose blood Pilate had mingled with their sacrifices. And he answered them, 'Do you think that these Galileans were worse sinners than all the other Galileans, because they suffered thus? I tell you, No; but unless you repent you will all likewise perish. Or those eighteen upon whom the tower in Siloam fell and killed them, do you think that they were worse offenders than all the others who dwelt in Jerusalem? I tell you, No; but unless you repent you will all likewise perish.' And he told this parable: 'A man had a fig tree planted in his vineyard; and he came seeking fruit on it and found none. And he said to the vinedresser, 'Lo, these three years I have come seeking fruit on this fig tree, and I find none. Cut it down; why should it use up the ground?' And he answered him, 'Let it alone, sir, this year also, till I dig about it and put on manure. And if it bears fruit next year, well and good; but if not, you can cut it down'" (Luke 13:1-9).

"If any one sees his brother committing what is not a mortal sin, he will ask, and God will give him life for those whose sin is not mortal. There is sin which is mortal; I do not say that one is to pray for that. All wrongdoing is sin, but there is sin which is not mortal" (1 John 5:16,17).

Early in my ministry, in 1974, while serving in the Marine Corps, I held a weekly Bible study at the Pearl Harbor Naval Station brig in Oahu, HI. Sometimes as many as ten prisoners, both Navy and Marine, would attend this Bible study. One evening just one sailor showed up. He was serving a sentence for drug abuse.

I would share the Gospel and encourage these prisoners. Most received the message of salvation humbly and thankfully. But this sailor became obnoxious and attacked God for allowing children to die. This young man could not understand how a loving God could sanction the death of children. He referred to the prophet Samuel, relaying from God instructions for king Saul to destroy all the people of the Amalekites.

"And Samuel said to Saul, 'The LORD sent me to anoint you king over his people Israel; now therefore hearken to the words of the LORD. Thus says the LORD of hosts, 'I will punish what Amalek did to Israel in opposing them on the way, when they came up out of Egypt. Now go and smite Amalek, and utterly destroy all that they have; do not spare them, but kill both man and woman, infant and suckling, ox and sheep, camel and ass'" (1 Samuel 15:1-3).

Not only this account, but he cited the following concerning the prophet Elisha:

"He went up from there to Bethel; and while he was going up on the way, some small boys came out of the city and jeered at him, saying, 'Go up, you baldhead! Go up, you baldhead!' And he turned around, and when he saw them, he cursed them in the name of the LORD. And two she-bears came out of the woods and tore forty-two of the boys" (2 Kings 2:23,24).

Frankly I struggled somewhat with such a challenging question, being new in ministry. If I remember correctly, I stuck to my guns emphasizing God's justice and wisdom, even in these seemingly cruel accounts found in Scripture.

Through the years I began to understand how God's tough love could be expressed even in the premature death of infants, children, sinners, and even Christian believers. It is God's will that no one dies prematurely and that all prosper. Sin and evil have power over all of mankind because we all have put ourselves outside of God's protection, for all have sinned. More importantly, God desires that no one lose eternal life. If given a free rein, evil can overtake our nature completely; even children can be trained in evil and become unredeemable when they reach the age of accountability.

Satan desires to corrupt human nature to the point of eternal damnation. The Scripture says that intuitively, we all receive from God a sense of right and wrong, even if we do not know God's ways or His plan of salvation. *"For it is not the hearers of the law who are righteous before God, but the doers of the law who will be justified. When Gentiles who have not the law do by nature what the law requires, they are a law to themselves, even though they do not have the law. They show that what the law requires is written on their hearts, while their conscience also bears witness and their conflicting thoughts accuse or perhaps excuse them on that day when, according to my gospel, God judges the secrets of men by Christ Jesus"* (Romans 2:13-16).

Understandably, God will not be mocked and the consequences of rejecting conscience and practicing evil may require judgment, even a premature death to stop the spread of evil and, if possible, one's spirit from the eternal fire.

In Acts, we have the account of Ananias and Sapphira, Elymas the Magician and the account of Paul turning a Christian believer over to Satan for the destruction of his physical being, that his spirit might be saved in the day of the Lord. (See Acts 5, 13, and 1 Corinthians 5).

Then there is the account where king Herod sought to kill the apostle Peter, opposing the word of the Lord from going forward. God miraculously rescued him from jail. Later, the angel of the Lord killed Herod,

"Now Herod was angry with the people of Tyre and Sidon; and they came to him in a body, and having persuaded Blastus, the king's chamberlain, they asked for peace, because

their country depended on the king's country for food. On an appointed day Herod put on his royal robes, took his seat upon the throne, and made an oration to them. And the people shouted, 'The voice of a god, and not of man!' Immediately an angel of the Lord smote him, because he did not give God the glory; and he was eaten by worms and died. But the word of God grew and multiplied" (Acts 12:20-24). (See also Acts 12:1-19).

These are difficult things to understand and Christ had many teachings that were hard to take, in fact many of his disciples (other than the 12) left near the end of His earthly ministry saying, *"This is a hard saying, who can listen to it?"* when Christ spoke, *unless you eat His flesh and drink his blood, one could not have the life in Christ.* (See John 6:42-69).

The Catholics turned this hard-to-understand teaching of Christ into the doctrine of transubstantiation, where the communion celebration during mass called the Eucharist, is mysteriously-miraculously turned into the actual body, blood and divine soul of Christ. Thus, every time a Catholic participates in communion, he or she believes in a superstitious man-made doctrine that claims that communion is the actual drinking and eating of Christ's blood and body—literally!

As Peter wrote concerning some of Paul's teaching, *"There are some things in them hard to understand, which the ignorant and unstable twist to their own destruction, as they do the other scriptures. You therefore, beloved, knowing this beforehand, beware lest you be carried away with the error of lawless men and lose your own stability. But grow in the grace and knowledge of our Lord and Savior Jesus Christ. To him be the glory both now and to the day of eternity. Amen"* (2 Peter 3:16b-18).

Indeed, in this case the error of this Catholic teaching missed the whole point of Christ's hard saying, which teaches that our nature must be changed into a nature like His, our life must come from Him and our attitudes of heart must be like His, and to do this one must abide in Him—spirit to spirit, being regenerated by the Spirit of Christ. He is not like the first Adam but gives life to all who believe and obey Him, for those who embrace all that He taught. (See 1 Corinthians 15:45). Christ finished this hard teaching by saying, *"It is the spirit that gives life, the flesh is of no avail; the words that I have spoken to you are spirit and life"* (John 6:63).

Jesus said, *"You have heard that it was said, 'You shall not commit adultery.' But I say to you that everyone who looks at a woman lustfully has already committed adultery with her in his heart. If your right eye causes you to sin, pluck it out and throw it away; it is better that you lose one of your members than that your whole body be thrown into hell. And if your right hand causes you to sin, cut it off and throw it away; it is better that you lose one of your members than that your whole body go into hell"* (Matthew 5:27-30).

Jesus was confronting the abuse by the men of Israel, how they exercised control over their wives and women in their culture. The priests gave out certificates of divorce to skirt around the commandment, *"You shall not commit adultery."* If a man lusted after another woman but was married, he was able to dump his current wife and marry another. Thus, the wives and women in Israel were dumped, traded and bargained for; they were treated like cattle.

Did Jesus mean to literally gouge out one's eye if a person could not stop lusting after the opposite sex? (Yes, women lust after men in their hearts as well).

Jesus used this figure of speech to bring home how serious lusting in the heart and acting out sin is. This is a fact, no fornicator, and envious, selfish, idolatrous person, Christian or otherwise, will have eternal life. (See Galatians 5:13-26).

If given a choice, which would you rather experience: missing an eye, a leg or a hand or spending eternity in hell?

Jesus taught, *"And do not fear those who kill the body but cannot kill the soul; rather fear him who can destroy both soul and body in hell"* (Matthew 10:28).

What would I say to a person who raised the same question concerning God's justice, as did the sailor in the Pearl Harbor brig?

Simply put, it is better to lose a leg, even die from the judgment of God in order to change the heart bent on sin, than to rot in hell!

The Amalekites practiced the sacrificing of their own children to Moloch, their false god. This wickedness was ingrained with demonic idolatry of the worst kind, which had to be stopped. Even the infant's and children's nature became polluted with this demonic vileness. Concerning the innocence of children and infants slaughtered by Israel—where are they now, Heaven, or hell? God is faithful and just, those infants and children whose nature was not polluted beyond redemption are safe in God's presence.

The 42 boys killed by the two she-bears came about because the prophet of the Lord cursed this group of children who were deriding the word of the Lord, not deriding Elisha. You see Elisha allowed his head to be bald as a message to all of Israel, to repent and return to the Lord. It was a shame to be bald. The scorn from these boys reflected the parent's contempt toward God's word brought forth by His faithful servant.

It is God's will that no one perishes eternally and sometimes death, even violent death, may purge enough evil from the heart bent for hell that perhaps true repentance is sought for and obtained during death's quick moment.

"One of the criminals who were hanged railed at him, saying, 'Are you not the Christ? Save yourself and us!' But the other rebuked him, saying, 'Do you not fear God, since you are under the same sentence of condemnation? And we indeed justly; for we are receiving the due reward of our deeds; but this man has done nothing wrong.' And he said, 'Jesus, remember me when you come into your kingdom.' And he said to him, 'Truly, I say to you, today you will be with me in Paradise'" (Luke 23:39-43).

It is obvious where the thief who railed at Christ went. Indeed, we must fear God and repent.

Revelation forewarns of the wrath of God to come, *"By these three plagues a third of mankind was killed, by the fire and smoke and sulphur issuing from their mouths. For the power of the horses is in their mouths and in their tails; their tails are like serpents, with heads, and by means of them they wound. The rest of mankind, who were not killed by these plagues, did not repent of the works of their hands nor give up worshiping demons and idols of gold and silver and bronze and stone and wood, which cannot either see or hear or walk; nor did they repent of their murders or their sorceries or their immorality or their thefts"* (Revelation 9:18-21).

Here is another passage predicting how obstinate men's hearts will become.

"And I heard the altar cry, 'Yea, Lord God the Almighty, true and just are thy judgments!' The fourth angel poured his bowl on the sun, and it was allowed to scorch men with fire; men were scorched by the fierce heat, and they cursed the name of God who had power over these plagues, and they did not repent and give him glory. The fifth angel poured his bowl on the throne of the beast, and its kingdom was in darkness; men gnawed their tongues in anguish and cursed the God of heaven for their pain and sores, and did not repent of their deeds" (Revelation 16:7-11).

You may say, this is in the past under the Old Covenant; God is love and does not do these terrible acts of judgment and wrath, nor use His servants to prophecy judgment.

In this you are deadly wrong. As mentioned earlier, Peter prophesied the death of Ananias and Sapphira. This was not an anomaly, but a recognized practice in the early church that instilled a healthy fear of God among Christians and respect for true leadership.

"And great fear came upon the whole church, and upon all who heard of these things. Now many signs and wonders were done among the people by the hands of the apostles. And they were all together in Solomon's Portico. None of the rest dared join them, but the people held them in high honor. And more than ever believers were added to the Lord, multitudes both of men and women, so that they even carried out the sick into the streets, and laid them on beds and pallets, that as Peter came by at least his shadow might fall on some of them" (Acts 5:11-15).

The apostles had respect from the church because they were trained by Christ, and walked in truth without pretense, arrogance or presumption, which God backed by true signs and wonders. This authority was not assumed, grasped or manipulated.

Some of the suffering and challenges a disciple in training will endure can seem strange and often unbearable. We share a few that we have endured to encourage the sincere disciple who is being trained for leadership.

Ministry case example: Departing Early

As I had mentioned previously, the special televised report entitled *"In the Name of God,"* presented a fairly accurate report covering different Church growth movements and revivals across America.

Much of the report was an exposé of the false spiritualistic activities in many churches, including John Wimber's Vineyard Church in California. As I sat and watched what Wimber condoned within the meetings of his church, chills went through me.

We had dealt with many people who were struggling with their walk with Christ, which directly related to these heretical teachings that the Vineyard movement and other such movements practiced. Such movements and activities are called Drunk in the Spirit, Holy Ghost Laughter and Toronto Blessing, Third Wave and Latter Rain.

The Holy Spirit immediately rose up inside me and I could sense God's disdain. Through that night, I wrestled with the thoughts I knew were coming from the Lord. Finally, in obedience, I prophesied what God commanded of me. "John Wimber, because of his error and continued dissemination of false doctrine, is now required to come home."

In 1997, because of a fall, Wimber died of a massive brain hemorrhage.

This is a difficult disclosure of what the Lord had me prophesy. It may be that God had others pray in the same manner. Regardless, I know what God commanded of me, and sadly I had to be obedient. I share this because God has commanded me to continue to warn. Those who persist in these false and empty manifestations, who promote the teachings that mislead the many, unless they repent, some will be called home early as well.

Ministry case example: The Ill-tempered Abuser.

"And Abigail came to Nabal; and, lo, he was holding a feast in his house, like the feast of a king. And Nabal's heart was merry within him, for he was very drunk; so she told him nothing at all until the morning light. And in the morning, when the wine had gone out of Nabal, his wife told him these things, and his heart died within him, and he became as a stone. And about ten days later the LORD smote Nabal; and he died" (1 Samuel 25:36-38). (For context read 1 Samuel 25:1-35).

We have made quite a few enemies over the last fifteen years of ministry. We have confronted abusers, pedophiles, false brethren, and evil people. Sometimes there are more people praying against us than for us. Most of our encounters have occurred in the process of helping victims of the evil perpetrated by evil people. We have had threats, hate letters, and hate phone calls and public denunciations of our ministry.

One person was abusive to his wife and family, even though he professed to be a Christian. We assisted his wife in confronting him, holding him accountable. Eventually he became so belligerent and threatening that he left no room for reconciliation, bringing upon himself removal from the house. He continued to contact her, harassing, stalking, and threatening.

To provide practical and spiritual support, I escorted her to the courthouse to obtain a restraining order.

Her husband somehow followed her or found out that she was at the courthouse, came to the courthouse and made a terrible scene in the waiting area. He verbally berated her publicly and forced me to stand between her and his in-your-face threats. He finally threatened me saying, *"I'll see you and your ministry burn in ashes,"* an inference to the Waco Cult, Branch Dividians, led by David Koresh.

This man was ill-tempered, rude, and abusive, like Nabal, Abigail's husband in the above Scripture passage. He continued to attack this woman, maligning her, undermining her relationship with their children, spreading base suspicions and lies. His attacks also continued against this ministry and like Nabal, he eventually died from a sudden heart attack.

This man projected from his own abusive, cult-like, oppressive heart onto his wife's actions and our support for her in holding him accountable. An evil heart often calls good evil and evil good.

Others, who have attacked, maligned, or opposed this work, have suffered and some have died prematurely. Still others opposing ours and other sound ministries often prosper. Though these were not judged as quickly by the Lord, nevertheless, they are in dire straits with the Lord, for He often abandons the wicked to prosperity, sealing their wicked hearts for the day of His wrath.

The challenge when standing up to evil and suffering from evil's backlash is not to take it personally and try to defend yourself or return threat for threat. God knows how to vindicate His servants—the right way and at the right time. It may be that a servant of the Lord will be inspired by the Holy Spirit to speak forth a stern judgment, such as Peter and Paul had to speak forth. Never pass a reviling or revengeful judgment.

Often one will experience extra suffering if there is hidden resentment, unforgiveness or fear residing within the heart. Discernment and understanding is paramount, for not all who practice evil and oppose truth are evil—some are just wayward sinners.

Some oppose the harder messages of Christ and the true Gospel out of ignorance, not understanding the harder teachings of Christ. When a Christian, a ministry or a pastor confronts evil many are shocked. Society and most

Christians have a caricature concerning servants of the Lord to be weak, milquetoast Christians who are supposed to tolerate evil.

Confrontations can become very testy when evil and evil people become exposed and are held accountable. They will slander, mock, ridicule and lie. They will enlist others and undermine relationships to blackmail, oppose and try ruining the reputation of those who stand up to their wicked ways. Thus, many are taken-in by evil's defense as they attack what God wants accomplished. Many are not discerning and often blame the pastor or true servant of the Lord for causing trouble.

Jesus said, *"Blessed are you when men hate you, and when they exclude you and revile you, and cast out your name as evil, on account of the Son of man! Rejoice in that day, and leap for joy, for behold, your reward is great in heaven; for so their fathers did to the prophets"* (Luke 6:22,23).

It is our hope that the enemies of truth and righteousness come to the light of the Gospel. Jesus teaches that we are not to return evil for evil. We are to bless, forgive and be conciliatory (peacemakers), but He also expects the true Christian to stand up for righteousness sake and hold evil and harmful wrong-doers accountable.

Again, these accounts are shared to encourage those ministries, young prophets, and true Christian workers not to threaten, use the term *"Don't Touch God's Anointed"* or any other offensive response to abuse. If God is leading you there is no need to defend yourself for being obedient, God will vindicate you. We kept silent, prayed for deliverance, and sometimes warned and confronted, but we did not threaten that God would smite them. Sometimes we spoke directly to the evil as the Holy Spirit gave utterance.

Sometimes God defended almost immediately and at other times we suffered for quite a while. Do not be afraid of man, false Christians or evil people who oppose truth and righteousness. God is faithful and vindicates His servants.

This all may seem arrogant on our part. We cannot minimize the seriousness of what God desires to accomplish in the coming days. Lives and the eternal life of many are at stake. This work and other ministries like ours must stand, confront and preach the true Gospel in the face of adversity and opposition.

When Christ began His earthly ministry, He stood up in the synagogues of His home in Nazareth and pronounced the mission God gave Him. He also perceived their scoffing underneath their flattering platitudes and pronounced what was in their heart—to their face.

"And all spoke well of him, and wondered at the gracious words which proceeded out of his mouth; and they said, 'Is not this Joseph's son?' And he said to them, 'Doubtless you will quote to me this proverb, 'Physician, heal yourself; what we have heard you did

at Capernaum, do here also in your own country.' And he said, 'Truly, I say to you, no prophet is acceptable in his own country. But in truth, I tell you, there were many widows in Israel in the days of Elijah, when the heaven was shut up three years and six months, when there came a great famine over all the land; and Elijah was sent to none of them but only to Zarephath, in the land of Sidon, to a woman who was a widow. And there were many lepers in Israel in the time of the prophet Elisha; and none of them was cleansed, but only Naaman the Syrian.' When they heard this, all in the synagogue were filled with wrath. And they rose up and put him out of the city, and led him to the brow of the hill on which their city was built, that they might throw him down headlong. But passing through the midst of them he went away" (Luke 4:22-30).

God's tough love is meant to awaken, constrain and prevent evil from destroying the faith of others.

The apostle Paul wrote, "So then he has mercy upon whomever he wills, and he hardens the heart of whomever he wills. You will say to me then, 'Why does he still find fault? For who can resist his will?' But who are you, a man, to answer back to God? Will what is molded say to its molder, 'Why have you made me thus?' Has the potter no right over the clay, to make out of the same lump one vessel for beauty and another for menial use? What if God, desiring to show his wrath and to make known his power, has endured with much patience the vessels of wrath made for destruction, in order to make known the riches of his glory for the vessels of mercy, which he has prepared beforehand for glory, even us whom he has called, not from the Jews only but also from the Gentiles?" (Romans 9:18-24).

Appendix B

The Human Psychic and Spirit Power Unleashed by Satan

A Brief Treatise

Satan and demons desire and gain access to the human spirit, even the Christian human spirit, to enlist this additional power to oppose God's will, inflict harm, control, and attack those who get in the way.

Many disagree with this statement. They search the Bible, looking for a passage that would indicate clearly that this is a true element of satanic spiritual influence and required understanding in Christian spiritual warfare. Since there is no such passage, they conclude that the teaching is irrelevant, and even false.

They could not be further from the truth! What opponents should look for is a clear and unequivocal passage that states Satan cannot use the human or carnal Christian human spirit in any manner to incite, carry out, and spiritually affect others with evil. Indeed, no passage of Scripture makes this claim.

The Bible does not provide graphic explanations or descriptive methods employed by those who practice sorcery, witchcraft, divination, and necromancy. Revelation 2:24 indicates that Jezebel, a self-proclaimed prophetess who practiced Christianity, was teaching other Christians at the Church of Thyatira the "deep things of Satan." Scripture is also silent on how and what Jezebel was teaching, other than beguiling Christ's servants to practice immorality and eat food sacrificed to idols. The Apostle Paul warns that certain Christian women, who were self-indulgent, lusting for a husband and grown wanton against Christ, strayed after Satan. (See 1 Timothy 5). Other scriptures also refer to people used by Satan to attack others, cause problems and require discipline and expulsion from fellowship. You recall the death of Ananias and Sapphira in Acts chapter 5. Simon the Magician tried to buy the power of God, and Peter rebuked him. The Holy Spirit spoke through the Apostle Paul to prophesy judgment upon Elymas the Magician for undermining the Gospel. (See Acts 13:4-12).

The Apostle Paul wrote to the Christians at Corinth, warning them about carnality and their lack of control with the gifts of the Holy Spirit.

In the book of James, we find that double-minded Christians were unstable, unfaithful, fighting, cursing and killing each other. James also reflects on the devilish acts practiced by Christians who suffer bitter jealousy and have selfish ambition. There must be a drawing near to God and resisting Satan. These Christians were carnal and divided in mind, spirit and heart.

Deaths were occurring at the hands of other Christians. This could mean that hatred of heart directed at others can kill. *"Anyone who hates his brother is a murderer, and you know that no murderer has eternal life abiding in him"* (1 John 3:15). James finalizes this part of his discourse, directing double-minded Christians to cleanse their behavior, purify their hearts, and allow remorse and emotional catharsis of their inner issues, humbling themselves so God could establish them and exalt them for His glory.

The intention of this teaching is not to teach the "deep things of Satan," but rather to help Christians become aware of his schemes and deceitful treachery employed through carnal Christians and evil people. *"For this is why I wrote, that I might test you and know whether you are obedient in everything. Any one whom you forgive, I also forgive. What I have forgiven, if I have forgiven anything, has been for your sake in the presence of Christ, to keep Satan from gaining the advantage over us; for we are not ignorant of his designs"* (2 Corinthians 2:9-11).

Unfortunately, many Christians are ignorant of Satan's designs. This is a grave error. Choosing to stay ignorant of the devil's schemes has cost lives, stopped the advancement of the Gospel, and allowed faithless people and carnal Christians to carry out evil. The devil does not want Christians to know about his designs. Christians walking with anger and unforgiveness, hidden in the heart and spirit become pawns for Satan. It is clear in Scripture that this gives an opportunity to Satan to use these issues of heart to attack Christians in such condition and use them to spiritually defile and attack others. What is more potent is Satan's use of faithless evil people who oppose truth and attack those who have faith.

The apostle Paul wrote, *"Finally, brethren, pray for us, that the word of the Lord may speed on and triumph, as it did among you, and that we may be delivered from wicked and evil men; for not all have faith. But the Lord is faithful; he will strengthen you and guard you from evil"* (2 Thessalonians 3:1-3) and he continues, *"For such men are false apostles, deceitful workmen, disguising themselves as apostles of Christ. And no wonder, for even Satan disguises himself as an angel of light. So it is not strange if his servants also disguise themselves as servants of righteousness. Their end will correspond to their deeds"* (2 Corinthians 11:13-15).

Since Scripture does not specifically indicate the human spirit has invisible power that is available for demonic use, we must look to Scripture that indicates the use of the human spirit and the effects of forbidden occult and carnal practices. We also must consider Christian witness to these effects and their understanding of its origin.

We should be able to agree that Scripture forbids the practice of sorcery, divination, soothsaying, fortune telling, spiritualism, magic, conjuring spells, necromancy, cultic and occult rituals. The main reason God outlawed these practices is the effect it has on those who practice these dark arts and those they attack.

All these activities open the human mind and human spirit to the invisible, but influential, spirit world, filled with demonic spirits. We also know that demons need human hosts for comfort and life, which is accessible through the human spirit.

The human spirit exists. *"May the God of peace himself sanctify you wholly; and may your spirit and soul and body be kept sound and blameless at the coming of our Lord Jesus Christ"* (1 Thessalonians 5:23). God desires to regenerate our spirit, clean it up and have it made Christ-like, to be one with Christ and God in spirit. God accomplishes this by the power of the Holy Spirit and through the Gospel of Jesus Christ. *"But he who is united to the Lord becomes one spirit with him"* (1 Corinthians 6:17).

Satan opposes God's will and promotes his own schemes to capture and harness the human spirit. He does this by exposing people to forbidden cultic and occult practices mentioned in Scripture. One account often overlooked by Christians is when the disciples asked if they should pray fire down on those who did not receive them, *"And he sent messengers ahead of him, who went and entered a village of the Samaritans, to make ready for him; but the people would not receive him, because his face was set toward Jerusalem. And when his disciples James and John saw it, they said, 'Lord, do you want us to bid fire come down from heaven and consume them?' But he turned and rebuked them. And he said, 'You do not know what manner of spirit you are of; for the Son of man came not to destroy men's lives but to save them"* (Luke 9:52-55).

This passage *"what manner of spirit you are of,"* added by other translations and ancient authorities, gives us another aspect to consider concerning the human heart and spirit molded by evil spirits.

The human spirit is dead to God before regeneration, but alive to the fallen spirit world. Satan wants to lure and deceive people to delve into their own spirit in order to gain access to the spirit world. Many Christians, before they came to Christ, were involved in these forbidden activities. These are defilements to our personal spirit and are avenues for demonic activity and influence.

Even after the initial regeneration by the Holy Spirit, the personal spirit may require additional cleansing. *"Since we have these promises, beloved, let us cleanse ourselves from every defilement of body and spirit, and make holiness perfect in the fear of God"* (2 Corinthians 7:1).

The personal spirit in each of us has spiritual power that Satan wants to use. Although, the human spirit is limited in power and captive within the human body, when mixed with the demonic it can project increased spiritual influence.

This is why Satan wants people to practice these forbidden activities and ensnare as many as possible. Casting spells and curses is effectual. Some who practice sorcery have learned how to allow their human spirit to travel out of body. This practice is *astral projection* and requires help from demons. Catholics are taught and believe this practice is a valid spiritual gifting.

Satan has enlisted various world religions, evil people, false Christians and carnal Christians to physically oppose and spiritually attack God and true Christians. This work of Satan is nothing new and will increase in effectiveness as the end of the age draws near. Remember how Jesus confronted Peter by saying, *"But he turned and said to Peter, 'Get behind me, Satan! You are a hindrance to me; for you are not on the side of God, but of men'"* (Matthew 16:23).

Carnal Christians, such as Peter's example, can be channels for Satan in action, in words and with carnal spiritual vibes or defilements. After what Peter went through, he knew that Satan could infill a believer's heart, *"Ananias, why has Satan filled your heart to lie to the Holy Spirit and to keep back part of the proceeds of the land?"* (Acts 5:3).

Satan also can enter a follower's heart. Judas followed Christ but his belief in Christ was shallow. When Christ began to preach dying to self, confronting evil and teaching people to give up the lust for power and recognition, the Scriptures indicate that many did not believe. Judas became a follower of Christ who no longer believed in Jesus as the Christ. Today, many who follow Christ do not allow His lordship to bring the discipline found in the work of the cross. They have unbelieving hearts leading them to fall away. The problem is these people form a religious persona, seek authority in fellowship and innately do Satan's bidding.

Satan has an army of false Christians implanted in the true body of Christ. The devil can enter their beings at will and use their unregenerate personal spirits to assault those who have genuine faith in Christ. *"Then Satan entered into Judas called Iscariot, who was of the number of the twelve; he went away and conferred with the chief priests and officers how he might betray him to them. And they were glad, and engaged to give him money. So he agreed, and sought an opportunity to betray him to them in the absence of the multitude"* (Luke 22:3-6).

The power an evil unbelieving follower of Christ has is effectual both in spiritual influence and in direct opposition to the genuine believer and God's will on earth. These false Christians oppose the work of the cross in their life as well as in the body of Christ. Satan knows that the work of the cross is the foundation for the true power of God wrought within the true child of God.

Further, the power operating through those who practice sorcery can also be very effective. We must believe the Word of God. False Christians and false leadership can operate spiritually in a powerful manner. The apostle Paul referred to a counterfeit faith that would grow and have great power at the end of the age.

"But understand this, that in the last days there will come times of stress. For men will be lovers of self, lovers of money, proud, arrogant, abusive, disobedient to their parents, ungrateful, unholy, inhuman, implacable, slanderers, profligates, fierce, haters of good, treacherous, reckless, swollen with conceit, lovers of pleasure rather than lovers of God, holding the form of religion but denying the power of it. Avoid such people. For among them are those who make their way into households and capture weak women, burdened with sins and swayed by various impulses, who will listen to anybody and can never arrive at a knowledge of the truth. As Jannes and Jambres opposed Moses, so these men also oppose the truth, men of corrupt mind and counterfeit faith; but they will not get very far, for their folly will be plain to all, as was that of those two men" (2 Timothy 3:1-9).

One of the hardest aspects to grasp is the fact that Satan can use the human spirit and mind to focus satanic power. The two mentioned in the above passage *Jannes and Jambres* were the Egyptian magicians who practiced magic and sorcery to discredit God's work and oppose Moses.

Here is an excellent example of the reality of satanic power. Two magicians who practice sorcery for the Pharaoh matched the miracles of God done by Aaron and Moses, at least for a while.

"So Moses and Aaron went to Pharaoh and did as the LORD commanded; Aaron cast down his rod before Pharaoh and his servants, and it became a serpent. Then Pharaoh summoned the wise men and the sorcerers; and they also, the magicians of Egypt, did the same by their secret arts. For every man cast down his rod, and they became serpents. But Aaron's rod swallowed up their rods. Still Pharaoh's heart was hardened, and he would not listen to them; as the LORD had said" (Exodus 7:10-13). (See also Exodus 7:20-22; Exodus 8:5-7 and Exodus 8:16-19).

These magicians performed three miracles, matching Moses and Aaron's first three plagues upon Egypt. The fourth they could not perform. Here is another biblical account on how sorcerers and witches can project spiritual power that affects the physical.

The apostle Paul states that in the last days, certain people, holding a form of religion (hypocrites), will oppose the truth and practice spiritual power through a counterfeit faith. These are people deceived and able to deceive others. We are to avoid this type of false Christian. They will grow worse as the end of the age approaches. Carnal Christians need instruction and support in the inner cleansing work of the Holy Spirit to close all defilements of spirit that Satan can use as a doorway. These doorways within carnal Christians can be very potent and insidious. Yes, Satan uses naïve and carnal Christians to spiritually influence others. He especially uses split or divided Christians, those who are double-minded. Again, the most powerful in this carnal work are false Christians.

We have encountered numerous people who claim Christianity as their "religion," but practice evil. When confronted, they wield a spiritual power that can cause headaches, nausea, dizziness, heart palpitations, shortness of breath and extreme weakness. At first, we did not know what was happening. As we studied and did research, we developed a scriptural understanding that these people developed a spiritual power to project their own spirit to attack us. The power came primarily from demons inside these people whose hearts were full of hate, jealousy and murder. We also discovered that many carnal, double-minded Christians had the same issues of heart but disassociated from the hate, jealousy, envy and murderous feelings. These carnal, double-minded Christians suffer from a divided spirit, heart and mind. Again, this condition allows demonic influences to use wounded and defiled parts of their heart and spirit to project part of their spirit onto others in spiritual attacks.

These books are good references for study: *War on the Saints* (unabridged), *Soul and Spirit;* both by Jessie Penn-Lewis, and *Earth's Earliest Ages* by G.H. Pember.

Jessie Penn-Lewis terms this power "soul-force" and the power of a true Christian as "spirit-force." I believe that a better term to describe the power harnessed by Satan through unregenerate people or carnal Christians can be termed "psychic-spirit" power. That is, the soul of man or *psuche* (Greek for soul) is connected to the unregenerate personal spirit *pneuma,* or partially regenerated spirit. Through various forbidden practices, along with demonic infestations, the ability to project a "psychic-spirit" force upon others can occur.

The following is an excerpt from *Soul and Spirit* that helped us realize psychic-spirit power is wrought through evil people but also through carnal, double-minded Christians.

> "...It appears that this generation of soul-force under the guise of prayer, is most likely to take place in those who have had great supernatural experiences and have in some way opened themselves to evil spirits. These souls seem, in some way, to get what might be called a fanatical spirit of insistence that other believers should come into the same experience that they have had, and if they in any way refuse to seek these experiences, or appear to these souls to be a block in the path of others obtaining these supernatural manifestations, they direct, as they think, 'prayer' upon them, that they should be punished by God with judgment, or that they should be compelled to yield to what these souls call 'the truth'.... So we would earnestly warn God's servants–truly God's servants–who seem to be concerned about others who will not seek their own particular line of "blessing"– and pray them to commit these other believers to God, and not to lay themselves open to the danger of generating soul-force by directing, what might be called **evil prayers** upon

them. In any case it behooves all who give themselves to intense prayer, to carefully avoid **praying for others what they think is the "will of God" for them**, and above all things, never to direct "prayer" **upon** others, but upward toward God, thus leaving those for whom they pray free from the possible danger of soul-force working upon them through the aerial currents of the hour. As an example, this minister writes:

'We have recently had a convention in this town and one of the 'speakers' was 'out' to enforce his own supernatural experience on others–his own particular line of 'blessing.' I was the subject of much 'prayer' on this line, and I have since seriously felt the effect…This concentrating the mind (i.e., soul-force) in prayer on something that one wants is fraught with evil…'

Let us remember that true Spirit-born prayer has its origination in the spirit, and that it is not the mind concentrating upon something the person desires under the cover of 'prayer' language." (Soul and Spirit, Jessie Penn-Lewis, Christian Literature Crusade, PA 1989. pp. 59,60).

Indeed, an attack by this *part human spirit* and *part demonic spirit* can be horrific and cause illness and even death.

Many Pentecostal and charismatic Christians embrace teachings that insist that one must speak in an unintelligible tongue as proof of the baptism of the Holy Spirit. Unfortunately, many have opened their own spirit up to a demonic presence that helps them utter a tongue, but not a true tongue.

Earlier in ministry, a few Pentecostal friends convinced me that speaking in tongues would allow my life in Christ and ministry to be successful. This drove me to seek this gift. Years later, when the Lord led me into the truth, He challenged me on this practice.

While praying in tongues during a morning devotional time, the Holy Spirit whispered to me, *"Chuck, stop that gibberish."* I said, *"Is that you Lord?"* and the Lord responded, *"Yes, I have been trying to get at something within your spirit and heart that is painful, and you have been getting a 'buzz' off your own spirit to avoid it."* Remember what Paul wrote. *"He who speaks in a tongue edifies himself, but he who prophesies edifies the church"* (1 Corinthians 14:4).

I sought confirmation and came to understand that I had received a false tongue years ago and I had to renounce this immediately and stop the practice. About two weeks later, the true gifts of the Holy Spirit began to manifest themselves in ministry and counseling.

Most charismatic or Pentecostal Christians do not realize that a false tongue for a prayer language is common. They have learned to allow their own spirit to pray without their minds being fruitful. Few learn to discern, as most do not bother to seek interpretation. The classic Pentecostal stance, where one must speak in a tongue to have evidence of the baptism of the Holy Spirit, has confused and alienated many Christians. The body of Christ must get the operation of the gifts of the Holy Spirit out of the carnal and into the pure work of God. The work of the cross and embracing fiery trials will straighten out many.

An excellent source to read concerning this error is *The Speaking in Tongues Controversy* by Rick Walston.

Paul corrected the Christians at Corinth by stating, *"So with yourselves; since you are eager for manifestations of the Spirit, strive to excel in building up the church. Therefore, he who speaks in a tongue should pray for the power to interpret. For if I pray in a tongue, my spirit prays but my mind is unfruitful. What am I to do? I will pray with the spirit and I will pray with the mind also; I will sing with the spirit and I will sing with the mind also. Otherwise, if you bless with the spirit, how can any one in the position of an outsider say the 'Amen' to your thanksgiving when he does not know what you are saying? For you may give thanks well enough, but the other man is not edified. I thank God that I speak in tongues more than you all; nevertheless, in church I would rather speak five words with my mind, in order to instruct others, than ten thousand words in a tongue. Brethren, do not be children in your thinking; be babes in evil, but in thinking be mature. In the law it is written, 'By men of strange tongues and by the lips of foreigners will I speak to this people, and even then they will not listen to me,' says the Lord. Thus, tongues are a sign not for believers but for unbelievers, while prophecy is not for unbelievers but for believers. If, therefore, the whole church assembles and all speak in tongues, and outsiders or unbelievers enter, will they not say that you are mad?"* (1 Corinthians 14:12-13).

The key phrase to focus on is Paul stating that *"my spirit prays but my mind is unfruitful."* How many Christians receive a false tongue and have no idea that they are in a carnal state spewing out demonic and carnal spirit prayers that inflict mind control and spiritual power on others. Often the interpretations are carnal and even false as well. When Christians do not pray according to God's specific will in a matter, then they are praying according to man's will or even Satan's. This has serious effect and can cause great harm. If led by the Spirit, we have peace and confidence in our prayer, for we pray according to God's will. Most who are deceived have a false peace, avoid the Spirit's check and pray amiss. (See Matthew 16:22-26, 1 John 3:18-24.)

When we first found out about this human psychic-spirit destructive power, it resulted in the derailment of a well-needed vacation. We had been working with a distraught Christian woman who was in a family crisis. Her problem was under control, so we had no qualms about going on our planned vacation, but she felt we were abandoning her. This woman was a carnal and double-minded Christian, but thought she was spiritual since she always spoke in tongues. Remember, Paul addressed the Christians at Corinth as carnal, though they practiced the gifts of the Holy Spirit. These Christians emphasized personal unknown tongues, which became an overindulgent activity.

One problem after another occurred during preparation to leave on our vacation. Finally, the camper van that we used broke down halfway to our destination. The alternator burned out and we had to limp back home, buying a new battery to keep the engine running. We realized this was a spiritual attack and started to seek the Lord concerning its source.

We were sure the spiritual attack came from this woman. Finally, a couple of nights after getting back home, I was praying and felt a strong spiritual oppression. The Lord gave a word of discernment and knowledge that it was a spirit of witchcraft that was attacking me through this woman. I couldn't imagine how this woman could pray such evil until the Lord revealed that her selfish and jealous heart, with the spirit of witchcraft, was gaining access to us spiritually by way of her own spirit speaking in a false tongue.

I rebuked her spirit off me and commanded the spirit of witchcraft to leave and the oppression went immediately. This woman believed the false doctrine that gave her license to pray with her spirit in an unknown tongue, leaving her mind blanked out and unfruitful. This so-called personal prayer language became a weapon in the hand of Satan.

This is not an isolated case. We have experienced many attacks by errant believers who speak in a false tongue, hosting a spirit of divination that promotes "Christian witchcraft." When we do not seek and discern God's specific will in a matter and then pray not according to His will, we can easily fall into practicing witchcraft. This is a doorway for Satan to inspire false and carnal prayers to oppose God's will. This indeed produces powerful and sometimes deadly results.

The book of James exhorts double-minded Christians to humbly submit to God, resist the devil by drawing near to God and God will then draw near to them. Satan harasses carnal, double-minded Christians. This demonic pressure, allowed by God, brings humility and awakens those who are ignorant and in denial of these inner issues.

King Saul was a believer in God who suffered from a severely divided heart. One moment he expressed affection for David, the next moment he attempted to murder him. Saul treated David treacherously and in Psalm 12, we see that David called those as such: double-hearted.

Saul had warnings from the Lord that he did not heed. *"Now the Spirit of the LORD departed from Saul, and an evil spirit from the LORD tormented him. And Saul's servants said to him, 'Behold now, an evil spirit from God is tormenting you. Let our lord now command your servants, who are before you, to seek out a man who is skilful in playing the lyre; and when the evil spirit from God is upon you, he will play it, and you will be well.' So Saul said to his servants, 'Provide for me a man who can play well, and bring him to me.' One of the young men answered, 'Behold, I have seen a son of Jesse the Bethlehemite, who is skilful in playing, a man of valor, a man of war, prudent in speech, and a man of good presence; and the LORD is with him.' Therefore Saul sent messengers to Jesse, and said, 'Send me David your son, who is with the sheep.' And Jesse took an ass laden with bread, and a skin of wine and a kid, and sent them by David his son to Saul. And David came to Saul, and entered his service. And Saul loved him greatly, and he became his armor-bearer. And Saul sent to Jesse, saying, 'Let David remain in my service, for he has found favor in my sight.' And whenever the evil spirit from God was upon Saul, David took the lyre and played it with his hand; so Saul was refreshed, and was well, and the evil spirit departed from him"* (1 Samuel 16:14-23).

Many Christians have a divided heart—one-part loving, the other full of murderous hate, bitter jealousy, and selfish ambition. These suffer from demonic torment, which are warnings from the Lord. These demonic attacks are not of God, but are allowed by God to keep the divided from falling headlong into the dark pit. Often they come to church and receive appeasement and false peace as pastors develop stronger doses of entertaining services and soothing worship. Eventually these wounded and deceived Christians become ensnared by false ministries and false prophets whose spirits channel lying demons. (See Ezekiel 13).

The root of these fanatical worship services and false revival meetings is the same root problem king Saul suffered: a double heart. Only through sound doctrine and teachings that penetrate denial and provide support for cleansing can these poor misled Christians obtain freedom. There is no condemnation when dealing with the hidden issues of the heart, rather most end-up self-condemned because they continue to harden their outer heart further and further, until they are cut off from the convicting work of the Holy Spirit. *"Be sober, be watchful. Your adversary the devil prowls around like a roaring lion, seeking someone to devour. Resist him, firm in your faith, knowing that the same experience of suffering is required of your brotherhood throughout the world. And after you have suffered a little while, the God of all grace, who has called you to his eternal glory in Christ, will himself restore, establish, and strengthen you. To him be the dominion for ever and ever. Amen"* (1 Peter 5:8-11).

"Behold, thou desirest truth in the inward being; therefore teach me wisdom in my secret heart.... Create in me a clean heart, O God, and put a new and right spirit within me.... The sacrifice acceptable to God is a broken spirit; a broken and contrite heart, O God, thou wilt not despise" (Psalm 51:6,10,17).

The Lord allowed lying spirits to speak through the false prophets to entice the wicked king Ahab to his death. (See 1 Kings 22:1-38).

The Lord told Ezekiel to prophesy against women of his own nation who practiced divination in the hunt for souls. They prophesied out of their own minds with destructive results. Somehow, these women found spiritual power by sewing magic bands and making veils. They saw delusive visions and practiced divination. In addition, the women betrayed good people, and lied to keep evil people alive. They disheartened the righteous falsely and encouraged the wicked to continue in evil. (See Ezekiel 13:17-23).

The spiritual power of the wicked can exercise influence, cause illness and even death. We read the account of Jezebel spiritually attacking Elijah in 1 Kings 19:1-18. When Jezebel heard what Elijah had done to the false prophets, she sent a death threat message to Elijah. Elijah, a great man of God became overwhelmed. This spiritual attack by Jezebel was so powerful Elijah wanted to die, and gave up on it all, so he laid down and slept. His sleep was not a normal sleep but rather an oppressive sleep due to his personal spirit being smothered by Jezebel's spiritual attack. An angel of the Lord awakened Elijah twice to eat in order to gain strength for the coming journey.

Often, when others have attacked us spiritually, we feel overwhelmed, become drained of energy and sleep a deep but restless sleep. As we understood the symptoms and characteristics as well as who was the source of our attack, we were able to fight off the attacks. Battling these attacks became easier as we continued to embrace His discipline and became more cleansed from our own defilements and hidden issues of heart. Jesus proved many times to be greater in power than those in the world attacking us, but in our initial spiritual training our strength and faith in Christ needed much purification and strengthening.

The preponderance of Scripture indicates that people who practice these things have a spiritual power that Satan harnesses and uses to attack God's work and others who get in their way. Further, Satan often enlists carnal and divided or double-hearted/minded Christians to cause trouble and even attack other Christians, especially through false gifts.

This is not a complete study, but an overview for the reader to consider, seek confirmation from the Lord, and do more research. Many have experienced these symptoms and wonder where the problems originated. God knows how to bear witness to truth. If you encounter this type of spiritual attack, we trust you will apply what we have learned and shared here. Take courage to stand and fight in the power of the Lord. We found that as we dealt with our own carnal issues and dividedness, the attacks were not as acute and were more easily fought off.

Many Christians who refuse to embrace sound doctrine that clearly gives instruction in these matters will suffer in the coming days, and some will die prematurely. The human psychic-spirit power unleashed by Satan is spreading, especially within the false movements and counterfeit faith ministries. Beware; the battle lines are drawn, and Satan is pulling out all stops.

God is allowing this to cleanse and heal His wayward people before it's too late. Now is the time to embrace the discipline of the Lord and grow up into Christ; our period of grace is running out. Soon the testing of millions of lost souls and Christians alike will come in the valley of decision!

About Pastor Charles Pretlow and MC Global Ministries

It was in 1973, when Charles accepted Christ, just after his reenlistment in the Marines for six more years. Then in 1974, after reading David Wilkerson's book The Vision, he accepted Christ's call to full time ministry and requested an early release from the Corps. Miraculously, his honorable discharge was granted.

In January of 1975 he began Bible College and accepted his first ministry appointment. His years of formal education and leadership training have helped him in ministry. However, his more in-depth training, wisdom, and character development were honed through years of ministering in a wilderness type training, facilitated by Jesus in the discipline of the Lord.

His call is helping Christians become tribulation proof and rapture ready. Most Christians are not prepared for the coming troubles that God will use to make His church "*without spot or blemish*" — if you will, to become rapture ready.

Contacting MC Global Ministries

If you are seriously looking for sound doctrine to help you get ready and desire genuine fellowship, then perhaps MC Global Ministries and MC Chapel Fellowship may be able to help you.

We mean business and our faces are set as flint concerning the call set before us. If you desire to change the direction God has given us or argue over the message of repentance, sanctification, and how to endure the coming Great Tribulation, then contacting us would not be beneficial.

However, if you are teachable and hungry to learn how to allow the true Christ to change you through his loving discipline, then this ministry can help you.

Ordering Additional Copies

www.mcgmin.com – click on Bookstore menu selection
Available online – Amazon, Barnes and Noble
Order at your local bookstore using:
ISBN 978-1-943412-04-4

Contact Information

Mailing address:
MC Global Ministries
PO Box 857, Canon City, CO 81215
(833) 695-1236
www.mcgmin.com

Fellowship address:
MC Chapel Fellowship
The Abbey/St. Joseph's Bldg.
2951 E. Hwy 50, Canon City, CO 81215
Sunday fellowship 10AM
www.mcgmin.com

Contacting the author, Pastor Charles Pretlow
PO Box 857, Canon City, CO 81215
(833) 695-1236
www.cpretlow.com ~ chuck@cpretlow.com

Note: The letters MC in our ministry and fellowship name stands for Message of the Cross, and reflects the Apostle Paul's statement concerning the power of God:

> "For the word [message] of the cross is folly to those who are perishing, but to us who are being saved it is the power of God" (1 Corinthians 1:18).

www.ingramcontent.com/pod-product-compliance
Lightning Source LLC
Chambersburg PA
CBHW081829170426
43199CB00017B/2686